COMPARING RELIGIONS
THROUGH LAW

Comparing Religions Through Law: Judaism and Islam offers a ground-breaking study which compares the two religions through shared dominant structures. In the case of Judaism and Islam the dominant structure is law. The legal systems of Judaism and Islam encompass all aspects of life, reflecting the shared view that there is nothing in human life beyond the scope of divine concern. But the uniqueness of the two religions is apparent in the areas where they disagree. The idea of the Land of Israel has no counterpart in Islam, while Islam's jihad is nowhere to be found in Jewish law.

The authors compare the classical statements of the two religions: those of the Torah, that set forth normative Judaism, and those of classical Sunni Islamic law, formulated by the Qur'an and oral tradition in the first three centuries of Islam. The religious bases in the concepts of "promised land" and "jihad" are also examined in detail.

Comparing Religions Through Law: Judaism and Islam presents an innovative and sometimes controversial study of the comparisons and contrasts between the two religions and offers an example of how comparative religious studies can provide grounds for mutual understanding.

COMPARING RELIGIONS THROUGH LAW

Judaism and Islam

Jacob Neusner and Tamara Sonn

London and New York

First published 1999
by Routledge
11 New Fetter Lane, London EC4P 4EE

Simultaneously published in the USA and Canada
by Routledge
29 West 35th Street, New York, NY 10001

Routledge is an imprint of the Taylor & Francis Group

Typeset in Garamond by RefineCatch Limited, Bungay, Suffolk
Printed and bound in Great Britain by
St Edmundsbury Press, Bury St Edmunds, Suffolk

British Library Cataloguing in Publication Data
A catalogue record for this book is available from the British Library

Library of Congress Cataloging in Publication Data
Neusner, Jacob, 1932–
Comparing religions through law: Judaism and Islam / Jacob
Neusner and Tamara Sonn.
p. cm.
Includes bibliographical references and index.
1. Jewish law. 2. Islamic law. 3. Jihad. 4. Palestine in
Judaism. 5. Zionism. I. Sonn, Tamara. II. Title.
LAW
296.1′8 – dc21 98–44111
CIP

ISBN 0–415–19486–5 (hbk)
ISBN 0–415–19487–3 (pbk)

CONTENTS

CONTENTS

PREFACE

Laws embody the norms by which societies live. They set forth in tangible and concrete form the practical consequences of abstract beliefs. An obvious example makes the point. A social order that deems all human life precious will forbid murder and punish the act without discrimination as to the victim. One that does not will build death factories. When we turn to religion we find the same thing. Religions that aspire to be realized in collective conscience, not only in individual conviction, will frame for themselves public policy through laws that define what is to be done or not done and they will enforce those laws in God's name. The history of Islamic, Christian and Judaic religious systems alike sets forth ample evidence that characteristic of monotheism from scripture forward is the aspiration to legislate theology and morality. And those religions that identify the entire social order as the setting for serving God will legislate, without differentiating the religious from the secular, norms of behavior for the whole of the society in which they find themselves. In that way theological conviction about God and what God wants of human beings will take the palpable form of rules that regulate conduct. Such rules will extend even to what outsiders deem the most minor and trivial action – a gesture required or forbidden, a bit of nourishing food deemed unclean.

This book takes up two religions of law; that is, religions that aspire to define the character of the social order of the faithful and who legislate in God's name. The two, Islam and Judaism, concur on much, and here we propose to compare their legal systems to discover the extent of their concurrence and the nature of their differences. In general, seen up close Judaism and Islam as religions of law exhibit significant divergence, but, viewed in the larger context of world religions, they stand side by side in their fundamental convictions about God and the social order. Accordingly, the work at hand compares religions that are sufficiently alike to sustain comparison, but also suitably different so as to yield interesting hypotheses about the character of each religion. The hypothesis set forth here is simple. The purpose of comparing religions is defining the religions that are compared, each in contrast with the other. However much religions have in common, in the end they never prove to be wholly like one another. Not concentric at all, each emerges as eccentric, making its distinctive statement in its own language. And where the eccentricities occur, there the religions find their definitions, their distinctive qualities. The points of concentricity then will emerge as routine; those of eccentricity, indicative.

Here the two comparable, in important ways concurring, religions turn out not to speak dialects of one language at all, even though both worship the one and only God, who, by their own word, is the very God they worship in common, and even though both deem worship to take place in the details of the workaday world. So where they do differ and sustain particular definition, it is on all that matters. The real question of comparison then arises from the contrast. Against the contrary view, that religions intersect and concur on what counts, we present this exercise in examining how the two monotheisms that come to expression in public policy and law compare so as to contrast. Accordingly, addressing the problem of comparing religions – what do we compare and why – requires us not only to theorize, but also to test theories of comparison and contrast. That is what we promise in this book. Our basic theory, then, is that when we see Islam and Judaism from a distance and in the perspective of other world religions, they concur on much, but when we set them side by side in close proximity, though they share an emphasis on law, they find difficult the identification of common thought and expression. And yet, both readily concur (along with Christianity) that they worship one and the same God, who is the only God of all creation, and who makes himself manifest through prophets that, at critical junctures, both deem authentic.

The plan of the book is simple. We have taken as our principal task the exposition of the facts of the two religions, set forth each in its own terms. Chapter 1 spells out the theory of comparing religions that guides us. We lay out some of the obstacles that impede the work and how we propose to overcome them. Chapters 2 through 5 define the terms of discussion here. These chapters, the shank of the book, provide the basic facts needed to see how Judaism and Islam compare and contrast. We cover the following topics: (1) the documentary sources, (2) the intellectual rules governing the formulation of law, and (3) the institutional and (4) personal media – courts, qualified religious judges – by which in theory the religions treated here take shape and enforce law. In these chapters we set forth the context in which we compare the religio-legal systems of the two religions.

We have omitted a sustained presentation of points of essential agreement on relationships between individuals and God (prayer, fasting, ablutions) and relationships among human beings (betrothal, marriage, inheritance, divorce, alms-giving and charity, commercial relations). Because the two religions concur on the large conceptions of the faith as they define the critical relationships and dimensions of life, both private and public, detailed treatment of these topics here would be redundant. The general outlines of these concurrences are referred to throughout the book, and details will be set out in a second volume.

Why stress difference in the process of comparison? It is because, in our view, the categories yielding the greatest insight into the natures of these two religio-legal systems are those in which their positions differ. In Chapter 6 we address categories treated disproportionately in the two traditions. Conceptions of temple ritual and sacrifice, for example, are very important in Judaism, but not in Islam. Slave laws are highly detailed in Islam, but are categorically inconsequential in Judaism. More significantly, both religions reserve certain times for religious activities, such as the Sabbath in Judaism and the month of pilgrimage in Islam, but their respective approaches to sacred time diverge. Although we would have compared the Islamic pilgrimage to the relatively minor category of Jewish pilgrimage, we have treated it in this chapter because both the Jewish Sabbath and the Muslim pilgrimage commemorate foundational events in the lives of the communities, but their respective treatments of these holy times differ in important ways from one another. In Judaism the time of Sabbath itself is sacred and the foundational events are not only commemorated, they are re-created. In Islam, on the other hand, it is the activities of the believers that sanctify the time. These activities commemorate historical events of monumental importance in the relationship between God and the community and as such refocus and inspire believers with confidence and dedication to their mission, but they do not re-create a past event. The significance of this disproportion becomes even more pronounced in the two religions' unique categories.

Having shown vast areas of general agreement and significant dispro-portion, we end at Chapter 7 with an account of how the two religions fundamentally differ. Both religio-legal systems recognize holy places and draw consequences from that fact, for example, for pilgrimage. But the sig-nificance of holy places in Islam is symbolic; Medina, Jerusalem and, most importantly, Mecca are sites of extreme religious significance, but what makes them holy are the events that took place there. The regular com-memoration of those events is the source of enormous spiritual strength for believers. But there is no counterpart, even in Islam's attachment to the three holy cities, to the notion of enlandisement in Judaism, the idea that the restoration to a particular piece of land forms an inevitable chapter in the story of the redemption of all humankind. Similarly, the notion of jihad – the ongoing struggle to bring all humanity to Islam (*islam*, submission to the divine will) has no place in Judaism. In both instances we hear how different people talk about different things to different people – no shared discourse whatsoever. These are points at which we see the two religions as not entirely concentric, or, even where concentric, not corresponding in proportions. In Chapter 7 and the Epilogue, therefore, we end with the difference, which the comparative study of religions as its principal task has to articulate and interpret in due course. That is, to make sense of religions in their concrete, historical power, we have finally to address the differences among them, understanding also their points of congruence and consensus. For it is the difference that makes history. That is the theory of this practicum. We conclude, in the Epilogue, with some reflections on the results of the comparison of the legal systems of Judaism and Islam, as well as insights afforded by the comparison of where these two systems fit into the community of world religions.

At every point – it hardly needs to be said – we approach with respect for the dignity and integrity of the religions that are described and compared. At no point do we mean to give offense to the faithful of either one, and we believe we never do so. Not only so, but we mean to treat each religion in every aspect in exact balance with the other. But, nonetheless, the problem of establishing the context for comparison arises. Specifically, when comparing religions, who speaks first sets the norm, and if one defines the norm to which the other responds, then to begin with the comparison is distorted. If we commence with the category formation of Judaism, Islam serves as the foil, and invidious comparisons may result. The contrary is also the case. How do we deal with that fact? Obviously we cannot permit Judaism always to define the norm and Islam to respond thereto. That cannot be allowed, even though Judaism fully set forth its legal system long before the advent of Islam, and even though scholars have hypothesized that in certain ways Islamic law makes its own, naturalizes for its purposes, the law of Judaism. Nor can we permit Islam always to define the norm. We may not permit such a pattern to emerge, even though the accumulated historical experience of Islam in defining through law the social order of enormous proportions of humanity makes Islamic law more dense and nuanced and experienced than that of Judaism. If each has its claim to priority in defining the discursive norm, if we are to accomplish our goal of comparing whole legal systems on a level plane, neither can exercise intellectual hegemony.

A simple solution suffices for the moment. To make provision for a complete equality of representation here, we have given the starting position – the one that defines the terms and issues for discussion, thus the norm – in an alternating pattern. At some points Judaism takes the lead, at others, Islam. In formulating our exact comparisons, therefore, at some points in the process of comparison and contrast Islam responds to Judaism, and at others, Judaism to Islam. In concrete terms, where Judaism is described at the outset, the issues raised by Judaism and those ignored by Judaism set the agenda, and where Islam takes the primary position, the presentation of Judaism is shaped by the Muslim program. We have divided matters in an equal way, as a glance at the contents page will indicate. But determining which of the two takes priority at a given topic represents a judgment on our part that one or the other of the two sets forth a more interesting definition of the topic and a more dense account of it. Still, throughout, our strategy of exposition aims to maintain a complete and perfect balance between the two religions, each given the same attention as the other, both allowed to define the framework of discussion in equal proportion.

"Judaism" stands for a variety of kindred religious systems, and so too, the more one learns about Islam, the more diverse and variegated the religious world of Islam emerges. How then do we compare? We have chosen the classical writings of each religion as these serve as a reference-point for all statements of systems that would emerge over time: the documents on which all Judaic and Islamic religious systems concur. That is why we compare only the classical, definitive statements of the two religions, those of the Torah, the written part as read by the oral part that sets forth normative Judaism, and of classical Islamic law (collectively known as Shari'a) formulated from scripture (the Qur'an) and oral tradition (Hadith, collectively known as the Sunna) in the first three centuries of Islam (by the tenth century CE). We seek to identify the generative logic that animates the law of the respective religio-legal systems as they originated. We do not deal with the later history of the halakhah of Judaism or of the Shari'a of Islam, and we certainly do not attend to the comparison and contrast of how the halakhah contributes to the religion and law of Judaism in the State of Israel or how the Shari'a does the same in the Islamic republics that girdle the middle of the globe. Certainly a comparison of the aspirations of the sages of the Torah of the State of Israel and the religious scholars (*ulama*) of the Islamic republics would produce important results, with profound implications for the study of the inner logic of the halakhah and the Shari'a that is revealed in this book. But the best is the enemy of the good, and we hope we will contribute a useful case to the broader work of framing a theory of the comparison of religions and executing that theory in concrete cases. Ending our story in the tenth Christian century, some three hundred years after Prophet Muhammad and four hundred years after the closure of the Talmud of Babylonia, we leave for others the work of telling what happened next.

This is not a book about politics but one that concerns the study of religion. We do not pretend that every line in these pages bears upon immediate and acutely contemporary issues of relationships concerning nations and peoples and power. But we realize that tensions of a political character spill over into the realm of religion, and some may represent the relationship between the State of Israel and its Muslim neighbors as a religious conflict. But both history and contemporary affairs testify that Islam and Judaism know how to co-exist in a comfortable and tolerant relationship, each honoring the other for its faith in the shared, one and only God. Not only in such Muslim countries as Turkey and Morocco, but also in the West, both secular and Christian, the faithful of Islam and Judaism, along with Christians of every communion, work at living together in harmony. To that aspiration to constitute a coherent social order out of the diversity of the monotheisms, we mean to contribute only an irenic exercise in academic description, analysis, and interpretation, such as the study of religion in the neutral academy makes possible. We hope that readers will find illumination and perhaps even a model of how learning affords grounds for mutual understanding. Long after the State of Israel and its Arab neighbors have found the path to peace, the religions, Judaism and Islam, along with Christianity, will continue to pursue their differences even as they seek to serve and love one and the same God.

It remains for the partners in this project to express their thanks to colleagues with whom they work at Bard College (for the first author), in particular Professors Bruce D. Chilton and Jonathan Brockopp, and at the University of South Florida (for both), in particular Professors John Morreall and James Strange. We consulted these colleagues, asking them to examine the first complete draft of the book. We taught a joint course on the basis of the manuscript and thank students at the University of South Florida who helped us identify points that require amplification and clarification. The first author did the same with Professor Brockopp and thanks Bard students who did the same. He further expresses thanks to both Bard College and the University of South Florida for valuable research support.

Jacob Neusner
Bard Collect and University of South Florida

Tamara Sonn
University of South Florida

1

COMPARING ISLAM AND
JUDAISM IN PARTICULAR

A Why compare religions and why compare
their laws?

"Who knows only one religion knows no religion," so Müller's familiar dictum maintains, and the learned consensus generally concurs. To understand a given religion, most people agree, requires comparison and contrast with some other(s). Only then do we gain perspective, a sense of proportion and balance, an account of the choices a religion makes: for example, why one makes choices the contrasting religion may well reject. To compare, moreover, requires seeing two things as whole and complete, then brought into juxtaposition and relationship. And the very exercise of seeing a religious system in its entirety, carried out with contrast in view, requires making judgments about structure and proportion that comparison with another whole makes possible. So we study religion in comparison or not at all. And we compare religions because we seek a perspective on each and on all of them all together; that is, for the same reason that natural historians compare and contrast beetles, to see how they are alike and how they are distinct and to find out what difference that distinction makes – and to explain it all. But in the study of religion we are not yet able to explain very much. Indeed, we discern little agreement on just what, at this time, we ought to want to explain. So for the moment we compare religions that sustain comparison in order better to understand each one.

But what does it mean to know more than a single religion, and (more to the point) what does it take to draw into juxtaposition, for purposes of comparison and contrast, two or more religions? To know a given religion means to form a conception of the whole of that religion, meaning to grasp how it is cogent and proportionate, what matters and what does not, its architectonics and its hermeneutics and animating logic. All of this may be expressed in one word, "rationality," meaning the cogency that imparts structure, the logic that propels the system. So to know a given religion means to grasp its principles of self-evidence and rationality, its category formation, its modes of thought and inquiry – to see the whole all at once

1

and all together. And to draw two religions into juxtaposition requires that the two wholes be cast in such a way as to correspond, to intersect, to pertain, to set forth the category formation of the one in a way that is coherent with, relevant to, the category formation of the other – and to do so without distortion.

These issues represent considerable demands upon the academic study of religion, and it is easier to demand than to respond. We do not claim to know all of the answers to the questions outlined above, only to be ready to undertake to find and instantiate some of them. Still, academic scholarship on the description of religions as systems of culture has progressed over the past generations. The conception of a religion as a system of the social order defines the requirements of description, analysis, and interpretation. Such a system is comprised by an account of a way of life, a world view, and a theory of social entity. Not only so, but what holds the whole together – an urgent question that provokes a self-evidently compelling answer – has been defined for one religious system after another. We know how to differentiate a given religion into its constituent, distinct systems, so we speak confidently about Judaisms and Christianities. But, in that same context of description, analysis, and interpretation of religions and their systems, comparing and contrasting have not yet attained a level of certainty: we are only just beginning. What justifies the choice we have made to compare the religio-legal systems, Judaism and Islam, in their classical, normative statements?

B The monotheist religions: Judaism, Christianity, Islam

What are monotheist religions, and what issues do they face in common? A monotheist religion asserts that there is only one God, transcendent over nature, who rules all creation and governs humanity in the here and now. Three religions take that view, all of them calling upon the Hebrew scriptures of ancient Israel ("the Old Testament" of the Christian Bible, "the written Torah" of the one whole Torah, oral and written, of Judaism). There, the three monotheist religions concur, God made himself manifest, principally through Moses, the prophet. And they agree that God further revealed himself and his will in other documents: the New Testament and Christ, for Christianity, the Qur'an and Muhammad, for Islam, and the Oral Torah and its sages, for Judaism, respectively. The three monotheisms, further, confront one and the same problem, and the basic logic of monotheism dictates the range of solutions that each of the monotheisms addresses: the problem of God's justice and mercy and how these are to be reconciled with the condition of the everyday world.

A religion of numerous gods finds many solutions to one problem; a religion of only one God presents one to many. Life is seldom fair. Rules rarely work. To explain the reason why, polytheisms adduce multiple causes of chaos, a god per anomaly. Diverse gods do various things, so, it stands to reason, ordinarily outcomes conflict. Monotheism by nature explains many things in a single way. One God rules. Life is meant to be fair, and just rules are supposed to describe what is ordinary, all in the name of that one and only God. So in monotheism a simple logic governs to limit ways of making sense of things. But that logic contains its own dialectics. If one true God has done everything, then, since he is God all-powerful and omniscient, all things are credited to and blamed on him. In that case he can be either good or bad, just or unjust – but not both. Within that framework, the three monotheisms pursue their distinctive expressions of the common faith in the one and only God, just and merciful, who created the world and made himself known through men of his choice and words of his own selection.

Judaism and Islam concur that culture and society cohere with religion, so there is no distinction between secularity and religiosity, state and church such as Christianity from Constantine's time forward contemplated. They in particular sustain comparison because they are sufficiently congruent in basic, indicative traits for the exercise to yield revealing contrast: alike, and then not alike, in that order. Both are religions of law, both monotheisms conceive of God in the same terms, both place heavy stress upon the formation of a society that conforms to God's will, expressed in verbal revelation having to do with social norms, and both set forth through jurisprudence an elaborate and articulated message. Furthermore in their unfolding history, in their nurture of distinct religious systems within the framework of the Torah for Judaism, and Shari'a for Islam, the diverse formations of both religious traditions appeal to authoritative and generative statements, which form a court of final appeal in the quest for the true faith. That means we may identify a specific body of authoritative formulations to which all formations of Judaism and of Islam respectively appeal, and if we compare the classical statement of Islam with the classical statement of Judaism, we go far toward a reliable exercise in juxtaposition and contrast of the two religions. Each presents itself for comparison with the other because of the shared trait of classicism: we compare the governing model of the one with that of the other. And, as it happens, the models belong to the same category, which comprises legal systems for religious communities.

Accordingly, through the juxtaposition of the classic, universally accepted legal systems of Judaism and Islam, we find ourselves able to answer questions of likeness and difference among comparable religious systems. Specifically, we are able to show where, in law, the distinct category formations set forth by the respective religio-legal systems converge and concur, where they converge and differ, and where they do not converge at all. These are the initial steps in comparing religions by showing where they are alike and where they are not alike.

That is not to ignore a further justification for the comparison and contrast of Islam and Judaism. From the very beginning of Islam to nearly the present day, in Muslim countries Judaism flourished side by side with Islam, and in the State of Israel today, the two religions are practiced as well. The comparison is therefore appropriate for historical and cultural reasons: we compare religions practiced under much the same cultural, political, sociological, and economic circumstances from the beginning to the present. We venture to hope that, at the dawn of peace between the State of Israel and its Arab, and mostly Muslim, neighbors, the historical interchange between the two religions, which bear so much in common, may renew itself. Certainly, as we show in this book, the two traditions concur on much, indeed on most matters that count.

It follows that two religions that for most of their shared history have co-existed in the same places and at the same times, past and present, offer many opportunities for illuminating juxtaposition. That is why we here undertake an elementary experiment in the systematic comparison of religions, with special attention to norms, expressed in law, of those religions. The work focuses upon comparing category formations. In that enterprise the authors mean to explore some basic procedures of comparing religions, with a focus on the normative law of the kindred faiths, Judaism and Islam.

Why not the third monotheist religion, Christianity? Why not, indeed! In theory our work should extend also to Christianity, for the three mono-theisms form a unique arena for comparative study. Different from all other religions, as we said above, Judaism, Christianity, and Islam share a common belief in one, unique God, creator of heaven and earth, whose self-manifestation is achieved through particular prophets, beginning with Moses, continuing, for Christianity and Islam, with Jesus, and ending, for Islam, with Muhammad. So far as Judaism is the religion of the written Torah, Christianity tells the story of Judaism within its own narrative, and Islam takes account of the stories of both Judaism and Christianity. For its part, Judaism in the confrontation with triumphant Christianity and Islam had to take account of the claim of the newcomers to worship the one and only God who made Himself known to holy Israel at Sinai. And Judaism did not classify the new monotheisms as idolatry, which category encompassed all other religions through all time. It follows that the three monotheisms accord recognition to one another, if not always unambiguously and if never enthusiastically. Not only so, but all three accord special status to the Hebrew scriptures of ancient Israel. All three concur that, in addition to the Israelite scriptures, a further revelation, another revealed scripture, is required. That additional revelation is the Oral Torah for Judaism, the New Testament for Christianity, the Qur'an for Islam. It has already been shown in several systematic works that the theologies of formative Christianity and Judaism build upon comparable category formations.[1] With so much in common, the comparison and contrast of each with the other two certainly promise considerable enlightenment.

But Judaism and Islam in one important way stand closer together than either does to the third companion in the trilogy of monotheism, Christianity. That way is their conviction that law embodying public policy as much as theology sets forth religious truth. In their classical statements, Islam and Judaism agree that the religious regulation of everyday life, extending to acutely detailed dimensions of ordinary conduct, is required to establish a godly society, a people and state formed in accord with God's will. Both stress norms of behavior as much as of belief, emphasis upon the formation, by the faithful, of a state governed by God's law as interpreted and applied by God's representatives. Judaism, appealing to the prophet Moses, and Islam, responding to the prophet Muhammad, concur that the community of the faithful form not only a religious but a political entity. The Israel envisioned by Moses governed itself by the law revealed by God to Moses at Sinai, and the abode of Islam envisioned by Muhammad would constitute a community meant to realize the law of God set forth in the Qur'an and associated teachings.

This is not to suggest that Christianity took the position of indifference to public policy or left law outside of its realm of governance; far from it. But Judaism and Islam tell themselves the story of origins within the framework of the godly state, the Israel called into being by God at Sinai through the prophet Moses, for example, being instructed about constructing courts and settling claims of damages for the goring ox, not only building a tabernacle and setting up an altar for offerings to God. Islam from the beginning understood itself as a political entity, with realization of the divine will through revealed law as its reason for existence. For its part, Christianity spent three centuries without thinking a great deal about law beyond the realm of Church order, paying slight attention, except as victim, to matters of public policy and politics. Then, from the time of Constantine, while aspiring to infuse politics with its vision, Christianity recognized a distinction between the state and the church that Judaism and Islam never contemplated and could never have conceived. That is why the halakhah for Judaism and Shari'a for Islam find no counterpart in a uniform legal code joining civil to canon law in Christianity. So while the Christian emperors worked out an autonomous position *vis-à-vis* Church authority (for example, the Emperor and the Pope in the West's Holy Roman Empire), in the theory of the halakhah and Shari'a religious and civil authority were joined. They were not to be distinguished in practice either. It follows that for Judaism and Islam, a single system of law, embodied in a single cadre of religio-legal authorities, would undertake to define the social order in conformity with God's revealed will. That in the ordinary, political sense, in the historical imagination of their respective faiths, Moses and Muhammad govern, but Jesus never does, suffices to differentiate Judaism and Islam from Christianity.

In the view of Islam and Judaism, it is through the conduct of everyday life under the aspect of the law of God that the faithful serve God. Both systems of religion and law concur, for example, that the marketplace, the bedroom, the fields and farms and factories, as much as the schools and the courts and the mosques and synagogues, all form arenas where God's will is meant to govern. That conviction carries the concrete consequence that laws set forth by religious authorities pertain and are to be enforced. To construct God's kingdom for Judaism on earth means to realize the teachings of the Torah, and for Islam, to implement the teachings of the Qur'an. So for Islam and for Judaism, sharing the conviction that to distinguish the secular from the sacred diminishes the realm of God's dominion, law forms a principal medium of religious action, thought, and expression, and law extends to the outer limits of ordinary life. From antiquity to our own time, learning in the law of the Torah for Judaism and in the Shari'a for Islam defined a principal qualification for religious authority, and study and application of the law of God in the here and now formed a main medium of religious activity. With so basic a definitive trait in common, Judaism and Islam present themselves as compelling candidates for systematic comparison. That is why we have undertaken an exercise in the comparison of religions through the comparison of the legal systems of the two religions treated here.

C Which Judaism, which Islam, and why?

Three problems define the initial task: two are closely related and treated here; the third is addressed in the next section. At the outset we propose a response to each of them, which is then fully exposed and realized in the core of this book.

First, people recognize that a given religion encompasses diverse systems of belief and behavior. "Judaism" stands for kindred religious systems. The recognition that these systems are to be differentiated, each by its generative myth and distinctive symbolic system, requires us to define not a single Judaism but multiple Judaisms. The indicative traits of a given system may emerge from the variables of time, space, or inner logic. So systemic description of Judaism demands that we treat as separate the Judaism of one period from that of another, the Judaism of one location from that of another, or the Judaic religious beliefs and practices of one group from those of another, whether separated in time or in space or living side by side, as in the contemporary world with its Reform and Orthodox Judaisms, and, among Orthodox Judaisms, many systems with less in common than in conflict.[2] That is why those who study religion today are accustomed to refer to "Judaisms," just as "Christianities" must be distinguished, whether Roman Catholic, Protestant or Orthodox.

Along the same lines when it comes to Islam, the more we learn about the complexity of the world of Islam, from Morocco to Indonesia, from the seventh century CE to the twenty-first, the more diverse that world appears.

True, the differences between Sunni and Shi'i Islam are not of the same order as the differences among Orthodox, Catholic, and Protestant Christianity, or among Orthodox Judaisms. But they do create, within Islam, two vast systems for the Islamic social and political order. There are other Islams as well, including sects described by the majority as heretical but whose adherents nonetheless describe themselves as Muslim (as much as Orthodox, Reform, Conservative, and Reconstructionist Judaism all call themselves Judaism). If, therefore, Islam to the uneducated eye presents a uniform visage, to the experienced, discerning vision Islam proves as plural in its distinctive way as do Judaism and Christianity in theirs. That is not to mention other academic constructions of complex things into simple compositions such as Buddhism or Hinduism. People now recognize that it is the outsider who sees uniformity, the insider who perceives difference; to study world religions, we treat as homogeneous what demands analysis and differentiation. And that defines the intellectual circumstance in which we carry out the work of comparing religions. The problem then becomes apparent when we compare religions: which Judaism to which Islam is subject to comparison? Whence the ideal type subject to inquiry?

Second, when we speak of a religion, we have to determine the evidence we deem definitive. Here we take account not only of different systems, but, within a given system and among the community of the faithful as a whole (however differentiated in way of life, world view, and theory of the social entity), diverse modes and types of religiosity, belief and expression. Within the body of the faithful co-exist the virtuosi, engaged in intellect, concerned for doctrine and law; the deeply spiritual, whose devotion to the transcendent lifts them beyond the concerns of daily life; and common folk, who bring to prayer their own practical concerns. Specifically, when we compare religions, to what exactly do we make reference: the beliefs and practices of books as set forth by the religious virtuosi (legal or spiritual), or the actualities of local practice and particular conviction of a given time and place? We may describe a religion by appeal to the official beliefs or the convictions of ordinary folk, who commonly take their own path to heaven. And when we turn from belief to behavior, we understand that what the books say does not dictate and therefore cannot be asked to describe what the people do. To take the familiar, Catholic case, the official teaching on birth control, endorsed by the Pope and the bishops, and the actualities of Catholic practice do not exactly coincide. So we have to address the issue: whose version of a given system within a particular religious tradition do we choose for comparison with which version in some corresponding system of that other religious tradition?

Third, we come to the question of category formation. Specifically, when we set side by side a particular Judaic religious system with a particular Islamic one, the classical with the classical, for instance, we may find not only areas in which the two overlap and address the same topics, but areas

7

in which each tradition speaks of a topic that the other does not treat at all, or does not treat in the same proportion. Religions in some ways prove concentric; in other ways each viewed against the model of the other will emerge as eccentric. The categories intersect only partially. If, for example, we wish to compare the Christology of Catholic Christianity with the Christology of Reform Judaism, we shall find little to say – and nothing that makes much sense. The apostle Paul's dietary laws – do not eat the remains of offerings made to idols – hardly compare in volume, density, or depth with the dietary laws we know in Rabbinic Judaism, so to compare the one with the other would be to ignore the matter of proportions. Then again, where two religions do address the same issue, what they say may prove unintelligible to the other. For example, the enlandisement of Judaism in reference to the Land of Israel does not correspond in any close or exact way to the standing, in Islam, of Mecca and Medina. So the possibility that one religion focuses upon topics utterly ignored by the other, or treats as central issues deemed marginal by the other, has to be addressed: whose category formation governs, and how do we compare two (or more) category formations that do not exactly form counterparts one to the other? The answer to that question derives from the decision made by those who undertake comparison: who takes the lead in defining matters, and who responds to whom? The one who speaks first dictates the norm; the respondent, the abnormal. Then comparison wrongly structured merely recapitulates theological apologetics. But how are we to preserve for both participants in the work of comparison the status of normality – norm-setting?

These three obstacles to the comparison of one religion to another, Judaism to Islam and Islam to Judaism, demand attention at the outset. If we ignore them, we may try to compare systems or parts of systems that are quite out of phase with one another and so do not sustain comparison at all. We shall be left merely to record the cacophony that results from different people talking about different things to different people. We may turn out to compare discourse and data of one kind deriving from a given religion with those of quite another order altogether deriving from the other religion: sophisticated theology with unreflective piety, for example. That hardly yields perspective on the things compared. Finally, we may end up comparing things that do not sustain comparison because they are not really comparable at all – apples to Australians, because both begin with an A, for instance. One set of categories, characteristic of one religion, may not afford the possibility of comparison and contrast with the utterly out-of-phase category formation of the other religion.

The three problems find a single solution, which is to focus upon the classical statements of the two religions, and that is what we do in this book. Let us explain.

Which Judaism, which Islam? Recognizing the diversity that the passage of time, the geographical expansion and (multi-)cultural development of the communities of the faithful have brought about, we focus on what by common agreement of the faithful governs through eternity. For Judaism that is the Torah, and for Islam, the Qur'an and the Sunna. Whatever other theology and law animate Judaisms over time, all Judaic religious systems from antiquity to nearly our own day, and the paramount ones today as well, appeal to the Torah for both authority and detailed law. Whatever the diversity of Islamic communities and orientations, the Qur'an and the example of the prophet Muhammad (the Sunna), however understood, together constitute the ultimate source of legal interpretation.

All Judaisms for all time, until nearly the present, have appealed to "the Torah," and each has defined itself by designating its particular and indicative reading of that Torah. When, therefore, we set forth the teachings of "the Torah," we portray Judaism in such a way that nearly all Judaic religious systems over time can have concurred, if not in every detail, then in the main. If what distinguishes one Judaism from another will be its definition of the Torah, still, from the formation of matters immediately prior to the advent of Islam to the present day, all Judaisms concurred about the law set forth in the writings called collectively "the Torah" that are set forth here. What, exactly, are those writings? By "the Torah," in the framework of normative Judaism, we speak of the Hebrew scriptures of ancient Israel, together with the interpretation of those scriptures produced by the ancient sages, or rabbis. In normative Judaism, the Hebrew scriptures are called "the Written Torah," and the documents that collectively authoritatively explain and augment those scriptures are called "the Oral Torah."

In Chapter 2 we present a more detailed definition of these writings. For the present it suffices to state that the Torah, the written as read by the oral part, served as authority and definition for most Judaic religious systems from its closure in late antiquity, by the seventh century CE, to the present time. The reason we restrict our account to the classical formulation of the law of the Torah is simple. As noted above however, various communities of Judaism may have differed in detail, whatever other distinctive practices or particular doctrines they may have adopted for themselves, nearly all representations of Judaic religious systems converged upon and accepted the authority and definition of the Torah, written and oral, that we portray in these pages. Since over time most Judaic authorities referred back to the writings at hand, we are justified in regarding those writings as representative of the law of Judaism, viewed whole and complete. That is why, when we compare Islam to Judaism, it is to the Judaism of the dual Torah, oral and written, as Judaism had reached its systematic statement in writings completed on the eve of the advent of Islam.

When we compare Judaism to Islam, it is to the Islam that we know through the Qur'an and the Sunna, or the normative example set by the prophet Muhammad and/or his close companions, as interpreted in the legal works of the founders of the official schools of Islamic law. Since the Qur'an states repeatedly that the prophet Muhammad is the best example to follow when trying to put those teachings into practice, his words and deeds beyond those recorded in the Qur'an (and, for Shi'i Muslims, those of his descendants) are considered essential to a full understanding of scripture. Collectively known as the Sunna ('way' or normative practice) of the prophet, reports (*ahadith*, singular: *hadith*) of these examples were originally transmitted orally, but by the second century after the prophet's death in 632 CE, scholars began to record these reports, screen them for authenticity, organize, and codify them. By the third century after the Prophet (late ninth/early tenth century CE), there were six major collections of hadith reports for Sunni Muslims. (Shi'i Muslims, a minority who differ from the Sunni Muslims on issues of community leadership, compiled other collections of hadith reports, and by the eleventh century CE had identified three major books of hadith.) Two of the Sunni collections were designated by the majority of scholars at the time as most authoritative. In addition to the Qur'an, then, the hadith collections, and especially those designated as most authentic, are the basis of Islamic law (collectively known as Shari'a). There are four major schools of Islamic law for Sunni Muslims, and another for Shi'i Muslims, all of which were established within the first three centuries of Islam (by the tenth century CE). The founders of the schools are accorded special status in Islam, as are their definitive works. Because Sunni Muslims comprise the vast majority (80–85 per cent) and because their first three schools (Hanafi, Maliki, and Shafi'i) have dominated historically, it is to their formulations of Islamic law, along with the Qur'an and Sunna, that we will compare Judaism.

Whose version of Judaism and of Islam? The one upon which all concur is our answer. The answer is the classical statement, held nearly everywhere to be authoritative among nearly all systems of the one, with the classical statement of the other, equivalently paramount in its context. This means that we are comparing the theoretical statement of the religious law of the one with that of the other – and that alone. Ours is a study in the history and comparison of religions viewed as intellectual constructions. We give an account of how sages imagine things, not how people actually conducted themselves. Since, second, we represent the classical law of the two religions, we portray the views of the religious virtuosi about how people should conduct themselves. We do not claim that ordinary folk kept the law in the way that the classical sources record, or in some other way, or not at all. To give an account of actualities would require, in addition to the laws, a vast amount of evidence of ordinary practice.

More to the point, even if we knew how and to what extent the religious law represents the actualities of the one religion or the other, what comparison between those actualities, respectively, will yield a cogent statement? If we learn, for example, that, in contemporary terms, the Islamic laws of prayer compel massive public response among the faithful, while those of Judaism on prayer do not, what does that comparison teach us about Islam or Judaism? At the outset we confess that, within the framework of the study of religion, we did not know how the work of comparison and contrast would proceed, what hypotheses we might set forth for investigation, what work of interpretation would be made possible, were we to try to describe how the faithful of Islam and of Judaism embodied their respective law codes. Our approach to the study of religion does not equip us to describe, analyze, and interpret actualities in the way that it does prepare us to investigate the ideal types of religion and religiosity portrayed by the classical documents. That is why we restrict ourselves to a portrait of the ideal types that the laws define, making no judgment upon the actualities of the faith. We leave to historians and sociologists the problem of describing, then interpreting, those actualities.

Our picture of the two religions therefore conveys the vision of the virtuosi, the ideal of the sages of the Torah and of the scholars who articulated the classical works of Islamic jurisprudence (*fiqh*). Anyone who wishes to compare the laws of the two religions will begin exactly where we do, but no one who then proposes to compare the two religions will end there. We compare the ideals, the laws as a matter of theory, not the social world formed by the faithful. We do not compare Muslim and Judaic faithful in their ordinary life, and we do not pretend to know how successfully the law of Islam or of Judaism accomplishes its goals in defining the holy community, the Israel imagined by the Torah, the just community contemplated by the Shari'a.

D Category formations: comparing incomparables

Now to the third and, for us, the most critical point: what makes us suppose that the ideal types themselves may be compared at all? That question carries us to the particular puzzle of comparing religions that are not wholly comparable – which is to say, comparing religions. For every religion sees itself in one way or another as unique; that is what the claim to teach truth implicitly alleges. And so far as a religion promises unique knowledge of, or access to, God, that religion by its own definition defies comparison with any other. But even if we turn from the rarified heights of theology and apologetics to the here and now of behavior, we discern among religions viewed as social and cultural systems a series of asymmetrical relationships, whether of belief or behavior. Specifically, some religions make their statement in philosophical–theological terms, others in law, others in yet other intellectual media. Some turn for principal media of religious expression to dance or drama or graphic art or song or story, others to silence and inner meditation. It is difficult to point to a single mode of human expression that is not deemed a critical medium of religious activity by some religions and utterly ignored by others.

11

This brings us to the matter of category formation. By "category forma-tion" we mean the process of setting up, by a religious system, classes of activity which belong together as particular kinds of significant religious expression; further, category formation designates the sets of such associated activities deemed consequential. Category formation tells us what sorts of data group together into a single cogent unit, and what sorts of data do not; what coalesce and sustain generalization, what remain random and unintelli-gible. Marshall Sahlins cites a zoological category formation fabricated by Borges – who attributed it to "a certain Chinese encyclopedia:"

> in which it is written that animals are divided into (a) belonging to the Emperor, (b) embalmed, (c) tame, (d) suckling pigs, (e) sirens, (f) fabulous, (g) stray dogs, (h) included in the present classification, (i) frenzied, (j) innumerable, (k) drawn with a very fine camel hair brush, (l) et cetera, (m) having just broken the water pitcher, (n) that from a long way off look like flies. In the wonderment of this tax-onomy, the thing we apprehend in one great leap, the thing that, by means of the fable, is demonstrated in the exotic charms of another system of thought, is the limitation of our own, the stark impossibility of thinking *that*.[3]

Borges's wonderful invention – no such Chinese encyclopedia ever existed except in his imagination! – calls attention to the centrality, for all rational thought, of the categories that we use for the organization of the inchoate facts, the data of workaday existence. Now the problem before us is that each religion organizes reality by appeal to its own set of categories, and these coalesce in statements intelligible solely within the system that to begin with organizes data in this way. Accounts of one religion are inevitably going to prove categorically inappropriate (incommensurate) to important parts of the data identified as consequential and organized in a particular way by the other religion; that yields results asymmetrical and disproportionate to the evidence. How do we propose to deal with that critical problem in the systematic comparison of religious systems, whole to whole?

Our solution to the problem derives from the data at hand. In basic structure – the kinds of sources used for legislation, the intellectual rules governing the formulation of law, the institutional structure, including its personnel – the two systems show remarkable similarity. Here, comparison, yielding contrast, takes place. The differences appear in detail, not in structure or system. The comparison identifies traits in common and also highlights specific, idiomatic points of difference. In actual legislation as well, the laws of Judaism and Islam often address the same topics and organ-ize data in comparable ways. At others, however, the two systems diverge. The two systems at some points say a different thing about the same topic. Then the contrast affords perspective on the points on which the two systems agree and also differ. Finally, there may be categories that do not intersect proportionately or do not intersect at all. That is, one system may deem a massive and complex topic, requiring much amplification and secondary and tertiary articulation, what the other sees as simple and even inconsequential; or the one system organizes massive legal inquiries into a topic the other treats casually and only in connection with other, more central and generative concerns. Or a topic may form a point of critical tension, a focus of much reflection for both, but for entirely different reasons; conversely, an issue of central concern to both religions may be treated in different categories by each of them. Then again, the one system may contain a heavy burden of legislation about a topic that lies wholly outside of the ken of the other.

All three results of the comparison of the religio-legal categories of classical Judaism and Islam are exposed in this book. We shall see that the legal category formation of classical Islam and that of Judaism intersect but also part company; that they prove concentric but not identical. The result shows the ways in which the two religions, in their authoritative statements, are alike and yet not alike. Out of the differences much will follow for the definition of the two religions and also for the formulation of hypotheses about how these two religions fit into the family of world religions.

How do we propose to face the fact that beyond points of common interest, the law of Judaism legislates for matters quite uninteresting to the law of Islam, and the law of Islam articulates rules for circumstances of slight interest or no relevance to Judaism? The shared trait of Islam and Judaism that makes comparison possible in the first place also defines what can be compared. Both are not only religions of law, but religions that legislate for the social order. They are political religions. Because both believe that God has revealed a design for a just and righteous community, the circle of Islam proves sufficiently concentric with the circle of Judaism that substantial areas of overlap emerge. It is there, in the recognition that Islam and Judaism are alike but not alike, that comparison takes place. They are alike in asking law to incorporate the theory of the design of the just society that they agree God means human beings to build. They therefore share a large corpus of categories, legislate about many of the same things, and do so in much the same way. And even where they differ in details of the law, they concur on the category formation that treats given topics together as significant for definition and encapsulation in normative rules. But each also defines for itself categories utterly outside of the religious imagination that animates the other, legislating for topics about which the counterpart is silent or legislates under a different category. These are the areas where each defines itself in its own terms. Let us briefly specify our view of areas of concentricity and eccentricity.

1 *Shared structures*

The most obvious area of comparison between Judaism and Islam is their very constitution as religio-legal communities. As systems based on belief in one God who reveals His will for humanity through prophets, Judaism and Islam share a common approach to their essential structural components. Each considers revelation – in both written and oral form – to be the ultimate source of law. Each incorporates specific intellectual methods for deriving legislation from the sources. Each establishes courts as central sociopolitical institutions, those empowered to administer the legal system and, as such, definitive of the community's identity. Finally, in view of the definitive role played by law in the community, both Judaism and Islam establish rigorous standards for its legal personnel. These structural similarities, each the focus of a chapter, provide the basis from which we may explore shared and unique categories of actual legislation.

2 *Shared categories*

(a) *Areas where they say the same thing about the same topic*

In the basic dimensions of religious life – relationships between individuals and God, and relationships between and among human beings – the two systems take up a common agenda and concur on much within that agenda; the differences turn out to pertain to details or to matters of proportion or context, not to the basic logic of the respective systems. Because of the general concurrence of the two systems in these areas, we have omitted detailed explication. Aspects of the following summary are referred to in passing throughout the core of the book.

Between individuals and God: Individuals' relationship to God comes to expression, first of all, in prayer. People mark time – the passage of the sun and moon through the heavens – as occasions of consecration, taking note of the times of day and holy seasons coincident with the movements of the sun and phases of the moon. So in both religions the advent of particular times and days, designated in relationship to the movement of celestial bodies, provokes religious activity of sanctification, expiation, and celebration. People reach out to God in prayer, and characteristic of both religions, which value the provision of norms and rules, is a significant corpus of laws governing the how-to's of common prayer and private devotions as well.

Like prayer, purity is a major category shared by Judaism and Islam. In both systems, certain foods are considered impure and must be avoided. Most human discharges are also considered polluting, such as those associated with sexual intercourse, menstruation, and childbirth. Purification from such ritual impurity requires specific bathing ceremonies. Major religious rituals must also be preceded by ritual bathing.

14

Fasting also defines a category common to both systems. Each recommends supererogatory fasting as a means of expiation, the extent and timing of which are left to the individual. Judaism and Islam both legislate specific times for required fasting as well. In Judaism, required fasting takes place on the Day of Atonement, in self-denial to atone for sin, on the ninth of the month of Ab, in mourning for the destruction of the Temple of Jerusalem, and on certain other, lesser occasions. Islam places far greater emphasis on fasting than does Judaism. Fasting is one of the five duties required of every Muslim. The ninth month of the lunar calendar, Ramadan, is designated as the month during which all able-bodied Muslims under normal circumstances are required to abstain from food, drink, smoking, and sexual activity during the daylight hours. The purpose of fasting is to gain spiritual renewal through awareness of the equality of all creation in its dependency upon God. To enhance the spiritual benefits of fasting, making a proper intention is required, and reading the entire Qur'an during Ramadan is recommended.

Between human beings: Both legal systems regard as critical the divine regulation of relationships between the sexes, legislating extensively for the conduct of family life. Both deem God to take a keen interest in the status of women in relation to men, with divine rites marking the changes in the status of their relationships: betrothal, marriage, and her divorce. Both regard the violation of the rules governing that status as a sin against God, not merely a crime (if that) against the husband or the family. Islam also legislates profusely about inheritance in this regard, specifying precisely who must receive inheritance and in what proportion. The law of Judaism contains provisions of a comparable character, resting in part on revelation in scripture, in part upon oral tradition. Judaism and Islam concur further that God has a heavy stake in the treatment of the poor, and each makes ample provision for care of the needy. Both regard giving alms as a principal religious obligation, one that pleases God.

(b) Areas where they say different things about the same topic

Systems may set forth shared categories but treat the subjects very differently or with a degree of importance disproportionate to the topic in the other system; they may also treat similar topics but under differing categories. We have selected several categories to show in concrete terms how proportionality affects the comparison of common categories. For example, Judaism offers detailed legislation concerning temple law and sacrifice. Islam, on the other hand, has no temple and legislates only sparingly on sacrifice. We also find differences of proportion between the two religions on legislation regarding slaves, for example, with Islam's treatment being far more extensive than that of Judaism.

Judaism and Islam both legislate copiously with regard to specific times considered extraordinary, yet their treatments differ categorically. We find, for example, that regulations regarding the sanctification of time are plentiful in Judaism. The Sabbath, for example, is time essentially sacralized through legislation. In Islam, specific times are dedicated to holy activities. Times of daily prayer, for example, are determined by solar positions; the beginnings of the months specified for fasting and pilgrimage are marked by the position of the moon. However, there is no specific legislation about the times. Holiness lies not in the times themselves but in the activities of the believers during those times. Prayer, fasting, and commemoration and renewal of commitment to the covenant bring people closer to God. Therefore, these activities are the object of legislation in Islam. Judaism does legislate concerning pilgrimage, but it does not occupy the place in Judaism that the hajj does in Islam. In order to find something comparable, we have therefore chosen to treat the Islamic pilgrimage as the counterpart of the Judaic Sabbath. That choice permits us to demonstrate the differing attitudes toward the sanctification of time. That difference will be shown to be paradigmatic when the two religions' unique categories are discussed.

3 Unique categories: areas where they do not intersect

Finally, we come to categories unique to their respective systems. Here we see how differences between the two communities' self-definitions reach concrete expression in the law. While both identify holy places and provide for pilgrimage, the category of enlandisement is of central importance in Judaism but does not exist in Islam. Jerusalem, Medina, and Mecca are of enormous significance in Islam, because they were the sites of formative historic events in the life of the community. Those events are commemorated regularly in the Islamic calendar. The annual pilgrimage to Mecca, site of the sanctuary believed to have been established by Abraham to commemorate the covenant and birthplace of the prophet Muhammad, as discussed above, is of central importance. However, the holiness of these sites differs fundamentally from the notion of inevitable restoration to the Land of Israel encompassed by the term enlandisement. Islam, by contrast, legislates uniquely on the ongoing struggle (*jihad*) to bring all humanity to submission (*islam*) to the divine will. Both sets of laws turn to the regulation of activities that embody the very heart and soul of the faith: the account of the origins of the community and the purpose of its existence. Here the contrast delivers the result of comparison. We turn out to hear the voices of different people talking about different things to different people.

We uncover what makes each unique among religions. Here, in the case of Judaism and Islam, is how generative myth and symbol come to concrete and tangible expression in category formations that encompass and hold together laws utterly unique to the system, the counterpart to the categories in Borges's wonderful joke, "(a) belonging to the Emperor, (b) embalmed, (c) tame, (d) suckling pigs, (e) sirens, (f) fabulous, (g) stray dogs, (h) included in

16

the present classification, (i) frenzied, (j) innumerable, (k) drawn with a very fine camel hair brush, (l) et cetera, (m) having just broken the water pitcher, (n) that from a long way off look like flies." But, as we shall argue in the conclusion, it is at that very point at which the two religious systems scarcely wish to intersect with any other, let alone with this other, that they turn out to exhibit remarkable consensus about how, in the end, people relate to God.

The distinguishing characteristics of Judaism and Islam are also reflected in their unique legislation concerning discipleship and Torah study, for Judaism, and *khilafah* or deputyship and legal scholarship, for Islam. Normative Judaism considered here maintains that at Sinai God gave to Moses the Teaching, or Torah, in two media: writing and memory. The former is transmitted in the Hebrew scriptures of ancient Israel (Christianity's "Old Testament," and then some) that Judaism calls "the Written Torah." The other is received and handed on from the master, Moses, to his disciple, Joshua, and onward in time to the present; the halakhah governing relationships of disciple to master then embodies the myth of origins contained within the simple statement at the head of the Sayings of the Founders (tractate Abot), "Moses received Torah at Sinai and handed it on to Joshua, Joshua to elders, and elders to prophets. And prophets handed it on to the men of the great assembly." The emphasis on generational continuity in scripture study is nowhere to be found in Sunni Islam; rather, the qualifications for expertise in the study of law are carefully articulated, with the understanding that this undertaking is among the duties of the community pledged to act as God's vicegerent (*khalifah*) on earth. Similarly, we find that Judaism and Islam concur that God has a heavy stake in history. Israel, the holy people of God, and the Islamic *ummat al-wasit* – the "median" or just community – take upon themselves a heavy responsibility to represent God's will, to accomplish God's purposes, in the here and now of history. However, in Judaism, the responsibility for living in accordance with God's law is undertaken by the Jewish community alone, which cherishes the hope that God will call all humanity to share in their eternal reward for doing so. In Islam, it is the believers' responsibility to try to transform all humanity into a just and godly society. All those who submit to the will of God will be rewarded on earth with the peace and security of knowing they are pleasing God, and in the afterlife, with eternal bliss. The two religions differ on the question of who is responsible for the transformation of all humanity into a peaceful, godly community. That they share this goal, however, as we shall discuss in the epilogue, allows us to see that, in the context of world religions, Judaism and Islam are as close as they can be without being identical twins. Now let us see how they differ.

2

THE AUTHORITATIVE LEGAL
DOCUMENTS OF JUDAISM
AND ISLAM

Ours is a task of describing the facts of the two religions subject to comparison, so organizing these facts as to permit comparison both explicit and otherwise. We begin with the basics: the law of Judaism, the law of Islam, and where we are likely to locate it.

A Where do we look for the law?

Both Judaism and Islam present themselves as traditional religions. In other words, they are religions that receive revelation from God through prophets and hand on that revealed truth from generation to generation. "Tradition," then, means that which is handed on out of the past; a traditional religion identifies a particular point at which, in the past, a truth was set forth to be preserved and handed on for generations to come, to serve as authority for all time. A traditional religion attributes to God the origin of such an enduring truth, and Judaism and Islam concur that God gives truth through prophets, men chosen for that purpose. Both agree, moreover, that God's revelation takes the form of specific, verbal statements; God reveals not only Himself but what He wants from human beings. Then the tradition of Judaism or of Islam addresses not only God's word, but God's exact words, sentences formulated in a particular language by God for the prophet to hand on ultimately to us.

When, therefore, a Judaic religious authority or rabbi wants to find the law, in the classical statement of Judaism he consults the record of the tradition, written and oral, of God's revelation to Moses at Sinai. Hence the word "tradition" carries a heavy apologetic charge. The law is represented, from start to finish, as a seamless, cogent, and harmonious statement of God's will, to be located in the Torah. The written tradition ("the Torah in writing") is set forth in the Hebrew scriptures, particularly in the Pentateuch ("Five Books of Moses"), and, within the Pentateuch, in Exodus, Leviticus, Numbers, and Deuteronomy. The oral tradition ("the Torah in memory") is ultimately preserved in a variety of documents that reached closure in the

18

first six centuries of the Common Era (CE = AD). These are the documents we consult for the law of Judaism. Over time these documents attracted numerous commentaries. Not only so, but when the faithful consulted sages over long distances, the replies, in writing, called "responsa," would accumulate as an additional source of law. Finally, as the laws unfolded, systematic codes would be created to afford ready access to them, and these codes would also be subjected to commentaries.

Opinions differed, and the most striking trait of the documents overall is their eagerness to preserve diverse opinion. But, as is clear from this description, the entire legal system developed in a cogent way and found its authoritative statement in a finite number of writings. Despite being scattered between Christian Europe and Muslim North Africa and the Middle East, because of the success of the ancient sages in setting forth the entire corpus of religious law in a coherent body of writings, the Jews maintained a highly cogent legal tradition. In the formative age with which we deal, the main structures of the law and the exegetical media for translating principles into the details of cases, if not uniform, cohered, and differences between authorities or schools of thought dealt with details. The main points of the law – the theory, the method, the basic philosophy and theology – proved uniform throughout the world of Judaism.

Islam, for its part, followed a similar pattern. The ultimate source of Islamic law is revelation, which is believed to have been in two forms. The written text is the Qur'an, delivered through the prophet Muhammad over a twenty-two- to twenty-three-year period in seventh-century Mecca and Medina in (currently Saudi) Arabia. It is complemented by oral tradition, carried in reports (*ahadith*; singular and collective: *hadith*) relating the words and deeds of the prophet Muhammad. On the basis of verses of the Qur'an describing Muhammad as the interpreter and exemplar of its teachings, Muslims believe that the Prophet's behavior is their best guide to understanding and implementing written revelation. His example is considered normative, as are the decisions he made in response to questions put to him outside of the confines of scripture. This normative example is called the Sunna (also spelled Sunnah). Collected and codified by the third century after the death of Muhammad (632 CE), there are now six official collections of Sunni hadith, two of which are considered to contain reports whose authenticity has been determined. While many hadith reports disagree with one another, and there remains disagreement among scholars regarding individual hadith reports' reliability and applicability, virtually all Muslims accept the principle that the Sunna of the Prophet, though secondary to the Qur'an, is essential to the understanding of scripture and therefore, like the written text, bears revelatory power. It acts as an authoritative explication of written scripture.

As Muslim rule spread beyond the Arabian peninsula – within one century of the prophet's death, it extended to Spain in the West and Central Asia in the East – issues arose that were not specifically covered in the Qur'an and the Sunna. A body of scholarship arose, therefore, deriving needed legislation from the revealed sources. The Qur'an and Sunna were believed to reveal the will of God for humankind; they embodied eternal and immutable divine law, Shari'a. But determination of specific applications of that law in the ever-changing circumstances of daily life fell to scholars devoted to gaining a clear understanding of the revealed divine will. Within the first three centuries of the Islamic era, a number of schools of legal thought developed in this regard. While all agreed on the ultimate sources and methodology for deriving legislation, they differed on the relative importance of sources as well as on specific points of interpretation and customary practice. Four of the schools survived to become classical Sunni law. (Shi'i Islam developed another school of law, surprisingly similar to Sunni law in detail, but based on its own collection of hadith literature. This volume will concern itself with Sunni law only.)

B The Written and the Oral Torah: scripture, the Mishnah and the Talmuds

1 Scripture: The Written Torah

By "the Written Torah," Judaism means the Hebrew scriptures of ancient Israel (what Christians know as the "Old Testament," plus a few books), beginning with the Pentateuch (the Five Books of Moses: Genesis, Exodus, Leviticus, Numbers, and Deuteronomy). The reason that this fact matters in the present context is that the last four named books contain important presentations of law, systematic accounts of the political and social institutions of the kingdom of priests and the holy people that Israel is supposed to constitute and the laws that are supposed to define that holy society.

Because the Written Torah is believed to be only part of the teaching of Sinai, classical Judaism never reads scripture on its own but only in dialogue with the Oral Torah, that is, the other part of that same teaching. Hence, to regard Judaism as "the religion of the Old Testament" and to suppose that the law of Judaism emerges directly from the Written Torah misrepresents matters. Judaism is the religion of "the one whole Torah of Moses," who is further called "our rabbi." But at the same time, the Written Torah, in the formation of the law, enjoys a privileged position. It defines most, though not all, of the legal categories of Judaism. It serves as the final authority in all disputes, in that if a verse of scripture or an authoritative interpretation thereof sustains one position in a dispute, the holder of the contrary position has either to overturn the interpretation with one supporting his view or to give up his position altogether.

A single example suffices to show how the Written Torah finds its place in the formulation of the law of Judaism. Exodus 21:24 declares that if one knocks out the eye of another, then the penalty is "an eye for an eye." But the

Oral Torah takes for granted that what is required is monetary compensation, not physical retribution: "He who injures his fellow is liable to [compensate] him on five counts" (Mishnah-tractate Baba Qamma 8:1A). The Talmud of Babylonia then finds evidence in both reason and the actual wording of the Written Torah to demonstrate that when the Torah speaks of "an eye for an eye," it refers to monetary compensation. The first proof provides an argument based upon reason; specifically, the rational reading of the rules of scripture:

> Might one suppose that if someone blinded a person's eye the court should blind his eye? Or if he cut off his hand, then the court should cut off his hand, or if he broke his leg, the court should break his leg? scripture states, "He who hits any man . . . and he who hits any beast" – just as if someone hits a beast, he is assigned to pay monetary compensation, so if he hits a man, he is required to pay monetary compensation.

Scripture treats as comparable the case of smiting a man and the case of smiting a beast, hence, by argument from analogy, just as someone who hits a beast compensates the owner, so someone who hits a man compensates the man. That, then, has to convey the intent of scripture when it speaks of "an eye for an eye." The Talmud, for its part, investigates just where and how scripture makes the point that is taken for granted in the process of analogical reasoning.

A second proof is offered, this time a reading of a verse of scripture itself. Here the language of scripture is closely parsed, producing the desired result:

> And if you prefer, then note the following: "Moreover you shall take no ransom for the life of a murderer, who is guilty of death" (Numbers 35:31) – for *the life of a murderer* you shall take no ransom, but you shall take a ransom for the major limbs, which will not grow back.

The italicized words are taken to exclude from the rule other components of the case in which someone has injured another person. Ransom for the limbs is explicitly encompassed through the exclusionary language that is used: the life, no; but the limbs, yes. In this way the language of the Written Torah itself yields the required clarification: "an eye for an eye" imposes the penalty of compensation for the eye, but not physical retribution. In this way we see how the Oral Torah takes over the law set forth by the Written Torah and imparts to the language of the Written Torah a meaning deemed implicit therein. That meaning may derive from a search for analogies or it may emerge from a close reading of the text. An uninterpreted scripture does not exist in Judaism, and the Hebrew scriptures read outside of the framework of the Oral Torah do not represent Judaism.

2 *Mishnah: the Oral Torah*

The initial and principal statement of that law, called in Hebrew "the hala-khah," the definition of its organizing categories of the halakhah, are set forth not in scripture but by the Mishnah. The Mishnah is a systematic law code with profound philosophical concerns that was produced in the Land of Israel at the end of the second century CE under the auspices of the ruler of the Jewish community of the country at that time. The patriarch, Judah, recognized by the Roman government as ethnarch, authority for a particular community, sponsored the collection of legal traditions, some deriving from very ancient times, beginning in scripture itself, others worked out over the previous two centuries, all of them set forth in a single literary form in a quite distinctive language. While it is in the form of a code of laws, the Mishnah's repertoire of topics encompasses matters that the secular West would not ordinarily include in a law code at all. Not only so, but the code is not merely informative. It does much more than collect and arrange random information. By its program of topics and by the questions it addresses in the exposition of those topics, the Mishnah pursues some few, profound concerns.

How exactly do we recognize the deep layers of abstract reflection that undergird the surface of detailed legal exposition and exegesis? To see how the law formulates in concrete terms principles of considerable abstraction, let us consider the way in which the Mishnah sets forth the debate between actualities and potentialities, such as Aristotelian philosophy considered in its study of causation. Here is the final paragraph of the Mishnah:

> A. Honeycombs: from what point are they susceptible to unclean-ness in the status of liquid?
> B. The House of Shammai say, "When one smokes out [the bees from the combs, so that one can potentially get at the honey]."
> C. The House of Hillel say, "When one will actually have broken up [the honeycombs to remove the honey]."
>
> (M[ishnah-tractate] Uqsin 3:11)

What is at stake in this rather odd dispute? At issue is the status, as to uncleanness or cleanness, of liquid, which is susceptible to the uncleanness deriving from sources of uncleanness specified by Leviticus, chapters 11 through 15. The premise of the question, "from what point does liquid become susceptible," is that liquid may or may not be susceptible to uncleanness at all.

Let us work our way back from the answer to the question, beginning with the shared principle. From the answers to the question we derive the principle shared by both parties. One party maintains that the liquid of honeycombs is susceptible to uncleanness when one has smoked out the bees; the other, when one has broken the honeycombs. Clearly, therefore, when I have access to the honey so that I may make use of it, the honey is susceptible; hence liquid that is not accessible to human use (in this context) is deemed insusceptible; Leviticus 11:34, 37 are read to make that point. So much for the concrete issue.

But what is the principle at hand? I have interpolated some words to make clear in context the issue of whether what is potential is real. That is to say, do I take account of what potentially may happen? Or do I treat as fact only what has happened? The House of Shammai say that once you have smoked out the bees, you have access to the honey. What is potential is treated as equivalent to what is actual. Since you can get at the honey, the honey can be useful to you and so is susceptible. The House of Hillel say that only when you have actually broken the honeycombs by a concrete deed is the honey susceptible. What is potential is not taken into account, only what is actual. So at stake in this odd passage is a very familiar debate. It specifically concerns the old philosophical problem of the acorn and the oak, the egg and the chicken, the potential and the actual. Discourse takes place at three dimensions all at once: (1) through *how* things are said, (2) through *what* is said, and (3) through *what lies beneath the surface* of things as well.

Now let us turn to the topical program – the category formation – of the halakhah, which the Mishnah defines for the classical statement of Judaism. The Mishnah comprises sixty-two tractates, divided by topics among six divisions as follows:

1 Agriculture (Zeraʿim): Berakhot (Blessings); Peah (the corner of the field); Demai (doubtfully tithed produce); Kilayim (mixed seeds); Shebiʿit (the seventh year); Terumot (heave offering or priestly rations); Maʿaserot (tithes); Maʿaser Sheni (second tithe); Hallah (dough offering); Orlah (produce of trees in the first three years after planting, which is prohibited); and Bikkurim (first fruits).
2 Appointed Times (Moʿed): Shabbat (the Sabbath); erubin (the fictive fusion meal or boundary); Pesahim (Passover); Sheqalim (the temple tax); Yoma (the Day of Atonement); Sukkah (the Festival of Tabernacles); Besah (the preparation of food on the festivals and Sabbath); Rosh Hashshanah (the New Year); Taanit (fast days); Megillah (Purim); Moʿed Qatan (the intermediate days of the festivals of Passover and Tabernacles); Hagigah (the festal offering).
3 Women (Nashim): Yebamot (the levirate widow); Ketubot (the marriage contract); Nedarim (vows); Nazir (the special vow of the Nazirite); Sotah (the wife accused of adultery); Gittin (writs of divorce); Qiddushin (betrothal).
4 Damages or civil law (Neziqin): Baba Qamma, Baba Mesia, Baba Batra

(civil law covering damages and torts, then correct conduct of business, labor, and real estate transactions); Sanhedrin (institutions of government; criminal penalties); Makkot (flogging); Shabuot (oaths); Eduyyot (a collection arranged on other than topical lines); Horayot (rules governing improper conduct of civil authorities).

5   Holy things (Qodoshim): Zebahim (everyday animal offerings); Menahot (meal offerings); Hullin (animals slaughtered for secular purposes); Bekhorot (firstlings); Arakhin (vows of valuation); Temurah (vows of exchange of a beast for an already consecrated beast); Keritot (penalty of extirpation or premature death); Me'ilah (sacrilege); Tamid (the daily whole offering); Middot (the layout of the temple building); Qinnim (how to deal with bird offerings designated for a given sacrificial purpose and then confused with other birds bearing different designations).

6   Purity (Tohorot): Kelim (susceptibility of utensils to uncleanness); Ohalot (transmission of corpse uncleanness in the tent of a corpse); Negaim (the uncleanness described in Leviticus 13–14); Parah (the preparation of purification water); Tohorot (problems of doubt in connection with matters of cleanness); Miqvaot (immersion pools); Niddah (menstrual uncleanness); Makhsirin (rendering susceptible to uncleanness produce that is dry and so not susceptible); Zabim (the uncleanness covered in Leviticus 15); Tebul-Yom (the uncleanness of one who has immersed on that selfsame day and awaits sunset for completion of the purification rites); Yadayim (the uncleanness of hands); Uqsin (the uncleanness transmitted through what is connected to unclean produce).

In volume, the sixth division covers approximately a quarter of the entire document. Topics of interest to the priesthood and the temple, such as priestly fees, conduct of the cult on holy days, conduct of the cult on ordinary days and management and upkeep of the temple, and the rules of cultic cleanness, predominate in the first, second, fifth, and sixth divisions. Rules governing the social order form the bulk of the third and fourth divisions. Of these tractates, only Eduyyot is organized along other than topical lines, rather collecting sayings on diverse subjects attributed to particular authorities. The Mishnah as printed today always includes Abot (sayings of the sages), but that document reached closure about a generation later than the Mishnah. While it serves as its initial apologetic, it does not conform to the formal, rhetorical, or logical traits characteristic of the Mishnah overall.

Main points of stress in the Mishnah: The stress of the Mishnah throughout on the priestly caste and the temple cult – the first, fifth, and sixth divisions – points to the document's principal concern, which centered upon sanctification, understood as the correct arrangement of all things, each in its proper category, each called by its rightful name, just as at the creation as portrayed in the priestly document, and just as with the cult itself as set forth in Leviticus. Further, the thousands of rules and cases (with sages' disputes thereon) that comprise the document turn out upon close reading to express in concrete language abstract principles of hierarchical classification. These define the document's method and mark it as a work of a philosophical character. Not only so, but a variety of specific, recurrent concerns, for example, the relationship of being to becoming, actual to potential, the principles of economics, the politics, correspond point by point to comparable ones in Graeco-Roman philosophy, particularly in Aristotle's tradition. This stress on proper order and right rule and the formulation of a philosophy, politics, and economics, within the principles of natural history set forth by Aristotle, explains why the Mishnah makes a statement to be classified as philosophy, concerning the order of the natural world in its correspondence with the supernatural world.

The Mishnah's philosophy: method and propositions: The system of philosophy expressed through concrete and detailed law presented by the Mishnah consists of a coherent logic and topic, a cogent world-view and comprehensive way of living. It is a world-view which speaks of transcendent things, a way of life in response to the supernatural meaning of what is done, a heightened and deepened perception of the sanctification of Israel in deed and in deliberation. Sanctification thus means two things: first, distinguishing Israel in all its dimensions from the world in all its ways; second, establishing the stability, order, regularity, predictability, and reliability of Israel in the world of nature and supernature in particular at moments and in contexts of danger. Danger means instability, disorder, irregularity, uncertainty, and betrayal. Each topic of the system as a whole takes up a critical and indispensable moment or context of social being. Through what is said in regard to each of the Mishnah's principal topics, what the system expressed through normative rules as a whole wishes to declare is fully articulated. Yet if the parts severally and jointly give the message of the whole, the whole cannot exist without all of the parts, so well joined and carefully crafted as they are. The details become clear in our survey of the document's topical program.

To understand the complete system set forth by the Mishnah, we review the six divisions as they were finally spelled out. This review provides a survey of the main themes of the law of Judaism in its definitive statement.

The Division of Agriculture treats two topics: first, producing crops in accord with the scriptural rules on the subject; second, paying the required offerings and tithes to the priests, Levites, and poor. The principal point of the division is that the land is holy, because God has a claim both upon it and upon what it produces. God's claim must be honored by setting aside a portion of the produce for those to whom God has designated it. God's ownership must be acknowledged by observing the rules which God has laid down for use of the land. In the temporal context in which the Mishnah was produced, some generations after the disastrous defeat by the Romans of Bar Kokhba and the permanent closure of Jerusalem to Jews' access, the stress of the division brought assurance that those aspects of the sanctification of

25

Israel – the Land of Israel, Israel itself and its social order, the holy cycle of time – that survived also remained holy and subject to the rules of heaven.

The Division of Appointed Times carried forward the same emphasis upon sanctification, now of the high points of the lunar–solar calendar of Israel. The second division forms a system in which the advent of a holy day, like the Sabbath of creation, sanctifies the life of the Israelite village through imposing on the village rules on the model of those of the temple. The purpose of the system, therefore, is to bring into alignment the moment of sanctification of the village and the life of the home with the moment of sanctification of the temple on those same occasions at appointed times. The underlying and generative logic of the system is expressed here in a concrete way. We recall the rule of like and opposite, comparison and contrast. What is not like something follows the rule opposite to that pertaining to that something. Here, therefore, since the village is the mirror image of the temple, the upshot is dictated by the analogical–contrastive logic of the system as a whole. If things are done in one way in the temple, they will be done in the opposite way in the village. Together, the village and the temple on the occasion of the holy day therefore form a single continuum, a completed creation, thus awaiting sanctification. The village is made like the temple in that at appointed times one may not freely cross the lines distinguishing the village from the rest of the world, just as one may not freely cross the lines distinguishing the temple from the world. But the village is a mirror image of the temple. The boundary lines prevent free entry into the temple, so they restrict free egress from the village. On the holy day, what one may do in the temple is precisely what one may not do in the village.

So the advent of the holy day affects the village by bringing it into sacred symmetry in such a way as to effect a system of opposites; each is holy, in a way precisely the opposite of the other. Because of the underlying conception of perfection attained through the union of opposites, the village is not represented as conforming to the model of the cult, but of constituting its antithesis. The world thus regains perfection when on the holy day heaven and earth are united, the whole completed and done: the heaven, the earth, and all their hosts. This moment of perfection renders the events of ordinary time, of "history," essentially irrelevant. For what really matters in time is that moment in which sacred time intervenes and effects the perfection formed of the union of heaven and earth, of temple, in the model of the former, and Israel, its complement. It is not a return to a perfect time but a recovery of perfect being, a fulfillment of creation, which explains the essentially ahistorical character of the Mishnah's Division on Appointed Times. Sanctification constitutes an ontological category and is effected by the creator.

This explains why the division in its rich detail is composed of two quite distinct sets of materials. First, it addresses what one does in the sacred space of the temple on the occasion of sacred time, as distinct from what one does in that same sacred space on ordinary, undifferentiated days, which is a subject worked out in holy things. Second, the division defines how for the occasion of the holy day one creates a corresponding space in one's own circumstance, and what one does, within that space, during sacred time. The division as a whole holds together through a shared, generative metaphor. It is the comparison, in the context of sacred time, of the spatial life of the temple to the spatial life of the village, with activities and restrictions to be specified for each, upon the common occasion of the Sabbath or festival. The Mishnah's purpose therefore is to correlate the sanctity of the temple, as defined by the holy day, with the restrictions of space and of action which make the life of the village different and holy, as defined by the holy day.

The Division of Women defines the women in the social economy of Israel's supernatural and natural reality. Women acquire definition wholly in relation to men, who impart form to the Israelite social economy. The status of women is effected through both supernatural and natural, this-worldly action. Women formed a critical systemic component because the proper regulation of women – subject to the father, then the husband – was deemed a central concern of heaven, so that a betrothal would be subject to heaven's supervision (Qiddushin, sanctification, being the pertinent tractate); documents, such as the marriage contract or the writ for divorce, drawn up on earth, stand also for heaven's concern with the sanctity of women in their marital relationship; so too, heaven may through levirate marriage dictate whom a woman marries. What man and woman do on earth accordingly provokes a response in heaven, and the correspondences are perfect. So women are defined and secured both in heaven and here on earth, and that position is always and invariably relative to men.

The principal interest for the Mishnah is interstitial, just as, in general, sanctification comes into play at interstitial relationships, those that require decisive classification. Here it is the point at which a woman becomes, and ceases to be, holy to a particular man; that is, entering and leaving the marital union. These transfers of women are the dangerous and disorderly points in the relationship of woman to man, therefore, the Mishnah states, to society as well. The division's systemic statement stresses the preservation of order in transactions involving women and (other) property. Within this orderly world of documentary and procedural concerns a place is made for the disorderly conception of the marriage not formed by human volition but decreed in heaven, the levirate connection. Mishnah-tractate Yebamot states that supernature sanctifies a woman to a man (under the conditions of the levirate connection). What it says indirectly is that man sanctifies too: man, like God, can sanctify that relationship between a man and a woman, and can also effect the cessation of the sanctity of that same relationship.

Five of the seven tractates of the Division of Women are devoted to the formation and dissolution of the marital bond. Of them, three treat what is done by man here on earth; that is, formation of a marital bond through betrothal and marriage contract and dissolution through divorce and its consequences. The division and its system therefore delineate the natural and supernatural character of the woman's role in the social economy framed by man: the beginning, end, and middle of the relationship. The whole constitutes a significant part of the Mishnah's encompassing system of sanctification, for the reason that heaven confirms what men do on earth. A correctly prepared writ of divorce on earth changes the status of the woman to whom it is given, so that in heaven she is available for sanctification to some other man, while, without that same writ, in heaven's view, should she go to some other man, she would be liable to be put to death. The earthly deed and the heavenly perspective correlate. That is indeed very much part of a larger system, which says the same thing over and over again.

The Division of Damages comprises two subsystems, which fit together in a logical way. One part presents rules for the normal conduct of civil society. These cover commerce, trade, real estate, and other matters of everyday intercourse, as well as mishaps, such as damages by chattels and persons, fraud, overcharge, interest, and the like, in that same context of everyday social life. The other part describes the institutions governing the normal conduct of civil society; that is, courts of administration, and the penalties at the disposal of the government for the enforcement of the law. The two subjects form a single tight and systematic dissertation on the nature of Israelite society and its economic, social, and political relationships, as the Mishnah envisages them. The main point of the first of the two parts of the division is that the task of society is to maintain perfect stasis, to preserve the prevailing situation, and to secure the stability of all relationships. To this end, in the interchanges of buying and selling, giving and taking, borrowing and lending, it is important that there be an essential equality of interchange. No party in the end should have more than what he had at the outset, and none should be the victim of a sizable shift in fortune and circumstance. All parties' rights to, and in, this stable and unchanging economy of society are to be preserved. When the condition of a person is violated, the law will secure the restoration of the antecedent status as far as possible.

The goal of the system of civil law is the recovery of the prevailing order and balance, the preservation of the established wholeness of the social economy. This idea is powerfully expressed in the organization of the three tractates that comprise the civil law, which treat first abnormal and then normal transactions. The framers deal with damages done by chattels and by human beings, thefts and other sorts of malfeasance against the property of others. The civil law in both aspects pays closest attention to how the property and person of the injured party so far as possible are restored to their prior condition; that is, a state of normality. So attention to torts focuses upon penalties paid by the malefactor to the victim, rather than upon penalties inflicted by the court on the malefactor for what he has done. When speaking of damages, the Mishnah thus takes as its principal concern the restoration of the

28

fortune of victims of assault or robbery. Then the framers take up the complementary and corresponding set of topics, the regulation of normal transactions. When we rapidly survey the kinds of transactions of special interest, we see from the topics selected for discussion what we have already uncovered in the deepest structure of organization and articulation of the basic theme.

The other half of this same unit of three tractates presents laws governing normal and routine transactions, many of which are of the same sort as those dealt with in the first half. At issue are deposits of goods or possessions that one person leaves in safe-keeping with another. Called bailments, for example, cases of such transactions occur in both wings of the triple tractate: first, bailments subjected to misappropriation, or accusation thereof, by the bailiff; second, bailments transacted under normal circumstances. Under the rubric of routine transactions are those of workers and householders; that is, the purchase and sale of labor, rentals and bailments, real estate transactions, and inheritances and estates. Of the lot, the one involving real estate transactions is the most fully articulated and covers the widest range of problems and topics. The three tractates of the civil law thus collectively provide a complete account of the orderly governance of balanced transactions and unchanging civil relationships within Israelite society under ordinary conditions.

The character and interests of the Division of Damages present probative evidence of the larger program of the philosophers of the Mishnah. Their intention is to create nothing less than a full-scale Israelite government, subject to the administration of sages. This government is fully supplied with a constitution and by-laws. It makes provision for a court system and procedures, as well as a full set of laws governing civil society and criminal justice. This government, moreover, mediates between its own community and the outside ("pagan") world. Through its system of laws it expresses its judgment of others and at the same time defines, protects, and defends its own society and social frontiers. It even makes provision for procedures of remission, to expiate its own errors. The (then non-existent) Israelite government imagined by the second-century philosophers centers upon the (then non-existent) temple, and the (then forbidden) city, Jerusalem. For the temple is one principal focus. There the highest court is in session; there the high priest reigns.

The penalties for law infringement are of four kinds, one of which involves sacrifice in the temple. (The others are compensation, physical punishment, and death.) The basic conception of punishment, moreover, is that unintentional infringement of the rules of society, whether "religious" or otherwise, is not penalized but rather expiated through an offering in the temple. If a member of the people of Israel intentionally infringes the law, that person must be removed from society and be put to death. And if there is a claim of one member of the people against another, that must be righted, so that the prior, prevailing status may be restored. So offerings in the temple are given up to appease heaven and restore a whole bond between heaven and Israel, specifically on those occasions on which without malice or ill will an Israelite has disturbed the relationship. Israelite civil society without a temple is not stable or normal, and not to be imagined. And the Mishnah is above all an act of imagination in defiance of reality.

The plan for the government involves a clear-cut philosophy of society, a philosophy that defines the purpose of the government and ensures that its task is not merely to perpetuate its own power. What the Israelite government, within the Mishnaic fantasy, is supposed to do is to preserve a perfect, steady-state society. That state of perfection which, within the same fantasy, the society to begin with everywhere attains and expresses forms the goal of the system throughout: no change anywhere from a perfect balance, proportion, and arrangement of the social order, its goods and services, responsibilities and benefits. This takes the form of at least five aspects.

First of all, one of the ongoing principles of the law, expressed in one tractate after another, is that people are to follow and maintain the prevailing practice of their locale. Second, the purpose of civil penalties is to restore the injured party to his prior condition so far as is possible, rather than merely to penalize the aggressor. Third, there is the conception of true value, meaning that a given object has an intrinsic worth, which, in the course of a transaction, must be paid. In this way the seller does not leave the transaction any richer than when he entered it, or the buyer any poorer (parallel to penalties for damages). Fourth, there can be no usury, a biblical prohibition adopted and vastly enriched in the Mishnaic thought, for money ("coins") is what it is. Any pretense that it has become more than what it was violates, in its way, the conception of true value. Fifth, when real estate is divided, it must be done with full attention to the rights of all concerned, so that, once more, one party does not gain at the expense of the other. In these and many other aspects the law expresses its obsession with the perfect stasis of Israelite society. Its paramount purpose is in preserving and ensuring that that perfection of the division of this world is kept inviolate or restored to its true status when violated.

The Division of Holy Things presents a system of sacrifice and sanctuary. The division centers upon the everyday and rules always applicable to the cult: the daily whole offering, the sin offering and guilt offering which one may bring any time under ordinary circumstances; the right sequence of diverse offerings; the way in which the rites of the whole, sin, and guilt offerings are carried out; what sorts of animals are acceptable; the accompanying cereal offerings; the support and provision of animals for the cult and of meat for the priesthood; the support and material maintenance of the cult and its building. We have a system before us: the system of the cult of the Jerusalem temple, seen as an ordinary and everyday affair, a continuing and routine operation. That is why special rules for the cult, both in respect to the altar and in regard to the maintenance of the buildings, personnel, and even the whole city, will be elsewhere – in Appointed Times and Agriculture. But from the perspective of holy things, those divisions intersect by supplying special rules and raising extraordinary (Agriculture: land-bound; Appointed Times: time-bound) considerations for that theme which holy things claims to set forth in its most general and unexceptional way: the cult as something permanent and everyday.

The Division of Purities presents a very simple system of three principal parts: sources of uncleanness, objects and substances susceptible to uncleanness, and modes of purification from uncleanness. So it tells the story of what makes a given sort of object unclean and what makes it clean. Viewed as a whole, the Division of Purities treats the interplay of persons, food, and liquids. We return to this matter in Chapter 6, in our discussion of ablutions in Islam and Judaism.

Omitted divisions: When we listen to the silences of the system of the Mishnah, as much as to its points of stress, we hear a single message. It is a message of a system that answered a single encompassing question, and the question formed a stunning counterpart to that of the sixth century BCE. The Pentateuchal system addressed one reading of the events of the sixth century, highlighted by the destruction of the Jerusalem temple in 586 BCE. At stake was how Israel as defined by that system related to its land, represented by its temple, and the message may be simply stated: what appears to be the given is in fact a gift, subject to stipulations. The precipitating event for the Mishnaic system was the destruction of the Jerusalem Temple in 70 CE, the question turned to obsession with the defeat of Bar Kokhba and the closure of Jerusalem to Jews. The urgent issue taken up by the Mishnah was, specifically: what, in the aftermath of the destruction of the holy place and holy cult, remained of the sanctity of the holy caste, the priesthood, the holy land, and, above all, the holy people and its holy way of life? The answer was that sanctity persists, indelibly, in Israel, the people, in its way of life, in its land, in its priesthood, in its food, in its mode of sustaining life, in its manner of procreating and so sustaining the nation.

This summary of the halakhah of Judaism – its legal system and its encompassing category formation – shows the purpose of the system as a whole. The Mishnah's formulation of Judaism's legal system focused upon the holiness of the life of Israel, the people brought into being by God at Sinai – a holiness that had formerly centered on the temple. The logically consequent question was: what is the meaning of sanctity, and how shall Israel attain, or give evidence of, sanctification? The answer to this question derived from the original creation, the end of the temple directing attention to the beginning of the natural world that the temple had embodied. For the meaning of sanctity the framers therefore turned to that first act of sanctification, the one in creation. It came about when, all things in array, in place, each with its proper names, God blessed and sanctified the seventh day on the eve of the first Sabbath. Creation was made ready for the blessing and the sanctification when all things were very good; that is to say, in their rightful order, called by their rightful name. An orderly nature was a sanctified and blessed nature, so dictated scripture in the name of the supernatural. So to receive the blessing and to be made holy, all things in nature and society were to be set in right array. Given the condition of Israel, the people, in its land, in the aftermath of the catastrophic war against Rome led by Bar Kokhba in 132–135, putting things in order was no easy task. But that is why, after all, the question pressed, the answer proving inexorable and obvious. The condition of society corresponded to the critical question that obsessed the system-builders. The legal system of Judaism is set forth by the Mishnah in such a way as to respond to that question.

3 The Talmuds

A talmud – generically defined – is a sustained, systematic amplification and analysis of passages of the Mishnah and other teachings alongside the Mishnah that are accorded the status of authoritative origin in the oral part of the Torah, the part repeated by memory from Sinai on. There are two talmuds: the Talmud of the Land of Israel (aka the Yerushalmi), c. 400 CE, and the Talmud of Babylonia (aka the Bavli), c. 600 CE. The former treats the first four divisions of the Mishnah; the latter, the second through the fifth; each is independent of the other, the two meeting only at parts of the Mishnah and sharing, further, some sayings attributed to authorities after the Mishnah; but these the documents' respective authorships read each in its own way. The second of the two Talmuds forms the definitive statement of the law of Judaism of the dual Torah and defines the curriculum of Torah study in the very centers in which the Torah is studied as God's word and will for Israel. The Talmuds propose to state in writing the basic rules of the social order, and to show us how to discover the right rule, based on the principles God has made known in the Torah, for the affairs of everyday life. In Chapter 3 we consider how that process of discovery takes place.

The Talmuds are documents full of debates on erudite and esoteric questions. But in the debates about fine points of law, ritual, and theology, "our sages of blessed memory" formulated through concrete examples the rules of right thinking and accurate formulation in words of God's will for the here and now. For they held that the Torah is given to purify the hearts of humanity, and that what God really wants is the heart. But there, in the center of life, in the streets and homes of the holy community, Israel, what does that mean? It is through close and careful thinking about little things that the legal authorities, called "our sages," brought the Torah's great principles into the everyday world of ordinary people. The media of language, logic, and law express the message of the Torah of Sinai. The Talmuds show us how, for the purposes of portraying the entirety of the social order, its culture and its politics alike, people write in signals an account of their modes of thought and how these are to be replicated any time and anywhere.

Both Talmuds, strictly speaking – the Yerushalmi, the Bavli – are formed into commentaries to some of the same passages of the Mishnah (tractates in the divisions of Appointed Times, Women, and Damages). The Yerushalmi treats most of the tractates of agriculture but not those of holy things. The Bavli takes up the tractates of holy things but not agriculture. And neither Talmud takes up purities, except for tractate Niddah, on a woman's status during her menstrual period. Both Talmuds are laid out in the same way; that is, as *ad hoc* treatments of phrases or even whole paragraphs of the Mishnah, the two Talmuds are identical in form, species of a genus. The two Talmuds defined Mishnah commentary in a distinctive way, through their active program of supplying not merely information but guidance on its meaning: a program of inquiry, a set of consequential issues, in place of mere information. That program would be fully realized only in the second, and last, of the two Talmuds.

But both Talmuds share the program of harmonizing one rule or principle with another. Both, furthermore, propose to uncover the scriptural foundation of the Mishnah's rules. In common therefore they undertake the sustained demonstration of the theology of the Torah: its perfection, on the one side, its unity (oral and written), on the other. Because of that fact we may properly speak of "the Talmuds," since both do one thing, though the second does another in addition. To begin with, the two Talmuds look alike. That is because both comment on the same prior text, the Mishnah. Both take up a few sentences of that prior text and paraphrase and analyze them. Both ask the same questions, for example, clarifying the language of the Mishnah, identifying the scriptural foundations of the Mishnah's rules, comparing the Mishnah's rules with those of the Tosefta or other texts of Tannaite status; that is, they are presented with attributions of sayings solely to names that occur also in the Mishnah or Tosefta. Furthermore, they are comparable because they organize their materials in the same way. They also take up much the same topical agenda, in common selecting some divisions of the Mishnah and ignoring others, agreeing in particular to treat the matters of everyday practice, as distinct from theory, covered by Mishnah's divisions of Appointed Times, Women, and Damages. Both documents moreover are made up of already-available compositions and composites, which we may identify, in each document, by reference to the same literary traits or indications of completion prior to inclusion in the Talmuds. So they exhibit traits of shared literary policy.

Both Talmuds invariably do to sense units of the Mishnah one of these four things, and each of these procedures will ordinarily be expressed in patterned language. It suffices here to classify the types of patterns: (1) text criticism; (2) exegesis of the meaning of the Mishnah, including glosses and amplifications; (3) addition of scriptural proof texts of the Mishnah's central propositions; and (4) harmonization of one Mishnah passage with another. Each of these types of compositions follows a well-defined form, so that if we were given only an account in abstract terms of the arrangement of subject and predicate or a simple account of the selection of citation language (for example, "as it is said," "our rabbis have taught"), we could readily predict the purpose of the composition or composite. So formal traits accompany the purpose of the commentary compositions and other compositions and composites and permit differentiation one type from another.

The first two of these four procedures remain wholly within the narrow frame of the Mishnah passage subject to discussion. Therefore, in the natural order of things, what the two Talmuds will find interesting in a given Mishnah passage will respond to the same facts and will commonly do so in much the same way. The second pair takes an essentially independent stance *vis-à-vis* the Mishnah pericope at hand. Part of the rhetorical convention of the Talmuds governs the order in which types of compositions – Mishnah text criticism, exegesis, scriptural proof texts, and the like – are set forth. Ordinarily, the order for both Talmuds is the same as given above. While both Talmuds conform to complex and distinctive rhetorical programs, what makes them different from all other documents of rabbinic literature is not only rhetoric but logic, to which we turn forthwith.

The composition of the two Talmuds: The two Talmuds are made up of compositions, complete in themselves, which have been formed into composites. The framers of the Talmuds then resort to two distinct logics of coherent discourse to form whole and cogent documents from their materials. Philosophical logic ordinarily holds together into cogent paragraphs the discrete sentences of a given composition. The logic of fixed association then connects into protracted statements of a cogent character otherwise unrelated sequential sentences, and also joins into sizable compositions entire paragraphs that on their own, through their own propositions, in no way coalesce. The authorship of the Talmuds in the making of medium- and large-scale logical connections thus resorted to two distinct principles of cogent discourse: the one of propositional connection within completed units of thought, a connection discovered through the pursuit of reasoned speculative inquiry; the second, the other of the fixed associative connection between and among those same completed units of thought, producing large-scale compositions.

Sizable numbers of the completed units of thought of the Talmuds find inner cogency through the development of a proposition concerning a given theme. Overall, these units of completed thought are linked to one another through the connections supplied for the Talmuds extrinsically by both the Mishnah and scripture. The framers of the Talmuds had in hand a tripartite corpus of inherited materials awaiting composition into a final, closed document. First, they took up materials, in various states and stages of completion, pertinent to the Mishnah or to the principles of laws that the Mishnah had originally brought to articulation. Second, they had in hand received materials, again in various conditions, pertinent to the scripture, both as the scripture related to the Mishnah and also as the scripture laid forth its own narratives. That fact points to the way in which the logic of fixed association governed their work.

Little of what the Talmuds' authorships present in a propositional form derives cogency and force from a received statement; most of it does not. True, many of the propositions of the two Talmuds, in the nature of things, address the meaning of paragraphs of the Mishnah, and most of the documents are laid out as a commentary to either the Mishnah or scripture. But the authorship of each of the compositions and the framer of the respective composites has selected out of scripture and the Mishnah the passages or topics it wishes to amplify. At stake is the re-formation of the (oral part of the) Torah in a way not envisaged by its writers. The Talmuds do not merely clarify the Mishnah; both of them in fact re-present the Torah – a very different thing.

The writers of the Mishnah created a coherent document, with a topical program formed in accord with the logical order dictated by the characteristics of a given topic, and with a set of highly distinctive formulary and formal traits as well. But these are obscured when the document is taken apart and reconstituted as were the Talmuds. The redefinition of the Torah accomplished by the Talmuds therefore represented a vast revision of the initial writing down of the oral component of the Torah – a point at which the hermeneutics shaded over into a profoundly theological activity.

What happens to the Mishnah in the Talmuds: The Mishnah is read by the Talmuds as a composite of discrete and essentially autonomous rules, a set of atoms, not an integrated molecule, so to speak. In so doing, the most striking formal traits of the Mishnah are obliterated. More important, the Mishnah as a whole and complete statement of a viewpoint no longer exists. Its propositions are reduced to details. But what is offered instead? The answer is a statement that, on occasion, recasts details in generalizations encompassing a wide variety of other details across the gaps between one tractate and another. This immensely creative and imaginative approach to the Mishnah vastly expands the range of discourse. But the consequence is to deny to the Mishnah both its own mode of speech and its distinctive and coherent message. So the two Talmuds formulate their own hermeneutics to convey their theological system: (1) defining the Torah, and (2) demonstrating its perfection and comprehensive character: unity, harmony, lineal origin from Sinai. What the second Talmud would subsequently add to that first stage in theological re-presentation of the Torah is instantiation of modes of analysis of the unity, lineal formation, and harmony of the Torah. But the framers of the first Talmud assuredly affirmed the same points.

Both authorships take an independent stance when facing the Mishnah, making choices, reaching decisions of their own. Both Talmuds' framers deal with Mishnah-tractates of their own choice, and neither provides a Talmud to the entirety of the Mishnah. What the Mishnah therefore contributed to the Talmuds was not received in a spirit of humble acceptance by the sages who produced either of the two Talmuds. Important choices were made about what to treat, hence what to ignore. The exegetical mode of reception did not have to obscure the main lines of the Mishnah's system, but it surely did so. The discrete reading of sentences, or, at most, paragraphs, denying all context, avoiding all larger generalizations except for those transcending the specific lines of tractates – this approach need not have involved the utter reversal of the paramount and definitive elements of the Mishnah's whole and integrated world-view (its "Judaism"). But doing these things did facilitate the revision of the whole into a quite different pattern. That represents a re-presentation of the Torah, one of considerable originality indeed.

A second trait joins with the foregoing. The Mishnah rarely finds it necessary to adduce proof-texts from the written Torah in support of its statements. The Talmuds, by contrast, find it appropriate whenever possible to cite scriptural proof-texts for the propositions of the Mishnah. While the various tractates of the Mishnah relate to scripture in different ways, the view of the framers of the Talmud on the same matter is not differentiated. So far as they are concerned, proof-texts for Mishnaic rules are required. These will be supplied in substantial numbers, and that is the main point. The Mishnah is now systematically represented as not standing free and separate from scripture, but dependent upon it. The authority of the Mishnah's laws is then reinforced. But the autonomy of the Mishnah as a whole is severely compromised. Just as the Mishnah is represented in the Talmud as a set of rules rather than as a philosophical essay, so it is presented, rule by rule, as a secondary and derivative development of scripture. It would be difficult to imagine a more decisive effort to re-formulate the Torah than is accomplished by this work.

The undifferentiated effort to associate diverse Mishnah laws with scripture is to be viewed together with the systematic breakup of the Mishnah into its diverse laws. The two quite separate activities produce a single effect in both Talmuds. They permit the Talmuds to represent the state of affairs pretty much as the framers of the Talmuds wish to do. Theology as a creative venture here determines to (re)define the Torah. And how is this done? Everything is shown to be continuous: scripture, Mishnah, the Tosefta where cited, the authoritative sayings labeled Tannaite where used, ending in – the Talmud itself (whichever Talmud we examine, the effect being the same)! Then all things, as now shaped by the rabbis of the Talmud(s), have the standing of scripture and represent the authority of Moses (now called "our Rabbi"). Accordingly, once the Mishnah enters either of the two Talmuds it nowhere emerges intact. It is wholly preserved, but in bits and pieces, shaped and twisted in whatever ways the Talmuds wish. The Torah now forms a single, continuous statement. And that is the work of the first Talmud, not only of the second.

The Talmuds as distinct from the Mishnah: The question has now to be asked: when do the Talmuds speak for themselves, not for the Mishnah? Second: what sorts of units of discourse contain such passages that bear what is "Talmudic" in the two Talmuds? These two questions produce the same answers for both Talmuds, allowing us to characterize the topical or propositional program of the two Talmuds.

1   Theoretical questions of law not associated with a particular passage of the Mishnah. In the first of the two Talmuds there is some tendency, and in the second, a very marked tendency, to move beyond the legal boundaries set by the Mishnah's rules themselves. More general inquiries are taken up. These of course remain within the framework of the topic of one tractate or another, although there are some larger modes of thought characteristic of more than a single tractate.
2   Exegesis of scripture separate from the Mishnah. It is under this rubric that we find the most important instances in which the Talmuds present materials essentially independent of the Mishnah.
3   Historical statements. The Talmud contains a fair number of statements that something happened, or narratives about how something happened. While many of these are replete with biblical quotations, in general they do not provide exegesis of scripture, which serves merely as an illustration or reference point.
4   Stories about, and rules for, sages and disciples, separate from discussion of a passage of the Mishnah. The Mishnah contains a tiny number of tales about rabbis. These serve principally as precedents for, or illustrations of, rules. The Talmuds by contrast contain a sizable number of stories about sages and their relationships to other people.

When the Talmuds present us with ideas or expressions of a world related to, but fundamentally separate from, that of the Mishnah, that is, when the Talmuds wish to say something other than what the Mishnah says and means, they will take up one of two modes of discourse. Either we find exegesis of biblical passages, with the value system of the rabbis read into the Scriptural tales; or we are told stories about holy men and paradigmatic events, once again through tales told in such a way that a didactic purpose is served. It follows that the Talmuds are composites of three kinds of materials: (1) exegeses of the Mishnah (and other materials classified as authoritative, that is, Tannaite), (2) exegeses of scripture, and (3) accounts of the men who provide both. Both Talmuds then constitute elaborate reworkings of the two antecedent documents: the Mishnah, lacking much reference to scripture, and the scripture itself. The Talmuds bring the two together into a synthesis of their compilers' own making, both in reading scripture into Mishnah, and in reading scripture alongside of, and separate from, Mishnah.

If, therefore, we want to point to what is Talmudic in either of the two

Talmuds it is the exegesis of scripture on the one side, and the narration of historical or biographical tales about holy men on the other. Since much of the biblical exegesis turns upon holy men of biblical times, we may say that the Talmuds speak for themselves alone as distinct from addressing the problems of the Mishnah, when they tell about holy men now and then. But what is genuinely new in the Talmuds, in comparison and contrast to the Mishnah, is the inclusion of extensive discourse on the meaning imputed to scripture.

It follows that the two Talmuds stand essentially secondary to two prior documents: Mishnah (encompassing for this purpose the whole corpus labeled Tannaite, whenever and wherever produced, much being later than the Mishnah and some being Babylonian) on the one side, and scripture on the other. The Mishnah is read in the Talmuds pretty much within the framework of meaning established by the Mishnah itself. Scripture is read as an account of a world remarkably like that of the rabbis of the Talmuds. When the rabbis speak for themselves, as distinct from the Mishnah, it is through exegesis of scripture. (But to them, any other mode of reading scripture would have been unthinkable. They took for granted that they and scripture's heroes and sages lived in a single timeless plane.)

The Mishnah's program and the Talmuds' program: Both Talmuds in common address the tractates of Appointed Times, Women, and Damages, the second, third, and fourth divisions of the Mishnah. That is then where the comparisons and contrasts have to take place. Interest in the division of Appointed Times involved extensive discussion of the conduct of the cult on extraordinary days. Perhaps at issue here was not what had to be omitted (the cult on appointed times) but what people wanted to discuss, the home and village on those same holy occasions. So the former came in the wake of the latter. Inclusion of the divisions of Women, on the family and the transfer of women from father to husband and back, and Damages, on civil law and institutions, is not hard to explain. The sages fully expected to govern the life of Israel, the Jewish people,[1] in its material and concrete aspects. These divisions, as well as some of the tractates of the division on Appointed Times, demanded and received attention. Ample treatment of the laws in the first division, governing the priests' rations and other sacred segments of the agricultural produce of the Holy Land, is to be expected among authorities living not only in, but also off, the Holy Land.

If we stand back and reflect on the Mishnah's program, we recognize how different is that of the respective Talmuds. The Mishnah covers a broad variety of topics which its compilers have identified as critical. The Talmuds contribute none of their own, but trawl across the entire surface of the Mishnah. The Mishnah is organized topically. The Talmuds may be broken down into discrete compositions and neatly joined composites, none of them framed as free-standing, topical formations, all of them in one way or another depending upon the Mishnah for order and coherence. The Mishnah lays out rules and facts about a world beyond itself. The Talmuds negotiate rules and recast facts into propositions that concern the Mishnah – a different focus of discourse and perspective altogether. Continuous with the Mishnah, the two Talmuds in point of fact redirect the Mishnah not only by destroying its integrity and picking and choosing with its topical (and propositional) program, but also by forming out of the detritus of the received writing a statement of their own. But it was not a statement that, in the end, concerned the Mishnah at all, but rather a statement about the Torah, and a statement of the Torah.

In accepting authority, in centering discourse upon the ideas of other men, in patiently listing even the names behind authoritative laws from olden times to their own day, the sages and framers of the Talmud accomplished exactly the opposite of what we might have supposed they wanted to do. They made a commentary. On the surface, that suggests they wanted merely to continue and strengthen the received tradition. But they obliterated the text. They loyally explained the Mishnah, but they turned the Mishnah into something else than what it had been. They patiently hammered out chains of tradition, binding themselves to the authority of the remote and holy past. But it was, in the end, a tradition of their own design and choosing; that is, it was not tradition but a new creation. And so these Talmuds of ours, so loyal and subservient to the Mishnah of Judah the Patriarch, turn out to be less reworkings of received materials than works – each one of them – of remarkably independent judgment. The Talmuds speak humbly and subserviently about received truth, always in the name only of Moses and of sages of times past. But in the end it is truth not discovered and demonstrated, but determined and invented and declared. That is what makes that discovery process so critical, as we shall see in Chapter 3.

The Mishnah speaks of a world in stasis, an unchanging, eternal present tense where all the tensions of chaos are resolved. The Talmuds address the real Israel in the here and now of ever-changing times, the gross matter of disorder and history. Clearly, the central traits of the Mishnah, revealed in the document at its time of closure in *c.* 200 CE, were revised and transformed into those definitive of the Talmud at its time of closure in *c.* 400 CE for the earlier Talmud, 600 for the later. When we compare the Mishnah to the Talmuds we find in each case two intertwined documents, quite different from one another both in style and values. Yet they are so tightly joined that the Talmud appears in the main to provide mere commentary and amplification for the Mishnah.

C Islamic counterparts

1 *Scripture: The Qur'an*

The Qur'an ("Recitation," i.e., of God's message) is the revealed scripture of Islam. According to orthodoxy, it is the uncreated word of God, believed to have been revealed word for word in the Arabic language by the only God through his prophet, Muhammad.

Unlike earlier scriptures, its history is both well known and considered to be of critical importance, for a number of reasons. First of all, the Qur'an claims to be the culmination of monotheistic scriptures. Its message does not differ from that of the Torah and the Gospels, to which it refers repeatedly and approvingly. Instead, it claims to be a confirmation and clarification of messages delivered to earlier prophets, and a correction of misinterpretations of those messages by followers of the prophets who delivered them. It is a unique and complete message in and of itself but, as such, it also completes and perfects the messages revealed through Muhammad's predecessors. Muhammad, accordingly, is not the originator of Islam. He is said to be the last prophet; and the Qur'an is the final installment in what has been a coherent plan of successive revelations of the divine will to humanity. Therefore, the Qur'an's historic appearance after earlier scriptures is essential to Islamic belief.

The Qur'an refers to the tradition of which it is the ultimate articulation as simply "the religion" (al-din), meaning the monotheistic religion that began with the initiation of the covenant between God and humanity in the deeds of Abraham:

> He has laid down for you as religion
> what He charged Noah with, and what
> We have revealed to you, and what We
> charged Abraham with, Moses and Jesus:
> "Practice the religion, and do not separate
> over it."
>
> (Sura 42:14)

The Qur'an chastises those who divide the din into sects:

> And they say, "Be Jews or Christians and
> you shall be guided." Say: "No, rather
> the creed of Abraham, a true believer;
>   he was no idolater."
> Say: "We believe in God, and
> in what has been revealed to us
> and revealed to Abraham, Ishmael,
> Isaac and Jacob, and the Tribes,
> and what was given to Moses and Jesus
> and the Prophets from their Lord; we
> make no division between any of them, and
>   to Him we surrender."
>
> (Sura 2:136–37)

The message of Muhammad is therefore believed to be the same as that of earlier prophets: "Truly [the Qur'an] is revelation from the Lord of the Worlds; the Trusted Spirit revealed it upon your heart, that you may be one of the warners, in a clear Arabic language. It is, indeed, in the scriptures of the forerunners. Is it not a sign for them that is known to the learned of the children of Israel?" (Sura 26:193–98). This din, the monotheistic religion, therefore, was accurately revealed before, the Qur'an affirms, but those communities who have received messages prior to the time of Muhammad became "doubtful and disconcerted" (Sura 42:13) about it. That is why there are separate groups claiming to follow the same God, and that is why there are disagreements even within those groups. Some deliberately ignored or abandoned the din; others distorted it.

> Which of the two parties has greater right
> to security, if you have any knowledge?
> Those who believe, and have not confounded
> their belief with oppression — to them belongs
> the security; they are rightly guided.
> That is our argument, which We gave
> to Abraham against his people.
> We raise up in degrees whom We will;
> Truly your Lord is wise, all-knowing.
> And We gave to him Isaac and Jacob —
>   each one We guided,
> And Noah We guided before; and of his progeny,
> David and Solomon, Job and Joseph,
>   Moses and Aaron —
> Thus We reward the good-doers —
> Zachariah and John, Jesus and Elias each
>   was of the righteous;
> Ishmael and Elisha, Jonah and Lot —
> each one We preferred above all beings;
> and of their fathers, and of their progeny,
>   and of their brothers;
> and We chose them, and We guided them
>   to a straight path.
> That is God's guidance; He guides by it
> whom He will of His servants; had they been
> idolaters, their deeds would have been
>   of no avail to them.
> Those are they to whom We gave the Book,
> and wisdom, and prophecy; so if these
> disbelieve, We have already
> entrusted them to a people who do not

disbelieve in it. . . .
This is a book We have revealed, blessed
and confirming that which was before it,
and for you to warn [Mecca]
and those around her; and those who believe
in the afterlife believe in it, and
    mind their prayers.

(Sura 6:82–93)

This confirmation and clarification of the historic divine message is how the Qur'an explains the mission of the prophet Muhammad: "This Qur'an narrates to the children of Israel most of what they disagree about. It is a guide and a merciful gift for believers" (Sura 27:77–78). Again, the historic line of prophets is essential. The Qur'an clearly presents Muhammad as an integral part of this same line, just as were Jesus and Moses before him: "And when Moses said to his people, 'O my people, why do you hurt me, though you know I am the messenger of God to you? . . . And when Jesus, son of Mary, said, 'Children of Israel, I am indeed the messenger of God to you, confirming the Torah that is before me, and giving good tidings of a messenger who shall come after me, whose name shall be Ahmad;' then when he brought them clear signs, they said, 'This is sheer sorcery'" (Sura 61:6–7). "Amhad" in this passage refers to Muhammad. It is believed that the prediction of the coming of Muhammad is one of the events deliberately suppressed in Christian scriptures. In fact, these examples are used to explain the predictability of doubters among Muhammad's audience. The historic integrity of the prophetic line represented by Muhammad is therefore basic to the claim to prophethood of Muhammad.

The Qur'an claims, furthermore, that Muhammad was perceived in seventh-century Mecca in this light. At least some of his listeners were aware of earlier prophets and judged him accordingly. Those who rejected him compared him negatively with his predecessors: "But when the truth came to them from Us, they said, Why has [Muhammad] not been given something like what Moses was given?" (Sura 28:49). Similarly, the Qur'an indicates that those who accepted him did so because they recognized his teachings to be in accord with those of earlier prophets: "Those to whom We had given the book rejoice at what is being revealed to you, but among the sectarians there are those who rejected a part of it" (Sura 13:37).

The Qur'an is not concerned with chronology when it mentions the earlier prophets. It prefers to stress the lessons to be learned from them; the unfortunate but inevitable fates of nations who ignored the teachings of their prophets – divine judgment in history – is a major theme of the Qur'an. Historical peoples and nations are mentioned, most of whom are familiar to readers of Judaic or Christian scriptures. But their stories are not laid out in historical detail; they are simply referred to, with the understanding that people are familiar with them, and listeners are reminded of what happened to them when they ignored the messages they were sent. An entire chapter (*Sura*), named after Hud, one of the Arab messengers unknown in Judaic and Christian scripture, is devoted to such a litany:

And We sent Noah to his people:
"I am a clear warner for you,
That you serve no one but God. I fear
for you the punishment of
   a painful day."
The heads of the unbelievers
of his people said, "We do not see you
as anything but a human being like ourselves,
and we do not see any but apparently the lowest of us
   following you.
We do not see you as
superior to us; no, rather we
   think you are liars."
. . . And it was revealed to Noah,
"None of your people shall believe
but who has already believed;
so do not be distressed
   by what they are doing.
Make the ark under Our eyes,
and as We reveal; and do not address me
about the oppressors;
   they shall be drowned."
. . . And to Ad [an Arab tribe] their brother Hud [their prophet];
he said, "O my people, serve God.
You have no god other than He;
   you are but forgers . . . .
O my people, ask forgiveness
of your Lord, then repent to Him,
and He sent skies over you with rain,
and will add strength to your strength,
and do not turn away sinners."
They said, "Hud, you have not brought
us a clear sign, and we will not leave
our gods for what you say; we are
   not believers in you . . . ."
He said, "I call God to witness;
. . . if you turn away, I have
shown you what I was sent with
and my Lord will make a people

other than you successors . . . ."
That was Ad; they denied the signs of
their Lord, and disobeyed His messengers,
and followed the command of every
    willful tyrant.
And there was sent following after them
in this world a curse, and upon the Day
of Resurrection: "Surely Ad disbelieved
in their Lord, so away with Ad, the
    people of Hud."
                      (Sura 11:26–61)

The sad story of the same community when it ignored the next messenger, Salih, is then recounted, with similar results. Then comes mention of the intransigent people of Lot, upon whom rained stones of baked clay. The Midianites are done away with when they rejected their messenger Shuʿaib, and so on. The same historic process is mentioned elsewhere in the Qurʾan. For example:

Now, if the hypocrites do not come around,
and those in whose hearts there is sickness
and those who make commotion in the city,
We shall assuredly provoke you against them
and then they will be your neighbors there
    but a short time;
accursed, wherever
they are found, they shall be seized
    and all of them slaughtered –
God's pattern with those who passed away
before; and you shall find no changing
    the pattern of God.
                    (Sura 33:61–63)

Finally, the current listeners are reminded of their historic role as recipients of the final clarification:

You are the best community brought forth
to people, enjoining good and forbidding
evil, and believing in God. Had the People
of the Book [those to whom earlier scriptures were sent]
believed, it would be better for them;
some of them are believers, but most of them are ungodly . . . .
[T]hey will be burdened with God's anger,
and stricken with sadness; because they disbelieved in

God's signs, and killed the prophets without right;
for they rebelled
    and were transgressors.

(Sura 3:111–13)

Thus, historic context is one of the bases for accepting Muhammad's mission. History is also essential to the Qur'an's claim that it not only completes but corrects misrepresentations made in the name of revelation. Many of those misrepresentations, like the one mentioned above concerning the prediction of the coming of Muhammad, are believed to have found their way into canonized versions of previous revelation. For example, Muslims believe that when Abraham committed himself to submission (*islam*) to the will of God by demonstrating willingness to sacrifice his son, the son in question was Isma'il (Ishmael), not Isaac, as Jews and Christians believe. Furthermore, and perhaps more importantly, Abraham's act was personal, but its reward was bequeathed to successive generations. However, the inheritance did not follow genetic lines. In Qur'anic teaching, no individual's actions can earn divine merit or retribution for others. Thus, the Qur'an recounts the story of Abraham:

Those to whom We gave the book
and who follow it accurately,
they believe in it; and whoever disbelieves in it,
    they are the losers.
People of Israel, remember my blessing
with which I blessed you, and that I
preferred you over all.
And beware the day that no one will redeem anything
for another, and no counterpoise
be accepted from him, nor any
intercession avail,
    and they will not be helped.
And when his Lord tested Abraham
with certain words, and he fulfilled them,
He said, "I will make you a leader
of people." He said, "And my offspring?"
He said, "My covenant does not extend to oppressors."

(Sura 2:122–25)

Another aspect of the importance which Muslims place on the historic role of Muhammad's mission is seen in the stress laid on fixing the written text. Because the Torah and the Gospels are believed to be true revelations but defective in their present form – containing verses that have been tampered with (*tahrif*) and excluding others that should have been included – Islam

45

emphasized accurate "recitation" (*qur'an*). That made it very important that the Qur'an be recorded quickly and accurately, before it fell victim to a similar fate. Originally transmitted orally by people (*huffaz*) who memorized the recitations, the Qur'an is widely believed to have been put in writing within the first few years after the prophet's death. The prophet's first successor (caliph), Abu Bakr, initiated the collection of various sections of it that had been recorded. A few years later, during the time of the third caliph, 'Uthman (644–56 CE), the task of codifying the text began. A committee headed by a close assistant of the prophet, Zayd ibn Thabit, working with Abu Bakr's personal copy which had been safeguarded by one of the Prophet's widows, an official text of the Qur'an was established.[2]

Finally, the historical context of the Qur'an is of central importance because of its claim to finality. The succession of prophets ends with Muhammad. The Qur'an calls him the "seal of the prophets" (Sura 33:41), in that his confirmation and clarification of God's will for humanity is final. It is believed that in the Qur'an God has made it clear that the purpose of human existence is to do the will of God, which has been revealed as the responsibility to re-create in society the equality which all human beings share in the eyes of their creator. This is considered the only appropriate response to recognition of God and is the overriding theme of the Qur'an. People are to remind themselves of their duty to do God's will on a regular basis, and are always to deal honestly and fairly with one another, establishing a socio-political order to ensure the well-being of even the most vulnerable members of society. As the Qur'an often puts it, those who submit to the will of God (the literal meaning of the Arabic word "muslim") are to "do good and prevent evil." Even the fact that the communities of earlier prophets have separated over their interpretations is accepted as the will of God: "If your Lord had so willed, He would have made mankind one community, but they continue to remain divided" (Sura 11:119; cf. 2:213, 10:19). Now, rather than disputing over doctrine, all who claim to believe should simply "vie with one another in good works," another common theme in the Qur'an. (Or as Sura (3:65) has it, all believers should "join on a position that may be common among us, that we may serve only God.") People do not need any more warnings; they must now simply practice what they have been preaching. Muslims believe this message is intended for all peoples and is sufficient for all time. Yet it could not cover in detail every possible situation that would ever be encountered by those wishing to implement the will of God in their daily lives. Instead, it is believed that the Qur'an lays down basic principles and some essential legislation, and that the prophet established a perfect example of how to create an equitable society in the specific circumstances of seventh-century Arabia. That example then stands as an inspiration for other communities, in different circumstances, to determine the best ways to establish communities pleasing to God.

It is important to Muslims that the Qur'an was revealed over a lengthy historical period, from about 610 CE until the prophet's death in 632 CE. During this period, the Prophet's community grew from being a small, beleaguered group in Mecca to being the dominant power in the region. As specific historical circumstances changed, so did the nature and tone of the Qur'an's teaching. This change is noticeable not only in the content and style of verses, but even in the Qur'an's judgment on specific topics. It often says different things about a single topic. In order to make sense of these shifts, scholars have emphasized the need to know the historic context of the verses in question.

An often-cited example of such transformation is in the Qur'an's statements about war. In Sura 16, Muslims are told that "those who emigrated in God's cause after they were wronged, We shall surely lodge them in this world in a goodly lodging, and the wage of the world to come is better" (Sura 16:42). They are not advised to seek any sort of retribution for having been oppressed or to interact in any way with their enemies. A little later, they are told to "call to the way of your Lord with wisdom and good admonition, and dispute with them in the better way. . . . And if you punish, do so as you have been punished; and yet assuredly if you are patient, it is better for those who are patient" (Sura 16:126–27). In this case, patience and forbearance are the appropriate response, along with efforts to influence the enemy with correct teaching. But in Sura 22:40, the Muslim community is told, "Permission is given to those [who fight] because they were wronged; surely God is able to help them." Similarly, "Fight in the way of God those who fight you, but do not commit aggression; God does not love aggressors" (Sura 2:191). Now, instead of patient forbearance, retaliation is allowed in cases of self-defense or defense of property. But then the chapter continues:

> And kill [those who fight against you] wherever you you find them
> and drive them out from where they drove you out;
> persecution is worse than killing.
> But do not fight them at the Holy Mosque
> unless they fight you there.
> Then, if they fight you, fight them.
> That is the recompense of unbelievers.
> But if they stop, surely God is
> all-forgiving and merciful.
> Fight them until there is no persecution
> and the religion [al-din] is God's. Then if they
> stop, there is no aggression
> except against the oppressors.
>
> (Sura 2:191–94)

In this verse, then, war is for self-defense, retaliation, and/or for ending persecution and spreading the monotheistic religion (al-din). How are believers to determine which of these revelations is supposed to govern their behavior? Historical context of the various verses provides the key to understanding their practical application. Scholars have therefore struggled to determine the order in which verses were delivered, since the Qur'an's verses are not recorded in chronological order. The Qur'an comprises 114 chapters, arranged in order of length; except for the first chapter, the chapters are ordered from longest to shortest. In general, the longer verses are believed to be of later origin, revealed after the emigration (*hijra*) from Mecca to Medina in 622 CE (the beginning of the Islamic calendar). The Meccan chapters (about ninety) tend to be deeply spiritual, richly poetic, and highly charged emotionally, while the Medinese chapters tend to be more prosaic disquisitions on practical matters. Though far fewer in number, the Medinese chapters contain most of the Qur'an's legislation. The more pacifist verses, it is believed, were delivered in Mecca, when the Muslim community's weakness would have made military efforts hopeless. As they gained strength, permission was granted for self-defense. Ultimately, when in Medina the Muslim community became the strongest power in the region, permission was granted to initiate armed conflict, provided that the motivation is correct. (Details of legislation on war will be discussed in Chapter 7.)

Interestingly, there is not always agreement among scholars about the chronological order of verses, which will account for some of the divergence of opinion among Muslim lawmakers. For example, scholars disagree on whether verses granting permission to retaliate against physical attacks were delivered in Mecca or Medina, which leads to varying opinions about the legal status of silent suffering in Islam. Nevertheless, it is unanimously agreed that the chronological order and historic context of revelation are essential to determining its implications for law. That is why chapters and verses are generally distinguished as Meccan or Medinan.

Furthermore, there is disagreement about how many verses have direct legislative impact. For example, the Qur'an declares that some later revelation abrogates earlier revelation (for example, "And when We exchange a sign [verse] in the place of another verse, and God knows what He is revealing" Sura 16:102; cf. 2:106, 13:39). Some scholars believe this applies only to the Qur'an's abrogation of earlier scriptures, but many legists believe it applies to verses within the Qur'an itself. This principle of abrogation (*naskh*) has been used, for example, to determine the Islamic prohibition on the consumption of alcohol, even though the Qur'an at one point says that the "strong drink" made from grapes is a sign of God's goodness (Sura 16:67), and, at another, simply that people should not pray under the influence (Sura 4:44) and, at still another, only that wine should be avoided (Sura 5:91). Nevertheless, the verses which state that drinking wine is a grievous sin whose evil outweighs its usefulness (e.g., Sura 2:220) are taken as definitive, superseding what are believed to be earlier verses. In other cases, however, such as the verses on war, many legists do not rely on the principle of abrogation, but maintain that all the verses dealing with it are applicable, depending upon the circumstances for which people are seeking guidance.

Overall, Qur'anic legislation is generally characterized, like all Islamic legislation, as of two kinds: those regulations concerning humans' responsibility to God (*'ibadat*), and those concerning human beings' interaction (*mu'amalat*). The former concern requirements for prayer, charitable giving, fasting, and pilgrimage. The latter deal with marriage, divorce, inheritance, orphans, slaves, murder, theft, retaliation, and war. In the Qur'an, however, these issues are not always simple to distinguish. The following verse, for example, was delivered when Mecca was established as the direction in which all Muslims should pray:

> It is not piety that you turn your faces
> to the East or the West.
> Pious is the one
> who believes in God and the Last Day,
> the angels, the Book, and the prophets,
> and spends for love of him
>   on relatives and orphans,
> poor people, travellers, the needy,
>   and for captives,
> performs the prayer, and gives charity;
> and the one who keeps promises,
>   is patient in poverty,
>   hardship and conflict.
> It is these who are truthful
>   and pious.
>
>   (Sura 2:178)

Instead of a neat division of duties into those concerned with the divine and those concerned with the mundane, then, the entire world for the Qur'an is of divine concern, and thus potentially sacred. Indeed, as the above verse shows, the task with which people are entrusted is to sanctify all aspects of human life by bringing them into accord with the will of God. Again, that will has been finally revealed. It is that human beings emulate the piety and dedication to justice demonstrated by the prophet Muhammad and his community at Medina.

2 Tradition: the Sunna

The disagreement among scholars concerning the legislative force of specific Qur'anic verses does not mitigate the agreement on the importance of

49

historical circumstances of revelation for determining legislation. That is one of the reasons why oral tradition is an essential source for Islamic legislation. Evidence for determining the chronological order of chapters and verses is taken from oral tradition, recorded in the hadith collections popularly known as the Sunna (normative practice established by the prophet Muhammad). Also derived from oral tradition are descriptions of the circumstances of revelation (*asbab al-nuzul*) of various verses. These amplify verses in order to allow legal scholars to determine whether or not they have legislative impact and, if so, to determine the specific precedent involved.

But oral tradition recording the Sunna has another role as well, one indicated by the Qur'an itself. As indicated above, the Qur'an, a text of finite physical proportions, could not provide specific directives for all possible situations which people would encounter for all time, even though its spiritual guidance is meant to govern them. That is why the Qur'an is not considered primarily a law book. While opinions vary regarding the amount of specific legislation in the Qur'an, there is overall agreement that in any case it is small. As already noted, it mandates the basic elements of Islamic practice — daily prayer, charity, kindness, fairness, fasting, pilgrimage, dietary restrictions. It also gives careful directives regarding human relations that are unlikely to change, given human nature. It prohibits, for example, murder, theft, lying, usury, and cheating. In discussions unique among monotheistic scriptures and addressed to one of the most glaring examples of injustice in seventh-century Arabia, the Qur'an also gives detailed instructions concerning women's rights. Specifying that women share human dignity and moral responsibility equally with men, it demands that women be allowed specific rights in inheritance, marriage, and divorce, owning and disposing of property, and giving legal witness. It also prohibits both female infanticide and prostitution. Similarly, slave-owners are instructed to let slaves purchase their freedom if they so desire.

But the vast majority of the Qur'an's verses which carry legal implications are not so specific. The Qur'an urges people to piety expressed not only in prayer and ritual but in social justice. Indeed, the Qur'an presents an overall world-view wherein the purpose of human existence is to fulfill the agreement or covenant made between human beings and God by creating a just society in which all human beings are accorded the dignity they deserve as God's creatures. In that context, it presents ethical behavior as even more important than prayer and ritual. An entire chapter, entitled "Charity" (Sura 107), is devoted to this topic:

> In the name of God, the Merciful, the Compassionate
> Have you seen the one who makes a mockery of faith?
> He is the one who sends away orphans
> and does not urge feeding the needy.
> Woe to those who pray

but are heedless of their prayers,
to who who make a show {of praying}
and yet refuse charity.

It is believed that these verses create obligations on human beings for
ethical behavior, but they do so by presenting a challenge to human beings to
figure out how to implement their implied laws in all circumstances. It is
further believed that the Qur'an accordingly presents the prophet Muhammad
as a guide on how to meet this challenge. The Qur'an at one point tells
believers that Muhammad can help explain revelation: "We have revealed to
you the reminder, so you may explain to people what has been revealed,
and so they may reflect" (Sura 16:45). He is also presented as an exemplar,
someone whose behavior can guide others in the best way to implement
the will of God on a daily basis: "Indeed in the messenger of God is a
good example for those who look to God and the Last Day and remember
God often" (Sura 33:21). In fact, Muhammad is presented as someone
whose example itself imposes an obligation. In response to a plea for
divine guidance, God says that divine mercy is for those who follow his
messenger, "the uneducated Prophet whom they find written down with
them in the Torah and the Gospel . . . enjoining for them good things and
forbidding for them evil. . . . Those who believe in him and support him and
help him and follow the light revealed with him, will prosper" (Sura 7:158).
The example set by the prophet Muhammad is therefore another source of
Islamic legislation.

It was on this basis that Muslims began collecting reports of the sayings
and deeds of the prophet. Because he was not only the divine messenger but
also the explainer, exemplar, and legislator of divine revelation, the community felt compelled to record what the prophet said and did, even when he
was not delivering revelation. These explanations and examples would serve
as models for posterity. Also included as supplemental material were reports
of the words and deeds of the prophet Muhammad's closest associates, on the
assumption that they would have been directly inspired by the prophet's
personal teaching and example. The task of collecting these reports (*hadith*,
pl. *ahadith*) quickly became specialized. The importance of the Qur'an and
prophetic example was such that pious scholars ("*ulama*") focused on the
careful collecting of hadiths. This meant attaching to each individual report
a source, identifying who witnessed the material related and by whom it
was passed along to the recorders. These reports would also become the basis
for Islamic history, dialectical theology, and biographies of the prophet
Muhammad, in addition to Islamic law.

Unlike Judaic law, which developed after the appearance of the Mishnah,
Islamic law was developing at the same time as hadith reports were being
generated and collected. Evidence of the reliance upon hadith material by the
early decision makers in the Muslim community is given by the proliferation

of hadith reports. By the mid-second century of the Islamic calendar (late eighth century CE), two centers of hadith collection had developed: Medina, the city where the Muslim community was first viable, and Kufa (in what is now Iraq), a political and cultural center established by the Muslims. It soon became evident to religious scholars that some control and order had to be established concerning hadith reports. Authenticity was of utmost importance, and so scholars made it their business to verify chains (*isnad*) of transmitters of hadith reports. Only those reports by people considered to be of upright character and who could actually have witnessed what they claimed to have witnessed were granted authenticity. Among the most authoritative reporters of hadiths collected in Medina were ʿAʾisha, the prophet's last wife, along with ʿUmar, a close companion of the prophet and his second successor (caliph), and ʿUmar's son. In Kufa, the prophet's cousin, close companion, and fourth successor, ʿAli, was a major authority, as was another companion of the Prophet, Ibn Masʿud.

It also became evident that authentic reports, originally transmitted orally, had to be recorded for posterity. Six scholars' collections were admitted as generally reliable, but only two collections were considered authentic on the basis of their isnads. Muhammad ibn Ismaʿil al-Bukhari's (d. 870 CE) collection and that of Muslim ibn al-Hajjaj (d. 875 CE) are considered to be sound (*sahih*), while those of Abu Daʾud of Basra (d. 888 CE), al-Tirmidhi (d. *c.* 892 CE), Ibn Majah of Qazwin (d. *c.* 886 CE), and al-Nasaʾi (d. 915 CE) are considered to be less reliable. Collectively, the hadith reports establish normative precedent, popularly known as the Sunna of the prophet Muhammad, although technically speaking, only the collections of al-Bukhari and Muslim are known as Sunna, while the other four collections are known as precedents or collections.[3]

It is important to note that even the careful collection and authentication of oral reports did not result in a body of mutually consistent reports. That is why even the two authoritative collections, though technically considered to convey the Sunna, are not necessarily coterminous with the authoritative example of the Prophet. In fact, there remain even in the official collections reports that contradict one another. For example, al-Nasaʾi reports that Muhammad rejected the propriety of a man pronouncing a final divorce from his wife without two preceding provisional divorces and efforts at reconciliation. He also presents a report allowing this procedure. Nor do the collections contain only reports that accord with the Qurʾan. For example, despite the Qurʾan's insistence on women's spiritual equality with men (e.g., Sura 33:35), there are numerous hadith reports concerning the inherent moral and religious defects of women. In Islamic jurisprudence, such differences are not unusual; it was one of the tasks of hadith literature to record a variety of views considered to be authoritative. As we shall see in Chapter 3, it was one of the tasks of legal scholars to examine such dissenting views and determine which is more authoritative and/or more appropriate given the specific circumstances of the case at hand. Differences in their conclusions will account for some of the variety in schools of Islamic law.

Contents and organization of the collections: The hadith collections include a wealth of material, including embellishment of Qur'anic stories, such as that of "the night visit." The chapter bearing this title begins with the verse: "Glory to Him who carried His servant by night from the holy mosque to the further mosque, the environs of which we have blessed, that we might show him some of our signs" (Sura 17:2; cf. 53:5ff). This verse was explained in hadith literature as referring to Prophet Muhammad's miraculous journey to Jerusalem, on the basis of which a shrine (the Dome of the Rock) and a mosque (the nearby Masjid al-Aqsa, "the farther mosque") were built in the late seventh century CE to commemorate the event. The hadith collections also include proverbs and anecdotes which allow them to be used as a source for theological discussions (*kalam*) and history, as well as minute details of daily behavior, such as whether or not to eat desserts and how to brush one's teeth. Hadith material is therefore also used to establish customary behavior without moral implications.

An important indication of the stature of this material is the fact that the basic "pillars of Islam," those duties required of all Muslims, are taken directly from the Sahih of Muslim. In a long report known as the hadith of Gabriel, Muhammad's knowledge is tested by the angel. In response to a series of questions, the Prophet establishes that "Islam means to bear witness that there is no god but God and that Muhammad is God's messenger, to perform the daily prayers, to give charity, to fast during Ramadan, and to perform the pilgrimage to [the Ka'ba in Mecca] if you are able to." The Qur'an advocates all the components of this hadith, but it does not list them consecutively or formalize them.

Equally revealing is the fact that while these practices are the minimum requirement of all Muslims, they are not codified into the kind of law with which Westerners are familiar. That is, civil authorities are not (in general) authorized to enforce their practice nor to inflict punishment for failure to practice the five pillars. They are, nonetheless, considered absolute requirements for Muslims. Literally thousands of other hadith reports lie somewhere between simple reports of custom, and reports with irrefutable moral and legal implications.

Similarly, this list of essential practices indicates that there is no clear distinction between the secular and eternal realms. As noted above, later thinkers divided Islamic legislation into the broad categories of duties to God (*'ibadat*), and responsibilities within society (*mu'amalat*). But as the hadith of Gabriel shows, the two are as deeply intertwined in the Sunna as they are in the Qur'an. The first pillar, for example, demands that Muslims "bear witness" to belief in God and the teachings of Muhammad. The verb used is important; it refers not to saying or believing but to manifesting in one's behavior that one recognizes divine authority. The second pillar, daily prayer (which was early on organized into five times indicated by the position of the sun), could be considered a "duty to God," although the Qur'an clearly states that God is not in need of anything. Therefore, God is not the beneficiary of prayer. Prayer is a means for human beings to maintain proper orientation or motivation in their daily behavior. Likewise, the third pillar, charity, could be considered a "duty to human beings," but in that it is the fulfillment of the divinely mandated responsibility, again, the line between the eternal and secular (literally, that bounded by time) becomes blurred. For the overall concern of the Sunna, like that of the Qur'an, is with the sanctification – or dedication to God – of all human life.

The primary purpose of authenticating and codifying oral tradition was as a source of legal precedent which could be used by legal scholars to establish law. Collections are therefore arranged according to categories so that legists may find their topics. The list of categories is specific to each collector, reflecting his judgment of which reports belong together. The most authoritative collection, for example, the *Sahih* of al-Bukhari, contains 7,397 reports divided among ninety-seven categories. The first category concerns revelation (or inspiration, *wahy*); the second, faith (*iman*); the third, knowledge (*'ilm*). The final category is "unicity" (*tawhid*, meaning not only that there is only one God, but that God is not divided into parts or personalities). Scattered among the remaining ninety-three categories are precedents concerning purity, charity or alms, pilgrimage, fasting, observance of various significant days in the Islamic calendar, charitable endowments, and medicine, as well as required shares of inheritance, commercial transactions, war, marriage, divorce, and punishments for infractions. Muslim's collection contains fifty-four categories containing reports, many of which are the same as al-Bukhari's but organized differently and citing different chains of authenticity.

Hadith reports were traditionally considered to be a second source of Islamic law. But with the development of formal schools of law, the question arose as to the status of this extra-Qur'anic material relative to the primary source of law. Early thinkers considered it supplemental to the Qur'an, able to be followed or not depending upon the opinion of the judge (*qadi*) in any given case. Eventually, however, it was elevated to the status of revelation, its precedents therefore considered binding – at least theoretically. That meant not that all hadith reports, even conflicting ones, must be followed – an obvious impossibility, but that only in cases in which no precedent could be cited from either the Qur'an or the Sunna were jurists to engage in personal judgment. In other words, the Sunna was not just an optional source of law; it was a formally required source of law.

3 FIQH

The term "Shariʿa" is commonly used to refer to Islamic law. But its reference is to the ideal law that guides human behavior, i.e., the will of God, rather than specific codes of law. The science of actual law is called *fiqh*, and the science of jurisprudence is *ʿilm usul al-fiqh*, science of the roots of law. A thirteenth-century scholar clearly distinguished between the two when he said, "Fiqh is knowledge of the commands of Shariʿa concerning human interaction, derived from their detailed proofs."[4]

Fiqh means knowledge or understanding. It is distinguished from the more general knowledge, *ʿilm*, in that it is considered to be a specialized kind of knowledge, legal knowledge. Scholars who deal in general religious topics, including the collection and study of hadith materials, are called *ʿulamaʾ* (those with *ʿilm*), while scholars dealing in legal applications and implications of religious knowledge are called *fuqahaʾ* (those who deal in fiqh). Indicative of the high value placed on reason in Islamic law, fiqh is often called "the queen of the sciences," carrying with it the connotation of being a result of active reasoning, while *ʿilm* connotes knowledge based on authority.

Opinions vary as to what was the first work of fiqh. *Kitab al-Raʾy* ("Book of Opinion") of Abu Hanifah (d. 767 CE) is sometimes cited as the first, but we have no copies of it. The earliest extant compendium of legal thought is that of Zayd ibn ʿAli (d. 743 CE), *Majmuʿ al-Fiqh* (ed. E. Griffini [Milan, 1919]), but the oldest surviving comprehensive work of fiqh is that of Malik ibn Anas (d. 795/96 CE), *Al-Muwattaʾ* ("the leveled path"). *Al-Muwatta* includes some 1,700 hadith reports circulating in the city of Medina, his home, and articulated the notion of *ijmaʿ*, consensus, as it was practiced in Medina in the process of determining legal judgments (see Chapter 3).

Fiqh at this time included what would later be called dialectical theology, *kalam*. Abu Hanifah, for example, is reputed to have written *Al-Fiqh al-Akbar* ("the greater fiqh"), dealing with the basic beliefs of Islam. The works based on Abu Hanifah's thinking, *Kitab al-Usul* of Abu Yusuf (d. 798/99 CE) and *Kitab Usul al-Fiqh* of Muhammad b. al-Hasan al-Shaybani (d. 804/5 CE), were the first works concentrating on fiqh alone.[5]

The earliest works of fiqh relied upon three major arguments in establishing their opinions. The Qurʾan, of course, was primary. Rules established in the Qurʾan were considered to have direct legal consequences. For subjects not specifically dealt with in the Qurʾan, or for amplification of those that were, hadith material was consulted. Legists then extrapolated from such precedent as was available, relying on their informed opinion (*raʾy*). Soon scholars called for more formal syllogistic reasoning (*qiyas*) in order to extract rulings from the sources for novel cases. For example, having determined on the basis of naskh (the theory of abrogation; see p. 48) that drinking wine (*khamr*, made from grapes) is forbidden by the Qurʾan, a question arose about the permissibility of drinking *nabidh* (a drink made from dates). The first task was to isolate the *'illah* (see p. 65), the common factor shared by a known case (precedent) and the case in question. The ruling in the precedent is then extended to the case under discussion. In that way it was determined that the offensive aspect of the wine is its intoxicating properties. By extension, then, other drinks which intoxicate, such as nabidh, are judged to be forbidden. (See Chapter 3 for further discussion of modes of legal reasoning.) Whether by means of ra'y or qiyas, however, the exercise of independent reasoning is called *ijtihad*' as distinguished from following precedent (taqlid), and was an important source of Islamic law.

Within the first two centuries of the death of the prophet Muhammad, a number of scholars throughout the central Islamic lands were recognized as so accomplished that their ijtihad was followed by others. These "mujtahids" (practitioners of ijtihad) became the founders of the major schools (*madhahib*, sing. *madhhab*) of Islamic law. In Iraq, Abu Hanifah gave his name to a school, the Hanafi madhhab, represented by his renowned disciples Abu Yusuf and al-Shaybani. Malik ibn Anas is credited with founding the Maliki school in Medina. It is important to recall, however, that these legists did not work in a vacuum. As noted above, there was an established body of hadith in each region, on the basis of which regional practice was generally established. This established practice, ijma', was, in fact, another source of Islamic law, following the Qur'an and Sunna. Ijma' means consensus, but in the context of early Islamic law it refers to practice that has been agreed upon as appropriate. "The ijma' of Medina," for example, was a common phrase, meaning that something or other was the agreed upon (legal) practice in Medina.

Some scholars go so far as to equate the early notion of ijma' with that of Sunna, i.e., the established behavior either of the Prophet himself or of others patterned on that of the Prophet. The argument is persuasive, based on certain usages in early fiqh. For example, Malik generally concludes his arguments in *al-Muwatta'*, after having cited an authoritative hadith, with sentences claiming that the practice in question is the one which his community in Medina usually follows. In these sentences Malik uses the terms *sunnah* and *amal* ("practice") and *al-amr al-mujtama' alayh* ("agreed upon practice") interchangeably.[6] In any case, it is clear that established practice was a source of legislation, so much so that in some cases, regional practice sometimes followed the "sunna" of a companion of the Prophet rather than that of the Prophet himself as reported in a hadith. Like the Sunna as represented in the hadith collections, therefore, admitting this type of communal ijma' into the sources of law allowed for differences of both opinion and practice in Islamic law.

The number and priority of sources of Islamic law as they are generally accepted today was established by the founder of a third legal school, al-Shafi'i (d. 820 CE).[7] The Qur'an, of course, remained the primary source of legislation, followed by the Sunna, assumed to be conveyed in the hadith collections. Next in importance came ijma', but for al-Shafi'i, ijma' did not refer to regional consensus. For him it meant the consensus of the entire Muslim legal community. This meant that very little could be established by consensus, given the extent of the Muslim world by that time and the relatively limited communication among scholars spread from Spain to Iran. The goal of this redefinition of ijma' was no doubt greater uniformity in Islamic law, but its effect was greater reliance on precedent (taqlid) in determining legislation. In fact, al-Shafi'i held that the soundest basis for law was precedent and that ijtihad should be used only as a last resort, and then it must be ijtihad narrowly interpreted as qiyas (Canalogical reasoning), for which he articulated rules, rather than the more liberal ra'y (personal opinion). Furthermore, he believed that the Sunna of the Prophet had to take priority over all others, even if it was contrary to the ijma' of a region. So insistent was al-Shafi'i on the importance of precedent in legislation that many scholars trace the proliferation of hadith reports to his influence. Whether or not he was the cause, the movement of hadith collecting and codification is traceable to this period, the official collections of hadith appearing after the death of al-Shafi'i. Indeed, it was al-Shafi'i who elevated the Sunna to the level of revelation. Since the Qur'an enjoins Muslims to obey the Prophet, he argues, Muslims must follow whatever the Prophet said or did as if it were law.[8] Indeed, the founder of the fourth official school of Islamic law, Ahmad Ibn Hanbal (d. 855 CE) was not known so much as a legal thinker as a compiler of hadith reports. Not surprisingly, his school, the Hanbali madhhab, places the greatest emphasis on taqlid of all the schools of Islamic law.

The four major schools of Islamic law allow for variety in Islamic law. The variety stems from differences of opinion regarding which verses of the Qur'an are actually legal precedents, which hadith reports establish legal precedent, and under what circumstances ijtihad may be used and to what extent. But all agree that (1) law is ultimately from God, although human beings have the responsibility to discern God's will; (2) that while its sources belong to a particular historical context and so are historically conditioned, the law must be flexible enough to deal with changing times and places; and (3) that law covers all aspects of human life and all kinds of behavior. There is no part of human life that is exempt from God's will. Therefore, not only does Islamic law cover many things that Western society would consider beyond the scope of legislation (such as details of personal hygiene and bodily functions), but Islamic law has a unique system of categorizing all behavior by degrees of propriety. Rather than just declaring some things lawful and some unlawful, Islamic law declares some things absolutely required, some simply recommended, some neutral, some discouraged, and some absolutely forbidden. The distinguishing characteristics are in the sphere of reward and punishment. Required acts are rewarded and failure to perform them is punishable. Recommended acts are rewarded, but failure to perform them incurs no punishment. Neutral acts bear neither reward nor punishment. Discouraged acts are not punished, but refraining from engaging in them is meritorious. Forbidden acts are punishable, and refraining from them merits no reward.

It is noteworthy that many of the punishments and rewards in question are beyond the jurisdiction of civil or state authorities. It is assumed that the reward or retribution is spiritual. For that reason, there is emphasis in Islamic law on intention. The merit or lack thereof of many actions can only be determined by the person's intention. Charity, for example, given begrudgingly or for show will not be rewarded.

The formative period of Islamic law has left us with some monuments of legal thought. Chief among them are Malik's *al-Muwatta* and al-Shafi'i's *Risala,* on which we will generally rely for this discussion. (We will also refer to works on specialized topics, such as al-Shaybani's *Siyar,* the Islamic "law of nations," for a discussion of laws pertaining to warfare.) As the following list of chapters indicates, as in the hadith collections, there is no unanimity in works of Islamic law regarding categorization of human behavior. *Al-Muwatta* is divided into sixty-one sections. The first fourteen concern prayer and ritual purity. Next comes the Qur'an, then Burials, (required) Charity, Fasting, the Retreat during Ramadan, Pilgrimage (by far the longest section), Jihad, Vows and Oaths, Sacrificial Animals, Slaughtering Animals, Game (dietary rules), Animals Killed to Celebrate the Birth of a Child, Fixed Shares of Inheritance, Marriage, Divorce, Suckling, Business Transactions, Trusts, Sharecropping, Rental Land, Pre-emption of Property, Judgments, Wills and Testaments, three categories concerning slaves, Punishments, (intoxicating) Drinks, two categories concerning blood-money, Medina, Pre-determination, Good Character, Dress, Description of the Prophet, The Evil Eye, Hair, Visions, Greetings, General (from "Asking Permission to Enter," and "Blessing a Person Who Sneezes," to "The Command to be Kind to Slaves," and "The Slave and His Reward"), The Oath of Allegiance, Speech, Hell, (voluntary) Charity, Knowledge, Supplication of the Unjustly Wronged, and Names of the Prophet. Al-Shafi'i's work is divided into only fifteen chapters, including an introduction, Declarations, Legal Knowledge, Qur'an, Authority of the Prophet, Abrogation, Duties, God's Orders of Prohibition and the Prophet's Orders of Prohibition, two chapters on the Sunna, Ijma', Qiyas, Ijtihad, Istihan (legal exceptions), and (legal) Disagreement. Clearly, Malik's work tends to follow the categories found in hadith collections, while al-Shafi'i's work reflects his concern with standardizing Islamic law. He subsumes many of the issues considered separately by Malik into single categories, especially that titled "Duties," and uniquely deals with issues of legal reasoning and methodology.

Nevertheless, Muslim commentators discern a common concern in both collections, perhaps characterized best by thirteenth-century Hanbali jurist Ibn Taymiyya as *maslaha*, the well-being of society. Pervading the works of all the classical jurists is an overriding concern for ritual propriety, in the private sphere, and justice, in the public sphere. The two – indeed, all aspects of life – are equally the concern of the Creator.

D Conclusions

Both Judaism and Islam believe that God governs in the here and now through revealed law. Each community of the faithful aspires to realize in this time and in this world God's will for humanity. Both make provision for human participation in, reception of, revelation, assigning to sages and masters of the law a role in the processes of reasoning and application of God's will, as will be shown below. Not only so, but, framed within the same logic of revelation, the sources of law in Judaism and Islam are similar. Each has two central components: written scripture directly revealed by God to the community through the prophet, and an oral tradition (now also recorded in written documents) which is accorded the binding status held by revealed literature for the formulation of law. Each, further, has developed a body of legal discussions in their respective formative periods, which establish both the nature and tone of all succeeding legal thought. Both value the difference of opinion preserved in those discussions and believe the decisions achieved in these discussions remain relevant throughout the history of the community.

There are also significant differences between Judaic and Islamic law. Among the most salient is that in Judaism the body of legal discussion – the oral part of the Torah – is considered timeless, like its scripture. By contrast, in Islam, the historicity of legal discussion, like that of its scripture and oral tradition, is of central importance. Context and specific incident prove determinative. Highlighting the importance of contextualization in Islamic law, al-Shafi'i developed a distinction in levels of responsibility within the community which became standard. Some duties are *fard al-'ayn*, meaning that each individual is responsible for fulfilling them, like the Five Pillars. Others are *fard kifaya*, meaning that, provided a sufficient number of people in the community are participating in the fulfillment of the responsibility that the job gets done, others are relieved of the duty for the time being. A common example is jihad, "strenuous effort to do the will of God" (see discussion in Chapter 7). Distinction of one from the other can only be made by the specifics of a given historic era. The nuancing of responsibility, public and personal, has no counterpart in the law of Judaism. Every Israelite – that is, member of the holy community of Israel called into being by God at Mount Sinai[9] – bears equal responsibility to realize the commandments of the Torah.

This difference between Judaism and Islam on the issue of historicity points to a major difference between the Judaic and Islamic communal self-images. The liturgy of Judaism considers holy Israel, that is, the supernatural community called into being by the Torah, not only the first but in the present age the only true community of God. Three times a day the faithful of Judaism pray that, at the end of time, all of humanity will recognize the one true God whom, even now, holy Israel serves. Judaic law, like its scripture, is concerned with the timeless realities of divinity and the community sacralized by its contact with divinity. Others are always welcome to accept the dominion of God revealed in the Torah, and the convert becomes fully part of that holy Israel called into being at Sinai. But Judaism does not assign to Israel the task of ensuring that the entire world submits to the one true God and his Torah. Holy Israel prays that God will accomplish his own goals, the faithful of the Torah striving to achieve the task of sanctification that God has set for them in particular.

The Muslim communal self-image, on the other hand, is that of a community charged with the mission of ultimately leading all humanity to submission to God, the literal meaning of the Arabic term "islam." The Qur'an is pre-eminently concerned with the moral perfection of all humanity, a task all believers are called upon to share. As Fazlur Rahman put it: "The Qur'an emerges as a document that from the first to the last seeks to emphasize all those moral tensions that are necessary for creative human action. Indeed, the center of the Qur'an's interest is [humanity] and [its] betterment."[10] It is for this reason that believers are repeatedly told not only to practice good themselves, but to make every effort to prevent evil. God has called all humanity through the Qur'an; those who accept its truth at the same time accept the challenge to spread it to the rest of humanity. The differences between these two self-images will become clearer through further analysis of their respective legal systems.

3

THE INTELLECTUAL SOURCES
OF THE LAW

A How do the authorities of the law reason?

We move from writing to reasoning. Judaic and Islamic law provide not only facts of what must or must not be done. In imposing upon a changing world the enduring principles of justice and truth, each system also appeals to rules of reason, modes of thought that guide people in dealing with the new and the unprecedented. What we now want to know is: do the Judaic and the Muslim lawyer-theologians think along the same lines, follow the same principles of logic, respond to the same types of criticism and challenge? That is what we investigate when we describe, analyze, and interpret the intellectual sources that sustain the law and theology of Judaism and Islam: how does the law intersect with everyday life?

Law codes and traditions form only the starting point in the exposition of the law. They supply facts and principles. But the law carries out its task in the myriad contexts of everyday life – which rarely match in exact detail the facts and principles of tradition. In the processes of reasoning, the doctors of law transform from theory to actuality the received religio-legal systems. At issue in this chapter is the comparison of the rules of rationality that guide Islamic and Judaic jurists in their analysis and exegesis of the law. Do they think or reason in essentially the same ways, or does each find guidance in a special and particular mode of thought, not shared by the other?

The role of reasoning is simple. Faced with a concrete problem, a legal authority undertakes the match between the case and the law that pertains; a process of reasoning will guide him in identifying and applying the governing principles. One familiar rule, deriving from ancient natural history, classifies diverse data within common classes, appealing for evidence to indicative traits of an objective character. Then things are like one another and follow the same rule, or they are unlike one another and follow a different rule. That is one mode of reasoning which extends to the solution of problems of law. Here we take up the way in which the law is turned from heritage and tradition in theory into concrete and palpable, workaday reality:

61

the intellectual sources of the law, seen in the setting of the traditional sources of the law set out in Chapter 2.

B Islam: consensus, reasoning, exceptions

Unlike its forebears in the monotheistic tradition, with their rich heritage of oral tradition prior to or even alongside the writing down of tradition as scripture, Islam began as a literate religion. The Qur'an, as noted in Chapter 2, refers to earlier revelation as "books," and clearly shows the respect for the written word characteristic of societies influenced by literacy. The Muslim community also demonstrated the impact of literacy in its institutions, especially in the area of law. The power of oral tradition cannot be denied; Islamic tradition clearly evinced modes of reasoning characteristic of oral societies: anecdotal rather than logical, and based on precedents established by patriarchs rather than on principles abstracted by reason. Yet in early Islam, oral tradition co-existed with the literate tradition and its characteristically abstract and logical modes of thought.[1] Indeed, the literate tradition ultimately dominated Islamic law. As a result, the task of identifying reasoning processes employed in Islamic jurisprudence is relatively simple. In analyzing oral traditions, scholars must intuit the modes of reasoning employed because the question of "how we reason" does not generally arise in such societies. In literate traditions, on the other hand, modes of reasoning are generally a major concern. The example often given by scholars of literacy is that of classical Greece, where the question of formal logic first arose. In the case of Islamic law, the legal scholars themselves, especially under the influence of al-Shafi'i (d. 820 CE), consciously articulated the intellectual processes employed in deriving specific laws from the ideal sources, the Qur'an and the Sunna.

1 Consensus (ijma')

As discussed in Chapter 2, ijma', as an early source of Islamic law, consisted of agreement of scholars within a given region on appropriate Islamic practice. That agreement was informal and based on hadith reports circulating in a specific locale. Some commentators go so far as to describe this type of consensus as the virtual equivalent of the customary practice of a given area, deemed by that area's leaders to be in keeping with Islamic norms. Regional customary practice no doubt influenced the development of Islamic law. According to hadith, judges were not to interfere with a people's customary practice provided it was consistent with Islamic law. Nevertheless, there is no place for it within the theories articulated by the founders of Islamic law. With the development of legal theory, ijma' as local practice was transformed from a de facto material source of Islamic law to a formal intellectual source. It became a process by which legal decisions were reached.

As noted above, the first change in conceptualizing ijma° initiated by al-Shafi°i was that it was no longer limited to the leaders of a certain area. Instead, the entire community was to agree on a particular issue. Al-Shafi°i believed that this was the only kind of consensus justified as a source of law by revelation. He seems to have accepted the popular hadith reporting that the Prophet assured his followers that the entire community would never agree on an error. This reorientation of ijma° by al-Shafi°i inevitably limited its actual use. In fact, al-Shafi°i believed that the era in which it was possible to determine true ijma° was over. The Muslim world had become so huge that it was no longer possible to determine the kind of general consensus he required. That, too, he found substantiated in the Sunna. He quotes a report from the prophet Muhammad:

> Believe my Companions, then those who succeed them, and after that those who succeed the Successors; but after them untruthfulness will prevail when people will swear [in support of their saying] without having been asked to swear, and will testify without having been asked to testify. Only those who seek the pleasure of Paradise will follow the community, for the devil can pursue one person, but stands far away from two.[2]

So difficult was the attainment of unanimity within the entire community that many scholars believe consensus was actually only used to determine the individual duties of all Muslims, such as the Five Pillars. A further limitation on the practical use of consensus as conceived by al-Shafi°i was that it became irrevocable. Formerly, ijma° seems to have been limited to the generation practicing it. In accordance with Islam's characteristic historicism, each generation was expected to determine its own agreement on the most effective ways to implement the will of God. But al-Shafi°i overruled this historicist element, believing that the later generations were further from the source of revelation and, as a result, more likely to be misled. He therefore insisted that no generation could overrule the ijma° of an earlier generation, even by ijma°.

This narrowing of ijma° was in many ways an inevitable development, given the changing situation of the Muslim community. After the first four successors of the prophet Muhammad as community leader (the "Rightly Guided" caliphs, *al-rashidun*), leadership of the community was taken over by dynasties. The Umayyads headed the community from their Damascus capital from 661–750 CE, and then the °Abbasids took over, building their capital at Baghdad and running the empire from 750–1258 CE. These imperial caliphs wielded enormous power, yet unlike their predecessors, correct Islamic practice did not seem to be their primary concern. The atmosphere in various regions therefore changed; there was often conflict between the legal (i.e., religious) and political authorities, and confidence that local practice continued to be modeled primarily on the Sunna began to wane. This reality is reflected in al-Shafi'i's explanation of his reforms:

> When the community spread in the land, nobody was able to follow its members who had been dispersed and mixed with other believers and unbelievers, pious and impious. So it was meaningless to follow the community, because it was impossible, except for what the [entire] community regarded as lawful or unlawful. . . . In the community as a whole there is no error concerning the meaning of the Qur'an, the Sunna, and analogy.[3]

The fact that al-Shafi'i's reforms, despite initial resistance, gradually came to be accepted indicates a growing concern on the part of the Muslim community that its legal structure maintain its integrity and, even more importantly, growing awareness that Islamic law was the backbone of the community.

2 Reasoning (ijtihad)

The limitation of the use of consensus as a source of law was consistent with al-Shafi'i's goal of greater reliance on the Qur'an and Sunna of the Prophet, and less reliance on the opinions of scholars. The goal of this reform seems to have been to curb the relatively free exercise of authority theretofore practiced by Islamic judges, in order to prevent deviations and innovations from marring the authenticity of Islamic legislation – to prevent gaps from developing between ideal law, the Shari'a, and real law, fiqh. But even al-Shafi'i acknowledged that there were times when the exercise of independent scholarly judgment was essential. In the absence of precedents considered relevant by legal authorities, scholars had to exercise their discretion: "On all matters touching the Muslim there is either a binding decision or an indication as to the right answer. If there is a decision, it should be followed; if there is no indication as to the right answer, it should be sought by ijtihad."[4] If there were no specific precedents set out in the Qur'an and authentic hadith reports, then scholars had to determine, in light of their understanding of the spirit and goal of revealed sources, what sort of behavior was appropriate in the novel case in front of them. This exercise of independent judgment is called *ijtihad*. It is noteworthy that the linguistic root of the term is the same as that of the term *jihad*. Both come from an Arabic root meaning "to exert strenuous effort." Ijtihad is considered to be strenuous intellectual effort dedicated to implementing the Shari'a, and even al-Shafi'i recognized that it was essential if Islamic law were to continue to be relevant to all aspects of human life.

(a) Ra'y

In its earliest manifestations, ijtihad was considered as simply the personal opinion (ra'y) of a person in authority or judge (often equivalent in the earliest days of Islam; see Chapter 5). The classic examples of judgment by ra'y are drawn from the time of the Rashidun and often demonstrate the historicist nature of Islamic law noted in Chapter 2. One manifestation of that historicism is concern with whether or not a particular practice of the Prophet, whether recorded in the Qur'an or hadith, constituted an immutable law or one contingent on the circumstances in which he lived. A well-known example involves judgment on how to distribute the charity which all Muslims contribute for the support of worthy causes. According to the Qur'an, it is to be spent for "the poor and the needy, and those who work with them, for those whose hearts are to be reconciled, for the freeing of slaves, for those in debt, in the cause of God, and for travellers" (Sura 9:60). 'Umar, the second caliph, decided that it was no longer necessary to give charity for "reconciliation" – that is, attracting people to join the Muslim community, because the circumstances of the community and its relationship to others had changed. At the time the verse in question was delivered, the Muslim community was new, small, and had relatively little in the way of material benefit to offer newcomers. But by the time of 'Umar, the Muslim community had become so strong that it was no longer necessary to resort to such measures to demonstrate the benefits of joining. It was 'Umar's judgment, therefore, that the essential part of the revealed verse was that people be attracted to Islam; the means described were contingent upon the historic circumstances in which that goal was revealed (*asbab al-nuzul*). He did not have to justify his opinion based on anything other than his personal authority in interpreting the meaning of the verse.

(b) Reasoning by analogy (qiyas)

By the close of the formative period of Islamic law, it was determined that mere opinion – even that of respected scholars – was not sufficient to prevent deviation from the spirit of the Qur'an and Sunna in Islamic legislation. Specific rules for the exercise of ijtihad were developed in an effort to ensure that the reasoning involved would produce results parallel to those in the revealed sources. As noted in Chapter 2, this form of ijtihad is called *qiyas*, syllogistic reasoning. It proceeds by determining a common factor ('*illah*; other terms used, especially by al-Shafi'i, were *ma'na* [meaning or key idea] and *asl* [root or basis]) between precedents in the Qur'an and Sunna and the case in question. When the common factor is identified, the ruling contained in the precedent is applied to the current case.

Qiyas is a step beyond merely judging a case to be similar to another one.

That type of reasoning was used, for example, by Malik in determining what to do about a thief who is caught in the act:

> Malik said, "The generally agreed on way of dealing among us with the thief who is found in a house and has gathered up goods and has not taken them out is that his hand is not cut off [the Qur'anically mandated punishment for theft]. That is like the man who places wine before him to drink and does not drink it. The [standard punishment for the crime] is not imposed on him. That is like a man who sits with a woman and desires to have [forbidden] intercourse with her and does not do it and he does not reach her. There is no [standard punishment] against that either."[5]

In this case Malik is pointing out a similarity among cases. However, qiyas must proceed not by mere analogy but by first determining a precedent, then deciding what aspect of that precedent is parallel to the case under discussion, and finally applying the judgment reached in the precedent to the present case. This mode of reasoning was used, for example, in a case in which Malik had to determine the appropriate punishment for knocking out someone's tooth. Some people in such cases apparently made different judgments depending upon whether the tooth in question was a molar, a front tooth, etc. Malik did not:

> Yahya related to me from Malik from Da'ud ibn al-Husayn that Abu Ghatafan ibn Tarif al-Murri informed him that Marwan ibn al-Hakam sent him to 'Abdullah ibn 'Abbas to ask him what there was for the molar. 'Abdullah ibn 'Abbas said, "There are five camels for it." He said, "Marwan sent me back again to 'Abdullah ibn 'Abbas." He said, "Do you consider all teeth as molars?" 'Abdullah ibn 'Abbas said, "It is enough that you take the fingers as the example for that, their [compensation] being all the same."[6]

In this case, the precedent is the punishment for cutting off someone's finger, established in reliable hadith. Since fingers are like teeth in that people have a number of them, and the Sunna treats all fingers as equivalently protected by law, then teeth shall also be treated as equivalently protected by law.

There is still a great deal of individual judgment involved in the practice of qiyas, of course. Identification of the 'illah is left to the judge, whose views undoubtedly influence the outcome of the case. The example of setting a minimum amount of dower is instructive in this regard. The Qur'an stipulated that brides must be given a dower (bridal gift) to do with as they will: "And give the women their dower as a gift" (Sura 4:5). Contemporary commentators generally describe this as part of the Qur'an's effort to elevate the status of women from their pre-Islamic status as mere property. By allowing brides to keep the dower, that institution was transformed from one where women were effectively being bought into one which guaranteed women at least a modicum of material independence. When it came to the process of creating legislation about the dower, however, the question arose as to the minimum amount required for a valid dower. But Malik did not consider precedent concerning economic freedom. Instead, he compared the dower to theft: "I do not think that women should be married for less than a quarter of a dinar. That is the lowest amount [of theft] for which cutting off the hand is obliged."[7] The fact that the precedent which the legal scholar chose was one of offense or interference in an individual's rightful wealth indicates, by qiyas, a difference in perspective between the eighth-century legal scholar and contemporary commentators. The Qur'an is full of references to generosity and goodwill offerings that might just as well have been chosen as relevant precedents for judging on this matter. Nevertheless, Malik's mode of reasoning is consistent with the controlled pattern of syllogistic reasoning insisted on by al-Shafi'i, rather than simple exercise of opinion.

Although earlier schools allowed ijtihad as a third source of Islamic law, whether by ra'y or qiyas, with al-Shafi'i's reforms only qiyas was to be used, and that only as a last resort. In all cases, a precedent in the Qur'an or Sunna was binding in the pattern established by al-Shafi'i, followed only by the precedent established by agreement of the entire legal community. That, as we saw, came to mean the first generation of Muslims – the revered companions of the prophet – since it was only in their time that it was possible to achieve such a consensus. Many contemporary Islamic reformers decry the demotion in priority of ijtihad among the sources of Islamic law. They attribute to it increasing inflexibility and thus decline in the viability of Islamic law. This may, in fact, have been the practical result of al-Shafi'i's reforms, but it does not reflect al-Shafi'i's rationale for the reorientation. Rather, he based his reforms on an important distinction in binding capacity between ijtihad/qiyas and the other three sources of law. The Qur'an, the Sunna, and the precedents agreed upon by the earliest generation are binding for all Muslims at all times; the results of ijtihad/qiyas are not. The results of jurists' reasoning become part of the lore of the school in which they are produced, and are then to be referred to by succeeding lawyers. But they remain subject to new ijtihad/qiyas in changed circumstances, which the Qur'an, the Sunna, and ijma' do not. Al-Shafi'i gives an example that demonstrates why this is so:

> Are we not obligated to accept the just character of a man on the basis of his outward behavior, and establish marital and inheritance relationship with him on [the basis of] his outward acceptance of Islam?
> . . . Yet he may not be just in character inwardly.

67

... So is it not lawful for us to establish marital and inheritance relationship with him, and to accept his testimony, and is it not unlawful for us to kill him on the basis of our explicit knowledge of him? But if others should discover him to be an [apostate, liable to capital punishment under Islamic law], would it not be lawful for them to kill him and to repudiate marital and inheritance relationship or whatever else he had been permitted to do?
... Thus the obligation imposed on us toward the same person differs in accordance with the degree of our understanding of it and others' understanding of it.
... Thus we hold concerning matters on which there is no binding explicit text that these should be sought by ijtihad – through qiyas – because we are under obligation to arrive at the right answers according to us [but others' knowledge may be different and more accurate].[8]

In other words, when relying on the Qur'an or authentic hadith reports, or even on the consensus of the community closest to Prophet Muhammad and imbued with his example, we assume that there are authorities higher than ourselves whose judgment is trustworthy. Among ourselves, however, the succeeding generations, none can claim infallible judgment. We must allow that errors of our judgment are possible. We must therefore remain open to further evidence and revised opinions.

Al-Shafi'i therefore ranks legal knowledge according to degrees of certainty. The highest or first order is knowledge derived directly from the Qur'an or a reliable hadith report concerning Prophet Muhammad. Legal knowledge based on these sources applies to all Muslims and is unquestionable. Of a lesser order is knowledge based on hadith material generally known only by specialists in law. It is still applicable to all Muslims, but its certainty is open to question. The example he gives is that legal scholars are bound to accept the testimony of two witnesses as conclusive, even though it remains possible that two witnesses could be mistaken. As noted above, knowledge based on the consensus of the generation among whom Prophet Muhammad lived is also considered authoritative by al-Shafi'i, and binding on all Muslims, even though it does not share the certainty of revelation. Finally, of the lowest order of certainty is knowledge derived from the indisputable sources by qiyas. "Such decisions are right in the literal sense to the person who applies analogy, not to the majority of scholars, for nobody knows what is hidden except God."[9]

Al-Shafi'i then justifies his limitation of ijtihad or juristic reasoning to qiyas, or reasoning by analogy from a known or certain precedent. When dealing with issues of questionable certainty, as in the cases for which there are no specific precedents in the Qur'an or reliable hadith literature, it is only reasonable to base the judgment on something that is known:

Do you not agree that if a man injured the slave of another the scholars would not ask a [third] man to fix the price of the slave, whether male or female, unless he were well informed about the market prices in order to estimate two prices [i.e., the market price and the estimated price] by which he would inform you of the price of a similar slave on that day? For such [pricing] cannot be done except on the basis of the knowledge of similar cases on the strength of which he applies analogy.[10]

To base legal reasoning on anything but a certain source would be like setting the price for something with no knowledge of the product in question or the current market conditions.

To further stress the need for restricting ijtihad to analogical reasoning, al-Shafi'i presents numerous examples demonstrating the lack of certainty even in this relatively restricted analytic method. He points out that this lack of certainty is evidenced by the possibility of reaching different answers depending upon what is chosen as a precedent and how clear its implications are. He then ranks the kinds of precedent chosen in order of certainty and establishes principles for choosing one kind of precedent over another. The most certain results will stem "from an order of prohibition by God or the Apostle involving a small quantity, which makes equally strong or stronger an order of prohibition involving a great quantity."[11] For example, he quotes a tradition prohibiting thinking anything but good about believers. Therefore, telling lies about a believer – "the thing greater than the thought implying in any way what is contrary to his good" – is even more unlawful. "Similarly," he continues, "the commendation of a small act of piety implies the presumably stronger commendation of a greater act of piety; and similarly an order of permission involving a great quantity would render permissible something of a smaller quantity."[12] Thus, when confronted with a case of the prohibition or permissibility of an act, a jurist should identify the act in question according to categories known to be prohibited or permitted. Then he should rank the act in question relative to the specific acts known to be prohibited or permitted. If the act under scrutiny is judged to be of greater significance than a known act, it will be either more prohibited or permissible (i.e., the punishment or commendation will be greater), depending upon the category.

Al-Shafi'i restricts analogical reasoning still further by excluding certain components of "the two roots," as he calls the Qur'an and Sunna, from those things which may be modified by human reason. First of all, ijtihad can be exercised only on a specific textual precedent, not on a general principle. For example, the Qur'an calls for prayer to be in the direction of Mecca. But if someone is unable to determine with certainty the direction of Mecca, then a judge may legitimately rule that prayer in the direction one has identified to the best of one's ability as Mecca's likewise fulfills the religious duty. But the judge could not rule out, for example, the general requirement for prayer or even for prayer in a certain direction.

Second, and more importantly, al-Shafi'i rejects the possibility of using ijtihad to reach a judgment on an issue that is already covered by what he calls *nass* ("something fixed"). Nass means, to al-Shafi'i, a specific textual ruling, and it may be used in ijtihad only to extend its ruling to a case judged to be similar. For example, the Qur'an stipulates and the Sunna reiterates that the complete suckling of children takes two years and that fathers must provide for their families during this time. Given such a specific ruling, and no countervailing verses or reports, al-Shafi'i could not envision a diminution of the ruling, such as a ruling in which men were not required, under normal circumstances, to provide for their families. But the ruling can be extended. Al-Shafi'i believes, in fact, that the ruling requires not only that fathers support their families for two years but, by extension, for as long as they are unable to provide for themselves. By yet further extension, children are obliged to support their father if he becomes incapable of supporting himself.[13]

Nor can a text be used as a basis for analogy if it is itself a modification of another ruling. For example, before people pray, they are required by the Qur'an to wash their faces and hands up to the elbows, and to wipe their heads, and feet up to the ankles (Sura 5:7). But the Prophet is reported to have practiced wiping of the shoes. Al-Shafi'i reasons that this is a modification of the prayer ruling and should not be used as a basis to assume that people should wipe other articles of dress, such as their turbans, veils, or gloves.[14]

The issue of determining which verses are clear texts (nass), however, is not a simple one. The Qur'an itself introduced a distinction between verses that are *muhkam* and those that are *mutashabih* (Sura 3:8). Many scholars today interpret muhkam verses as those containing legal rulings with a single, obvious meaning, and mutashabih verses that are ambiguous or equivocal. Yet there is little unanimity historically concerning the meanings of these terms. Al-Tabari (d. 923 CE), among the most respected Qur'anic commentators and the most aware of hermeneutical issues in his day, discusses at length possible meanings of these terms.[15] He says that the muhkamat are "those [verses] which are fortified (*ahkama*) by clarity (*bayan*) and detail (*tafsil*)."[16] These include verses dealing with what is lawful and what is forbidden, he says, what is promised and what is threatened, what is commanded and what is criticized, direct as well as metaphorical information, and moral exhortation and admonition. The mutashabihat are those verses that sound like others but have different meanings, with the implication that their real meanings can be twisted by those so inclined. But he then offers multiple groups of hadith reports that allow for different understandings of these terms. The majority of hadith reports describe muhkam verses as those that abrogate the mutashabih verses. Among others he describes are those that characterize the muhkam verses as God's proofs or evidence, while the mutashabih verses serve as tests for believers. The position he favors is that expressed in hadith reports describing the muhkam verses as those understandable to religious scholars, while the mutashabih verses are those very few verses that can be understood only by God, although he recognizes that the other opinions on the distinction between the two types of verse remain options. There is even less unanimity among scholars regarding which verses fall into which categories.

Determining which texts are clear or determined is also complicated by the issue of abrogation. As noted above (see p. 55), the Qur'an refers to its power of abrogation or supersession of previous revelation. "Whatever of our revelations as we abrogate or cause to be forgotten, We bring [in place] one better or the like thereof" (Sura 2:107). Elsewhere: "God effaces what he will, and establishes [what he will], and with Him is the source of all revelation [Mother of the Book]." (Sura 13:40). But, again, there is no agreement among scholars concerning either what these terms mean exactly or which verses are involved. Some scholars believe that the only revelation abrogated by the Qur'an is that which preceded the Qur'an. According to this inter-pretation, the Torah and the Gospels are abrogated by the Qur'an. Other scholars believe that the verses abrogated by the Qur'an are no longer in existence, i.e., that they were obliterated before the Qur'an was enunciated. The most famous example is that of the so-called "Satanic verses." According to tradition, while the Prophet was reciting the Surat al-Najm ("Chapter of the Star," Sura 53), in which he mentions three favorite goddesses of the region, Satan intervened and persuaded him to say that it was acceptable to pray for their intercession. As the verse is actually revealed, these goddesses are described as "mere names . . . for which God has sent down no authority" (Sura 53:24), the erroneous verses having been lost or obliterated before the Qur'an was recorded.

The interpretation of abrogation (naskh) that became incorporated into Islamic law, however, is the one according to which later verses of the Qur'an abrogate earlier verses. For example, the Hanafi legal scholar al-Shaybani claims that Sura 5:107 was abrogated: "O believers, the testimony among you when any of you is faced with death, when you make a bequest, shall be two just men from among you, or of two others not from among you if you are travelling in the land and the tragedy of death befalls you." That verse allows a non-Muslim to be a valid witness regarding the last wishes of a Muslim who dies in a foreign land. Al-Shaybani claims that by the time of Abu Hanifa it was believed that Muslims may only allow other Muslims to be witnesses on their behalf, that verse having been abrogated. The Malikis also use the theory of abrogation of Qur'anic verses. For example, they believe Sura 2:181 ("[A]ny of you visited by death and if he leaves much wealth, must make a testament in favor of his parents and relatives. . . . Then if anyone changes it after hearing it, the sin shall rest upon those who change it. . . . But if anyone fears injustice or sin from such testament and so makes things right between them, then it is no sin for him") is no longer in effect. Malik says that a will can be changed only with the permission of all those to whom a man is obliged to bequeath his property.

A widely accepted example of a variation on the theory of abrogation as it operated in legislation concerns the punishment for adultery. According to the Qur'an, the punishment for adultery is whipping: "The adulteress and the adulterer, whip each of them one hundred times" (Sura 24:3). But by the time of Malik, it was determined that the punishment was stoning instead:

> Malik related to me from Nafi' that 'Abdullah ibn 'Umar said, "The Jews came to the Messenger of God, may God bless him and grant him peace, and mentioned to him that a man and woman from among them had committed adultery. The Messenger of God, may God bless him and grant him peace, asked them, "What do you find in the Torah about stoning?" They said, "We make their wrong action known and flog them." 'Abdullah ibn Salam, "You have lied. It is stoning for it, so bring the Torah." They spread it out and one of them placed his hand over the verse of stoning. Then he read what was before and after it. 'Abdullah ibn Salam told him to lift his hand. He lifted his hand and there was the verse of stoning. They said, "He has spoken the truth, Muhammad. The verse of stoning is in it." So the Messenger of God, may God bless him and grant him peace, gave the order and they were stoned."[17]

The punishment of stoning instead of whipping, at least for properly married Muslims, was thus incorporated into Islamic law, an apparent case of a hadith report abrogating a Qur'anic verse.

According to al-Shafi'i, this type of abrogation is technically unacceptable. He did accept the idea of abrogation in general:

> God indeed created mankind for whatever His established knowledge desired in creating and for whatever [its destiny] should be. There is no reversal at all of His judgement, He being swift of reckoning [Sura 14:51]. And He revealed to them the Book that explains everything, as a guide and a mercy [Sura 16:91]. In it He laid down some duties which He confirmed, and others which He abrogated, as a mercy to His people so as to lighten their burden and to comfort them in addition to the favors which He had begun to bestow upon them. For the fulfillment [of the duties] He confirmed, He rewarded them with Paradise and with salvation from his punishment. His mercy has included all of them in what He confirmed and what He abrogated. Praise be to Him for His favors.[18]

Al-Shafi'i even accepted the idea that certain Qur'anic verses abrogate others, rather than limiting the Qur'an's abrogating effect to earlier scriptures alone. However, according to al-Shafi'i, only the Qur'an can abrogate the Qur'an. A Qur'anic command cannot be abrogated by a hadith:

> God has declared that He abrogated [communications] of the Book only by means of other communications in it; that the sunna cannot abrogate [a text in] the Book but it should only follow what is laid down in the Book, and that the sunna is intended to explain the meaning of communications of general [nature] set forth [in the Book].[19]

The principle al-Shafi'i articulates is that something can only be abrogated by something of equal status. Thus, even though he was responsible, as we have seen, for elevating the hadith to the level of revelation, making it an essential component of understanding the Qur'an, he nevertheless insists that it is secondary to the Qur'an:

> Thus God informed that He had commanded His Prophet to obey what was communicated to him, but that He did not empower him to alter [the Book] of his own accord. For there is in His saying: "It is not for me to alter it of my own accord" [Sura 10:16], an evidence for what I stated, that nothing can abrogate the Book of God save His Book. Since [God] is the originator of His [own] commands, He [alone] can repeal or confirm whatever of it He wills – glorious be His praise – but no one of His creatures may do so. For He also said: "God repeals what He wills, or confirms; with Him is the Mother of the Book" [Sura 13:39].[20]

Similarly, al-Shafi'i points out that only a hadith can abrogate another hadith (and he bases that on a hadith). How, then, does he deal with the hadith regarding stoning for adultery, rather than the Qur'anically mandated whipping? He claims that a hadith cannot be abrogated by the Qur'an unless there is another hadith making the abrogation clear, again, on the principle that something can be abrogated only by something of equal status. This is, he says, because:

> Were it permissible to hold that what the Apostle has laid down in the sunna was abrogated by the Qur'an and that he has transmitted no abrogating sunna, it would be permissible to hold a similar view concerning [the tradition relating to] the prohibition of all kinds of sale [of property], by holding that [the Prophet] had prohibited them before God had laid down [the rule] that "God has permitted sale and forbidden usury" [Sura 1:276]. The same might be held

about [the tradition concerning] the stoning of adulterers, namely, that stoning may be regarded as abrogated in accordance with God's saying: "The fornicatress and the fornicator – scourge each one of them with a hundred stripes" [Sura 24:2].[21]

He goes on to give a number of other examples of hadiths that differ from the Qur'an in specific legislative details and yet were the basis of legislation, overriding the Qur'anic position on the subject. In all the cases he mentions, he believes there is ample evidence in the hadith material that the Prophet had indeed abrogated an earlier hadith, presumably one agreeing with the Qur'an's position on the subject. Thus, the hadiths are not actually abrogating the Qur'an but earlier hadiths – on the principle he articulated. In other words, he says, it is not permissible to think that the Qur'an abrogates individual hadiths because that would allow rejection of all the hadith reports if they disagreed with something in the Qur'an. While such a position may seem reasonable on the face of it, so strong was the conviction that the Sunna is necessary for understanding the Qur'an that, to al-Shafi'i and the majority of his successors, it was impossible that hadith reports which were accepted as reliable could really contradict the Qur'an.

It should be noted that the idea of abrogation is another aspect of the historicity of Islamic revelation (see Chapter 2). The rationale for abrogation is not that mistakes were made in revelation. On the contrary, revelation is believed to be perfect. Yet part of its perfection is its being suited to the circumstances in which it is meant to be effective. While the overall message of revelation is meant for all peoples and for all time, it is above all a message of reform, and many of its components are examples of that reform in process. It is therefore to be expected that, as circumstances change, so will specific aspects of legislation. Nevertheless, the notion of abrogation immeasurably complicates the process of legislation, opening up endless debate about which verses are abrogated and which are abrogators. Even among those scholars who accept the theory that later Qur'anic verses abrogate earlier Qur'anic verses, there is no agreement either on the mode of abrogation or the number of verses involved. Some believe later verses can only make temporary exceptions to earlier verses, others believe they can only clarify or make earlier verses more explicit, while still others believe later verses can completely overrule earlier ones.

Thus, even restricting legal reasoning to syllogism based on specific texts considered to be univocal does not result in consensus among scholars. In addition to the issues of interpreting which verses are clear and which are general, and which are abrogated and which are abrogators, there are texts that can be interpreted as univocal or contradictory, depending upon the opinion of the judge. One example given by al-Shafi'i involves two reliable sets of hadith reports. In the first, Prophet Muhammad is quoted as saying: "Let no one exchange gold for gold save in equal quantities, or increase the quantity against the other. Let no one exchange silver for silver save in equal quantities, or increase one quantity against the other. Let no one exchange anything at hand for another not in evidence." But other reports have the Prophet declare, "*Al-riba* (usury) is to be found in *al-nasi'a* (deferred payment)." Al-Shafi'i explains that these two positions "may be regarded as both contradictory and not contradictory." They may be considered in agreement if we assume the latter concerned the exchange of two different kinds of property; the prohibition of unequal amounts of the same thing and of selling anything that the buyer cannot see is consistent with the prohibition of deferred payment. But if it is assumed that the latter allows any sale as long as the exchange takes place immediately, then it contradicts the first report.[22] He prefers to assume the two reports are in agreement but allows that other legal thinkers may see things otherwise. Elsewhere, he discusses that the same prohibition on transactions involving anything but the immediate exchange of equal amounts when dealing with gold, dates, wheat, and barley could result in a number of different 'illas or precedents for qiyas. A judge could assume that only the things mentioned are thus restricted, or he could assume that the prohibition applies to all edibles, or edibles and potables, or to basic foodstuffs, or to plentiful foodstuffs. One could also equivocate on whether the prohibition applies to things that are normally weighed or measured, as well. Al-Shafi'i concludes that the prohibition means that "nothing edible or potable can be [exchanged lawfully] for other kinds of things to be delivered at an appointed time. For the rule of [exchanging] foodstuffs by measure applies to [exchanging] foodstuffs by weight."[23] But, again, he acknowledges that other opinions are also arguable.

Such differences in legal opinion even within the controlled framework of Islamic jurisprudence as articulated by the scholars explain some of the differences between the various official schools of law mentioned above. Al-Shafi'i explains that in the practice of law it is sometimes necessary to establish several ways of determining the truth. Some of those means will be more reliable than others, and legal scholars must be sensitive to that. For example:

> If a man admits an obligation on his part to God or to another person, I should take a decision against him on the strength of his admission; if he does not admit, I should take the decision on the evidence established against him; if no evidence can be established against him, I should take the decision on the basis of an oath taken by him which might acquit him; if he refuses [to take the oath], I should ask the other party to take an oath and I should make the decision against him on the basis of the oath of the other party. It is understood that [one's own] admission against himself – owing to covetousness and greed – is more certain than the evidence of others, since they might make a mistake or tell a lie against another. The

evidence of witnesses of just character against a person should be regarded as nearer to the truth than refusal [by the accused] to take an oath, or [nearer to the truth] than the oath taken by the other party [against him], since the latter might not be just in character. Thus the decision is taken on several grounds, some of them stronger than others.[24]

The Hanafis, al-Shafi'i reports, would consider the accused's refusal to take an oath as grounds for finding against him, and points out that he believes theirs is a weaker basis of certainty than the one he has established. The Hanafis, by contrast, feel theirs is a stronger basis of certainty.

Given these degrees of certainty in legal knowledge, the question arises regarding the cases in which differences of opinion among legal scholars are permissible. Al-Shafi'i does not allow any difference of opinion regarding issues covered by specific texts from the Qur'an or Sunna. Only in matters determined by qiyas, according to him, is there any room for disagreement (ikhtilaf). But given that qiyas produces the uncertain results he has described, then legal scholars will inevitably disagree on its results. Typically, al-Shafi'i points out the degrees of certainty even in the exercise of qiyas. If qiyas is used to derive a ruling from a single precedent that is almost identical to the circumstances in the case at hand, then its results should be obvious and there should be no disagreement. But if there are several precedents and it is not obvious which is closer to the circumstances of the case under discussion, then there is likely to be disagreement despite the scholars' best efforts to determine which precedent is most appropriate. Furthermore, when there is disagreement on the interpretation of terms, disagreement within acceptable limits will result. For example, the Qur'an stipulates that divorced women "shall keep to themselves for three periods (quru')" (Sura 2:229). That verse seems specific, but the question arises over the interpretation of the term quru'. It could mean menstruation, meaning that the woman may marry again after the third menstrual period. Or it could mean the states of "purity" between menstrual courses, in which case she would have to wait until the end of three periods between menstruation, meaning until the just before the fourth menstrual cycle.

Overall, the tendency to rely on the Qur'an and Sunna – interpreted as that which is conveyed in reliable hadith collections – stressed so vehemently by al-Shafi'i appears to be a reversion to an oral model of reasoning by precedent, rather than on the basis of principle. In fact, however, al-Shafi'i demonstrated an unprecedented privileging of literacy in his reforms, especially in the development of specific qualifications for the practice of ijtihad. Those claiming this right first had to demonstrate a thorough knowledge of Arabic grammar and style, the Qur'an, hadith literature, logic, and the legal precedents established in one's school of law, and the customary law of the land in which one's judgments would be effective (see Chapter 4). What the reforms represent, then, is an abiding concern with institutionalizing legal practice for future generations in a changing political climate. The closer legal scholars stayed to the precedent established by the Prophet and his close companions, the more likelihood they thought there would be of maintaining the integrity of the Prophet's message. Further evidence of the literate pattern of Islamic jurisprudence is that even with the increasing concern for precedent represented in the Shafi'i and Hanbali schools, Islamic law continued to focus on the overall goal of legislation, rather than following precedent for its own sake (a pattern characteristic of oral culture). This concern is demonstrated in the principle of "juristic preference" (*istihsan* and *istislah*), whereby judges are allowed to make exceptions to the results of strict legal reasoning for the sake of the common good.

3 Exceptions: istihsan and istislah

Al-Shafi'i says that istihsan as practiced by the earlier schools "is merely doing what is agreeable," by which he seems to mean following the easiest route. He therefore limits isithsan to qiyas.[25] In fact, his treatment of istihsan is simply a continuation of his discussion of qiyas. But the Hanafi school treated istihsan in the same way as the Malikis treated istislah: as "juristic preference," the right of the judge to deviate from the letter or direct implication of an established precedent if strict adherence would not, in his opinion, result in justice. In other words, it was a deviation from the letter of the law in order to remain faithful to the spirit of the law.

There are several well-known examples of deviation from precedent exercised by the second caliph, 'Umar. For example, when Iraq and Egypt came under Islamic rule, 'Umar deviated from the Prophet's practice of distributing conquered territory to the army. He justified this innovation on the basis of his responsibility to fulfill his Qur'anic obligation to provide for later generations of Muslims (Sura 59:11). Accordingly, the "juristic preference" or judge's prerogative here is based on a perceived conflict between two specific precedents. In cases where it is not possible to follow both precedents simultaneously, the judge must choose a means to fulfill the obligations considered most pressing.

Further clarification of this device is provided in perhaps the best known example of 'Umar's istihsan, and the one most formative for later legal reasoning. It concerns the punishments for theft called *hudud*. As mentioned above, the Qur'an stipulated that the punishment for theft was amputation of the hand: "The thief, male and female, cut off their hands as retribution for what they have earned, and as an exemplary punishment from God" (Sura 5:39). But when confronted with a situation where theft results from hunger, it is assumed that the amputation is not imposed. This is expressed as a precedent, in fact, by Malik when discussing punishment for eating carrion:

Malik, when asked whether or not a man who had been forced by necessity to eat carrion, should eat it when he also found the fruit, crops or sheep of a people in that place, answered, "If he thinks that the owners of the fruit, crops or sheep will accept that it was a necessity so that he will not be deemed a thief and have his hand cut off, then I think that he should eat from what he finds whatever will remove his hunger but he should not carry any of it away."[26]

In this case, the judgment is based on a simple deviation, initiated by the Caliph 'Umar, from a clear ruling of the Qur'an. Yet it is accepted as an important precedent in Islamic law because it is believed that 'Umar's decision was based on the Qur'an's ultimate concern: justice. It is believed that justice was better served by 'Umar's waiving of the severe punishment in the case of theft due to hunger than it would have been by following the letter of the Qur'an's ruling. Indeed, many scholars believe that 'Umar's juristic preference in this case itself constituted a precedent, so that thenceforth the hudud would not be imposed for theft in periods of famine.

Clearly, such judgments could only be made in light of an understanding of the overall spirit of the law. Lacking such a notion, application of the established law, adherence to the letter of the law, would become a goal in itself, as may have been the case with the Shafi'is. But the supporters of juristic preference demonstrated a concern beyond the letter of the law. The Hanifis, for example, identified justice ('adl) as the overriding concern of Islamic legislation. In fact, they use the term hukumah 'adl for ijtihad, meaning decision or judgment based on justice. The Malikis focus on social well-being (maslaha), using the term istislah, rather than istihsan, for juristic preference: concern for maslahah, or social well-being. Included in Malik's Muwatta is a section designed to inspire scholars to correct judgment based on maslaha. Most tellingly, he relates that the Prophet claimed that even his own judgments are subject to scrutiny:

> Yahya related to me from Malik from Hisham ibn 'Urwa from his father from Zaynab bint Abi Salama from Umm Salama, the wife of the Prophet, may God bless him and grant him peace, that the Messenger of God, may God bless him and grant him peace, said, "I am but a man to whom you bring your disputes. Perhaps one of you is more eloquent in his proof than the other and so I give judgment according to what I have heard from him. Whatever I decide for him which is part of the right of his brother, he must not take any of it for I am granting him a portion of the Fire."[27]

In other words, an unfair judgment even from the prophet himself is as bad as tasting hell and therefore should not be followed. Nor should anyone be privileged on the basis of communal identity. Malik's second example, related in order to stimulate judgment according to principles of justice, concerns a case in which 'Umar had to judge in a dispute between a Muslim and a Jew. Malik makes a point of saying that 'Umar judged in favor of the Jew simply because he thought his case had more merit.[28] This position reflects a Qur'anic verse considered to be paradigmatic of Islamic standards of justice: "O you believers, establish justice, being witnesses for God, even if the evidence goes against yourselves or against your parents or relatives, and irrespective of whether the witness is rich or poor" (Sura 4:136).

Other scholars have identified a number of themes of Islamic law which indicate a variety of dominant concerns. A major one is the universalism of Islam, perhaps best articulated in what is known as Prophet Muhammad's farewell speech. After reminding his listeners *inter alia* that their lives and property are inviolable, that they will be called to account for their actions on the Last Day, that husbands and wives each have rights and that wives especially must be treated with kindness and love, and that usury is forbidden, and that slaves should be fed and clothed as their owners are, Muhammad made a pronouncement about the equality of all Muslims believed to encapsulate the spirit of the Islamic community:

> O people, your Lord is one and your ancestor is [also] one. You are all descended from Adam and Adam was [born] of the earth. "The noblest of you all in the sight of Allah is the most devout. Allah is knowing and all-wise" (Sura 44:13). An Arab is superior to a non-Arab in nothing unless it is devotion.[29]

Reinforcing the self-perception of Muslims as a potentially universal community, the principle of privilege within the Islamic community according to tribe or nation is rejected throughout Islamic legislation.

Thus, the law itself becomes the unifying factor of the Muslim community. The Islamic legal system is everywhere conscious of itself as supreme, holding precedence even over its own leaders. The Qur'an describes all prophets, including Muhammad, as subject to the law, having been enjoined to judge only in accordance with it. Speaking of people to whom earlier revelations were sent, the Qur'an says:

> If they come to you, judge between them,
> or turn away from them; if you turn
> away from them, they will not hurt you;
> and if you judge, judge justly among them;
>   God loves the just ones.
> And how will they make you judge
> when they have the Torah, wherein is God's

judgement, and nevertheless turn their backs?
   They are not believers.
Indeed We sent down the Torah, wherein is
guidance and light; thereby the prophets
who had submitted [to God] gave judgement
for the Jews, as did the pious people
and the learned, preserving such of
God's book as they were witnesses to.
So do not fear people,
but fear Me; and do not trade my signs
for a little price. Whoever does not judges
according to what God has revealed,
   they are the unbelievers.
(Sura 5:43–45)

The law is universal, and indeed is the one thing all people may share. And, although it has taken a variety of forms, it is eternal, its eternal element being piety and justice as service to God.

One final theme dominant in Islamic law, considered to be an essential correlate of justice, is mercy, as expressed in the conclusion of the above passage:

And therein We prescribed for them:
"A life for a life, an eye for an eye,
a nose for a nose, an ear for an ear,
a tooth for a tooth, and for wounds
retaliation"; and whoever forgoes it
in charity, that is an expiation.
Whoever does not judge
according to what God has revealed,
   they are the oppressors.
(Sura 5:46)

The Qur'an, overall, refers to itself as "a mercy" or a gift to humanity, given by God for our well-being. Every chapter of the Qur'an begins with the phrase, "In the name of God, the Merciful, the Compassionate." Without the knowledge of God's will and the inspiration to submit to it supplied by revelation, human beings abide in ignorance and war. In fact, as we shall see below (Chapter 7), those regions not ruled by Islamic law are referred to by the legal scholars as "the abode of war" (*dar al-harb*). But this means not that they are involved in active war. Rather, the concern is that those who are not protected by the ultimate justice of Islamic law recognize that, for their own well-being, they must eventually submit to the will of God, "the Benevolent, the Merciful."

In conclusion, then, the ambiguity built into Islamic law – due to acceptance of the need for human input with regard to appropriate means of implementing clear principles in changing circumstances (ijtihad), due to acceptance of the notions of abrogation and clarification, due to acceptance of multiple viewpoints – does not appear as a weakness or fault in the legal system. Instead, it is a function of Islam's inherent historicity, itself a function of its intended universality. Above and beyond ambiguity in the human sphere is the belief in an abiding divine justice that must inevitably manifest itself in a variety of ways, depending upon the circumstances. Again, therefore, we see the distinction between the eternity of God's will, the ideal law – Shari'a – and the time-bound and fallible nature of human efforts to implement that will – fiqh.

C Judaic counterparts: exegesis, logic, argument, dialectics

Judaic law deals more with the what than the how, with the contents of the law than with the methods by which those contents are delineated. When we come to ask about the intellectual sources of Judaism, we have to work back from the exposition of the law to the principles which guide that exposition. In the classical sources of the law, Mishnah, Tosefta, two Talmuds, and the exegetical compilations of legal passages of scripture, there are only a few points at which the how of legal theory is addressed. While some rather opaque principles of exegesis are totted up, seven on one list, thirteen on another, these by no means yield a coherent account of the intellectual working of the law. Yet, as we shall now see, reason, logic, and rationality form a well-defined and fully exposed corpus of principles of thought. Talk to a yeshiva-sage about ijtihad and he will not know what you mean, but ask about tradition versus logic, the authority of a verse of scripture as against that of a case, and he will respond right to the point. One of the great points of tension for example, contrasts massive erudition with acute reasoning. But the very appeal to reason in legal thinking – reason, not only explicit rule – is the starting point of the law of Judaism.

With halakhah, or law, set forth by the Written Torah, particularly in Exodus, Leviticus, Numbers, and Deuteronomy, as well as in the Oral Torah beginning with the Mishnah, a vast labor of harmonization and analysis was required to produce a coherent legal system. Human reasoning enjoys an exalted position within the law of Judaism. A famous story of the Talmud tells how, when a heavenly voice interfered in the sages' debate, a sage addressed heaven and insisted that sages now take charge of the law through their own processes of thought:

> So he [Eliezer] went and said to the other sages, "If the law accords with my position, let the Heaven prove it!"

An echo came forth, saying, "What business have you with R. Eliezer, for the law accords with his position under all circumstances!"

R. Joshua stood up on his feet and said, "'It is not in heaven' (Deuteronomy 30:12)."

What is the sense of, "'It is not in heaven' (Deuteronomy 30:12)"?

Said R. Jeremiah, "[The sense of Joshua's statement is this:] For the Torah has already been given from Mount Sinai, so we do not pay attention to echoes, since you have already written in the Torah at Mount Sinai, 'After the majority you are to incline' (Exodus 23:2)."

R. Nathan came upon Elijah and said to him, "What did the Holy One, blessed be he, do at that moment?"

He said to him, "He laughed and said, 'My children have overcome me, my children have overcome me!'"

God accepts the priority of reason and affirms the universal authority of rational discourse. So much is at stake in the intellectual resources of law in Judaism.

Four distinct modes of thought characterize the mind of Judaic jurisprudents when they addressed the tradition of the halakhah. One involved a close reading of the received Torah, exegesis; the second required the construction, out of the data of the Torah, of generalizations of broad consequence, logic; the third demanded reasoned argument concerning the propositions that were adduced; and the final one set forth modes of analysis of those arguments and their results, dialectics. Each is briefly introduced in what follows.

1 Exegesis: midrash halakhah

The Hebrew word "midrash" refers to the close reading of verses of scripture in order both to clarify the intent of scripture and to answer urgent questions brought to scripture by successive generations of the faithful. "Midrash halakhah" refers to the exegesis of legal passages of the Pentateuch. In Chapter 2 we have already examined a classical example of midrash halakhah. The word "midrash", translated "exegesis," presents confusion, since it is routinely used to convey three distinct, if related, meanings. If people say "the midrash says," they may mean to refer to (1) a distinctive *process* of interpretation of a particular text, thus, the hermeneutic, (2) a particular compilation of the results of that process, thus, a book that is the composite of a set of exegeses, or (3) a concrete unit of the working of that process, of scriptural exegesis, thus the write-up of the process of interpretation as it applies to a single verse, the exegetical composition on a particular verse (or group of verses).

The main, but not the sole task of halakhic midrash – exegesis of legal passages of scripture – was to link the Mishnah to scripture. The character of the Mishnah, with its disinclination to cite verses of scripture to sustain its propositions, defines one important task undertaken by midrash halakhah. Specifically, the midrash compilations that deal with Exodus, Leviticus, Numbers, and Deuteronomy measure the distance between the Mishnah and scripture and aim to close it. The question is persistently addressed in analyzing scripture: precisely how does a rule of the Mishnah relate to, or rest upon, a rule of scripture? That question demanded an answer, so that the status of the Mishnah's rules, and, right alongside, of the Mishnah itself, could find a clear definition. Collecting and arranging exegeses of scripture as these related to passages of the Mishnah first reached literary form in Sifra, to Leviticus, and in two books, both called Sifré, one to Numbers, the other Deuteronomy. All three compositions accomplished much else. For, even at that early stage, exegeses of passages of scripture in their own context and not only for the sake of Mishnah exegesis attracted attention. But a principal motif in all three books concerned the issue of Mishnah–scripture relationships.

A second, still more fruitful path in formulating midrash clarifications of scripture also emerged from the labor of Mishnah exegesis. It was the work of generalization, of discovering general rules in scripture's cases. As the work of Mishnah exegesis got under way, in the third century, exegetes of the Mishnah and others alongside undertook a parallel labor. They took an interest in reading scripture in the way in which they were reading the Mishnah itself. That is to say, they began to work through verses of scripture in exactly the same way – word for word, phrase for phrase, line for line – in which, to begin with, the exegetes of the Mishnah pursued the interpretation and explanation of the Mishnah. Precisely the types of exegesis that dictated the way in which sages read the Mishnah now guided their reading of scripture as well. And, as people began to collect and organize comments in accordance with the order of sentences and paragraphs of the Mishnah, they found the stimulation to collect and organize comments on clauses and verses of scripture.

2 *The Mishnah's applied logic of hierarchical classification*

The main modes of reasoning involved not exegesis of texts but abstract, logical inquiry and reflection. These produced, in succession, rational propositions treated here, arguments and analysis of the arguments. The generalizations emerged out of the logic of natural history – classification and hierarchization of data, arguments out of the application of analogy and contrast, and analysis out of the construction of dialectical inquiry, as we shall see in this and the following two sections.

The Mishnah, the fullest statement of the halakhah and its principles, is worked out through the modes of inquiry of natural history – classification of genera and species in a hierarchical structure. These modes of producing intelligible, rational propositions come to expression solely through the nitty-gritty of ordinary everyday life. The Mishnah's rhetoric, balanced and orderly and proportionate – is testimony to its conception that within the everyday are contained the highest and most abstract truths of not merely wisdom but knowledge, in our language, natural philosophy or science. If things are orderly, then out of the chaos of the here and now, we must show it. Just as in contemporary empirical, experimental science the case stands for the principle, which is to be inferred and tested, so in the Mishnah, cases bear the entire burden of analytical and principled thought. The Mishnah's mode of making connections – the details of its practical logic and applied reason – conforms to the rules of natural history set forth by Aristotle. In that science, the Mishnaic component of the Talmud proposes to investigate science in everyday life, identifying the data that follow the same rule, excluding those that do not, and setting the whole into a great chain of being.

Making connections means, specifically, investigating the properties of things and classifying like together with like. The method of natural history formulated by Aristotle rests upon the classification of things conducted in just that way. Moving from the known to the unknown, whether in science or in philosophy, requires that we employ what is known to solve the problem of the unknown, the certain imparting sense to the uncertain. This means we must discover the pertinent point of comparison, the governing analogy, that allows us to invoke the principle governing the known in the disposition of the unknown. If we can determine that to which the unknown is comparable, then we may impose upon the unknown the rule that governs the known, so classifying the unknown within the larger system of sense. Those taxonomically indicative traits inhere in the things themselves.

Let us consider a concrete text to see how the Mishnah puts forth a syllogism. In the following passage, drawn from Mishnah-tractate Sanhedrin, Chapter 2, the authorship wishes to say that Israel has two heads, one of state, the other of cult, the king and the high priest, respectively, and that these two offices are nearly wholly congruent with one another, with a few differences based on the particular traits of each. The traits associated with the one are then compared with those pertinent to the other, and out of this classification of shared, indicative traits also emerges the hierarchization of the one over the other. Broadly speaking, therefore, our exercise is one of setting forth the genus and the species. The genus is head of holy Israel. The species are king and high priest. Here are the traits in common and those not shared, and the exercise is fully exposed for what it is, an inquiry into the rules that govern, the points of regularity and order, in this minor matter, of political structure. My outline, imposed in bold type, makes the point important in this setting:

1   **THE RULES OF THE HIGH PRIEST: SUBJECT TO THE LAW, MARITAL RITES, CONDUCT IN BEREAVEMENT**

2:1 A.   A high priest judges, and [others] judge him;

B.   gives testimony, and [others] give testimony about him;

C.   performs the rite of removing the shoe [Deuteronomy 25:7–9], and [others] perform the rite of removing the shoe with his wife.

D.   [Others] enter levirate marriage with his wife, but he does not enter into levirate marriage,

E.   because he is prohibited to marry a widow.

F.   [If] he suffers a death [in his family], he does not follow the bier.

G.   "But when [the bearers of the bier] are not visible, he is visible; when they are visible, he is not.

H.   "And he goes with them to the city gate," the words of R. Meir.

I.   R. Judah says, "He never leaves the sanctuary,

J.   "since it says, '*Nor shall he go out of the sanctuary*' (Leviticus 21:12)."

K.   And when he gives comfort to others

L.   the accepted practice is for all the people to pass one after another, and the appointed [prefect of the priests] stands between him and the people.

M.   And when he receives consolation from others,

N.   all the people say to him, "Let us be your atonement."

O.   And he says to them, "May you be blessed by Heaven."

P.   And when they provide him with the funeral meal,

Q.   all the people sit on the ground, while he sits on a stool.

2   **THE RULES OF THE KING: NOT SUBJECT TO THE LAW, MARITAL RITES, CONDUCT IN BEREAVEMENT**

2:2 A.   The king does not judge, and [others] do not judge him;

B.   does not give testimony, and [others] do not give testimony about him;

C.   does not perform the rite of removing the shoe, and others do not perform the rite of removing the shoe with his wife;

D.   does not enter into levirate marriage, nor [do his brother] enter levirate marriage with his wife.

E.   R. Judah says, "If he wanted to perform the rite of removing the shoe or to enter into levirate marriage, his memory is a blessing."

F.   They said to him, "They pay no attention to him [if he expressed the wish to do so]."

G.   [Others] do not marry his widow.

H.   R. Judah says, "A king may marry the widow of a king.

I.   "For so we find in the case of David, that he married the widow of Saul,

J.   "For it is said, '*And I gave you your master's house and your master's wives into your embrace*' (II Samuel 12:8)."

2:3 A. [If] [the king] suffers a death in his family, he does not leave the gate of his palace.

    B. R. Judah says, "If he wants to go out after the bier, he goes out,

    C. "for thus we find in the case of David, that he went out after the bier of Abner,

    D. "since it is said, '*And King David followed the bier*' (2 Samuel 3:31)."

    E. They said to him, "This action was only to appease the people."

    F. And when they provide him with the funeral meal, all the people sit on the ground, while he sits on a couch.

(Mishnah-tractate Sanhedrin 2: 1–2)

Clearly, scripture plays a subordinate role here, not a taxonomically-indicative one. The topic is organized within its own logic, not in accordance with the order or data of scriptural references. Scripture supplies facts. What proves decisive in both the ordering of data and the conclusions drawn from the specific juxtapositions set forth? It is the traits of things – kings, high priests – that dictate classification categories on their own, without scripture's dictation.

Here we see a striking contrast to the power of Islamic philosophical lawyers to explain in abstract terms what they intend to do, as against the preference of their Judaic counterparts to speak through cases about large generalizations of rational thought. We should not mass the abstraction that is embedded in the concrete case before us. For the philosophical cast of mind is amply revealed in this essay, which in concrete terms effects a taxonomy, a study of the genus, national leader, and its two species, (1) king, (2) high priest: how are they alike, how are they not alike, and what accounts for the differences. The premise is that national leaders are alike and follow the same rule, except where they differ and follow the opposite rule from one another. But that premise is also subject to the proof effected by the survey of the data consisting of concrete rules, those systemically inert facts that here come to life for the purposes of establishing a proposition. By itself, the fact that, for example, others may not ride his horse, bears the burden of no systemic proposition. In the context of an argument constructed for nomothetic, taxonomic purposes, the same fact is active and weighty. The whole depends upon three premises: (1) the importance of comparison and contrast, with the supposition that (2) like follows like, and the unlike follows the opposite rule; and (3) when we classify we also hierarchize, which yields the argument from hierarchical classification: if this, which is the lesser, follows rule X, then that, which is the greater, should surely follow rule X. And that is the whole sum and substance of the logic of *Listenwissenschaft* as the Mishnah applies that logic in a practical way.

What we accomplish in list making is to seek connection between fact and fact, sentence and sentence, and this we find, in the subtle and balanced rhetoric of the Mishnah, by comparing and contrasting two things that are like and not alike. At the logical level, too, the Mishnah falls into the category of familiar philosophical thought. Once we seek regularities, we propose rules. What is like another thing falls under its rule, and what is not like the other falls under the opposite rule. Accordingly, as to the species of the genus, so far as they are alike, they share the same rule. So far as they are not alike, each follows a rule contrary to that governing the other. So the work of analysis is what produces connection, and therefore the drawing of conclusions derives from comparison and contrast: the *and*, the *equal*. The proposition that then forms the conclusion concerns the essential likeness of the two offices, except where they are different, but the subterranean premise is that we can explain both likeness and difference by appeal to a principle of fundamental order and unity. To make these observations concrete, we turn to the case at hand. The important contrast comes at the outset. The high priest and king fall into a single genus, but speciation, based on traits particular to the king, then distinguishes the one from the other. This whole exercise is conducted essentially independently of scripture; the classifications derive from the system, are viewed as autonomous constructs; traits of things define classifications and dictate what is like and what is unlike.

What is it that the second century rabbis regarded (in general terms) as subject to their speculative inquiry? In respect to society, they want to know what people usually do, how various classes of society may be expected to behave. In respect to happenings in the natural world, for example, the world of animals, they ask about what are the likely principles by which we may interpret events we do not know have taken place. In respect to material processes, they wish to speculate on the nature of mixtures. If I have a substance of one sort and it is joined to a substance of another, how do the traits of the one combine with the traits of another? Then whence come interesting questions? The answer, of course, is from the interstitial cases, in the case of human beings, the person bearing sexual traits of both genders, or the one bearing no discernible sexual traits; the person in the transition period, for example, a boy nine years and one day old, or a girl between one status, as to maturity and marriage, and the next. In the case of beasts, it will be the one that falls between the two established categories, domesticated and wild. In the case of time, it will be dusk. In the case of the sabbatical year, it will be a crop that matures over two or three growing seasons and hence cannot be definitively assigned to any one year. The list of interstitial possibilities is endless. In all cases, we find represented mixtures of things: something that falls into two or more classifications within a given system.

The Mishnaic system repeatedly invokes three principles of classification. The first is (1) to identify the correct definition or character of something and to preserve that essence. So we begin with the thing itself. Our premise is that we can identify the intrinsic or true or inherent traits of a thing, once more, the thing seen by itself. But, having our answer, we (2) then ask in what way something is like something else, and in what way it differs. Our premise is that in some ways things are like other things, traits may be shared. So we proceed to the comparison of things. That requires us to identify the important traits that impart the definitive character or classification to a variety of distinct things. So we proceed to a labor of comparison and contrast. The third principle is that (3) like things fall into a single classification, with its rule, and unlike things into a different classification, with the opposite rule. That conception, simple on the surface, defines the prevailing logic throughout the entire philosophy. At no point do we find any other logic in play.

The system of ordering all things in their proper place and under the proper rule maintained that like belongs with like and conforms to the rule governing the like, the unlike goes over to the opposite and conforms to the opposite rule. When we make lists of the like, we also know the rule governing all the items on those lists, respectively. We know that and one other thing; namely, the opposite rule, governing all items sufficiently like to belong on those lists, but sufficiently unlike to be placed on other lists. That rigorously philosophical logic of analysis, comparison and contrast, served because – so it would seem – in that context it was the only logic deemed able to sustain a system that proposed to make the statement concerning the social order.

Natural philosophy, out of which natural science has evolved, dictates the labor of classification in accordance with a simple procedure. Faced with a mass of facts, we are able (1) to bring order – that is to say, to determine the nature of things – by finding out which items resemble others, and (2) determining the taxic indicator that forms of the lot a single classification, and then (3) determining the single rule to which all cases conform. That method of bringing structure and order out of the chaos of indeterminate facts pertains, on the very surface, to persons, places, things; to actions and attitudes; to the natural world of animals, minerals, vegetables, the social world of castes and peoples, actions and functions, and the supernatural world of the holy and the unclean, the possession of heaven and the possession of earth, the sanctified and the common. A necessary principle of classification is that things are always what they are, never anything else. It comes second in logical order because, once we maintain that taxic indicators are inherent and intrinsic, only then does the complementary principle emerge. One way of expressing that conception of the *Ding an Sich* is the notion of intrinsic classification. Something bears intrinsic and inherent traits, which are not relative to the traits of other things and furthermore are not imputed by function or extrinsic considerations of any other kind.

Hierarchical classification embodies the purpose of the philosophy as a whole: not only to classify diverse things, which yields mere information. It is to establish a hierarchy of classes. This serves to make the point that things are not only orderly, but stand in hierarchical sequence to one another, everything in a single frame of order. This is worked out by showing that the rule applying in one class relates to the rule applying in some other: *all the more so*, in the case of what is of a higher station in the hierarchy to what is of a lower station, for example. The medium by which we move from *this*, to *why this, not that*, is through the argument, *if this, then surely that*, or *if this, then obviously not that.* On its own, that medium presents a mere point of logic. But the medium should not obscure the message, for here the system makes its real point, as I shall make abundantly clear.

What is at stake in classification? The answer points us toward the source of the philosophy's dynamic. If we draw no conclusions, then nothing – by definition – happens. We have organized information. But if we do draw conclusions, then much happens, and we have so framed information as to produce conclusions of consequence. When we contemplate the Mishnah's conception of the realm of reality, the social order of humanity, the metaphysical order of nature and supernature, we ask: what makes all things move? How do we account not for a steady-state tableau, in which nothing happens, but for the realm of activity, in which, rightly ordered, everything happens the way it should happen? The answer to that question derives from the point at which classification is accomplished. That is when we must ask: so what? And the point is, from classification we must draw conclusions, the rule that animates all rules. Then what conclusions are we to draw from our power to classify? They derive from hierarchization of the classes of things, as I said at the outset.

Showing that all things can be ordered, and that all orders can be set into relationship with one another, we of course transform method into message. The message of hierarchical classification is that many things really form a single thing, the many species a single genus, the many genera an encompassing and well-crafted, cogent whole. Every time we speciate, we affirm that position. These are intellectual aspirations natural to monotheism, which posits one God, creator of heaven and earth, from which all things flow, to which all things return. Each successful labor of forming relationships among species, for example, making them into a genus, or identifying the hierarchy of the species, proves it again. Not only so, but when we can show that many things are really one, or that one thing yields many (the reverse and confirmation of the former), we state in a fresh way a single immutable truth, the one of this philosophy concerning the unity of all being in an orderly composition of all things within a single taxon. Exegesis is always repetitive – and a sound exegesis of the systemic exegesis must then be equally so, everywhere explaining the same thing in the same way.

3 The argument of analogy and contrast

So much for the discovery of the law through a process of hierarchical classification. What about constructing arguments on behalf of a legal proposition? Arguments based on analogy and contrast serve as the medium for settling moot points. The Tosefta, a corpus of supplementary laws joined to the Mishnah, *c.* 300 CE, presents us with a striking case in which the governing analogy is introduced in an explicit manner. What we see is how argument by analogy and contrast works. The case concerns the disposition of what is subject to doubt. In the following case, what we do not know is the status of objects immersed in a pool that, at a given point in time, is found to be lacking in the requisite volume of water and so unable to effect the purification of what is immersed. Specifically, how do we dispose of those objects immersed in the time from the last point at which it was known that the pool had a valid volume of water?

A. An immersion-pool which was measured and found lacking – all the acts requiring cleanness which were carried out depending upon it
B. whether this immersion-pool is in the private domain, or whether this immersion-pool is in the public domain – [Supply: objects that have been immersed are unclean.]
C. R. Simeon says, "In the private domain, it is unclean. In the public domain, it is clean." '

Thus far we have the statement of the case. Now comes the dispute and debate:

D. Said R. Simeon, "There was the case of the water-reservoir of Disqus in Yabneh was measured and found lacking.
E. "And R. Tarfon did declare clean, and R. Aqiba unclean.
F. "Said R. Tarfon, 'Since this immersion-pool is in the assumption of being clean, it remains perpetually in this presumption of cleanness until it will be known for sure that it is made unclean.'
G. "Said R. Aqiba, 'Since this immersion-pool is in the assumption of being unclean, it perpetually remains in the presumption of uncleanness until it will be known for sure that it is clean.' "

The principle is, do we focus upon the prevailing assumption as to the status of the pool and confirm that status, or do we declare the governing analogy to be the status of the unclean object that was immersed in the pool, and confirm that status? The former status is confirmed as valid, since we have assumed the pool was valid until we discovered that it was lacking in the requisite volume of valid water; the latter status is confirmed as unclean, since we assume objects that have been declared unclean remain so until they are validly purified. Now at stake is: which is the governing analogy?

H. "Said R. Tarfon, 'To what is the matter to be likened? To one who was standing and offering [a sacrifice] at the altar, and it became known that he is a son of a divorcee or the son of a woman who has undergone the rite of removing the shoe,

I.   " 'for his service is valid.'

J.   "Said R. Aqiba, 'To what is the matter to be likened?'

K.   " 'To one who was standing and offering [a sacrifice] at the altar, and it became known that he is disqualified by reason of a blemish —

L.   " 'for his service is invalid.' "

Thus far we have the conflict between relevant analogies. Now how is the argument articulated? It is through the challenge of each party to the pertinence of the analogy introduced by the other:

M.   "Said R. Tarfon to him, 'You draw an analogy to one who is blemished. I draw an analogy to the son of a divorcee or to the son of a woman who has undergone the rite of removing the shoe [and is invalid for marriage into the priesthood].

N.   " 'Let us now see to what the matter is appropriately likened.

O.   " 'If it is analogous to a blemished priest, let us learn the law from the case of the blemished priest. If it is analogous to the son of a divorcée or to the son of a woman who has undergone the rite of removing the shoe, let us learn the law from the case of the son of the divorcee or the son of a woman who has undergone the rite of removing the shoe.' "

In fact, as we shall now see, Tarfon's statement of the issue of which analogy governs proves to set matters up to allow Aqiba to settle the question. He does so by differentiating the analogical cases, showing where the true point of similarity – now, he insists, not mere similarity but identity! – is to be located:

P.   "R. Aqiba says, 'The unfitness affecting an immersion-pool affects the immersion-pool itself, and the unfit aspect of the blemished priest affects the blemished priest himself.

Q.   " 'But let not the case of the son of a divorcee or the son of a woman who has undergone the rite of removing the shoe prove the matter, for his matter of unfitness depends upon others.

R.   " 'A ritual pool's unfitness [depends] on one only, and the unfitness of a blemished priest [depends] on an individual only, but let not the son of a divorcee or the son of a woman who has undergone the rite of removing the shoe will prove the matter, for the unfitness of this one depends upon ancestry.'

S.   "They took a vote concerning the case and declared it unclean."

T.   "Said R. Tarfon to R. Aqiba, 'He who departs from you is like one who perishes.' "

(Tosefta Miqvaot 1:16–19)

91

Aqiba finds no difficulty in acknowledging the similarity, but he criticizes the use of the analogy by differentiating, in the manner of Socrates, between similarity and identity. He is able to differentiate ("divide") the analogy into its operative components, and, in so doing, he shows that the analogy as he proposes to apply it sustains his position. Hearing the language, "Let us now see to what the matter is appropriately likened," will have pleased the Classical philosophers. True, sages' debates on differentiating like into unlike categories will not have challenged the intellect of the philosophers, for whom the question was one of practical, not theoretical interest. But with the details properly explained, they will have fully appreciated the modes of analytical argument before them and found no reason to dismiss them as other than philosophical.

4 The Talmuds' dialectics

Both Talmudic analyses of daily affairs greatly valued argument, the one as a test of knowledge, the other as a sure guide to deep inquiry into truth. And argument demanded not merely set-piece presentation of propositions, pro and con, but challenge and response, analytical reasoning on the spot. Well-reasoned demonstration did not suffice, only rigorous dispute between responsive, reasonable players. And, as we shall see, all parties deemed contention in quest of truth to form the path to a well-considered position.

Dialectical argument – the movement of thought through contentious challenge and passionate response, initiative and counter-ploy – characterizes the Talmud of Babylonia in particular. "Dialectical" means moving, and for the Talmud a dialectical argument is a systematic exposition, through give and take, moving from point to point; the argument is the thing, since the dialectical argument strays from its original, precipitating point and therefore does not ordinarily undertake the demonstration, but rather the exploration of a fixed proposition. Argument moves along, developing an idea through questions and answers, sometimes implicit, but more commonly explicit. That mode of analysis through media of question–answer and contentious argument imparts to the Talmud its distinctive characteristics of thought. Called in the language of the Talmud *shaqla vetarya*, give and take, dialectics requires definition in neutral terms.

What, exactly, do we mean by a "moving argument"? It is one that transcends the juxtaposition of propositions, arguments, and evidence. This it does by treating propositions, arguments, and evidence to a process of interchange and challenge, composing out of the pronouncement of differences of opinion an ongoing, unfolding argument, one in which one point is countered by another, so that what then follows is not a recapitulation of what has been said, but an interchange of reason and argument. Then because the players listen thoughtfully to one another and respond to the point, the "moving argument" may, and should, change course. This is always in response to the arguments that are set forth, the obstacles placed in the original path of thought. The purpose of the dialectical argument is not to advocate but to explore, not to demonstrate truth but to discover truth out of a process of contention and confrontation. The successful argument formed dialectically will deal with all possibilities and reach not a climax but a laconic conclusion: all things having been said, we end up here rather than somewhere else.

The rabbinic dialectical argument – the protracted, sometimes meandering, always moving flow of contentious thought – raises a question and answers it, then raises a question about the answer, and, having raised another question, it then gives an answer to that question and continues in the same fashion until a variety of issues has been sorted out. So it moves hither and yon; it is always one and coherent but it is never the same, and it flows across the surface of the document at hand. The dialectical character derives not from the mere rhetorical device of question and answer, but from the pursuit of an argument, in a single line, but in many and diverse directions: not the form but the substantive continuity defines the criterion. And the power of the dialectical argument flows from that continuity. We find the source of continuity in the author's capacity to show connections through the momentum of rigorous analysis, on the one side, and free-ranging curiosity, on the other.

Those second, third and fourth turnings therefore differentiate a dialectical from a static argument, much as the bubbles tell the difference between still and sparkling wine. The always-sparkling dialectical argument is one principal means by which the Talmud or some other rabbinic writing accomplishes its goal of showing the connections between this and that, ultimately demonstrating the unity of many "thises and thats." These efforts at describing the argument serve precisely as well as program notes to a piece of music: they tell us what we are going to hear; they cannot play the music. What "moves" therefore is the flow of argument and thought, and that is – by definition – from problem to problem. The movement is generated specifically by the raising of contrary questions and theses. What characterizes the dialectical argument in rabbinic literature is its meandering, its moving hither and yon. It is not a direct or straight-line movement, for example, the dialectical argument with which we are familiar in the modern West: thesis, antithesis, synthesis. It also does not correspond to any propositional or syllogistic argument, even though such arguments may take place in three or more steps, inclusive of counter-arguments.

The dialectical argument imparts flavor to the whole Talmud by imposing tension and supplying movement, focus and purpose. By its movement, from question to answer, point to point, problem to problem, case to case, the dialectical argument also gives the Talmud the quality of dynamism. The rigor required to participate in a challenging exchange defines the intellectual quality of the whole document, even though most of the sustained discussions prove merely illuminating, not contentious. For its part the dialectical argument asks for not merely information but analysis, not merely acute reading of existing language but formulation of new points of interest altogether.

The character of the Mishnah defined the challenge that was met by the selection and utilization of the dialectical argument, which, in all writings of all Judaisms from the beginnings to the third century CE, has no precedent. Nor does the dialectical argument appear elsewhere than in the two Talmuds. Dialectics predominates only in the final compilation of the rabbinic canon, the Talmud of Babylonia. A large-scale structure of lists, the Mishnah's generalizations (for example, the king ranks higher in the political hierarchy than the high priest) rarely come to articulation; the mass of detail invited close study and analysis. The general had to emerge out of the concrete and specific, and generalizations valid at one point had to be tested against those emergent elsewhere; implications of generalizations for encompassing principles here required comparison and contrast with those that formed the foundations of a legal unit on an unrelated topic elsewhere. All this work of construction would turn the Mishnah's details into large-scale compositions of encompassing significance.

But the Mishnah by itself did not exhaust the resources of normative rulings that formed the heritage of its time and sages. And the Talmud, for its part, though organized around the Mishnah, in fact took as its problem the law of the Mishnah, along with other law not found in the Mishnah. The privileging of the Mishnah did not extend to the laws that it set forth. If the framers of the Mishnah hoped to bring order out of chaos by giving the authoritative selection of the law – not merely a collection of their preferences and choices among laws – they were to find only disappointment. Repudiating the privileging of the Mishnah, reducing the document to a mere framework for the organization of something greater, the writers of the Gemara's compositions and compilers of its composites redefined matters and assigned to themselves a far more important task than merely glossing a fixed code.

That choice formed their response to a simple fact: the Mishnah collected only a small portion of the law that had come into being in the first and second centuries. A sizable corpus of opinion, rulings, cases, and disputes, circulated from the period in which the Mishnah emerged but found (or was given) no place within the Mishnah. Some of these materials came to rest in the compilation of supplements to the Mishnah called the Tosefta. Corresponding to the Mishnah in its topical organization and program, the Tosefta exceed the Mishnah in sheer volume by approximately at least four times – perhaps more. Other laws were formulated along with attributions to the same authorities, called Tannaite sages, who occur in the Mishnah. These laws scarcely differentiated themselves from those in the Mishnah, except in content. Still more laws circulated, whether or not they were attributed to the names of authorities which also occur in the Mishnah, bearing the mark yielding "it was formulated as a Tannaite rule." These too enjoyed the same standing and authority as Tannaite sayings collected in the Mishnah or the Tosefta.

Therefore, if a coherent and uniform, principled system of norms was to reach full articulation, the laws, and not the Mishnah, would form the arena for systematic study. That is to say, if a cogent system was to emerge out of the heritage of normative rulings of Tannaite sponsorship, the entire mass of normative rulings would require analysis; points of contradiction would have to be sorted out; harmony between and among diverse laws would have to be established. To accomplish the task of analysis of sayings, formulation and testing of generalizations, above all the discovery of the principles embedded in the normative rules governing discrete cases, the Talmud resorted to the dialectal argument. That would make possible the transformation of the Mishnah's lists, limited by their nature to data of a single kind, into the starting points for series capable of infinite extension across data of diverse kinds. Accordingly, the sages of blessed memory addressed a dual challenge, (1) both subjecting a well-crafted document to exegesis, amplification, and theoretical inquiry, (2) but also sorting out conflicting data on the same matters that said document took up.

The Mishnah's character as a mass of petty rulings defined a third task, one that was natural to the rigorous intellects who comprised the cadre of the sages of blessed memory. This was to require the quest for not only harmony but also generalization, the encompassing principle, the prevailing rule emerging from concrete data. For intellectuals of sages sought not only information about details, but guidance on the main lines of thought. Not only so, but, engaged as they were in the administration of the life of the Jewish communities of Babylonia, theirs proved to be a practical reason and applied logic. They had not only to rule on cases covered by the Mishnah – and laws of its standing in addition – but also on cases not envisaged at all within the framework of the Mishnah. These cases of new kinds altogether, involving not only application of the law but penetration into the principles behind the law that could be made to cover new cases, demanded the formation of an analytical logic capable of generating principles to produce new laws.

And that is where dialectics entered, for both practical and theoretical reasons. Theoretical considerations come first. Crafted to begin with to produce clarity of definition, the mode of dialectical argument of Classical philosophy defined a reliable method to secure compelling definitions of important principles. To deal with conflicting opinion on definition, two or more rulings on the same problem had to be set side by side and each given its hearing. Perhaps the conflict could be resolved through making a distinction; in that case let one party challenge the other, with a harmonizing opinion then registering. Perhaps the conflict revealed principles that were at odds. These required articulation, analysis, juxtaposition and then, if possible, harmonization, reformulation at a higher level of abstraction. Perhaps rulings on one topic rested on a principle that also affected rulings on another topic altogether. Then the principle expressed by rulings on that unrelated topic had to be made articulate and brought into relationship with the underlying principle operating elsewhere. And again, a given set of rulings served to illustrate a single point in common, and that point in common was to be formulated as a hypothesis of general intelligibility and applicability. Rulings on one topic rested on a principle that also affected rulings on another topic altogether. Then the principle expressed by rulings on that unrelated topic had to be made articulate and brought into relationship with the underlying principle operating elsewhere.

And again, a given set of rulings served to illustrate a single point in common, and that point was to be formulated as a hypothesis of general intelligibility and applicability. How better to test a hypothesis than in a dialogue between proponents and opponents, the latter raising contrary cases, the former overcoming contradiction, the former amplifying and extending their hypothesis, the latter proposing to limit it. The upshot is that the very character of the corpus of law received by the sages in Babylonia ensured that a vast repertoire of conflict and contention would define the work of those responsible for the orderly application of the law – the Mishnah's law but not that alone – to the everyday affairs of the community of holy Israel. Given the range of data to be addressed, the mode of question–answer, challenge out of conflicting data and response through resolution of conflict, served as the principal medium of thought. The very character of the corpus of norms generated the kind of conflict best resolved through the challenge and response embodied in question–answer rhetoric of dialectics. The specific purpose of our sages' reading of the norms – the formulation of an internally coherent, proportionate, and harmonious statement – coincided with the promise of dialectic, which is to expose conflict and find ways through reasons of resolving it. But if theory made dialectics the method of choice, politics re-enforced the theoretical usefulness of that method of thought and expression.

The mode of argument made possible through dialectics – two or more positions fully exposed, with arguments pro and con, a complete repertoire of positions and possibilities, laid out in the form of an exchange between and among equals, with point-by-point *Auseindersetzungen*, allowing for the full articulation of generalizations, exceptions based on cases, counter-arguments, and competing generalizations – that mode of argument alone could prove congruent to the politics of powerful intellects lacking worldly position to sustain their hypotheses. Accordingly, the sages chose wisely when they determined that argument in dialogic form, within dialectical logic, defined the best possible instrument with which to accomplish their task of explanation, analysis, and amplification of the law that they had received not only from the Mishnah but from other sources of the same status or origin.

Let us give a single example of the power of the dialectical argument to expose the steps in thinking that lead from one end to another: principle to ruling, or ruling to principle. In the present instance, the only one where we require to see a perfectly routine and obvious procedure, we mean to prove the point that if people are permitted to obstruct the public way, if damage was done by them, they are liable to pay compensation. First, we are going to prove that general point on the basis of a single case. Then we shall proceed to show how a variety of authorities, dealing with diverse cases, sustain the same principle.

TALMUD BABA MESIA 10:5/O-X

O. He who brings out his manure to the public domain –

P. while one party pitches it out, the other party must be bringing it in to manure his field.

Q. They do not soak clay in the public domain,

R. and they do not make bricks.

S. And they knead clay in the public way,

T. but not bricks.

U. He who builds in the public way –

V. while one party brings stones, the builder must make use of them in the public way.

W. And if one has inflicted injury, he must pay for the damages he has caused.

X. Rabban Simeon b. Gamaliel says, "Also: He may prepare for doing his work [on site in the public way] for thirty days [before the actual work of building]."

We begin with the comparison of the rule before us with another Tannaite position on the same issue, asking whether an unattributed, therefore authoritative, rule stands for or opposes the position of a given authority; we should hope to prove that the named authority concurs. So one fundamental initiative in showing how many cases express a single principle – the concrete demonstration of the unity of the law – is to find out whether diverse, important authorities concur on that principle, each ruling in a distinctive case; or whether a single authority is consistent in ruling in accordance with the principle at hand, as in what follows:

I.1 A. *May we say that our Mishnah-paragraph does not accord with the view of R. Judah? For it has been taught on Tannaite authority:*

B. R. Judah says, "At the time of fertilizing the fields, a man may take out his manure and pile it up at the door of his house in the public way so that it will be pulverized by the feet of man and beast, for a period of thirty days. For it was on that very stipulation that Joshua caused the Israelites to inherit the land" [TBM 11:8E–H].

C. You may even maintain that he concurs with the Mishnah's rule [that while one party pitches it out, the other party must be bringing it in to manure his field]. R. Judah concedes that if one has caused damage, he is liable to pay compensation.

In line with the position just now proposed, Judah will turn out to rule every which way on the same matter. And that is not an acceptable upshot.

D. *But has it not been taught in the Mishnah:* **If the store-keeper had left his lamp outside the store-keeper is liable [if the flame caused a fire]. R. Judah said, "In the case of a lamp for Hanukkah, he is exempt"** [MBQ 6:6E–F], because he has acted under authority. *Now surely that must mean,* under the authority of the court [and that shows that one is not responsible for damage caused by his property in the public domain if it was there under the authority of the court]!

The dialectic now intervenes. We have made a proposal. Isn't it a good one? Of course not; were we to give up so quickly, we should gain nothing:

E. *No, what it means is, on the authority of carrying out one's religious obligations.*

By now, the reader is able to predict the next step: "But isn't the contrary more reasonable?" Here is how we raise the objection.

F. *But has it not been taught on Tannaite authority:*
G. in the case of all those concerning whom they have said, "They are permitted to obstruct the public way," if there was damage done, one is liable to pay compensation. But R. Judah declares one exempt from having to pay compensation.
H. *So it is better to take the view that our Mishnah-paragraph does not concur with the position of R. Judah.*

The point of interest has been introduced: whether those permitted to obstruct the public way must pay compensation for damages they may cause in so doing. Here is where we find a variety of cases that yield a single principle:

2. A. *Said Abayye, "R. Judah, Rabban Simeon b. Gamaliel, and R. Simeon all*

take the position that in the case of all those concerning whom they have said, 'They are permitted to obstruct the public way,' if there was damage done, one is liable to pay compensation.

B.   *As to R. Judah, the matter is just as we have now stated it.*

Simeon b. Gamaliel and Simeon now draw us to unrelated cases:

C.   *"As to Rabban Simeon b. Gamaliel, we have learned in the Mishnah:* **Rabban Simeon b. Gamaliel says, 'Also: He may prepare for doing his work {on site in the public way} for thirty days {before the actual work of building}.'**

D.   *"As to R. Simeon, we have learned in the Mishnah:* **A person should not set up an oven in a room unless there is a space of four cubits above it. If he was setting it up in the upper story, there has to be a layer of plaster under it three handbreadths thick, and in the case of a stove, a handbreadth thick. And if it did damage, the owner of the oven has to pay for the damage. R. Simeon says, 'All of these measures have been stated only so that if the object did damage, the owner is exempt from paying compensation if the stated measures have been observed'** [MBB 2:2A–F]."

We see then that the demonstration of the unity of the law and the issue of who stands or does not stand behind a given rule go together. When we ask about who does or does not stand behind a rule, we ask about the principle of a case, which leads us downward to a premise, and we forthwith point to how that same premise underlies a different principle yielding a case – so how can X hold the view he does if that is his premise, since in a different case he makes a point with a principle that rests on a contradictory premise. The Mishnah and the Talmud are comparable to the moraine left by the last ice age, fields studded with boulders. For the Talmud, reference is made to those many disputes that litter the pages and impede progress. That explains why much of the Talmud is taken up with not only sorting out disputes but also by showing their rationality and meaning, reasonable people have perfectly valid reasons for disagreeing about a given point, since both parties share the same premises but apply them differently; or they really do not differ at all, since one party deals with one set of circumstances, and the other with a different set of circumstances.

The main consequence for the Talmud of formation through dialectical arguments is simply stated. It is the power of that mode of the representation of thought to show us – as no other mode of writing (without abstract symbols) can show – not only the result but the workings of the logical mind. By following dialectical arguments, we ourselves enter into those same thought processes, and our minds are then formed in the model of rigorous and sustained, systematic argument. The reason is simply stated. When we follow a proposal and its refutation, the consequence thereof, and the result of that, we ourselves form partners to the logical tensions and their resolutions; we are given an opening into the discourse that lies before us. As soon as matters turn not upon tradition, to which we may or may not have access, but reason, specifically challenge and response, proposal and counter-proposal, "maybe matters are just the opposite?" and we find an open door before us.

Here then are the traits of the dialectical argument. First, we test every allegation by a counter-proposition, so serving the cause of truth through challenge and constant checking for flaws in an argument. Second, we survey the entire range of possibilities, which leaves no doubts about the cogency of our conclusion. That means we move out of our original case, guided by its generative principle, to new cases altogether. Third, quite to the point, by the give and take of argument, we ourselves are enabled to go through the thought processes set forth in the subtle markings that yield our reconstruction of the argument. We not only review what people say, but how they think: the processes of reasoning that have yielded a given conclusion. Sages and disciples become party to the modes of thought; in the dialectical argument, they are required to replicate the thought-processes themselves.

The dialectical argument forms the means to an end. The distinctive character of the Gemara's particular kind of dialectical argument is dictated by the purpose for which dialectics is invoked. Specifically, the goal of all argument is to show in discrete detail the ultimate unity, harmony, proportion, and perfection of the law – not of the Mishnah as a document but of all the law of the same standing as that presented by the Mishnah. The hermeneutics of dialectics aims at making manifest how to read the laws in such a way as to discern that many things really say one thing. The variations on the theme then take the form of detailed expositions of this and that. Then our task is to move backward from a result to the reasoning process that has yielded said result: through regression from stage to stage to identify within the case not only the principles of law that produce that result, but the processes of reasoning that link the principles to the case at hand. And, when we accomplish our infinite regression, we move from the workings of literature to its religious character and theological goal: it is to know God in heaven, represented, on earth, by the unity of the law, the integrity of the Torah.

D. Conclusions

Here the promise and the puzzle of comparing religions through law emerge. On the one side, when we see things close up, we realize that the differences present formidable barriers to mutual comprehension. We seem to deal with different people talking about different things to different people. But as we take a step back, we identify from a distance the shape of parallel structures. In abstract rather than visual terms, we may say, a common core of rationality, a shared conception of logic – these characterize the vastly different legal-theological traditions of Judaism and Islam when the sages and legists undertake to analyze rules and solve problems. At their foundations the two religions share a fundamental logic and rationality.[30]

How would Judaism respond to Islam's modes of reasoning? Point by point, a sage of the Torah would have found himself quite at home in the principles that govern in Islamic jurisprudence. When it comes to consensus, the sages held that the prevailing custom rules, and the authority of a place defines the norm. When it comes to reasoning (ijtihad), the stress on appeal to analogy would find instant recognition among the Talmudic sages. This we have already noted in connection with the passage of the Tosefta we examined above. They too invoked analogy to precedent or to prevailing principle. If they had a settled case and one subject to doubt, the settled one would guide. If they had an established principle governing a class of things, that would resolve matters.

To move from law to philosophy we enter comparable territory. Many of the Judaic sages' most searching debates concerned whether or not two classes of things really were analogous at all, and, if so, what governing analogy pertained. An entire, classical document, Sifra, on the book of Leviticus, pursues exactly the problem of analogy and difference. Sages took up precedents alongside, but as between a powerful argument from analogy and a precedent, the analogical argument would ordinarily prevail. But, as with Islamic reasoning so in the Judaic, where the Written Torah or a strong tradition of the Oral Torah settled a question; even in violation of supposed analogies the matter was deemed settled; analogy then took second place to tradition.

Can Judaic judges make exceptions to the results of strict legal reasoning for the sake of the common good? The matter comes under debate in the Talmud and related writings. On the one hand, the strict results of reasoning are to prevail, come what may: "Let the law pierce the mountain," as the saying goes. On the other hand, sages found numerous ways to work out urgent practical problems, and not only those posed by the results of rigorous reasoning but also by the law of the Torah itself. Great authorities had (and have) the power to make *ad-hoc* ordinances in response to urgent need. For example, in the Holocaust during World War II, great authorities of the Torah completely abrogated the dietary laws and permitted the people to eat whatever food they could get – and even on the Day of Atonement, a strict fasting day, preservation of life took priority. But they would not abrogate the laws against murder, fornication, or idolatry, even at the cost of death.

If we had to choose a point at which the intellectual traits of Judaic and Islamic law differ, it emerges in the contrast between the ahistorical and the highly historical modes of thought and reasoning of Judaic and Islamic jurisprudents, respectively. The sages of the Talmud set forth abstract and analytical arguments about concrete matters. To these arguments, cases proved useful but not essential; principles governed. By contrast, as we have seen, Islamic law paid much closer attention to the conditions of everyday life, and, alongside, invoked historical authority and precedence as principal media of legal thinking. Judaic law is set forth through analysis reaching its climax in sustained, dialectical arguments, Islamic law through narrative as much as through reasoning. The Judaic sages may have found the Islamic arguments unrealized and even simple; the Islamic counterparts may have accused the Judaic sages of an excess of abstruse, recondite theorizing about things with no concrete consequence. As between Judaic and Islamic intellectual life, the latter emerges as more practical and more political, the former as more theoretical and more abstract. But in actuality, both systems showed the same traits of applied reasoning and practical logic, such as a living society required for its governance. If we explained to the one side the details of a case facing the judges of the other, chances are the jurisprudents of both religions would reach a decision in accord with the same rules of reasoning – and would reach the same decision.

We conclude with a story out of our own experience. The first of the two authors was approached by a Muslim student for a fatwa on whether or not she was to be condemned if she was required to remove her hair-covering against her will. Calling upon nearly the whole of the law of Judaism, the response was, "God knows the difference between what we do as an act of will, and what we do despite our own intentionality." She responded, "Yes, that is what Islam maintains as well."

4

THE WORKING OF THE LAW
Institutions

A Institutional authority

From classical theories of legal theory, we proceed to classical theories of legal practice. How, in theory, do the Judaic and Islamic religio-legal systems conceive law to work in the social order that each aspires to realize? That is a political question, concerning the institutions of law enforcement and the character of legal sanctions.

The answer to that question requires that we consider politics, meaning the exercise of legitimate coercion, who has the right legitimately to do what to whom, which is the standard (secular) definition of politics. We deal not with how things worked themselves out here and there, but with the stories that the two systems tell to portray the politics of the law. In the case of Judaism we see how power is differentiated, parceled out between God and human beings, explaining the division of sanctions among a variety of institutional centers. In the case of Islam it is assumed that all law originates with God, but that human beings are entrusted with the challenge of understanding and implementing the law. The science of Islamic law therefore determines the relationship of law to the state and its leaders. The issue confronting Islamic and Judaic legal theory is thus the same: the realization of power in concrete form.

We take up two questions. First, what theory – or, more really, what story – accounts for the institutional arrangements that regulate the community in accordance with the law, and how is the law enforced? Second, to what sorts of persons do the systems assign the task of law enforcement? What explains who has the credentials and authority to enforce the law? The first question draws our attention to the matter of how the legal systems explain their institutional arrangements; that is, the court system and the penalties it imposes. The second question, dealt with in Chapter 5, requires attention to the qualifications required of those who enforce the law, the personal gifts they are supposed to possess, and similar matters of individual credentials and charisma. That is where law, religious sentiment and conviction, and theology intersect: in the person of the sage and the saint.

B The Israelite court system in the legal narrative of Judaism

Politics in Israelite law takes place because God assigns to man the responsibility to form a just and holy society, providing the legitimate power to also enforce the law. The halakhah – the law of Judaism – provides for three correlated but autonomous institutions to exercise the power to inflict sanctions in the enforcement of the law: God, the court, and the Temple, the three agencies with the power to bestow or take away life and property and to inflict physical pain and suffering, work together in a single continuum and in important ways cooperate to deal with the same crimes or sins. But who does what to whom? The politics of the halakhah, then, demands a labor of differentiation of power, indicating what agency or person, in connection with which infraction of the halakhah, has the power to precipitate the working of politics as legitimate violence at all. The encompassing framework of rules, institutions, and sanctions is explained and validated by appeal to God's shared rule. That Israel, the holy people, lives under God's law and accepts the yoke of God's rule, is the theological foundation of all else. But if that dominion, exercised by God and his surrogates on earth, is focused partly in the royal palace, partly in the temple, and partly in the court, then which part falls where and why?

Since, we already realize, the Mishnah sets forth the main lines of the halakhah, we focus on its data. There, power comes to brutal expression when the state kills or maims someone or deprives a person of property through the imposition of legal sanctions for crime or sin (the halakhah does not differentiate between them). But the Mishnah presents rules and does not contain the story that the rules embody, so where shall we begin? In the absence of a story of power – who does what to whom – we begin with cases of the exercise of power itself. We work our way back from the facts of power to the intimations, within the record of legitimately violent sanctions, of the intellectual and even mythic sources of legitimation for the exercise and use of that legitimate violence. For it is at the point of imposing sanctions, of killing, injuring, denying property, excluding from society, that power operates in its naked form. Then how these legitimate exercises of violence are validated will set before us such concrete evidence of the story. And, so far as there is such evidence, that will identify the political theology of rabbinic Judaism: its justification for the institutional expression of the law.

Analyzing the political theory of matters by explaining sanctions draws our attention to the modes of legitimate violence that the system identifies. There we find four types of sanctions, each deriving from a distinct institution of political power, each bearing its own mythic explanation. The first comprises what God and the heavenly court can and does do to people. The second comprises what the earthly court can do to people. That type of

104

sanction embodies the legitimate application of the worldly and physical kinds of violence of which political theory ordinarily speaks. The third comprises what the cult can do to the people. The cult through its requirements can deprive people of their property as legitimately as can a court. The fourth comprises conformity with consensus – self-imposed sanctions. Here the issue is: whose consensus, and defined by whom? Across these four types of sanction, four types of coercion are in play. They depend on violence of various kinds – psychological and social as much as physical. Clearly, then, the sanctions that are exercised by other than judicial-political agencies prove violent and legitimately coercive, even though the violence and coercion are not the same as those carried out by courts.

On this basis we can differentiate between types of sanctions – and hence trace evidence of how the differentiation is explained. Since our data focus upon who does what to whom, the story of politics must explain why various types of sanctions are put into effect by diverse political agencies or institutions. As we shall see, the exercise of power, invariably and undifferentiatedly in the name and by the authority of God in heaven to be sure, is kept distinct. And the distinctions in this case signal important differences which require explanation. Concrete application of legitimate violence by (1) heaven covers different matters from parts of the political and social world governed by the policy and coercion of (2) the this-worldly political classes. Both sorts of violence have to be kept distinct from the sanction effected by (3) the community through the weight of attitude and public opinion. Here again, we find a distinct set of penalties applied to a particular range of actions.

Our task is therefore to figure out, on the basis of sanctions' distinct realms, Heaven, earth, and the mediating range of the temple and sacrifice, which party imposes sanctions for what crimes or sins. Where heaven intervenes, do other authorities participate, and if so, what tells me which party takes charge and imposes its sanction? Is the system differentiated so that where earth is in charge there is no pretense of appeal to heaven? Or do we find cooperation in coextensive jurisdiction, such that one party penalizes an act under one circumstance, the other the same act under a different circumstance? A survey of the sanctions enables us to differentiate the components of the power structure before us. So we wonder whether each of these three estates that enjoy power and inflict sanctions of one kind or another – heaven, earth, temple in-between – governs its own affairs without the intervention of the others, or whether, working together, each takes charge in collaboration with the other, so that power is parceled out and institutions simultaneously differentiate themselves from one another and also intersect. The survey of sanctions will allow us to answer these questions and so identify the story of politics and the exercise of power that rabbinic Judaism promulgated through the Mishnah.

Why not turn directly to the Written Torah? The reason is that scripture presents for a political story pretty much everything and its opposite; it allows for government by the prophet (Moses), the king (David), the priest-scribe (Ezra). But the picture of the halakhah does not coincide with that of scripture, even though it has a heavenly court, a sages' court (corresponding to David's), and a priests' source of sanctions as well. Simply knowing that everything is in accordance with the Torah and that God wants Israel to keep the laws of the Torah does not reveal the systemically active component of the political story. On the one hand, the propositions are too general; on the other hand, they do not address the critical question. The sequence of self-evident premises that runs: (1) God revealed the Torah, (2) the political institutions and rules carry out the Torah, and therefore (3) people should conform, hardly sustains a concrete theory of just where and how God's authority serves the systemic construction at hand. The appeal to scripture, therefore, reveals no incisive information about the Mishnah's validating theology of politics.

Let us start with the first question: is God's direct intervention (for example, as portrayed in scripture) represented as a preferred or even available sanction? Yes and no, but mostly no. No one in the rabbinic literature prays to have God supply a decision in a particular case. More to the point, no judge appeals to God to put a convicted felon to death. If the judge wants the felon killed, he kills him. When God intervenes, it is on the jurisdiction assigned to God, not the court, and then the penalty is a different one from execution. True, the repertoire of sanctions does encompass God's direct intervention, but that is hardly a preferred alternative or a common one. Still, God does commonly intervene when oaths are violated, for oaths are held to involve the person who invokes God's name and God. Further, whereas when faced with an insufficiency of valid evidence under strict rules of testimony, the earthly court cannot penalize serious crime, the heavenly court can and does impose a penalty. Clearly, then, God serves to justify the politics and account for its origin. Although God is never asked to join in making specific decisions and effecting policy in the everyday politics of the state, deliberate violation of certain rules provokes God's or the heavenly court's direct intervention. Thus, obedience to the law clearly represents submission to God in heaven. Further, forms of heavenly coercion such as we shall presently survey suggest a complex mythic situation, with more subtle nuance than the claim that, overall, God rules, would indicate. A politics of rules and regulations cannot admit God's *ad-hoc* participation, and this system did not do so. God joined in the system in a regular and routine way, and the rules took for granted God's part in the politics of rabbinic Judaism.

Precisely how does the intervention of God into the system come to concrete expression? By appeal to the rules handed down at Sinai as an ultimate reference in legal questions, for instance. This is the case in the story about R. Simeon of Mispah, who sowed his field with two types of wheat. Simeon's problem is that he may have violated the law against sowing mixed seeds in a single patch. When the matter came before Rabban Gamaliel, the passage states:

C. They went up to the Chamber of Hewn Stone and asked [about the law regarding sowing two types of wheat in one field].
D. Said Nahum the Scribe, "I have received [the following ruling] from R. Miasha, who received it from his father, *who received {it} from the pairs, who received {it} from the prophets, {who received} the law {given} to Moses on Sinai,* regarding one who sows his field with two types of wheat."

(Mishnah-tractate; Peah 2:6; my emphases)

Here, the law's legitimacy clearly depends on its descent by tradition from Sinai. But that general principle of descent from Sinai was invoked only rarely. Indeed, R. Simeon's case undermines the Mishnah's relation to God's intervention. R. Simeon's problem is minor. Nothing important requires so drastic a claim to be made explicit. That is to say, it is a mere commonplace that the system appeals to Sinai.

Now come the data of real power, the sanctions routinely imposed, not by a miracle. We may divide sanctions just as the authorship of the Mishnah did, by simply reviewing the range of penalties for law-infraction as they occur. These penalties, as we mentioned above, fall into four classifications: what heaven does, what political institutions do, what religious institutions do, and what is left to the coercion of public opinion, that is, consensus, with special attention to the definition of that "public" that has effective opinion to begin with. The final realm of power, conferring or withholding approval, proves constricted and, in this context, not very consequential.

Let us begin with the familiar, with sanctions exercised by the earthly court as they are fully described in Mishnah-tractates Sanhedrin and Makkot. We will review the imposition of sanctions as it is represented by the earthly court, the temple, the heavenly court, the sages. This review allows us to identify the actors in the system of politics – those with power to impose sanctions, and the sanctions they can inflict. Only from this perspective will the initial statement of Rabbinic Judaism, in its own odd idiom, be able to make its points in the way its authorship has chosen. When we take up the story to which that statement implicitly appeals, we shall have a clear notion of the character of the evidence, in rich detail, on which our judgment of the mythic substrate of the system has been composed.

The most impressive mode of legitimate violence is killing; it certainly focuses our attention. The earthly court may justly kill a sinner or felon. This death-dealing priority accorded to the earthly court derives from the character of the power entrusted to that court. The earthly court enjoys full power to dispose of the property and life of all subject to its authority – in the context imagined by Rabbinic Judaism, of all residing in territory that comes under the state's control. Imposing the death penalty is described in the following way:

A. Four modes of execution were given over to the court [in order of severity]:
B. (1) stoning, (2) burning, (3) decapitation, and (4) strangulation.
C. R Simeon says, "(2) Burning, (1) stoning, (4) strangulation, and (3) decapitation."

Mishnah-tractate Sanhedrin 7:1)

The passage leaves no doubt that the court could put people to death. Only the severity of suffering imposed by each mode of execution is in question. Thus, Simeon's hierarchy of punishments (C) differs from that of B in the degradation and suffering inflicted on the felon, not in the end result. The passage details four modes of execution, that is, four forms of legitimate violence. In the account, the following is of special interest. I have emphasized the key words.

A. The religious requirement of decapitation [is carried out as follows]:
B. They would cut off his head with a sword,
C. just as the government does.
D. *R Judah says, "This is disgusting.*
E. "But they put the head on a block and chop it off with an ax."
F. *They said to him, ""There is no form of death more disgusting than this one."*
G. The religious requirement of strangulation [is carried out as follows]:
H. They would bury him in manure up to his armpits, and put a towel of hard material inside one of soft material, and wrap it around his neck.
I. This [witness] pulls it to him from one side, and that witness pulls it to him at the other side, until he perishes.

(Mishnah-tractate Sanhedrin 7:3)

In among all the practical detail, Judah's intervention stands out. It leaves no doubt that carrying out the law realizes a particular world-view. Specifically, his language implies that the felon remains a human being, in God's image. Clearly, then, at stake in the theoretical discussions at hand is how to execute someone in a manner appropriate to his or her standing after the likeness of God. This problem obviously presupposes that in imposing the penalty in the first place and in carrying it out, the court acts wholly in conformity with God's will. This being the case, a political story of a dominion belonging to God and carrying out God's plan and program certainly stands behind the materials at hand.

How to proceed? By close attention to the facts of power and by sorting out the implications of those facts. A protracted journey through details of the law of sanctions leads us to classify the sanctions and the sins or crimes to which they apply. What precisely do I think requires classification? Our project to see who does what to whom and, on the basis of the consequent perception, to propose an explanation for that composition. For from these sanctions of state, that is, the legitimate exercise of coercion, including violence, we may work our way back to the reasons adduced for the legitimacy of the exercise of coercion, which is to say, the political story. The reason is that such a classification will permit us to see how in detail the foci of power are supposed to intersect or to relate: autonomous powers, connected and related ones, or utterly continuous ones, for instance, joining heaven to earth, in the person of this institutional representative or that one. What we shall see is a system that treats heaven, earth, and the mediating institution, the temple, as interrelated, thus connected, but that insists, in vast detail, upon the distinct responsibilities and jurisdiction accorded to each. Once we have perceived that fundamental fact, we may compose for ourselves the story, or at least the point and propositions of the story, that accounted for the political structures of rabbinic Judaism and persuaded people to obey or conform even when there was no immediate threat of penalty.

A survey of (1) types of sanctions, (2) the classifications of crimes or sins to which they apply, and (3) who imposes them, now yields these results. First come the death penalty on earth and its counterpart, which is extirpation (death before one's allotted time) imposed by heaven. "Heaven" refers to the heavenly court, "earth" to the sages' court, "temple" to the sanctions imposed by the temple and its priesthood, and "community" to the common consensus (e.g., ostracism).

Heaven	Earth	Temple	Community
Extirpation for deliberate actions	*Death penalty*	*Death penalty*	
Sexual crimes incest violating sex taboos (bestiality, homosexuality)	*Sexual crimes* in improper relationships incest		
Religious crimes against God blasphemy idolatry magic sorcery profaning Sabbath	*Religious crimes against God* blasphemy idolatry magic sorcery profaning Sabbath		

109

Heaven	Earth	Temple	Community
Extirpation for deliberate actions	*Death penalty*	*Death penalty*	
	Religious sins against family cursing parents		
	Sexual crimes murder communal apostasy kidnapping		
	Sexual crimes public defiance of the court false prophecy		
Religious sins deliberately committed, against God unclean person who ate a holy thing uncleanness in sanctuary violating food taboos making offering outside of temple violating taboos of holy seasons replicating temple incense or oil outside			

Next we deal with court-inflicted sanctions carried out against property or persons (for example, fines against property, flogging or other social or physical violence short of death for the felon or sinner):

Heaven	Earth	Temple	Community
	Flogging, exile	*Obligatory offering and/or flogging for inadvertent action*	*Shunning or approbation*
	manslaughter incest violation of menstrual taboo marriage in violation of caste rules	uncleanness eating temple food in violation of the law replicating temple oil, incense outside	repay moral obligation (debt cancelled by sabbatical year) stubbornly rejecting majority view

110

Heaven	Earth	Temple	Community
	Flogging, exile	*Obligatory offering and/or flogging for inadvertent action*	*Shunning or approbation*
		violating temple food taboos	opposing majority will
			opposing the patriarch
		violating taboos of holy days (Passover, atonement)	obedience to majority or patriarch
		uncleanness (Zab, mesora, etc.) Nazirite	
	violating food taboos	sex with bondwoman unclean Nazirite false oath of testimony	
	removing dam with offspring violating negative commandments	false oath of deposit	

The operative distinction between inflicting a flogging and requiring a sacrifice (temple sanctions against a person or property), and the sanction of extirpation (heavenly death penalty), is made explicit as follows: "For those [transgressions] are people liable, for deliberately doing them, to the punishment of extirpation, and for accidentally doing them, to the bringing of a sin-offering, and for not being certain of whether or not one has done them, to a suspensive guilt-offering." This summary yields a simple and clear fact, and on the basis of that simple fact we may now reconstruct the entire political story on which the politics of rabbinic Judaism rested. Let us emphasize: *Some of the same crimes or sins for which the heavenly court imposes the penalty of extirpation are those that, under appropriate circumstances (for example, sufficient evidence admissible in court) the earthly court imposes the death penalty.*

That is, the heavenly court and the earthly court impose precisely the same sanctions for the same crimes or sins. The earthly court therefore forms down here the exact replica and counterpart, within a single system of power, of the heavenly court up there. This no longer looms as an empty generalization; it is a concrete and systemically active and indicative detail, and the system speaks through its details. But this is not the entire story. There is a second fact, equally indicative of our recovery of the substrate of the story. We note that there are crimes for which the earthly court imposes penalties but for which the heavenly court does not, as well as vice versa. The earthly and heavenly courts share jurisdiction over sexual crimes and over what I classify as serious religious crimes against God. The Heavenly court penalizes with its form of the death penalty religious sins against God, in which instances a person deliberately violates the taboos of sanctification.

That fact calls our attention to a third partner in the distribution and application of power, the temple, with its system of sanctions that cover precisely the same acts subject to the jurisdiction of the heavenly and earthly courts. The counterpart on earth is now not the earthly court but the temple. This is the institution that, in theory, automatically receives the appropriate offering from the person who inadvertently violates these same taboos of sanctification. But this is an odd choice for the Mishnah, since there is now no temple on earth. The juxtaposition appears then to involve courts and temple, and the upshot is that both are equally matters of theory. In the theory at hand, then, the earthly court, for its part, penalizes social crimes against the community that the heavenly court, on the one side, and the temple rites, on the other, do not take into account at all. These are murder, apostasy, kidnapping, public defiance of the court, and false prophecy. The earthly court further imposes sanctions on matters of particular concern to the heavenly court, with special reference to taboos of sanctification (e.g., negative commandments). These three institutions therefore exercise concrete and material power, utilizing legitimate violence to kill someone, exacting penalties against property, and inflicting pain. The sages' modes of power, by contrast, stand quite apart, apply mainly to their own circle, and work through the intangible though no less effective means of inflicting shame or paying honor.

The facts we have in hand draw us back to the analysis of our differentiation of applied and practical power. In the nature of the facts before us, that differentiation tells us precisely for what the systemic story will have to give its account. Power flows through three distinct but intersecting dominions, each with its own concern, all sharing some interests in common. The heavenly court attends to deliberate defiance of heaven, the temple to inadvertent defiance of heaven. The earthly court attends to matters subject to its jurisdiction by reason of sufficient evidence, proper witnesses, and the like, and these same matters will come under heavenly jurisdiction when the earthly court finds itself unable to act. Accordingly, we have a tripartite system of sanctions – heaven cooperating with the temple in some matters, with the court in others, and, as noted, each bearing its own distinct media of enforcing the law as well. What then can we say concerning the systemic theology of politics? The forms of power and the modes of mediating legitimate violence draw our attention to a single political story, one that we first confronted, if merely as a generality and commonplace to be sure, at the very outset. The unity of that story is underlined by the simple fact that the earthly court enters into the process right alongside the heavenly court and the temple; as to blasphemy, idolatry, and magic, its jurisdiction prevails. So a single story must serve all three correlated institutions.

112

It is the story of God's authority infusing the institutions of Heaven and earth alike, an authority diffused among three principal foci or circles of power: heaven's court, the earthly court, and the temple in-between. Each focus of power has its own jurisdiction and responsibility, heaven above, earth beneath, the temple in the position of mediation – transmitting as it does from earth to heaven the penalties handed over as required. And all media of power in the matter of sanctions intersect at some points as well: a tripartite politics, a single story drawing each component into relationship with a single source and origin of power, God's law set forth in the Torah. But the story has not performed its task until it answers not only the question of why, but also the question of how. Specifically, the details of the story must address questions of the details of power. Who then tells whom to do what? And how are the relationships of dominion and dominance to compliance and obedience made permanent through the story?

It is where power is differentiated and parceled out that we see the workings of the political story. So we ask: how do we know who tells whom to do, or suffer, what sanction or penalty? It is the power of the story to differentiate that defines the generative question. The key lies in the criterion by which each mode of power, earthly, mediating, and heavenly, identifies the cases over which it exercises jurisdiction. The criterion lies in the attitude of the human being who has done what he or she should not: did he or she act deliberately or unintentionally? I state the upshot, again with heavy emphasis: *The point of differentiation within the political structures, supernatural and natural alike, lies in the attitude and intention of a human being.*

We differentiate among the application of power by reference to the attitude of the person who comes into relationship with that power. A person who comes into conflict with the system, rejecting the authority claimed by the powers that be, does so deliberately or inadvertently. The story accounts in the end for the following hierarchization of action and penalty, infraction and sanction: (1) If the deed is deliberate, then one set of institutions exercises jurisdiction and utilizes supernatural power. (2) If the deed is inadvertent, another institution exercises jurisdiction and utilizes the power made available by that same supernatural being. A sinner or criminal who has deliberately violated the law has by his or her action challenged the politics of rabbinic Judaism. Consequently, God or God's surrogate imposes sanctions – extirpation (by the court on high), or death or other appropriate penalty (by the court on earth). A sinner or criminal who has inadvertently violated the law is penalized by the imposition of temple sanctions, losing valued goods. People obey because God wants them to and has told them what to do, and, when they do not obey, a differentiated political structure appeals to that single hierarchizing story. The components of the story are twofold: first, God's will, expressed in the law of the Torah, second, the human being's will, carried out in obedience to the law of the Torah or in defiance of that law.

In scripture there is a very precise answer to the question of how to differentiate among sins or crimes and the reason to do so. Given the position of the system of the Mishnah, the point of differentiation must rest with one's attitude or intention. And, indeed, I do have two stories of how the power of God conflicts with the power of humanity in such ways as to invoke the penalties and sanctions in precisely the differentiated modes we have before us. Where do I find such stories of the conflict of wills, God's and humanity's? The first such story of power differentiated by the will of the human being in communion or conflict with the word of the commanding God comes to us from the Garden of Eden. We cannot reread the following astonishing words too often:

> The Lord God took the man and placed him in the garden of Eden . . . and the Lord God commanded the man, saying, "Of every tree of the garden you are free to eat; but as for the tree of knowledge of good and bad, you must not eat of it; for as soon as you eat of it, you shall die."
>
> . . . When the woman saw that the tree was good for eating and a delight to the eyes, and that the tree was desirable as a source of wisdom, she took of its fruit and ate; she also gave some to her husband, and he ate. . . .
>
> The Lord God called out to the man and said to him, "Where are you?"
>
> He replied, "I heard the sound of You in the garden, and I was afraid, because I was naked, so I hid."
>
> Then He asked, "Who told you that you were naked? Did you eat of the tree from which I had forbidden you to eat?"
>
> . . . And the Lord God said to the woman, "What is this you have done!"
>
> So the Lord God banished him from the garden of Eden.

Now a reprise of the exchange between God, Adam, and Eve tells us that what was at stake was responsibility: who has violated the law, but who bears responsibility for deliberately violating the law:

> "The woman You put at my side – she gave me of the tree, and I ate."
> "The serpent duped me, and I ate."
> Then the Lord God said to the serpent, "because you did this. . . ."

The ultimate responsibility lies with the one who acted deliberately, not under constraint or on account of deception or misinformation, as did Adam and Eve. Then the sanction applies most severely to the one who by intention and an act of will has violated God's intention and will.

Now the political story that generates the law of Judaism coincides with the theological story of God's relations with Man, Adam, and Eve. The halakhah's politics presents a reprise of the story of God's commandment, humanity's disobedience, God's sanction for the sin or crime, and humanity's atonement and reconciliation. The Mishnah omits all explicit reference to myths that explain power and sanctions, but invokes in its rich corpus of details the absolute given of the story of the distinction between what is deliberate and what is mitigated by an attitude that is not culpable, a distinction set forth in the tragedy of Adam and Eve, in the failure of Moses and Aaron, and in countless other passages in the Pentateuch, prophetic books, and writings. Then the Mishnah's is a politics of life after Eden and outside of Eden aimed at restoring Eden. The upshot of the matter is that the political story of rabbinic Judaism sets forth the constraints of freedom, the human will brought to full and unfettered expression, imposed by the constraints of revelation, God's will made known. Since it is the freedom of humanity to make decisions and frame intentions that forms the point of differentiation among the political media of power, we are required, in my view, to return to the paradigmatic exercise of that same freedom; that is, to Eden, to the moment when Adam and Eve exercise their own will and defy God. Since the operative criterion in the differentiation of sanction is the human attitude and intention in carrying out a culpable action, we must recognize that the politics before us rehearses the story of Adam and Eve in Eden – it finds its dynamic in the correspondence between God's will and humanity's freedom to act however it chooses, thus freely incurring the risk of penalty or sanction for the wrong exercise of freedom.

Power comes from two conflicting forces: the commanding will of God and the free will of the human being. Power expressed in immediate sanctions is also mediated through these same forces: heaven above, human beings below, with the temple mediating between the two. Power works its way in the interplay between what God has set forth in the law of the Torah and what human beings do, whether intentionally, whether inadvertently, obediently, or defiantly. That is why the politics of rabbinic Judaism is a politics of Eden, and why the institutions of the law express the restorationist theology of Eden.

C The Islamic court in the legal narrative of Islam

1 Legitimacy

Islamic legal theory did not initially distinguish between those empowered to interpret the law and those empowered to execute it. Prior to there being a carefully articulated legal or political theory in Islam, the eighth-century Hanafi legal scholar Abu Yusuf was asked by Harun al-Rashid, the famous 'Abbasid caliph, to advise him on taxation. Abu Yusuf defined the context of his response within the overall framework of the purpose of Islamic government. He wrote, "God in His benevolence and mercy has appointed the holders of authority as deputies [*khulafa'*] on His earth and has given them a light to illuminate for the subjects those of their affairs that are obscure to them and to clarify those duties about which they are in doubt."[1] Thus, the leader is, above all, delegated the task of ruling justly:

> Cause right to prevail in those matters where God has empowered and authorized you, if only for an hour of the day, for the happiest of shepherds before God on Judgement Day is the shepherd who made his flock happy. . . . Be cautious in the fear of God, and in God's command let all men, near or far, be equal before you. In God's work do not fear the blame of any man. Be cautious, with the caution of the heart, not the tongue; fear God, for the fear of God is a safeguard, and God protects those who fear Him. . . . Know that the steps of no man shall pass from before Almighty God save after questioning. As the Prophet, God bless and save him, has said, "On the Day of Judgement, no creature shall pass beyond until he has been asked four questions concerning his knowledge and the use he has made of it, his life and the way he passed it, his wealth and the way he earned and spent it, his body and the way he used it." Prepare, therefore, O Commander of the Faithful [title used by early caliphs], an answer for each question, for what you have done and established will be read out against you tomorrow. Remember that the veil between you and God will be removed at the gathering of witnesses.[2]

The ruler therefore rules only by delegation of divine authority; like all God's creatures he is subject to the law. Even in the context in which Abu Yusuf wrote, the task of the head of state was conceived as primarily executive, based on the assumption that divine law had been revealed through Prophet Muhammed:

> The illumination of the light of the holders of authority consists of enforcing the penalties for offenses as laid down in the holy law and the rendering of what is due to those to whom it is due, resolutely and by clear command. The maintenance of traditional practices [*sunan*] established by worthy men is of the greatest importance, for the maintenance of traditions is one of those good deeds which lives and does not die.[3]

Thus, the ideal Islamic state is one dominated by laws derived from divine revelation. Indeed, implementing Islamic law is the purpose of the state's existence since, as we saw in Chapter 3, the goal of Islamic law is to create a just society. This is the basis of the classical distinction between *dar al-islam*, *dar al-sulh* (or *'ahd*), and *dar al-harb*; the abode of Islam and the abodes of truce (or covenant) and war. Dar al-Islam, the most common designation of the Muslim political entity among the classical legal scholars, refers specifically to those territories in which the law of Islam prevails. Dar al-ʿahd and dar al-sulh are both regions whose leaders have agreed to pay the Muslim leaders a certain tax and to protect the rights of any Muslims and/or their allies who dwell there, but who otherwise maintain their autonomy, including their own legal systems. Dar al-harb, contrary to popular opinion, does not refer to an entity at war with the Muslim state. It is a region whose leaders have made no agreement concerning the safety of Muslims and their allies and where, unprotected by law, they are therefore technically under threat.

As we saw in previous chapters, however, it gradually became apparent that the task of legislation was more complex than simply executing revealed law. Situations arose for which there were no exact precedents. Accordingly, the role of extracting specific legislation from the revealed sources became a specialized task for religious scholars, and the division of authority between the executive and legislative came into focus in legal theory.

This division of labor in the Sunni Islamic state had its roots in distinct roles of the first leader of the Islamic political entity, Prophet Muhammad. He was considered both a source of divine revelation and a just arbiter, but the two roles were not fused. The Qur'an commanded that the prophet make decisions on practical issues in consultation (*shura*) with members of the community. In addition, the Prophet elicited periodically from the community an oath of allegiance to his political leadership (*bay'a*); acceptance of his prophetic role was a matter of faith. The political leaders who succeeded Muhammad (the caliphs, meaning "successors") took up his role as political leader, and ideally were just arbiters and judges as well. However, they did not inherit his prophetic role.

The prophet's successors were generally expected to behave according to the guidance left by the Prophet and to be personally pious as well, but there was no formal theory upon which to either determine leadership of the community or judge its legitimacy. The Qur'an had simply commanded, "Obey God and the Messenger and those among you in authority" (Sura 4:60). We have no record that the early Muslim community believed it was doing anything more or less than that. In 661 CE, following violent confrontation, the descendants of a leading Meccan family, the Umayyads, assumed control of the caliphate and established their headquarters in Damascus. This move brought the distinction between political or executive (coercive) authority and religious (legal) authority into sharper contrast; Damascus was only the political capital of the empire, while Mecca remained the religious center. The distinction was emphasized again when the Umayyads were overthrown in another revolution, by the ʿAbbasid family in 750 CE who moved the capital to Baghdad.

During the lifetime of the Prophet and his first four immediate successors (his closest companions, who are regarded by Sunni Muslims as having been of exemplary character and judgment, and are therefore called the Rashidun or "rightly guided" caliphs), the model of governance was that described in a document believed to have been dictated by Muhammad when he established the community at Medina, the "Constitution of Medina." In that document, preserved in extra-Qur'anic literature, the Prophet's political role is described as that of arbiter of disputes. Clearly, it was assumed that Muhammad's behavior was divinely guided and that his judgment was sound. The only monotheists referred to in the Constitution were Jews and, although they were designated as part of the community of the Prophet, it was stipulated that they retain their own religious laws and practice. Those who declared themselves Muslim, in lieu of a developed legal system, deferred to the Prophet's judgment on a case-by-case basis. Apparently, the Rashidun followed this same model.

With the expansion of the Islamic political entity and the development of a dynastic caliphate (starting with the Umayyads in 661 CE), it was no longer possible for the head of state to settle all disputes. The need arose for an organized Islamic legal infrastructure and further delegation of authority. The Umayyads established the first official Islamic courts, overseen by political appointees given the title of judge (*qadi*). The qadis had varied administrative responsibilities, including police and treasury work, but were generally charged with settling disputes in accordance with local custom, provided that it did not interfere with Islamic principles. They were accorded a great deal of latitude, exercising their own discretion with regard to what was permissible in view of Islamic principles and administrative necessities.

By the mid-eighth century, there was a discernible body of religious scholars who were popularly regarded as having the authority to identify and interpret the sources of normative Islamic practice (Islamic law). When the 'Abbasid dynasty overthrew the Umayyads in 750 CE, they incorporated those religious scholars who specialized in legal matters (*fuqaha'*) into their administration. Abu Yusuf's comments on his own role when he advised Harun al-Rashid illustrates the developing role of legal scholars:

> I have written for you as you commanded and have explained it to you and interpreted it. Study it and reread it until you know it by heart. I have striven for you in this and have not withheld advice from you and from the Muslims, who aspire to the countenance of God and His reward and fear His punishment. I hope that, if you act in accordance with my explanations, God will increase for you the yield of your land tax, without the oppression of any Muslim or tributary ally [*mu'ahad*], and that He will prosper your subjects for you.[4]

It is clear, then, that within the first century of Islam, executive power was being distinguished from legislative authority. It was in this context that al-Shafi'i articulated the components of Islamic law, an articulation that would ultimately become the basis of Islamic political thought as well. As legal historian N.J. Coulson put it, "The legal scholars were publicly recognized as the architects of an Islamic scheme of state and society which the 'Abbasids had pledged themselves to build, and under this political sponsorship the schools of law developed rapidly."[5] Indeed, when regional powers challenged the central authority of the 'Abbasid caliphs, it was a Shafi'i jurist, al-Mawardi (d. 1058 CE), who articulated Islam's first comprehensive theory of state.[6] This theory reinforces the separation of powers, but again, by delegation of authority that ultimately comes from God.

According to al-Mawardi, the office of the caliphate was established in order to continue the work of the Prophet in his capacity as defender of Islam and in worldly governance. The very purpose of the Islamic state – to create and maintain social justice – makes it obligatory upon the community that someone be placed in the position of caliph. Al-Mawardi says scholars' opinions are divided as to whether that obligation is based on reason or revelation. Reason tells us that "it is in the nature of reasonable men to submit to a leader who will prevent them from injuring one another and who will settle quarrels and disputes, for without rulers men would live in anarchy and heedlessness like benighted savages." Revelation tells us, as noted above, that we must "obey God, the Messenger, and those in authority among you" (Sura 4:60). Furthermore, there is a hadith report that the Prophet said, "Other rulers after me will rule over you, the pious according to his piety, the wicked according to his wickedness. Hear them and obey in all that accords with the truth. If they do good, it will count for you and for them. If they do evil, it will count for you and against them."[7]

Either way – whether on the basis of common sense or revelation – there must be a political head of state, says al-Mawardi, a view reiterated by later scholars as well. If no one is in the position of caliph, then the community must come up with a group of candidates eligible for the position and a group of electors to choose from among the candidates. The electors must have integrity, enough intelligence to recognize the qualifications of the candidates, and the ability to choose wisely from among the candidates.

The duties of the caliph fall into three categories: defense, treasury, and executive. He is to defend the community from attack (article 3), maintain frontier defenses (article 5), and wage war against those who refuse to either become Muslims or enter into treaty with Muslims (article 6); regarding fiduciary responsibility, he is to collect both the alms payments required of all Muslims to be spent on the needs of the community at large and the legitimate spoils of wars (article 7), fairly determine and pay salaries from the treasury (article 8), and make sure those he appoints to handle treasury moneys do so honestly (article 9). Most importantly, he is to make sure that

119

the established principles of religion are safeguarded (article 1), and that legal judgments and penalties are enforced (articles 2 and 4).[8]

The candidates for the position of caliph – in addition to having sound hearing, vision, speech, limbs, and judgment, and being courageous, vigorous (male) members of the Quraysh tribe (the tribe of the Prophet Muhammad) – must be of honorable character and able to practice ijtihad. But it seems to have been recognized that the actual caliph was rarely endowed with the ability to practice ijtihad. Therefore, he could delegate his authority in this regard to the legal scholars. This idea was reflected in the work of Shafi'i scholar al-Juwayni (d. 1085 CE), who claimed that the real authority in the community belongs to the legal scholars anyway, since they are the articulators of divine law, which is the source of all authority. Therefore, the caliph could be a muqallid (follower of precedents or imitator, rather than an independent thinker), so long as he consulted the religious scholars.[9] (This will be discussed further in Chapter 7.)

Thus, the primary role of the chief Islamic political authority was to safeguard and execute Islamic law. That he acts in this capacity through delegation of authority from God had been established from the earliest days of Islam. Even when the political leader delegated legislative and judicial authority to legal specialists, he was still charged with the responsibility "to execute judgements given between litigants and to settle disputes between contestants so that justice may prevail and so that none commit or suffer injustice."[10]

The caliph, therefore, in delegating his legislative power, relegates himself to a position logically subservient to those to whom he has delegated authority. So we have the anomalous situation wherein the executive authority is subject to the laws articulated by legists whose authority rests ultimately in the executive. On a practical level, of course, this can lead to conflict: the executive can take back the authority he has delegated from any legal scholar whose rulings he finds distasteful. On the theoretical level, however, there is no inherent conflict: the source of both the law and the authority to articulate and execute it come from the single, divine source. The conflict results from the fact that the legal authority is delegated secondarily; it comes through the executive, rather than directly from God. This produces an inevitable tension between the executive and legislative branches, a tension that will characterize virtually all of Islamic history. Yet it is creative tension; as discussed in Chapter 3, the self-image of the Islamic community is one of potential universality. It is charged with the mission of bringing all humanity to submission to the will of God. That mission requires considerable political organization and the orderly exercise of power. The task of the legal scholars is the "eternal vigilance" described as the cost of democracy. That is, the legal scholars' role is to assure that whatever authority is exercised and whatever laws are executed are in the service of the greater goal of Islamic law: the creation and maintenance of social justice. It is in this spirit that we read Abu Yusuf reminding Harun al-Rashid:

Al-Fadl ibn Marzuq told me, on the authority of ʿAtiyya ibn Saʿid, on the authority of Abu Saʿid, who said: The Prophet of God, may God bless and save him, said, "The dearest of men to me, and the nearest to me in station on the Day of Judgement, is a just Imam. The most hateful of men to me on the Day of Judgement and the recipient of the severest punishment is the tyrannical Imam.[11]

2 Courts' jurisdiction

Under the highly articulated legal system developed by the time of al-Shafiʿi, a regular court system was established. The role of the courts was a formalized version of the role of the just arbiter of disputes. Once permissible and impermissible behavior had been established, it was a short step to determining lawful and unlawful behavior. Once that had been established, it was necessary to lay down mechanisms whereby innocence or guilt could be determined, and appropriate punishments meted out.

It was noted in Chapter 2 that Islamic law covers all aspects of human life; it seeks to regulate all human behavior. Islamic law therefore deals not just with what is illegal, as do modern secular legal systems; it specifies what is required, recommended, neutral, discouraged, and forbidden. In all cases, the basis of determination is morality. In Islamic legal theory there is no distinction between legality and morality. In fact, the early Islamic law courts were physically located in mosques, yet Islamic courts could not deal practically with all the classifications of moral/legal acts. Meritorious actions, first of all, exceed their jurisdiction, since the rewards for moral behavior are believed to be eternal, not secular. Therefore, although rewards are a part of Shariʿa, the courts' jurisdiction is limited to dealing with actions deserving punishment. The jurisdiction of Islamic courts is further limited to acts that are forbidden outright. Medieval Islamic administrations included officials known as muhtasibs, generally in charge of public decency and fair measures in the marketplace. They could oversee general behavior and discourage acts considered to be less than virtuous. However, they were under no part of the Islamic court system; their authority stemmed directly from the political leadership.

Therefore, the jurisdiction of Islamic law is much greater than that of Islamic courts. Not only are the four degrees of behavior other than the illicit excluded, but so are the majority of issues of state, such as taxation and war. As we saw in the cases of Abu Yusuf and al-Mawardi, legal scholars offered their advice on administrative matters, and pious leaders accepted it. But they were not required to do so; there were no specific injunctions available to the courts to dissuade them from rejecting good advice.

In general, Islamic courts' jurisdiction was limited to those matters specifically forbidden by the Qurʾan: physical injury and wrongful death, theft, illicit sexual relations and false allegations thereof, apostasy, and the consumption of intoxicants. The Islamic legal system is predicated on the belief that people's clear understanding of what is required and forbidden is a major component of justice. Obviously a reaction to arbitrariness in coercive power, the concern for precision in law and its relationship to justice is elegantly expressed by Abu Yusuf. In advising Harun al-Rashid, he expresses hope that the sovereign's subjects will prosper. He then says that "their prosperity lies in the enforcement of the established legal penalties [hudud] and the prevention of oppression and injustice arising from uncertainties concerning their obligations."[12] In other words, good law is precise law.

3 Evidence

The emphasis on the need for precision in Islamic law is also apparent in the rules of evidence. The system was based on the assumption of innocence. The plaintiff (mudda'i) had to have another adult male (or two female) Muslim witnesses, besides himself, to testify in person concerning the charge against the defendant (mudda'a 'alayhi). The witnesses had to be able to demonstrate their own integrity ('adalah) and have immediate, personal knowledge of the charge. If the plaintiff could not produce such witnesses, the defendant was offered the opportunity to swear his innocence on the Qur'an. The only deviations from these strict rules of evidence were in the direction of greater strictness. For guilty verdicts in accusations of adultery (zina'), for example, the plaintiff must produce four witnesses of the actual sexual union, a requirement based on direct Qur'anic revelation (Sura 24:5). As we saw in Chapter 3, false accusations and defective judgments were so abhorrent in Islamic law that the Prophet is quoted as equating even his own faulty judgments against others with the fires of hell.

4 Punishments

The punishments prescribed in classical Islamic law fall into two general categories: fixed (hadd, pl. hudud), and discretionary (ta'zir). The specific punishments found in these categories include corporal punishment (whipping, stoning, amputation of the hand or foot), death (by stoning, crucifixion, or with a sword), retaliation, financial obligation to the injured party or her/his family (including liability for damage to property and payment of a certain amount in place of retaliation for injury or death, the so-called "blood money"), and expiation. Imprisonment is another punishment inflicted at the judge's discretion.

The crimes for which hadd punishments are due are those specifically forbidden by revelation. These sanctions are considered unchangeable, having been prescribed by God. The severity of the punishments, such as stoning to death for unlawful intercourse, or amputation of the hand or foot for theft, is considered a strong deterrent to the crimes involved, as well as a powerful inducement to repentance for those who have committed them.

Indeed, Islamic law shows a marked tendency to avoid the severest of punishments. In most cases, repentance and restitution are sufficient to preclude their application. The law also takes into consideration a wide variety of mitigating circumstances, including intention, the legal and mental status of the accused, and the degree of her/his responsibility. In such circumstances, punishments are inflicted according to the judge's discretion. Examples of such cases include: unlawful intercourse with a slave rather than a free person; unintentional intoxication; theft of trifling amounts or of things not properly guarded; and inflicting various levels of bodily injury indirectly, rather than directly. The hadd punishments are therefore only applied in cases of crime through deliberate intent, by a free, sane, and otherwise decent adult.

An example from Malik's *Muwatta* is instructive in this regard:

> Malik related to me from Yahya ibn Sa'id from Sa'id ibn al-Musayyab that a man from the Aslam tribe came to Abu Bakr as-Siddiq and told him, "I have committed adultery." Abu Bakr said to him, "Have you mentioned this to anyone else?" He replied, "No." Abu Bakr told him, "Then cover it up with the veil of Allah. Allah accepts repentance from His slaves." He was still unsettled, so he went to 'Umar ibn al-Khattab and told him the same as he had said to Abu Bakr and 'Umar gave him the same answer as Abu Bakr had done. He was still unsettled so he went to the Messenger of Allah, may Allah bless him and grant him peace, and said to him insistently, "I have committed adultery." The Messenger of Allah, may Allah bless him and grant him peace, turned away from him three times. Each time the Messenger of Allah, may Allah bless him and grant him peace, turned away from him until it became too much. The Messenger of Allah, may Allah bless him and grant him peace, questioned his family, "Does he have some illness which affects his mind or is he mad?" They said, "Messenger of Allah, he is well." The Messenger of Allah, may Allah bless him and grant him peace, said, "Unmarried or married?" They replied, "Married, Messenger of Allah." The Messenger of Allah, may Allah bless him and grant him peace, then gave the order for him to be stoned.[13]

We have seen above the precedent for suspension of the hadd punishment for theft in times of famine. In discussing the punishments for adultery and theft, al-Shafi'i likewise reflects the effort to restrict hadd punishments to only the most blatant cases:

And God said:

> The fornicatress and the fornicator – scourge each of them with a hundred stripes [Sura 24:2].

And He, concerning slave-women, said:

> If they, having been taken under ihsan [good reputation], commit an indecency, they shall be subject to half the punishment to which those under ihsan are subject [Sura 4:30].

Thus the Qur'an indicated that scourging with a hundred stripes is intended [only] for the free, not the slave-women. And when the Apostle stoned rather than scourged the [non-virgin] adulterer, the sunna of the Prophet specified that the hundred stripes are [the penalty] for the free fornicatress and fornicator; and that cutting off the hand of the thief was intended to be [the penalty] for one who steals [a thing] from a secure place and that the price [of the theft] should be [at least] a quarter of a dinar, excluding other things covered under the terms "theft" and "adultery."[14]

The goal of Islamic law, therefore – to produce an equitable, upright society – is reflected in its system of punishments. It is designed to make the difference between right and wrong, between righteous and unrighteous behavior perfectly clear, reflecting the belief that lack of such clarity is among the reasons why people are led astray. Its severity is mitigated not only by the effort to encourage repentance, as we saw above, but also by a clear concern for mercy, inspired by the Qur'anic advice to Prophet Muhammad to treat people gently: "It is by God's grace that you [the Prophet] have dealt kindly with them" (Sura 3:160).

It is worth noting, again, the very practical intent of Islamic law, reflected in the continuation of this verse: "Had you been harsh and hard-hearted, they would have dispersed from around you. Therefore, forgive them and pardon them and consult them in affairs. When you have made a decision, put your trust in God, for God loves those who put their trust in Him." Islamic law was intended to be the foundation for a practical, effective, universal movement of piety and justice. It was an ongoing struggle (jihad) to fulfill the covenant established between God and humanity with the initial act of Abraham's submission to the will of God. The purpose of Islamic law is to achieve this goal, overcoming the impediments which have kept it elusive thus far. It is a goal that cannot be achieved by the court system alone, of course. But the courts were an integral part of that effort.

D Conclusions

In both Judaic and Islamic classical legal theory, political authority rests on the delegation by God to humanity of the task of creating a just and therefore holy society. There are important differences, however, in how that authority is conceived. In Judaic law, God's role is incorporated into a coherent system of justice that includes as well the religious and political institutions, and both social and psychological pressure imposed by the community. That coherent system of justice, just as in the case of Islam, defies the division of concerns into the eternal and secular; the one is meaningless without the other. It is not articulated as such in documents dealing with specific law or political theory. Yet a comprehensive reading of the oral Torah, the Mishnah, reveals a cohesive system of justice designed to restore the ideal relationship between God and humanity represented in the scriptural description of Eden.

The Islamic legal system is likewise a coherent system of justice based on revelation. Its components are clearly articulated in written documents, which envision authority as derived from or delegated by God to humanity. Unlike the Judaic system, God remains outside the system; God is its *fons et origo,* but is neither subject to it nor a participant in it. The very purpose of human existence is to do the will of God. On that the Torah of Judaism concurs. The legal system and its courts are components in the effort to meet that challenge. It is believed that the justice and mercy institutionalized in that system reflect the nature of God, and the guidance in that effort provided by revelation is a gift of God, but the challenge itself must be met by human beings.

As in Judaic law, in the world-view of Islamic law, the courts are only a part of the overall system. But unlike the Judaic system, the other components of the Islamic system include political power which is beyond its authority to control. The Judaic system does not contemplate political institutions beyond the ken of the Torah, probably because the Judaic system set forth in the Mishnah and amplified in the Talmud deals with the theory of matters, but much less with practicalities.

Perhaps the most significant difference between the Judaic and Islamic court system, however, lies in their respective views of the ultimate goal of legislation. In the Judaic system, as we saw above, the overall goal is to bring humanity back to its original, perfect relationship with the Creator. In the Islamic system, by contrast, the goal is to achieve what has never been achieved before, the challenge set out for humanity at creation. That challenge is to re-create in society the equality which all humanity shares in the eyes of the Creator. But in the Judaic vision, that was once achieved. The court system, with its cosmic world-view, is a vestige of that perfect relationship. In the Islamic system the challenge has yet to be met. The court system is among the means which human beings have established in an effort to do so.

Perhaps we may best explain the difference by an appeal to historical facts. Islam quickly attained authority over, and responsibility for, large populations of believers and non-believers alike. Judaism ruled over small numbers, who formed subordinate communities. Islam could theorize but also had to govern. The sages of Judaism had the luxury of thinking about matters far beyond their control. The one confronted the intractables of the here and now, the other had the possibility of theorizing about a long-ago perfection without actually testing the theory against the practicalities of large-scale politics. These fundamental differences between the institutional responsibilities of Islam and Judaism make all the more striking the points on which they coincide and even concur. For Islam and Judaism in their classical statements agree on what counts: the state, the entire social order — these form the setting for humanity's service to God and endeavor to carry out God's will. Both theories of the working of the law take shape within not the everyday necessities of the workaday world but the rigors of rational, logical thought. Judaism and Islam concur that in the beginning is God's word, and only then, in response thereto, people devise a political construction to realize God's will in the real world.

5

THE WORKING OF THE LAW
Personnel

A Bases of authority

What preparation are judges to have, what qualities of mind and character are they to possess, in order to undertake to administer the affairs of the community in Judaism and Islam? Clearly, both religious legal systems require faith and intellect, and neither can take the one without the other. These gifts of the soul and scholarly training constitute another mode of validation of the authority of the law: for Judaism, intellectual and charismatic; for Islam, intellectual. The definition of the requirements for legal scholars and judges in Islam, and the disciple of sages (*talmid hakhamim*), who bears the honorific title "rabbi" in Judaism, completes the account of how the law works in the two religions. Once more we see how the law serves as the medium of the theological system and religious convictions of each of them, and how levels of literacy distinguish the two systems. As noted in Chapter 2, recent studies have identified key differences between oral and literate cultures. In our discussion of modes of reasoning, the tendency for oral cultures to reason anecdotally (by precedent), and for literate cultures to reason logically (by syllogism) was indicated. Another characteristic distinction between orality and literacy will become evident in this chapter. Oral cultures tend to place authority in persons; something is true because the person we recognize as authoritative said it. In literate cultures the process is reversed: we recognize as an authority someone who says something we believe is true based on other sources, primarily text and logic. Since Judaism lays heavy emphasis upon formulation and transmission through memory of the oral part of the Torah, gifts of the spirit are to be anticipated; since Islam rests upon a wholly written tradition, we should find heavier emphasis upon intellectual ability. The formal difference then turns into an expression of a deeper theological disagreement on how human beings know God's will in words.

B Islam

1 *Legal scholars* (Fuqaha')

The earliest works of Islamic law reflect both oral and literate influences in their scant references to the qualifications required for proper legal judgments. On the one hand, there is evidence that correct judgment was considered to be somehow spiritually guided. Malik cites the following approvingly:

> [It was] related to me from Yahya ibn Sa'id from Sa'id ibn al-Musayyab that 'Umar ibn al-Khattab [the second caliph] had a dispute brought to him between a Muslim and a Jew. 'Umar thought that the Jew was in the right and gave judgement in his favor. The Jew said to him, "By Allah! you have judged correctly!" So 'Umar ibn al-Khattab struck him with his whip and said, "How can you be sure?" The Jew said to him, "We find that there is no judge who judges correctly but that there is an angel on his right side and an angel on his left side who guide him and give him success in the truth as long as he is with the truth. When he leaves the truth, they rise and leave him."[1]

On the other hand, Malik cites even Prophet Muhammad's insistence that he is merely a human being when it comes to arbitrating disputes, and that human judgments are based on evidence and the way it is presented, and may indeed be in error, even when pronounced by the most pious of human beings, as in the example noted previously:

> Yahya related to me from Malik from Hisham ibn 'Urwa from his father from Zaynab bint Abi Salama from Umm Salama, the wife of the Prophet, may Allah bless him and grant him peace, that the Messenger of Allah, may Allah bless him and grant him peace, said, "I am but a man to whom you bring your disputes. Perhaps one of you is more eloquent in his proof than the other and so I give judgement according to what I have heard from him. Whatever I decide from him which is part of the right of his brother, he must not take any of it for I am granting him a portion of the Fire."[2]

In this vein, the importance of knowledge and training for clear judgment is stressed:

> Yahya related to me from Malik that he heard that Luqman al-Hakim made his will and counselled his son, saying, "My son! Sit with the learned men and keep close to them. Allah gives life to the

hearts with the light of wisdom as Allah gives life to the dead earth with the abundant rain of the sky."[3]

The stress on the necessity for intellectual training for jurisprudents eventually came to dominate as the Islamic legal system develops. By the time al-Shafi'i regularized the legal system in the early ninth century CE, literacy had clearly left its mark. In his detailed account of the steps in legal training, references to supernatural guidance of a chosen few have been replaced by intellectual requirements theoretically achievable by any man.

As noted in Chapter 3, legal reasoning (ijtihad) for al-Shafi'i is limited to syllogism (qiyas) starting from a case believed to have been divinely revealed. He then lays out the training required before a man is qualified to practice ijtihad.

> No one except a well-informed scholar fully acquainted with the [binding] narratives should exercise [analogy]. And he who exercises it should do so only on the basis of [legal] knowledge, and legal knowledge consists of the binding narrative on the strength of which analogy may be applied by means of certain indications as to what is right.[4]

Again, the stress here is on certainty as an essential component of justice. As indicated in Chapter 4, judges (qadis) were originally political appointees of the caliph. By the time of al-Shafi'i, judges were to be chosen only from among properly trained legal scholars. And that proper training was rigorous, at least partly as a result of his articulation of the bases (*usul*) of Islamic legislation:

> Nobody should apply analogy unless he is competent to do so through his knowledge of the commands of the Book of God: its prescribed duties and its ethical discipline, its abrogating and abrogated [communications], its general and particular [rules], and its [right] guidance. Its [ambiguous] communications should be interpreted by the Sunna of the Prophet; if no Sunna is found, then by the consensus [ijma'] of the Muslims; if no consensus is possible, then by analogical deduction.[5]

Therefore, legal training requires knowledge of the Qur'an, first of all, both its general principles and the specific rules it has determined as binding on all people, as well as a thorough knowledge of the collections of authenticated hadith materials, and decisions concerning what is legal and illegal made unanimously by the pious ancestors.

In the clearest indication that literacy had come to dominate the orality of Arab culture, al-Shafi'i specified that legal scholars must not rely on memory alone: "And he who possesses the [legal] knowledge I have described [solely] through memory, and is uncertain of its correctness, should not be permitted to express an opinion based on analogy, for he may not comprehend the meaning [of that knowledge]."[6] Mere rote memory of a text is not sufficient, therefore, to demonstrate understanding of its implications, a judgment that could only be made from the standpoint of literacy. This literacy requirement produced the further requirement that prospective legal scholars must be highly proficient in the Arabic language, including its rules of grammar, a feature of written, rather than oral language.

Literacy and intimate knowledge of the Qur'an and Sunna are necessary to qualify as an Islamic legal scholar, but not sufficient. Beyond these skills, one must be astute in logic and careful to survey all the sources before determining an opinion. Furthermore, the potential jurisprudent must show sufficient strength of character to seek the opinions of others, particularly those who disagree with him, "for he might be warned against [possible] forgetfulness or be confirmed in his right [judgment]." In this exercise, the scholar must make an effort to defend his own position and, at the same time, be open to valid arguments:

> In so doing he must exert his utmost power not to be misled by personal [bias], so that he knows on what ground he has given one opinion and on what ground he has rejected another. Nor should he be more preoccupied with the opinion he has given than with the one with which he disagrees, so that he knows the merits of what he accepts as compared with that which he rejects.[7]

Literacy, intelligence, and maturity, therefore, seasoned through careful training in the Qur'an, the Sunna and precedents based on consensus of the early community of Muslims, are the requirements established by the time of al-Shafi'i for joining the ranks of legal scholars. They are the basis of the kind of specialized knowledge required to render valid legal decisions. There is a more general kind of legal knowledge, according to al-Shafi'i, of which no "sober and mature" Muslim should be ignorant. It is knowledge of the basic responsibilities and prohibitions that guide daily life, for example:

> that the daily prayers are five, that men owe it to God to fast the month of Ramadan, to make the pilgrimage to the [Sacred] House whenever they are able, and to [pay] the legal alms in their estate; that [God] has prohibited usury, adultery, homicide, theft, [the drinking of] wine, and [everything] of that sort which He has obligated men to comprehend, to perform, to pay in their property, and to abstain from [because] He has forbidden it to them.[8]

Al-Shafi'i considers all this to be legal knowledge, but because it is unquestionable, based on specific texts, and not susceptible to interpretation, it is everyone's responsibility to know. But the kind of knowledge accessible only to specialists is that concerning rules not based on specific, unquestionable texts, and "subject to different interpretations arrived at by analogy."[9] There is also an even more specialized knowledge, al-Shafi'i says, accessible only to very gifted specialists. He is referring to the kind of knowledge that allows the practice of ijtihad; even the majority of fuqaha' are capable only of following precedent (taqlid). Yet even this highest level of legal knowledge is a matter of intelligence and training, rather than social standing or charisma. This is evident in al-Shafi'i's insistence that achievement of legal knowledge is a religious duty. Gaining the first level of knowledge is a duty required of all Muslims, but highly specialized legal knowledge is the kind of duty he describes as collective. (This will also be discussed in Chapter 7.) It is necessary that someone pursue this level of knowledge; provided that enough do so to supply the community with the guidance it needs, the others are relieved of the personal responsibility:

> So far as I have been informed, the Muslims have continued to act as I have stated, from the time of the Prophet to the present. Only a few men must know the law, attend the funeral service, perform the jihad and respond to greeting, while others are exempt. So those who know the law, perform the jihad, attend the funeral service, and respond to a greeting will be rewarded, while others do not fall into error since a sufficient number fulfill the [collective] duty.[10]

Thus, the qualifications for the specialized role of legal scholar – if not the highest level required for ijtihad – are considered achievable by anyone of sound judgment (dhu'l-ra'y). This category excluded women, at least those who are fertile, in the opinion of al-Shafi'i. This opinion is based on the belief that such people are not in full control of their capacities. He quotes a hadith according to which three categories of people are excluded from religious obligations: "the one asleep, until he awakes; the child, until he comes of age; and the lunatic, until he recovers." But he then goes on to comment that "menstruant women during the period of menstruation" are in the same category as those asleep, those below the age of reason, and lunatics.[11]

It is interesting to note that there is some confusion among commentators regarding al-Shafi'i's views on ijma' (consensus). We saw in Chapter 3 that al-Shafi'i rejected the earlier notion of ijma' whereby the consensus of a region was authoritative. He says the only ijma' he recognizes is that wherein the entire Muslim community reaches consensus. Therefore, ijma' is no longer possible; the Muslim community is too large for it to be possible to determine anything upon which everyone agrees. But when al-Shafi'i later says that only legal scholars may practice ijtihad, many commentators describe his definition of ijma' as consensus among the legal scholars

131

(fuqaha') rather than the entire community, even though the position of faqih had not been institutionalized during the formative period where he locates legitimate ijma' historically.

Similarly, there is concern over his answer to the question of who may practice ijtihad. Some treat his description of the requirements for the practice of legal reasoning as establishing a veritable clergy in Islam, a class of religious scholars whose prerogative it was to interpret the religion for the less educated majority. An argument can be made, however, that his goal was not to limit the practice of responsible legal reasoning, but to promote it. It is indeed the case historically that Islamic education declined, leaving very few capable of meeting the qualifications of the faqih (legal scholar). Yet it remains arguable whether or not that development can be attributed to al-Shafi'i. Given the fact that, despite some dissent at the time over al-Shafi'i's views, they were ultimately adopted by the majority of Muslims, it appears that his position was not a complete innovation. He seems to have been making official what had already become established practice. The qualifications he listed technically exclude only those considered mentally incompetent, including women, from potentially engaging in legal reasoning. The development of an exclusive class of legal scholars need not have been the result of al-Shafi'i's reforms.

Nevertheless, the practice of the most creative and responsive aspect of Islamic law – ijtihad – was eventually limited. During the formative period of Islamic law, what would become the official schools of law were differentiated primarily by region and the oral materials dominant within them, although the Iraqi scholars were often characterized as more reliant on reasoning than those in Medina, known for a stronger reliance on precedent conveyed in regionally popular hadith reports. Legal thinkers were generally identified as either Medinese or Iraqi. Al-Shafi'i, who was from Gaza, studied with scholars from both regions. By the tenth century, however, schools of thought began to be identified by the names of their reputed founders. The Iraqis became the Hanafis; the Medinese became the Malikis; those who embraced al-Shafi'i's framework became Shafi'is; later, the followers of a former traditionalist (hadith collector), Ahmad Ibn Hanbal, became the Hanbalis. With this development came two corollaries. First, the development of schools of legal thought (*madhahib*) was associated the tendency to attribute the decisions reached within the various schools to the thought of their namesakes. In other words, with this development came the tendency not to claim that one's position had been achieved through independent reasoning (ijtihad). Legal scholars claimed that their positions were the result of following the precedents established within their schools (taqlid). Second, the development of the official schools of Islamic legal thought was associated with the growing conviction that only the founders of the schools had been capable of true ijtihad. That came to be known as absolute ijtihad, the highest degree of ijtihad. Beyond that were lower degrees of ijtihad, for example, a kind of legal reasoning that resulted in new input within the limited framework of a particular legal school. But even these limited degrees of ijtihad were considered difficult to achieve and few claimed for themselves the right to exercise them. A hadith report according to which the Prophet claimed that as time progressed, Islamic thought would degenerate precipitously, became widely accepted as an explanation for the decline of ijtihad.

These developments came after the formative period of Islamic law. It is possible to see al-Shafiʿi's reference to the highest level of legal reasoning – the one achievable by only some specialists – as the first step on the path to limiting ijtihad. Yet the actual decline in its practice seems to reflect more the reversion to oral models of reasoning – based entirely on precedent established by an unassailable personal authority – rather than any direct effect of al-Shafiʿi's work. Indeed, his rigorous standards are a monument to the literacy of his era; that is, the requirements for the position of legal scholar were a strictly intellectual matter. Of course, one had to be of generally upright character, just as is required of all legal witnesses, but the job required no special status or charisma.

2 Judges

With the passing of Prophet Muhammad and his closest companions passed also the model of the religio-political leader who could also be called upon to render just arbitration in disputes. The spread of the Islamic administrative system far beyond its original confines in the Arabian peninsula, and the growth of dynastic leadership under the Umayyads (beginning in 661 CE), gave rise to the need for arbitrators or judges in the various regions of the Islamic empire. These positions were orignally filled, as noted, by political appointees of the Umayyads. Under the ʿAbbasid caliphate, however (beginning in 750 CE), legal scholars were incorporated into the administration. Beginning with the ʿAbbasids, then, judges were chosen from among the legal scholars.

This transition represents a pronounced division of labor within the Islamic community, again reflective of literate patterns rather than oral. The ancient tribal arbitrator was known as a *hakim*. His role was undifferentiated religious and sociopolitical leadership; his behavior normative. He was chosen on the basis of a number of factors, including family lineage, reputation, and leadership skills (the ability to inspire confidence in his wisdom and guidance, i.e., charisma). In the ʿAbbasid system, which came to be identified as the Islamic system, legislative work was specialized. Individuals could qualify on the basis of carefully articulated requirements, essentially involving a high degree of literacy, achievable by people regardless of their tribal affiliation and standing, and whether or not they had a reputation. Eleventh-century legal scholar al-Mawardi gives the most detailed description of the qualifications required for the position of qadi. According to him, qadis had to have integrity, but this was required of all Muslims in good standing:

> [Integrity] is a requirement for any position of authority. This means that a man speaks truth, is manifestly trustworthy, virtuously refrains from forbidden things and avoids sin, is beyond suspicion, can be trusted in both approval and anger, and conducts himself as befits a man like him in both religious and worldly matters. The fulfillment of all these requirements constitutes ['adala], which qualifies him to testify and to exercise authority. If any of these qualities is lacking, he may neither testify nor exercise authority; his words shall not be heard nor his judgement executed.[12]

Al-Mawardi specifies six other qualifications for the position of qadi. First, "he must be a man." Al-Mawardi admits that some have disagreed with him, but he argues his position this way:

> This condition [maleness] consists of two qualities, puberty and masculinity. As for the child below puberty, he cannot be held accountable, nor can his utterances have effect against himself; how much less so against others. As for women, they are unsuited to positions of authority, although judicial verdicts may be based on what they say. Abu Hanifa said that a woman can act as qadi in matters on which it would be lawful for her to testify, but she may not act as qadi in matters on which it would not be lawful for her to testify. Ibn Jarir al-Tabari, giving a divergent view, allows a woman to act as qadi in all cases, but no account should be taken of an opinion which is refuted by both the consensus of the community and the word of God. "Men have authority over women because of what God has conferred on the one in preference to the other" [Qur'an 4:38], meaning by this, intelligence and discernment. He does not, therefore, permit women to hold authority over men.[13]

Since there were no special courts for women, presumably al-Mawardi considered it inevitable that a woman judge would have to sit in judgment of men, and that he considered unthinkable. Therefore, to be a qadi one had to be a man.

The second requirement for the position of qadi, according to al-Mawardi, was intelligence, "the importance of which is universally recognized." The basic use of the five senses was not enough for him. Intelligence meant as well "discriminating judgement and great perspicacity," as well as a good memory and "sufficient acumen to clarify difficulties and resolve obscure cases."[14]

Third, the qadi must be free and not involved in any degree of slavery.

(There are several degrees of slavery recognized in Islamic law, including those who are considered only partially enslaved because they will become free upon the death of their owners or upon the completion of a contract. This will be discussed in further detail in Chapter 6.) However, once freed, a former slave can become a qadi.

It is perhaps surprising that al-Mawardi lists the requirement that a man be Muslim as only fourth in the list of qualifications for the position of qadi. Perhaps he considered it self-evident. In any case, he reasons that the judge must be a Muslim on the same basis as he reasons a judge must be a male: the question of who has the right to exercise authority over Muslim men. Thus, "The fourth condition is Islam, because this is a necessary condition for the right to testify and because of the word of God, 'God will not give the unbelievers the advantage over believers' [Qur'an 4:140]." To further clarify the point, al-Mawardi then specifies that non-Muslims appointed to legal positions among their co-religionists must not be considered qadis. According to Islamic law, Jews are free to follow Judaic law, Christians to follow Christian law, and so on, but they are not required to do so:

> It is not lawful for an unbeliever to exercise judicial authority over Muslims or over unbelievers. Abu Hanifa said that an unbeliever may be appointed to dispense justice among his co-religionists. Though it is common practice for rulers to appoint unbelievers in this way, it is an appointment as chief or head and not appointment conferring judicial authority. His decisions bind them because they voluntarily submit to him, not because he has binding authority over them, and the Imam does not assent to his rulings in judgements rendered by him among his co-religionists. If his people do not resort to his jurisdiction, they are not compelled to do so, and they will then be subject to Islamic judicial authority.[15]

In other words, if non-Muslims were considered judges, then, at least theoretically, the Muslim political leader ("the Imam") would be bound to accept their judgments among their co-religionists. Since that would put a Muslim (the leader) in the position of being subject to the judgments of non-Muslims (the judges under his jurisdiction), it could not be allowed. Non-Muslims were still free to submit to their own legal authorities, but their legal practitioners were not to be considered judges.

There is some dispute among the authorities regarding the necessary physical capacities of qadis. Al-Mawardi says they must have good hearing and eyesight. He cannot imagine a judge who cannot distinguish visually between a plaintiff and defendant, and thinks these faculties are also essential in distinguishing between a person telling the truth and a liar. But he acknowledges that Malik allows a blind man to be a judge, just as the blind may give valid legal testimony. He also acknowledges that some scholars do not require hearing for the position. And he notes that "soundness of limb is not a requirement . . . although freedom from physical defects gives greater dignity to those exercising authority."[16]

Finally, al-Mawardi identifies detailed legal knowledge as necessary for the judgeship. Recapitulating almost verbatim al-Shafi'i's standard requirements, he says:

> The sources of the rules of the Holy Law are four:
>
> > 1. Knowledge of God's book, so that he has a sound understanding of the rules contained in it, both abrogating and abrogated [nasikh and mansukh], both precise and equivocal [muhkam and mutashabih; Sura 3:7], both general and specific, and both unexplained and clearly interpreted.
> > 2. Knowledge of the authentic tradition [Sunna] of the Prophet of God, may God bless and save him, of his words and his deeds, how they were transmitted, by many or by few, which are genuine and which false and which refer only to a specific occasion and which are of general application.
> > 3. Knowledge of the interpretations of the first generation of Muslims, whether unanimous or divergent, conforming to the consensus or exercising independent judgement [ijtihad] in cases of disagreement.
> > 4. Knowledge of analogy, the method used to deduce implicit consequences from explicit and agreed principles, so as to attain the knowledge required to settle lawsuits and to distinguish true from false.[17]

So insistent is al-Mawardi on these intellectual requirements that he says that judgments, whether just or not, from someone lacking these qualifications must be rejected, and that anyone who appoints someone lacking these qualifications to a judgeship, and anyone lacking them who accepts a judgeship, commits a sin.

The position of qadi had one more requirement, beyond that of being a legal scholar, not mentioned by al-Mawardi. Eligible individuals had to have the rigorous training of the fuqaha' (legal scholars). But, in reality, whether or not one was chosen as qadi depended upon one's standing with the political leader under whom one worked. The same is true for one's length of tenure once chosen. Judges could be appointed or dismissed at the will of the political (executive) leader. Al-Mawardi makes some reference to this reality when he distinguishes between two types of qadi. He says the first kind is one whose authority is general and absolute ('aimmah mutlaqah). This is the judge who decides cases; imposes punishments for infractions of religious law; acts as guardian for orphans, minors, and lunatics; and administers religious endowments (*awqaf*). But there is also the special (*khassah*) judge, whose authority is limited by the terms of his appointment by the ruler. The distinction was more theoretical than practical, however, since all judges served at the pleasure of the ruler.

The 'Abbasids also instituted the office of chief qadi (*qadi al-qudat*), a title first held by Abu Yusuf. As we saw in Chapter 4, Abu Yusuf was the advisor to Umayyads caliphs, including Harun al-Rashid. Because of the high regard in which Abu Yusuf was held by Harun, he was involved in choosing qadis for the outlying provinces. But this was the prerogative of the caliph, and one not necessarily followed by other rulers.

Nevertheless, the qadi was technically independent of the political rulers, and we have evidence that even as early as the eighth century, under Umayyad rule, that independence was recognized and at least sometimes respected. The following is from the annals of the court at Cordoba:

> The amir 'Abd al-Rahman ibn Mu'awiya [the Umayyad caliph in Spain], may God have mercy on him, had need to appoint a qadi for the district of Cordova. He had heard of a man in Merida, of probity, firmness, and piety. He sent for him and appointed him, and he conducted himself worthily in the office of qadi.
>
> Muhammad ibn 'Abd al-Malik ibn Ayman said: One of those who served as qadi for 'Abd al-Rahman ibn Mu'awiya, may God be pleased with both of them, was 'Abd al-Rahman ibn Tarif, an inhabitant of the city of Merida and an honorable man of praise-worthy conduct. . . .
>
> Muhammad said: Khalid ibn Sa'd said: I heard Muhammad ibn Ibrahim ibn al-Jabbab repeat the following story: Habib al-Qurashi appeared before the amir 'Abd al-Rahman ibn Mu'awiya, may God have mercy on him, to complain against the qadi 'Abd al-Rahman ibn Tarif. He said that the qadi intended to record a verdict against him in a case about an estate on which al-Qurashi was living and concerning which a claim had been brought against him, alleging that he had misappropriated it by force. The amir sent a messenger to the qadi, who spoke with him on the matter. He ordered him to proceed with caution and forbade him to act in haste. Thereupon the qadi Ibn Tarif went out immediately, sent for the jurisconsults and legal witnesses, pronounced a verdict against Habib, recorded it, and had it witnessed. Habib went to the amir and incited him against the qadi, saying that he hated the amir and made light of him. The amir was very angry and sent for the qadi Ibn Tarif. He had him brought into his presence and said to him, "Who impelled you to pronounce a verdict after I had ordered you to proceed with caution?"
>
> "I was impelled to do it," replied Ibn Tarif, "by the same one who seated you on this throne, but for whom you would not sit there."

"Your words," said the amir, "are even stranger than your deeds. Who seated me on this throne?"

"The Prophet of the Lord of the Universe," replied the qadi. "Were it not for your kinship with him, you would not sit on this throne. He was sent with the Truth to dispense justice to all, far and near. O amir," said the qadi, "what induces you to favor one of your subjects at the expense of another? You could find a way of satisfying the one who interests you by using your own money."

"If those," said the amir, "who are the rightful owners of the estate are willing to sell it, I would buy it for Habib with my own money and satisfy them in the price."

"I shall send for them," said Ibn Tarif, "and put this to them. If they are willing to sell, well and good, but if not, my verdict stands."

The qadi went away and sent for the owners. He spoke to them about the estate and they agreed to sell it if the price were good.

Habib used to say thereafter, "May God reward Ibn Tarif for my sake. I held an estate unlawfully, and Ibn Tarif made it lawful for me."[18]

In this case the political leader submitted to the judgment of the qadi he himself appointed. Whether or not this was common, the fact that this instance was considered important enough to have been recorded for posterity indicates that it was considered admirable.

3 Muftis

A mufti is a specialist in Islamic law who can give authoritative opinions (fatwas) on specific issues of doctrine or practice. The position of mufti is a reflection of both historic circumstances and the nature of Islamic law. Concerning the former, the position is a carryover from the earliest stages of Islamic law, before the institutionalization of requirements for legal scholarship. In that context, virtually anyone with the interest and ability to inspire the confidence of the community could assume this position, essentially an advisory, rather than legislative, one. The position was actually superseded by the institutionalization of the requirements for legal scholarship, and the resultant development of a body of legal scholars, effectively integrated into the Islamic administrative system, and from among whom judges were chosen. Nevertheless, governments continued to appoint muftis, due to the second basis mentioned above, the nature of Islamic law itself. As discussed in Chapter 4, institutionalized Islamic law was limited on a practical level to enforceable prohibitions, even though Islamic law actually covers all aspects of life, including things that are recommended but not required, and things that are discouraged but not forbidden. In other words, the courts could not handle all aspects of Islamic law. The mufti was able to respond in an advisory capacity to those extra-judicial aspects of Islamic law. His advice could also be sought on issues within the courts' jurisdiction, and presented as arguments before the court, although the judge was not required to accept his advice. While muftis' views were considered authoritative, they remained outside the enforceable legal structure.

Accordingly, the qualifications for being a mufti were not quite as stringent as those for being a legal scholar (faqih) or qadi. This is perhaps predictable, given the fact that the position of mufti evolved before the institutionalization of Islamic law. But not as predictably, a mufti could even be a slave. In his discussion of the requirements for the position of qadi, al-Mawardi explained that in order to qualify for the position of mufti one must be thoroughly versed in the four sources of Islamic law. "If he masters these four sources of the rules of the Holy Law, he becomes a mujtahid [practitioner of independent legal reasoning, ijtihad] in religion, and is allowed to act as mufti or qadi, and may be asked to act in either capacity. But if he is deficient in them or in any part of them, he cannot be a mujtahid and may not act as mufti or qadi."[19] But muftis need not meet all the other requirements for the position of qadi. Specifically, al-Mawardi notes that judges must be autonomous, since they exercise authority over others. But this is not the case with muftis, who only render legal advice: "[T]he state of slavery does not prevent a man from giving [fatwas] or from relating traditions, since neither of these involves the exercise of authority."[20] By the same reasoning, it would follow that a woman may be a mufti, since women were prevented from holding judgeships due to the prohibition on their exercising binding authority over men. But al-Mawardi does not draw this conclusion.

C Judaism: the sage

Since Judaism in the formulation of the sages of late antiquity invokes the conception of revelation handed on as oral tradition, we cannot find it surprising that the sage who is in charge of the court and administration of the community by reason of his learning is held to constitute a living Torah, an embodiment of the Torah of Sinai. He is a sacred text, as much as the scroll of the Torah is a sacred text. For God did not resort solely to a book to convey and preserve the divine message. It was through teachings, which could be transmitted in more than a single form. Consequently, the sage could be received as a Torah and treated as such. An important and simple statement of that fact will prove the point. A sage himself was equivalent to a scroll of the Torah – a material, legal comparison, not merely a symbolic metaphor.

> He who sees a disciple of a sage who has died is as if he sees a scroll of the Torah that has been burned.
>
> (Y. Moed Qatan 3:7.X)

> R. Jacob bar Abayye in the name of R. Aha: "An elder who forgot his learning because of some accident which happened to him – they treat him with the sanctity owed to an ark [of the Torah]."
>
> (Y. Moed Qatan 3:1.XI)

The sage is therefore represented as equivalent to the scroll of the Torah, and, turning the statement around, the scroll of the Torah is realized in the person of the sage. The conception is not merely figurative or metaphorical, for, in both instances, actual behavior was affected. Still more to the point, what the sage *did* had the status of law; the sage was the model of the law, thus once again enjoyed the standing of the human embodiment of the Torah. Since the sage exercised supernatural power as a kind of living Torah, his very deeds served to reveal law, as much as his word expressed revelation. That is a formidable component of the argument that the sage embodied the Torah, another way of saying that the Torah was incarnated in the person of the sage.

The capacity of the sage himself to participate in the process of revelation is illustrated in two types of materials. First of all, tales told about rabbis' behavior on specific occasions are immediately translated into rules for the entire community to keep. Accordingly, he was a source not merely of good example but of prescriptive law.

X.   R. Aha went to Emmaus, and he ate dumpling [prepared by Samaritans].

Y.   R. Jeremiah ate leavened bread prepared by them.

Z.   R. Hezekiah ate their locusts prepared by them.

AA.   R. Abbahu prohibited Israelite use of wine prepared by them.

> (Y. Abodah Zarah 5:4:III)

Along with hundreds of parallels in the halakhic literature, these reports of what rabbis had said and done enjoyed the same authority, as statements of the law on eating what Samaritans cooked, as did citations of traditions in the names of the great authorities of old or of the day. What someone did served as a norm, if the person was a sage of sufficient standing. The precedent entered the Torah, and what a sage said became part of the oral component of the one whole Torah that God gave to Moses at Sinai.

Charismatic authority – authority by reason of the gifts of the soul and the spirit – takes many forms. By reason of the character of the Torah, oral and written, the model of charismatic authority coincided with the model of political authority, namely, the person of Moses, ruler and prophet at once. And what made Moses charismatic was his supernatural gifts, on the one side, and the repeated allegation that the laws that he set forth in the Torah were dictated to him by God on Mount Sinai: "The Lord spoke to Moses saying, speak to the children of Israel and say to them . . ." forming the definitive statement of matters. Not only so, but a long line of prophets from

Moses forward likewise spoke in God's name and on that basis demanded that people obey their instructions.

When it came to setting norms of behavior, however, Judaism emphasized the sages' power of rational analysis, rarely invoking direct revelation of the law. The reasons and traditions sages could muster decided matters, and a heavenly echo was explicitly dismissed as source of authority over the formation of the law. That view is stated explicitly in the famous story of the debate on the status, as to cultic cleanness of uncleanness, of the oven of Akhnai, an oven built in pieces joined by sand. The claim that it was subject to uncleanness rested on the view that the oven was complete, whole, and functioning, even though in form it was in pieces. The claim that it was not subject to uncleanness held that because the oven was broken down and not a complete utensil, it did not have the capacity to receive uncleanness. The course of the debate, not the law in particular, is what matters, and here is how the issue is represented. Two points are important. First, the echo may not intervene in the reasoned debate of sages. However, second, sages themselves possessed charismatic power, in the present context, the power to do supernatural deeds themselves. So the sages are represented as holy men, able to do miracles, but the law is set forth by sages in their capacity as masters of tradition and reasoning concerning tradition.

I.15 A. *There we have learned:* **If one cut [a clay oven] into parts and put sand between the parts,**

B. **R. Eliezer declares the oven broken-down and therefore insusceptible to uncleanness.**

C. **And sages declare it susceptible.**

D. **[59B] And this is what is meant by the oven of Akhnai [M. Kel. 5:10].**

E. *Why* the oven of Akhnai?

F. Said R. Judah said Samuel, "It is because they surrounded it with argument as with a snake and proved it was insusceptible to uncleanness."

G. *A Tannaite statement:*

H. On that day R. Eliezer produced all of the arguments in the world, but they did not accept them from him. So he said to them, "If the law accords with my position, this carob tree will prove it."

I. The carob was uprooted from its place by a hundred cubits – and some say, four hundred cubits.

J. They said to him, "There is no proof from a carob tree."

K. So he went and said to them, "If the law accords with my position, let the stream of water prove it."

L. The stream of water reversed flow.

M. They said to him, "There is no proof from a stream of water."

N. So he went and said to them, "If the law accords with my position, let the walls of the school house prove it."

O. The walls of the school house tilted toward falling.

P. R. Joshua rebuked them, saying to them, "If disciples of sages are contending with one another in matters of law, what business do you have?"

Q. They did not fall on account of the honor owing to R. Joshua, but they also did not straighten up on account of the honor owing to R. Eliezer, and to this day they are still tilted.

R. So he went and said to them, "If the law accords with my position, let the Heaven prove it!"

S. An echo came forth, saying, "What business have you with R. Eliezer, for the law accords with his position under all circumstances!"

T. R. Joshua stood up on his feet and said, "'It is not in heaven' (Deuteronomy 30:12)."

U. *What is the sense of, "'It is not in heaven' (Deuteronomy 30:12)"?*

V. Said R. Jeremiah, "[The sense of Joshua's statement is this:] For the Torah has already been given from Mount Sinai, so we do not pay attention to echoes, since you have already written in the Torah at Mount Sinai, 'After the majority you are to incline' (Exodus 23:2)."

W. *R. Nathan came upon Elijah and said to him, "What did the Holy One, blessed be he, do at that moment?"*

X. *He said to him, "He laughed and said, 'My children have overcome me, my children have overcome me!'"*

Y. They said:

Z. On that day they brought all of the objects that R. Eliezer had declared insusceptible to uncleanness and burned them in fire [as though they were unclean beyond all purification].

AA. They furthermore took a vote against him and cursed him.

BB. They said, "Who will go and inform him?"

CC. Said to them R. Aqiba, "I shall go and tell him, lest someone unworthy go and tell him, and he turn out to destroy the entire world [with his curse]."

DD. What did R. Aqiba do? He put on black garments and cloaked himself in a black cloak and took his seat before him at a distance of four cubits.

EE. Said to him R. Eliezer, "Aqiba, why is today different from all other days?"

FF. He said to him, "My lord, it appears to me that your colleagues are keeping distance from you."

GG. Then he too tore his garments and removed his shoes, moved his stool and sat down on the ground, with tears streaming from his eyes.

HH. The world was blighted: a third olives, a third wheat, a third barley.

II. And some say, also the dough in women's hands swelled up.

JJ. *A Tannaite authority taught:*

KK. There was a great disaster that day, for every place upon which R. Eliezer set his eyes was burned up.

LL. And also Rabban Gamaliel was coming by ship. A big wave arose to drown him.

MM. He said, "It appears to me that this is on account only of R. Eliezer b. Hyrcanus."

NN. He stood upon his feet and said, "Lord of the world, it is perfectly obvious to you that it was not for my own honor that I have acted, nor for the honor of the house of my father have I acted, but it was for the honor owing to you, specifically, so that dissension should not become rife in Israel."

OO. The sea subsided.

(Talmud of Babylonia Tractate Baba Mesia 59A–B)

Clearly, this passage treats Eliezer as a holy man who has remarkable powers to pray, bless, and curse. And people took account of those powers, but when it came to authority over the law the acknowledged charismatic gifts were null.

The sages' own mastery of traditions and power of reasoning then constitute sages' credentials; they are what qualifies the sage to rule on matters of halakhah. This picture of matters is expressed in so many words in a striking passage, which represents the sage as a party to the discussions of not only the earthly, but also the heavenly court. The sage now participates in that process of learning and practical reason that the study of the Torah inaugurates, and heaven – engaged in the same issues, confirming above what sages declare below – now does more than (merely) reach the same conclusions that sages have reached. It finds itself unable – so sages present matters – to conduct its affairs without the participation of sages themselves.

We find an explicit statement that it is reasoning about revelation, inclusive of the exegesis of the Written Torah, rather than new revelation, that forms the basis of the law. That is expressed at the conclusion of a debate on a problem that need not detain us here. At the end, an authority chooses between the contending positions, and this ruling is rejected in so many words:

2. A. Said R. Adda bar Ahbah said Rab, "The decided law is in accord with R. Hananiah b. Gamaliel."

B. Said R. Joseph, "Well, who has gone up to heaven and 'said' [that is, returned and made this definitive statement]?!"

143

C. Said to him Abbayye, "But then, in line with what R. Joshua b. Levi said, 'Three rulings were made by the earthly court, and the court on high concurred with what they had done,' ask the same question — who has gone up to heaven and returned and 'said' [made this definitive statement]?! Rather, we expound verses of Scripture [to reach dependable conclusions], and in this case, too, we expound verses of Scripture."

(Talmud of Babylonia Makkot 11b)

For our purpose the interesting point comes at 2.B, Joseph's (sarcastic) statement that he thinks it unlikely that sages possess direct knowledge of heaven's will in a given point of law. Abbayye's reply in the name of Joshua b. Levi provides us with the key to the way in which, in this Judaism, people know heaven's will: sages do not have to go to heaven on consultations because they have direct access to God's will as expressed in scripture. The Holy Spirit, or prophecy, gives way to another medium for communication between heaven and earth, although, as we shall see below, prophecy retains a critical position for itself. The issue then becomes subtle: at what point does heaven communicate for which purpose? And the first part of the answer is, when it comes to the determination of law, it is by the correct exposition of scripture that sages have an accurate and reliable picture of heaven's will. The upshot, in so many words, and in the exact context at hand, is then simply stated: study of the Torah for sages has now replaced prophecy. Here, masters of Torah enter into communion with heaven through their knowledge of the Torah, its traditions but also its logic.

The story that follows states in so many words that sages are required for heaven to do its work of Torah study. I take this statement to mean that prophecy ended in one form, continued in many forms, but found its true fulfillment in the mastery of the Torah that (some) sages accomplished. Not only so, but, as we saw in so many words, sages maintained that the court in heaven confirmed precisely what sages' court on earth determined, on the basis of the correct exposition of the Torah, to be the law. Each time sages declared the decided law emerging from controversy, Joseph's remark pertains: "Who has gone to heaven," and Abbayye's reply comes into play: the earthly court made its rulings, the heavenly court confirmed them. But sages went still further. They maintained that God in heaven studies the Torah just as they do, and that communication from heaven to earth takes place on that account. In so many words they specify that something very like prophecy takes place when the Torah is studied on earth as it is in heaven, and the following story is explicit in that regard.

I.39 A. *Said R. Kahana, R. Hama, son of the daughter of Hassa, told me that Rabbah b. Nahmani died in a persecution. {And here is the story:}"*

144

B. *Snitches maligned him to the government, saying, "There is a man among the Jews who keeps twelve thousand Israelites from paying the royal poll-tax for a month in the summer and for a month in the winter."*

C. *They sent a royal investigator {parastak} for him but he did not find him. He fled, going from Pumbedita to Aqra, from Aqra to Agma, from Agma to Shehin, from Shehin to Seripa, from Seripa to Ena Damim, from Ena Damim back to Pumbedita. In Pumbedita he found him.*

D. *The royal investigator happened by the inn where Rabbah was located. They brought him two glasses of liquor and then took away the tray {and this excited the ill-will of demons}. His face was turned backward. They said to him, "What shall we do with him? He is the king's man."*

E. *{Rabbah} said to them, "Bring him the tray again, and let him drink another cup, and then remove the tray, and he will get better."*

F. *They did just that, and he got better.*

G. *He said, "I am sure that the man whom I am hunting is here. He looked for him and found him."*

H. *He said, "I'm leaving here. If I am killed, I won't reveal a thing, but if they torture me, I'm going to squeal."*

I. *They brought him to him and he put him in a room and locked the door on him. But {Rabbah} sought mercy, the wall fell down, and he fled to Agma. He was in session on the trunk of a palm and studying.*

J. *Now they were debating in the session in the firmament the following subject:* **If the bright spot preceded the white hair, he is unclean, and if the white hair preceded the bright spot, he is clean. [The Mishnah paragraph continues: and if it is a matter of doubt, he is unclean. And R. Joshua was in doubt] [M. Neg. 4:11F-H]** –

K. The Holy One, blessed be he, says, "It is clean."

L. *And the entire session in the firmament say, "Unclean."*

M. *They said, "Who is going to settle the question? It is Rabbah b. Nahmani."*

N. For said Rabbah b. Nahmani, "I am absolutely unique in my knowledge of the marks of skin-disease that is unclean and in the rules of uncleanness having to do with the corpse in the tent."

O. *They sent an angel for him, but the angel of death could not draw near to him, since his mouth did not desist from repeating his learning. But in the meanwhile a wind blew and caused a rustling in the bushes, so he thought it was a troop of soldiers. He said, "Let me die but not be handed over to the kingdom."*

P. *When he was dying, he said,* "It is clean, it is clean." An echo came forth and said, "Happy are you, Rabbah bar Nahmani, that your body is clean, and your soul has come forth in cleanness."

Q. *A note fell down from heaven in Pumbedita:* "Rabbah bar Nahmani has been invited to the session that is on high."

R. *Abbayye, Raba, and all the rabbis came forth to tend to his corpse, but they did not know where he was located. They went to Agma and saw birds hovering over and overshadowing the corpse. "This proves that he is there."*

S.   *They mourned him for three days and three nights. A note fell down: "Whoever refrains [from the mourning] will be excommunicated." They mourned for him for seven days. A note fell down: "Go to your homes in peace."*

T.   *The day on which he died a strong wind lifted a Tai-Arab who was riding on a camel from one side of the Pappa canal and threw him down onto the other side. He said, "What is this?"*

U.   *They told him, "Rabbah bar Nahmani has died."*

V.   *He said before him, "Lord of the world, the whole world is yours, and Rabbah bar Nahmani is yours. You are Rabbah's, and Rabbah is yours. Why are you destroying the world on his account?" The wind subsided.*

(Babylonian Talmud Tractate Baba Mesia 86A)

It would be difficult to find more plainly stated the view that God does communicate with sages; the communication is explicit and substantive, and the medium of communication, if not prophecy, is then comparable to prophecy: "the Lord spoke to . . ." is here replaced by a letter falling to earth. But what is communicated is a matter of halakhah, and what is required, in particular, is the reasoning behind the rule. The modes of thought – God's and the sage's – are the same, a single rationality joining heaven and earth.

The Torah, then, is the medium for communication from heaven to earth, not only way back in the time of Moses, but also in the here and now of sages' own day. The sages' knowledge and acumen link their minds to God's. And it is God's intellect that animates the whole, that is revealed in the words of the Torah. Were we to close at this point, the resulting account would distort the actualities of rabbinic Judaism. We should give the impression that only intelligence and learning formed valued credentials in the legal system of the Torah. But sages accorded recognition not only to the charisma accruing to mastery of the Torah, but also, and especially, to the gifts of the spirit attained by unlettered people, not only men but also women. Indeed, at the very heart and center of Judaism we find the systemic reversal – from Torah to ignorance, from man to woman – which places above sages' Torah learning a remarkable gift of character and conscience, the gift of humility and self-sacrifice. That gift represents a spiritual power far above the power of the Torah. It is portrayed in a set of stories that scarcely require exposition, so unmediated is the power of the narrative.

The stories address the question of how simple folk are able to perform miracles that learned rabbis cannot carry out, and they deal with the conception of zekhut, the word that stands for the empowerment, of a supernatural character, that derives from the virtue of one's ancestry or from one's own virtuous deeds of a very particular order. If we wanted a single word to represent charismatic power and moral authority, that word for rabbinic

Judaism would have to serve: that moral authority is attained through acts of will consisting of submission, on one's own volition, to the will of heaven. Such acts performed by the holy people endowed Israel with a lien and entitlement to heaven. When done by individuals, these same types of acts of omission or commission provoke heaven to acts of special favor – prayers are answered, miracles are done. Here is moral authority signified by charismatic power, set forth in the purest sense: what we cannot by will impose, we can by will evoke. What we cannot accomplish through coercion, we can achieve through submission. God will do for us what we cannot do for ourselves, when we do for God what God cannot make us do. In a wholly concrete and tangible sense, love God with all the heart, the soul, the might we have. Here is the clearest doctrine of charismatic authority that rabbinic Judaism puts forth, and it is a charisma not attached to Torah or assigned to judges.

Even though a man was degraded, one action sufficed to win for him that heavenly glory to which rabbis in lives of Torah study aspired. The mark of the system's integration around zekhut lies in its insistence that all Israelites, not only sages, could gain zekhut for themselves (and their descendants). A single remarkable deed, exemplary for its deep humanity, sufficed to win for an ordinary person the zekhut that elicits supernatural favor enjoyed by some rabbis on account of their Torah study. The centrality of zekhut in the systemic structure, the critical importance of the heritage of virtue together with its supernatural entitlements therefore emerge in a striking claim. Even though a man was degraded, one action sufficed to win for him that heavenly glory to which rabbis in general aspired. The rabbinical storyteller whose writing we shall consider assuredly identifies with this lesson, since it is the point of his story and its climax.

In all three instances that follow, defining what the individual must do to gain zekhut, the point is that the deeds of the heroes of the story make them worthy of having their prayers answered, which is a mark of the working of zekhut. It is deeds beyond the strict requirements of the Torah, and even the limits of the law altogether, that transform the hero into a holy man, whose holiness served just like that of a sage marked as such by knowledge of the Torah. The following stories should not be understood as expressions of the mere sentimentality of the clerks concerning the lower orders, for they deny in favor of a single action of surpassing power sages' lifelong devotion to what the sages held to be the highest value, knowledge of the Torah:

F. A certain man came before one of the relatives of R. Yannai. He said to him, "Rabbi, attain zekhut through me [by giving me charity]."

G. He said to him, "And didn't your father leave you money?"

H. He said to him, "No."

I. He said to him, "Go and collect what your father left in deposit with others."

J. He said to him, "I have heard concerning property my father deposited with others that it was gained by violence [so I don't want it]."

K. He said to him, "You are worthy of praying and having your prayers answered."

(Taanit 1:4.I)

The point of K, of course, is self-evidently a reference to the possession of entitlement to supernatural favor, and it is gained, we see, through deeds that the law of the Torah cannot require but must favor: what one does on one's own volition, beyond the measure of the law. Here I see the opposite of sin. A sin is what one has done by one's own volition beyond all limits of the law. So an act that generates zekhut for the individual is the counterpart and opposite: what one does by one's own volition that is also beyond all requirements of the law. The passage records another such narrative and then proceeds as follows:

Q. In a dream of R. Abbahu, Mr. Pentakaka ["Five sins"] appeared, who prayed that rain would come, and it rained. R. Abbahu sent and summoned him. He said to him, "What is your trade?"

R. He said to him, "Five sins does that man [I] do every day, [for I am a pimp:] hiring whores, cleaning up the theater, bringing home their garments for washing, dancing, and performing before them."

S. He said to him, "And what sort of decent thing have you ever done?"

T. He said to him, "One day that man [I] was cleaning the theater, and a woman came and stood behind a pillar and cried. I said to her, 'What's with you?' And she said to me, 'That woman's [my] husband is in prison, and I wanted to see what I can do to free him,' so I sold my bed and cover, and I gave the proceeds to her. I said to her, 'Here is your money, free your husband, but do not sin.'"

U. He said to him, "You are worthy of praying and having your prayers answered."

Q moves us still further, since the named man has done everything sinful that one can do, and, more to the point, he does it every day. So the singularity of the act of zekhut, which suffices if done only one time, encompasses its power to outweigh a life of sin – again, an act of zekhut as the mirror-image and opposite of sin. Here again, the single act of saving a woman from a "fate worse than death" has sufficed.

V. A pious man from Kefar Imi appeared [in a dream] to the rabbis. He prayed for rain and it rained. The rabbis went up to him. His householders told them that he was sitting on a hill. They went out to him, saying to him, "Greetings," but he did not answer them.

W. He was sitting and eating, and he did not say to them, "You break bread too."

X.   When he went back home, he made a bundle of faggots and put his cloak on top of the bundle [instead of on his shoulder].

Y.   When he came home, he said to his household [wife], "These rabbis are here [because] they want me to pray for rain. If I pray and it rains, it is a disgrace for them, and if not, it is a profanation of the Name of Heaven. But come, you and I will go up [to the roof] and pray. If it rains, we shall tell them, 'We are not worthy to pray and have our prayers answered.'"

Z.   They went up and prayed and it rained.

AA.   They came down to them [and asked], "Why have the rabbis troubled themselves to come here today?"

BB.   They said to him, "We wanted you to pray so that it would rain."

CC.   He said to them, "Now do you really need my prayers? Heaven already has done its miracle."

DD.   They said to him, "Why, when you were on the hill, did we say hello to you, and you did not reply?"

EE.   He said to them, "I was then doing my job. Should I then interrupt my concentration [on my work]?"

FF.   They said to him, "And why, when you sat down to eat, did you not say to us 'You break bread too'?"

GG.   He said to them, "Because I had only my small ration of bread. Why would I have invited you to eat by way of mere flattery [when I knew I could not give you anything at all]?"

HH.   They said to him, "And why when you came to go down, did you put your cloak on top of the bundle?"

II.   He said to them, "Because the cloak was not mine. It was borrowed for use at prayer. I did not want to tear it."

JJ.   They said to him, "And why, when you were on the hill, did your wife wear dirty clothes, but when you came down from the mountain, did she put on clean clothes?"

KK.   He said to them, "When I was on the hill, she put on dirty clothes, so that no one would gaze at her. But when I came home from the hill, she put on clean clothes, so that I would not gaze on any other woman."

LL.   They said to him, "It is well that you pray and have your prayers answered."

The pious man, finally, enjoys the recognition of the sages by reason of his lien upon heaven, able as he is to pray and bring rain. What has so endowed him with zekhut? Acts of punctiliousness of a moral order: concentrating on his work, avoiding an act of dissimulation, integrity in the disposition of a borrowed object, his wife's concern not to attract other men, and her equal concern to make herself attractive to her husband. None of these stories refers explicitly to zekhut; all of them tell us about what it means to enjoy not an entitlement by inheritance but a lien accomplished by one's own supererogatory acts of restraint. In the end, it is not only, or mainly, Torah study that endows a person with charismatic power. The principals of the story are not the men who can pray and have their prayers answered, but the women who are the heroines but, even in the stories, take a secondary role.

What we see is a careful differentiation between the qualifications for law-enforcement, which encompass piety, and the power of all persons, women as much as men, ignorant as much as learned, to attain piety. In Judaism the pious are marked by gifts of the spirit involving remarkable self-sacrifice and generosity. But when it comes to the courts, the pious judge must be a man of acknowledged learning, probity, and intelligence. These represent the particular gifts of the spirit that qualify the personnel of the courts of Israel, the holy people, because, in these particular capacities, man gains access to the intellect and will of God. Much of the later history of normative Judaism spins out the tension between learning and charisma, gifts of intellect and gifts of the soul and the spirit.

D Conclusions

In both Judaism and Islam, the position of the judge is one that requires intelligence, learning, and integrity. In Judaism, however, there is far greater emphasis on spiritual gifts than there is in Islam. The notion of zekhut, supernatural power resulting from extreme piety (occasionally so intense it could be inherited), has a parallel in Islam. *Barakah* in Islam refers to that elusive quality of being blessed, often with the gift of supernatural abilities, believed to result from an individual's (or his ancestors') submission to the divine will. But this capacity is not one associated with legal scholars or judges, as it is in Judaism. Barakah is a feature of folk Islam. Accounts of the miraculous wisdom and deeds of various Sufi leaders and tribal elders, for example, are extremely popular in rural communities, where they are taken as the basis for the legitimacy of authority. Legal authorities, whether scholars, judges, or muftis, must meet, above all, the intellectual requirements established by such authorities as al-Shafi'i and al-Mawardi. In Judaism, the sage must have mastery of the traditions, but his role as the embodiment of Torah is far beyond that accorded legal scholars in Islam. In Islam, that role is reserved for the Prophet alone.

How to account for the difference? In Islam the Prophet is incomparable and unique. In Rabbinic Judaism, Moses is called "our rabbi," and he is the model of how rabbis are to conduct themselves. So sages strive to become like God through the model of Moses, "our rabbi." Moses is not unique but exemplary; only God is unique. But, more to the point, sages participate in the formation of the Torah, their processes of analysis, argument, and reasoning permit them – as we saw in an earlier chapter – even to engage in debate with God Himself. So while not all sages are described as holy men, to qualify as a sage every aspirant must master those processes of rationality and logic that to begin with bring the Torah into being. The sage participates in the process of revelation, using his powers of reasoning to extend and amplify the Torah. In so doing he is assigned gifts of a sacred order, because to begin with, the very processes of God's reasoning in framing and giving the Torah are accessible to the sage.

Overall, there are two key differences between the Judaic and Islamic legal structures. The first is structural. While both systems incorporate written and oral material, in Islamic law the characteristics of literate culture predominate, although, as we have seen, some oral patterns are still evident. Judaic law, by contrast, retains the characteristics of oral culture. That is why the debates in the Talmud can and must be reconstructed, using the hints of the written record to regain access to the processes of thought and reasoning behind a given debate. Talmudic culture is not only oral, it is personal, in that the Talmud cannot be merely "read" as a book is read but must be "learned" with a master who himself is a disciple; so we deal with a continuing tradition that endures in the very persons of the sages, the masters and their disciples, tracing themselves upward to Sinai, to Moses, God's disciple.

This distinction in the status of legal scholars is a reflection of that difference. In oral cultures, authority rests primarily with individuals who may consult texts but whose authority transcends those texts, while in literate cultures, authority rests primarily with texts. Thus, in Islam, individuals derive authority by virtue of their relationship with or mastery of the texts. In the Judaic culture of the Talmud, by contrast, individuals derive authority by reason of mastery of the texts in a relationship of discipleship.

The second key difference between Judaic and Islamic law is an ideological or, better, theological, one, and it is also evident in the differences between the Judaic and Islamic structures of legal authority. In the Islamic system, care is taken to disqualify non-Muslims from holding religious authority over Muslims. This is important because Islamic law does make provisions for non-Muslims. Non-Muslims may choose to subject themselves to their own legal systems, although they are given the option to submit to Islamic legal authorities. In the Judaic system, by contrast, no specific requirements that legal authorities be Judaic are evident. It is taken for granted that sages and their disciples derive from that holy people, Israel, to whom God gave the Torah at Sinai. While providing commandments for gentiles to obey, the massive corpus of Judaic law is for Jews alone. In concrete terms, seven commandments are assigned to the children of Noah, but 613 are assigned to the children of Abraham. While details of the halakhah take account of the possibility of gentiles' coming under the authority of Judaic courts, the anticipated reality is different. The Judaic legal system rarely conceives that gentiles will come under the law; no court of Judaism had, or anticipated having, the power to subject gentiles to the law of Judaism, even in connection with the seven obligations that apply to the children of Noah, that is, to gentiles after the Flood.

This distinction between the two systems reflects the enormous difference between the two communities' perceptions of their roles. As we have noted, the Judaic community's self-perception is of a people chosen by God to receive Torah and live within it. For Judaism, the moment of universal knowledge of the one and only God is prayed for; it will take place at the end of time. So Judaic universalism is eschatological. The Muslim community's perception is that of an expansive community, living in accordance with Shariʿah and bound by the responsibility to spread its way of life ultimately to the entire human race. Islamic universalism is immediate and shades over into the concrete and the political. So both monotheist religions address all of humanity and aspire to reveal the one, unique God to every people and nation. But while Judaism has prayed for that end – the restoration of humanity to God – Islam has acted, in this world, to bring it about.

Despite these two differences, a study of Judaic and Islamic legal systems reveals a significant overlap in structure and category formations. Yet this difference in self-perception will account for categorical differences, as we shall see in the remaining chapters.

6

DISPROPORTIONS

In the foregoing chapters we have compared the structures of legal systems and given examples of congruent category formations, for example, shared categories of holy books of law and of theological lawyers, characteristic of both religious traditions. What results have we produced up to this point? In general outline, we have shown that that congruence is proportionate as well as topical and in important ways also substantive; to the category formations considered until now each religio-legal system assigns an equivalently formidable corpus of law. Both systems appeal to law as much as to theology to accomplish their goals. Both concur that God has plans for the social order of the faithful. Both agree upon the types of writing that convey those plans. And both put forth religious virtuosi possessed of a common core of qualifications. We might also have identified, as shared category formations, a variety of specific topics of public piety. For example, both Islam and Judaism legislate extensively concerning prayer, ablutions, fasting, and the family. Islam and Judaism agree that betrothal, marriage, inheritance, and divorce form primary concerns of their respective religious law, as does philanthropy, defining as a principal religious obligation ongoing support for the poor.[1] In all of these category formations the two religio-legal systems more or less match, even though, in details, they differ – and are bound to differ.

But the circles of Islam and of Judaism are only partially concentric, and now we turn to two ways in which each religion defines its own categories in its own way, so that comparison and contrast expose disproportions. The first way, set forth here, involves topics common to both religious traditions, in which one tradition assigns importance to a subject treated as routine and of minor consequence by the other.

In dealing with disproportions, the second way entails our identifying comparable categories; that is, finding out what functionally compares on the one side to some other, different category altogether on the other side. That involves a much more subtle exercise in taste and judgment, which we do carry out when we turn to the matter of sacred time in Islam and in Judaism. We here impose our own theoretical category – sacred time – and ask how each religious tradition legislates for an enchanted occasion delineated by the movement of heavenly bodies ("time"). When we do, we come up with a category of Islam that barely intersects with what we deem its counterpart in Judaism. Specifically, to find a counterpart to the Judaic Sabbath we turn to the Islamic pilgrimage – hardly an obvious point of comparison at all. Then, in Chapter 7, we take up categories important to the one religious tradition that have no counterpart at all in the other.

A Temple law and sacrifice

In one kind of disproportion, Judaism and Islam talk about the same subject but not with the same intensity. That is to say, one religion accords enormous importance to a topic that the other religion treats casually or unsystematically or, in any event, not as a principal component of the law. Judaism, for example, treats the temple and sacrifice law in great detail, while Islam has no temple and its treatment of animal sacrifice is minimal.

1 Temple law and sacrifice in Judaism

If cultic purity forms a principal concern of the halakhah, that is because the blood cult – sacrifices, the priesthood and their families, marriages, and income, the temple and its layout and upkeep, all unique to Jerusalem – defines the critical locus of God's relationship to man. That is why, by contrast to Islam, a disproportionate part of the halakhah is devoted to temple law and sacrifice. Two of the Mishnah's six divisions are devoted to the Temple of Jerusalem and the conduct of its sacrificial rites, the fifth, Holy Things, to the everyday procedures, and the sixth, Purities, to the sources of uncleanness that can disqualify the temple rites. The first division, on Agriculture, also pays ample attention to the upkeep of the temple, to its personnel, to provision of rations for its priesthood, and to making sure that a steady supply of produce reaches the Jerusalem markets, so keeping food prices low. The second division, Appointed Times, treats as the focus of interest on the observance of certain holy days the conduct of the temple sacrifices. The Day of Atonement, for example, is set forth in a systematic account of how the sacrifices ordained in Leviticus, Chapter 16, are to be carried out. So in proportion, in its classical statement, the halakhah devotes about half of its entire discussion to temple law, sacrifice, and the maintenance of the cult.

The sort of law that is set forth, the detail that is encompassed in the exegesis – these are difficult to summarize in a few words. It suffices to present two representative examples of the halakhah of sacrifice in the Temple of Jerusalem:

2:1 A. All animal offerings, the blood of which (1) a non-priest, (2) [a priest] mourning his next of kin, (3) a [priest who was] tebul yom,

(4) [a priest] lacking proper garments, (5) a [priest] whose atonement is not yet complete, (6) a [priest] whose hands and feet are not washed, (7) [an] uncircumcised [priest], (9) [a priest] who was sitting down, (10) [a priest] standing on utensils, on a beast, on the feet of his fellow, received, has he rendered invalid.

B. [If] he received it in his left hand, he has rendered [the sacrifice] invalid.

C. [If] it [the blood] was poured onto the floor and one [then] collected it, it is invalid.

D. [If] one [who was fit] sprinkled it on the ramp, not by the [altar] base –

E. [if] one sprinkled those [drops of blood] which are to be sprinkled below, above,

F. and those which are to be sprinkled above, below,

G. those which are to be sprinkled inside, outside,

H. and those which are to be sprinkled outside, inside –

I. it is invalid.

(Mishnah-tractate Zebahim 2:1)

The rule covers the status of the person who collects the blood of an animal that has been slaughtered as a sacrifice. The offering is invalidated if the priest in any way lacks the proper credentials, garments, cultic status as to ritual cleanness, and the like. The blood has to be sprinkled properly at a section of the high altar, above or below a red line painted around the altar, as the particular sacrifice required. Above all, the officiating priest had to carry out the action with the proper motivation. If he slaughtered the beast or did other of the key-actions with inappropriate intentionality, the act is null:

4:6 A. For the sake of six things is the animal offering sacrificed: (1) for the sake of the animal offering, (2) for the sake of the one who sacrifices it, (3) for the sake of the Lord, (4) for the sake of the altar fires, (5) for the sake of the odor, (6) for the sake of the pleasing smell.

B. And as to the sin offering and the guilt offering, for the sake of the sin expiated thereby.

(Mishnah-tractate Zebahim 4:6)

Clearly, a complex web of relationships is spun around the altar and its offerings, scripture being explicit that God has commanded the building of the one and the provision of the other. How are we to account for the enormous proportion of the halakhah that is occupied by sacrifice?

The answer derives from the principal concerns of the system as a whole, which identifies the Holy Land, called "the Land of Israel," as the surrogate and future Garden of Eden, and Israel, the people, as the surrogate and

155

replacement of the First Man. Israel through submission to God's will corrects the catastrophic error and sin of Adam, committed by his rebellion against God's will. Now at the Temple in Jerusalem, God and Holy Israel meet. That is the highest point on earth, where God receives His share of the natural gifts of the Holy Land: meat, grain, wine, and olive oil; and where through the presentation of these gifts, the Israelite fulfills his obligations to God, inclusive of atoning for sin. It is in the temple that in the here and now Israel exhibits before God its punctilious acceptance of God's will, serving God in exactly the way that God, in the Torah, has commanded. The sin of man – a sin of rebellion against God's will – is atoned for in the Temple.

Take, for example, the elaborate garments of the high priest and why the law takes so seriously that the priest be properly garbed. The garments that the priest wore signified atonement and forgiveness for sins of various classifications, so says Song R. XLVIII:v.3: The high priest serves in eight garments, and an ordinary priest in four: tunic, underpants, head-covering, and girdle. The high priest also wears the breastplate, apron, upper garment, and frontlet (M. Yoma 7:5A–C). The tunic would atone for bloodshed: "And they dipped the coat in the blood" (Genesis 37:31). Some say, "It atoned for those who wear mixed varieties: 'And he made him a coat of many colors' (Gensis 37:3)." The underpants atone for fornication: "And you shall make them linen underpants to cover the flesh of their nakedness" (Exodus 27:42). The head-covering atones for arrogance: "And he set the head-covering on his head" (Leviticus 8:9). For what did the girdle atone? For the double-dealers. Others say, "For thieves." The one who says that it was for thieves maintains that view because the garment was hollow, standing for thieves who work in hiding. The one who says that it was for the double-dealers is in accord with that which R. Levi said, "It was thirty-two cubits long, and he would twist it on either side." The breastplate would atone for those who pervert justice: "And you shall put in the breastplate of judgment the Urim and the Thummim" (Exodus 28:30). The apron ephod would atone for idolatry: "And without ephod or teraphim" (Hosea 3:4). The upper garment robe would atone for slander. The frontlet would atone for impudence. Some say, "It was for blasphemy." The one who says it was for impudence cites the following verse of scripture: "And it shall be upon Aaron's forehead" (Exodus 28:38), and also, "Yet you had a harlot's forehead" (Jeremiah 3:3). The one who says it was for blasphemy cites the following verse of scripture: "And it shall always be upon his forehead" (Exodus 28:38) alongside "And the stone sank into his forehead" (1 Samuel 17:49). The elaborate corpus of law devoted to the temple and its rites proves indicative of the importance accorded to these matters by the governing theology of Judaism in its classical statement.

2 Sacrifice in Islam

Since there is no temple or synagogue in Islam, there is no category of law concerning them. Muslims pray in mosques (*masajid*), which are "places of prostration"; that is, places of prayer (which involves prostration). The prescribed five-times daily prayer (*salat*) may take place in virtually any available place, inside or outside, provided it is clean. What are at issue in fulfilling the duty for prescribed prayer are the ritual purity of the believer, having the proper intention, the time (indicated by the position of the sun) and the direction of prayer (*qibla*), not the building. Only the Friday midday prayer is supposed to be performed communally (*salat al-jum'a*), at least by the males of the community.

The treatment of sacrifice is more extensive in Islamic law but, again, is not elaborate. Sacrifice is not a significant category; the subject is treated primarily within the context of the required pilgrimage, discussed below. The important issues concerning animal sacrifice, moreover, are generally related to concerns for purity and hygiene. Thus, animals must be slaughtered properly, beginning with their dedication to the one God (and not to the other deities popular in pre-Islamic Arabia). The jugular vein must be cut and the blood drained from the animal. Beyond that, only healthy and sound animals should be offered for sacrifice:

> Yahya related to me from Malik from Amr ibn al-Harith from 'Ubayd ibn Fayruz form al-Bara' ibn 'Azib that the Messenger of Allah, may Allah bless him and grant him peace, was asked what animals should be avoided as sacrifices. He indicated with his hand and said, "Four." Al-Bara' pointed with his hand and said, "My hand is shorter than the hand of the Messenger of Allah, may Allah bless him and grant him peace. A lame animal whose lameness is evident, a one-eyed animal which is clearly one-eyed, an animal which is clearly ill, and an emaciated animal with no fat on it."[2]

The other rules concerning animal sacrifice have to do with consuming, sharing, and storing the meat. Animals sacrificed during the Hajj (pilgrimage), for example, must be shared with neighbors and poor people. According to Malik:

> Yahya related to me from Malik from Abu'z-Zubayr al-Makki from Jabir ibn 'Abdullah that the Messenger of Allah, may Allah bless him and grant him peace, forbade that the meat from sacrificial animals be eaten after three days. Then later he said, "Eat, give [charity], provide for yourselves and store up."
> Yahya related to me from Malik from 'Abdullah ibn Abi Bakr that

ʿAbdullah ibn Waqiq said, "The Messenger of Allah, may Allah bless him and grant him peace, forbade eating the meat from sacrifical animals after three days."

ʿAbdullah ibn Abi Bakr continued, "I mentioned that to ʿAmra bint ʿAbd ar-Rahman, and she affirmed that he had spoken the truth as she had heard ʿAʾisha, the wife of the Prophet, may Allah bless him and grant him peace, say, 'Some people from the desert came at the time of the sacrifice in the time of the Messenger of Allah, may Allah bless him and grant him peace, so the Messenger of Allah, may Allah bless him and grant him peace, said, "Store up for three days, and give what is left over as [charity]." ' "

She said that afterwards someone said to the Messenger of Allah, may Allah bless him and grant him peace, that people had been accustomed to make use of their sacrificial animals, melting the fat and curing the skins. The Messenger of Allah, may Allah bless him and grant him peace, said, "I only forbade you for the sake of people who were coming to you. Eat, give [charity], and store up."

By these people, he meant the poor people who were coming to Madina.[3]

Here, then, we see that what is central to the classical legal system of Judaism is peripheral to the Islamic counterpart. Now we turn to a case of the opposite: importance in Islamic, categorical unimportance in Judaism.

B Slave laws in Islam and in Judaism

Islam richly elaborates the law of slavery, treating those categories involving slaves as autonomous and devoting detailed analysis to its problematic in other categories. Judaism, by contrast, sets forth laws about the slave but does not focus on that category and contains no counterpart to Islamic law's dense and subtle consideration of its ramifications. Consequently, while the legal systems intersect on a common topic, the importance accorded to that topic by the one is not matched by the other's view of matters.

1 Slave laws in Islam

Islamic law treats the category formation of the slave in a systematic way. The socioeconomic system in which Islam developed was one of which slavery was an integral part. Islam intervened in this system, most obviously with its insistence on the equality of all human beings in the sight of God. But rather than prohibit slavery altogether, which would have required an overhaul of the economic and social structure of Arabian society, the Qurʾan established the principle of human dignity and, based on that principle, made recommendations for the treatment of slaves:

We have surely created the human being in difficulties.
Does he think that no one has power over him?
He says, "I have spent a great deal of money."
Does he think that no one sees him?
. . . And We have indicated to him two ways.
But he did not attempt the high road.
And what indicates the high road?
Freeing a slave
Or feeding on a day of hunger
an orphaned member of the family
or a poor person in trouble.

(Sura 90:5–17)

Clearly, there is recognition that slavery is a source of inequality to be corrected, just as are hunger and being orphaned. Righteousness consists in making effort to overcome such evils. The Qur'an therefore establishes an ideal which believers must strive to achieve. Indeed, it claims that one demonstrates one's "islam," one's commitment to the will of God, precisely by engaging in such efforts.

While the Qur'an does not prohibit slavery outright, it does establish laws for personal piety, and prescribes the emancipation of slaves as expiation for transgression of divine laws:

God will not hold you to empty oaths, but He will hold you to serious oaths. The expiation for them is to feed ten poor people with the average of what you feed your families, or to clothe them, or to free a slave. But whoever does not find the means shall fast for three days. That is the expiation for your oaths you have sworn.

(Sura 5:90)

Thus, freeing slaves is not only a means to demonstrate awareness of and submission to the divine will, but it is one of the required ways to make up for transgressions. Again, charity and freeing slaves are established as means of creating the society envisioned by the Qur'an, and the Qur'an in this instance establishes as law the means of achieving that goal. Freeing of a slave is also established by the Qur'an as a recompense for mistreating wives: "God has heard the words of the one who pleads with you about her husband and complains to God. Indeed, God is all-seeing and all-hearing" (Sura 58:2). The verse goes on to describe the complaint of women about husbands who divorce them and those who divorce them and then revoke their divorces. The Qur'an prescribes for such offenses the freeing of a slave, or fasting for two months, or feeding sixty poor people. It is interesting to note that the practice of buying a slave in order to fulfill the obligation to free a slave is expressly prohibited. The legal sources also deem it preferable to free a Muslim slave:

159

Malik said, "The best of what I have heard on the obligation of freeing slaves is that it is not permitted to free a Christian or a Jew to fulfill it. . . . There is no harm in freeing a Christian, Jew, or Magian voluntarily because Allah, the Blessed, the Exalted, says in His Book, '. . . either as a favour then or by ransom' (Sura 47:4). The favour is setting free."

Malik said, "As for obligations of freeing slaves which Allah has mentioned in the Book, one only frees a believing slave for them."

Malik said, "It is like that when feeding poor people for [expiation]. One must only feed Muslims and one does not feed anyone outside the [religion] of Islam."[4]

Classical Islamic law incorporates the Qur'an's prescriptions and thus introduces several categories of slaves. The general category consists of those who were slaves at the time Islam was introduced as well as their offspring; that is, those born into slavery; and those non-Muslims captured in war or war zones. Islamic law stipulates that slaves have rights. Some of those rights are of the order of the rights of a minor within the family, as Joseph Schacht notes: "[T]he Islamic law of slavery is patriarchal and belongs more to the law of family than to the law of property."[5] Slaves must not be mistreated or overworked, and must be properly maintained. They may sue for failure to abide by those rules and the court may free the slave if the owner is in flagrant violation of the law. Thus, according to the earliest surviving legislation on the matter, "Malik related to me that he had heard that a slave-girl who had been beaten by her master with a red-hot iron came to 'Umar ibn al-Khattab and he set her free."[6] Further, slaves may own property, including owning their own slaves, and may marry with the permission of the owner; they may also be given in marriage by the owner without their permission. Slaves' spouses and children are not treated as property of the slave but as individuals with their own rights. Thus, when a slave is sold, his spouse and children are not. According to Malik, "[W]hen a slave is sold and the person who buys him stipulates the inclusion of his property, his children are not included in that property."[7]

Also according to the model of family law, slaves are treated like minors in criminal offenses and are not punished to the full extent of the law for hudud offenses, such as theft and fornication or false accusations of forbidden sexual relations. Similarly, slaves may be delegated by their owners to contract business under specific circumstances. There are variations on the family model, of course. The owner is responsible for damages incurred by the slave, but may take the slave's property for it or even offer the slave in payment. Female slaves become the concubines of their owners, but the law clearly expresses a bias in favor of freedom. For example, if a female slave bears a child fathered by the owner, the child is free and the mother (*umm walad*) becomes free upon the death of the master. Thus: "Malik related to me from

Nafi' from 'Abdullah ibn 'Umar that 'Umar ibn al-Khattab said, 'If a slave-girl gives birth to a child by her master, he must not sell her, give her away, or bequeath her. He enjoys her and when he dies, she is free.' "[8]

Reflecting the Qur'an's recommendation that righteous people free slaves, classical Islamic law offers legislation regarding the freeing of slaves under various circumstances and the status of freed slaves. For example, many slaves were co-owned. Questions therefore arose about what to do if one owner wanted to free the slave, but the other owner(s) did not. The recommendation is that the owner who wishes to free the slave buy out the co-owner's share and then free the slave, if he can afford to do so:

> Malik related to me from Nafi' from 'Abdullah ibn 'Umar that the Messenger of Allah, may Allah be pleased with him, said, "If a man frees his share of a slave and has enough money to cover the full price of the slave justly evaluated, he must buy out his partners so that the slave is completely freed. If he doesn't have the money, then he partially frees him."[9]

Legislation is also offered to protect slaves from manipulation of the law of manumission. The possibility of temporarily freeing a slave, to enable him to testify on behalf of the owner, for example (since, as we saw, only free people may testify concerning Muslims), is dealt with:

> Malik said, "A master who frees a slave of his and settles his emancipation so that his testimony is permitted, his inviolability is complete, and his right to inherit confirmed, cannot impose stipulations on him like those imposed on a slave about property or service, nor can he get him to do anything connected with slavery because the Messenger of Allah, may Allah bless him and grant him peace, said, "If a man frees his share of a slave and has enough money to cover the entire price of the slave justly evaluated for him, he must give his partners their shares so that the slave is completely free."
>
> Malik commented, "If he owns the slave completely, it is more proper to free him completely and not mingle any slavery with it."[10]

The practicality of Islamic law concerning slavery is expressed in a discussion about the impermissibility of freeing all of one's slaves on one's deathbed if one has no other property to leave one's family. While freeing slaves when on one's deathbed is recommended, it is mandated that one provide for one's family through specified inheritance shares (see Chapter 7), a prior responsibility in Islamic law. Therefore:

> Malik related to me from Yahya ibn Sa'id and somebody else from al-Hasan ibn Abi al-Hasan al-Basri and from Muhammad ibn Sirin

that a man in the time of the Messenger of Allah, may Allah bless him and grant him peace, freed six of his slaves while he was dying. The Messenger of Allah, may Allah bless him and grant him peace, drew lots between them and freed a third of those slaves.

Malik added that he had heard that the man did not have any property besides them.[11]

Al-Shafi'i expounds on this well-known case:

We have found that the Apostle made a decision [concerning] six slaves owned by a man who possessed no other property and who had set them free at the time of his death. The Prophet divided them into three groups, freeing two [slaves] and leaving four in slavery. . . . Thus the indication of the sunna, as provided in the tradition of 'Imran b. Husayn, is that the Prophet's decree to free [the slaves] at the time of death constitutes a bequest. Since the person who freed the slaves was an Arab – and the Arabs own foreign [slaves] with whom they had no blood relationship – the Prophet allowed a bequest to them to be valid. This [precedent] indicates that if a bequest in favor of persons other than relatives were void, it would be void concerning the freed slaves [too], as they were not blood relatives of [the man] who set them free.

It also indicates that the bequest of the deceased cannot exceed one third of his estate; that what exceeds one third is illegal; that bequests in favor of freeing slaves [already] earning money for their freedom (*istis'a*') are void; and that [the choosing of two freed slaves [out of six] by dividing them [into three groups] is confirmed [on the basis of] the casting of lots.[12]

In other words, freeing slaves is good and contributes to the fulfillment of God's will, but it cannot take precedence over obligations to support one's family properly.

The centrality of the family model of social responsibility is reflected in Islamic law in a number of other ways. For example, Malik holds that one may not free a minor, nor someone requiring assistance in managing his property: "A boy is not allowed to be set free until he has reached puberty. The young person whose affairs are managed cannot be set free with his property, even when he reaches puberty, until he manages his property."[13] This is because, when slaves are freed, so is their property: "Malik related to me that he heard Ibn Shihab say, 'The precedent of the sunna is that when a slave is set free, his property follows him.' Malik said, 'One thing which makes clear that slave's property follows him when he is freed is that when the contract is written for his freedom, his property follows him even if he does not stipulate that.'"[14]

The basis of this legislation is the relationship established by law between freed slaves and their former masters. To simply free them and expel them from the household would impose a hardship on them; instead, freed slaves enter into a relationship with their former owners similar to a family relationship of dependency. This relationship is called *wala'*, clientship or patronage, which carries with it certain rights for the client and responsibilities on the part of the patron. The right to maintain one's property is one of the rights of clientship. The primary responsibility of the patron is to protect the clients as they would members of their own families, including paying the recompense if the client commits a crime. Clients have the status of free people under the law and are not subject to capture or re-enslavement. It should be noted, however, that the relationship of clientship does not apply to the freed slave's children:

> Malik said, ". . . [W]hen a slave is freed, his property follows him and his children do not follow him, and when [a slave who buys his own freedom] writes the contract for his freedom, his property follows him and his children do not follow him." Malik said, "One thing which makes this clear is that when a slave or [one buying his freedom] are bankrupt, their property is taken but the mothers of their children and their children are not taken because they are not their property."[15]

Early Islamic law also developed two categories of slaves who will eventually be freed. The first is the mukatab, a slave who has been given a contract (*kitaba*) by the owner according to which s/he may buy her/his freedom on an installment plan. This is based on a Qur'anic injunction to allow those slaves who desire freedom to purchase it: "And those of your slaves who desire a document [giving them freedom], write it for them if you see any good in them, and give them out of the wealth which God has given to you" (Sura 24:34). Malik quotes this verse, and notes that granting slaves the right to purchase their freedom is not an absolute duty; it is only recommended, meaning it will be rewarded, but those who do not have the means to do it will not be punished. But Malik adds that it is also recommended that when the deed has been granted, the owner help pay the price:

> Malik said, "I heard one of the people of knowledge say about the words of Allah the Blessed, the Exalted, 'Give them of the wealth which Allah has given you,' that it meant that a man give his slave a kitaba and then reduce the end of his kitaba for him by some specific amount."
>
> Malik said, "This is what I have heard from the people of knowledge and what I have seen people doing here."[16]

The laws concerning the kitaba are extremely detailed, dealing with inheritance of the kitaba in case the mukatab or mukataba (male or female slave who has contracted with the owner to buy freedom) dies; the status of children in the contract; details concerning co-ownership of slaves and what happens if one of the owners wants to grant a kitaba and the other one does not, and refuses to allow his portion to be bought out; and what happens if a group of slaves contract to buy their freedom together and one of them dies; and other possible circumstances. One of the more interesting areas covered is that of a mukatab who grants his or her own slave a kitaba. Malik holds that the case must be examined: "If he wanted to do his slave a favour, and it was obvious by his making it easy for him, it was not permitted. If, however, he was giving him a kitaba from desire to find money to pay off his own kitaba, then he was permitted to do so."[17] The rationale behind this opinion is obscure, but Malik returns to more predictable opinions in dealing with the case of a mukatab who is sold. He holds that the mukatab's right to buy his freedom takes precedence over the purchaser's right to buy his slavery:

> Malik said, "The best of what I have heard about a mukatab when he is sold is that he is more entitled to buy his kitaba than the one who buys him, if he can pay his master the price for which he was sold in cash. That is because his buying himself is his freedom, and his freedom has priority over whatever bequests accompany it."[18]

Similarly, Malik holds, "There is no harm in a mukatab paying towards his kitaba with coin or merchandise other than the merchandise for which he wrote the kitaba if it is identical with it, on time (for the installment) or delayed."[19] Such rulings again reflect the Qur'an clear preference for freedom.

Another category of slave in classical Islamic law is the *mudabbar*, one who will be freed upon the death of the master. Once the *tadbir* (the declaration that manumission will occur upon the death of the owner) has been declared, the mudabbar cannot be sold or given in recompense for an offense. When the owner dies, the manumission of the mudabbar is considered part of the one-third of his estate he is allowed to bequeath beyond the inheritance shares which Islamic law requires people to guarantee for members of their families. This is the only limit to the tadbir; if the owner's property is not sufficient to cover the required inheritance and the value of the mudabbar, then the mudabbar does not get his freedom:

> Malik said that if a man who made his slave a mudabbar died and he had some property on hand and some absent property, and in the property on hand there was not enough to cover the value of the mudabbar, the mudabbar was kept there together with the property, and his tax was gathered until the master's absent property was clear. Then if a third of what his master left would cover his value, he was

freed with his property and what had gathered of his tax. If there was not enough to cover his value in what his master had left, as much of him was freed as the third would allow, and his property was left in his hands.[20]

Similarly, if someone makes all his slaves mudabbars and they are his only property, only one-third of them will be freed on the death of the owner. According to Malik, those freed will be the ones first granted tadbir.

Upon the death of the owner, the mudabbar becomes fully free, as described in the case of a mudabbar who contracted a kitaba:

> Malik, speaking about a mudabbar who says to his master, "Free me immediately and I will give you fifty dinars which I will have to pay in installments." His master says, "Yes, you are free and you must pay me fifty dinars and you will pay me ten dinars every year." The slave is satisfied with this. Then the master dies one, two or three days later. Malik said, "The freeing is confirmed and the fifty dinars becomes a debt against [the mudabbar]. His testimony is permitted, his inviolability as a free man is confirmed, as are his inheritance and his liability to the full hudud punishments. The death of his master, however, does not reduce the debt for him at all."[21]

This ruling reflects the irrevocability of the tadbir, unlike a simple promise to free a slave. Because the Qur'an recommends freeing slaves as a supererogatory and meritorious act of charity, it was common for Muslims to promise to free a slave in times of distress. Such promises can be rescinded, unlike the tadbir, according to Malik:

> Malik said, "The generally agreed on way of doing things in our community is that any setting-free which a man makes in a bequest that he wills in health or illness can be rescinded by him when he likes and changed when he likes as long as it is not a tadbir. There is no way to rescind a tadbir once he has made it."[22]

As with other classes of slaves, if they are owned by non-Muslims and become Muslim, they are separated from their non-Muslim owners and sold to Muslims. If the non-Muslim slave owner dies owing a debt, the debt is paid from the price of the slave if there is insufficient property in the deceased's estate to cover the debt.

Thus, the legislation surrounding slaves is rich and complex. In addition to the categories described, slaves are dealt with in numerous other categories, such as penal law and inheritance. The fact that slavery is a major concern in Islamic law no doubt stems from the prevalence of slavery at the time when Islam was instituted combined with the fact that the Qur'an clearly presents universal freedom and human dignity as its ideal society. Its recommendation that slaves be freed is on the same plane as its recommendation that the poor be clothed and the hungry be fed. Prohibiting slavery in the context of seventh-century Arabia apparently would have been as useful as prohibiting poverty; it would have reflected a noble ideal but would have been unworkable on an immediate basis without establishing an entirely new socioeconomic system. Rather than legislating against slavery, then, the Qur'an recommended measures to be taken to gradually diminish and perhaps ultimately eliminate it.

2 Slave laws in Judaism

While Islamic law systematically investigates the logic of the slave within the social order, in the initial statement of the halakhah, the slave, or bondman, does not define a principal category formation at all. Numerous laws attend to the slave, but only as a subdivision of some other topic; no tractate or composite of laws finds in the topic of slavery a generative problematic sufficient to sustain large-scale and fully articulated exposition. The slave then is an item on a list, sharing traits with other such items, but rarely, if ever, in the halakhic classics does the slave define the focus of interest of a list. He is inert, like an ox, and not active and complex, like a woman – the other categories with which he is commonly joined on lists.

In the halakhah of classical Judaism, a person is classified as a slave by reason of his relationship to the householder, not from any natural features of his own.[23] In this regard a scholar of the subject of slavery in Judaism, Paul Flesher states:

> Although the Mishnah's framers view the slave as physically, mentally and spiritually equivalent to his master, the master has supreme power of the slave. . . . The slave possesses the capacity to classify objects, just like a citizen-householder. But the master's power over the slave gives him the capacity to determine the effectiveness of his slave's acts of classification.[24]

In fact, the halakhah recognizes four classes of Israelite society: householders, minor sons, women (adult and minor), and slaves, and, as is clear, the first three are defined by intrinsic features, the fourth by relationship. The slave may be equivalent to three other species of the same genus, oxen, women, and citizens, says Flesher:

> Oxen and slaves belong to the genus of property, women and slaves belong to the genus of subordinate human beings, and citizens and slaves belong to the overall genus of human beings. . . . The ultimate category to which the slave must be compared lies not outside the

system of slavery but within, namely, the ex-slave or freedman . . . defined as a slave who has been released from his subjugation to a householder. He now constitutes a free man or woman, but one whose past stems not from individual human beings but from slavery.[25]

So much for the facts of the matter. Why so?

Specifically, since the halakhah means to classify things in hierarchical order, we must wonder why slaves do not, on their own, form a category. The answer is clear from the category pertaining to their counterpart: women. There, as we have seen, the halakhah has business to do, a problem to solve, namely, to answer a very particular question in classification: How does a woman move from one category to another? In that very context, as we noted, the slave is included (e.g., at Mishnah-tractate Qiddushin 1:1ff.), but he is not the focus, the important questions arising from the matter of the woman. A slave is acted upon; his status is the result of others' exercising power. In that regard he is comparable to an ox, to which, too, the halakhah devotes no systematic statement. To define a principal category formation, a class of persons must require acute differentiation, says Flesher: "Foreigners . . . remain outside the focus of the system of the Mishnah and thus stand beyond its system of classification." As we noted in connection with idolatry, the gentile comes under sustained analysis in relationship with Israel and only in those aspects of that relationship that have a bearing upon Israelite existence. The same is so of the slave.

The law concerning slaves, therefore, is going to focus upon the slave in relationship to the master. For example, a slave owned by a priest has the right to eat priestly rations; he loses that right when the master dies:

8:1 A. The wife [of a priest] who was eating heave offering,

　　 B. [and] they came and told her, "Your husband has died," or, "[Your husband] has divorced you" [such that the woman no longer has the right to eat heave offering];

　　 C. and so [in the case of] a slave [of a priest] who was eating heave offering,

　　 D. and they came and told him, "Your master has died," or, "He sold you to an Israelite," or, "He gave you [to an Israelite] as a gift," or, "He has made you a freeman" [in any of which cases, the slave no longer may eat heave offering];

　　　　 R. Eliezer declares [all of these individuals] liable to payment of the principal and [added] fifth [of the heave offering they unintentionally had eaten as non-priests].

　　 H. But R. Joshua exempts.

(Mishnah-tractate Terumot 8:1)

Here is a fine example of how the slave forms a subordinated category, not generating the kind of problems that attract sustained attention from the lawyer-theologians of the halakhah.

For the purposes of hierarchical classification, a category that does not participate in the process will not define a generative category formation. As a matter of fact, the bondman does not participate in the caste system, and that suffices to exclude him from serving as a focus of legal exposition and exegesis:

A. Ten castes came up from Babylonia: (1) priests, (2) Levites, (3) Israelites, (4) impaired priests, (5) converts, and (6) freed slaves, (7) mamzers, (8) Netins, (9) "silenced ones" [shetuqi], and (10) foundlings.
B. Priests, Levites, and Israelites are permitted to marry among one another.
C. Levites, Israelites, impaired priests, converts, and freed slaves are permitted to marry among one another.
D. Converts, freed slaves, mamzers, Netins, "silenced ones," and foundlings are permitted to marry among one another.

(Mishnah-tractate Qiddushin 4:1)

Flesher observes, "The category of bondmen lacks the features belonging to categories of the caste system." Flesher explains the matter in this language:

> The framers use the householder's power as a taxonomic criterion to distinguish species within a genus. . . . The taxonomic criterion of the householder's control defines the bondman as a human being subject to the full power of a householder . . . the bondman is a human being whose capacity to classify objects in his world is controlled by his master.[26]

Such a person is not going to form the center of a halakhic disquisition, because nothing important is going to be learned from him for the purposes of fully exposing the system. Sages define the slave as property, "as the private possession of an Israelite. Just as an ox or a bed belongs to a householder, so the bondman constitutes the property of his master,"[27] and while the halakhah deals with oxen and beds, it defines no category formations around oxen and beds.

C Sacred time/Sabbath in Judaism and sacred time/ pilgrimage in Islam

In this section, we see an example of a different kind of disproportion in the categories of Judaism and Islam: the treatment of sacred time. Not only do their respective conceptions of the sanctity of specific times differ significantly, but the categories under which those conceptions are expressed vary as well. We shall consider legislation concerning the Judaic Sabbath in order to understand the nature and source of Judaism's concept of sacred time. Islam, however, has no Sabbath as such. As noted, Muslims pray together once a week, but the day of communal prayer does not fit the pattern of a Sabbath day – a day commemorating creation, an event considered by Judaism to be of supreme significance. On the other hand, Islam does set aside certain months during the year for sacred activities. We have noted, for example, that the ninth month of Islam's lunar calendar, Ramadan, is designated as the time for the required fast. In addition, Islam designates the month Dhu al-Hijja for the required pilgrimage to Mecca. Because the performance of the pilgrimage commemorates events considered foundational in Islam – the establishing of the covenant by Abraham – we shall consider the Hajj (pilgrimage) as the counterpart to Judaism's sacred time of the Sabbath. (It should also be noted that Judaism does legislate concerning pilgrimages, but they are of minor significance and therefore could not be considered as counterparts of Islam's required pilgrimage.)

1 Judaism: sacred time/Sabbath

Judaism correlates the movement of the sun and the moon, so that the holy seasons of the Torah remain synchronized with the solar seasons. This is accomplished by matching the two principal holiday seasons, the lunar months of Tishré, in the autumn, and Nisan, in the spring, with the equinoxes, autumnal and vernal, respectively. The fifteenth of the lunar month of Tishré, marking the advent of the festival of Tabernacles (Sukkot), and the fifteenth of the lunar month of Nisan, marking the advent of the festival of Passover (Pessah), cannot fall prior to September 21 and March 21, respectively, and when that is going to happen, an additional lunar month is added to the year. In this way Tabernacles remains an autumnal festival, Passover a vernal one, the first marking the advent of the rains in the autumn, the second the appearance of the earliest spring crops. But the single most important moment of time is not the festival season but the Sabbath, that is, the seventh day, which celebrates the perfection, completion, and sanctification of creation. The scriptural account of the Sabbath stands behind the halakhah that pertains to the correct celebration of that day, sundown to sundown.

The advent of the Sabbath transforms Israelite life, imposing restrictions that encase the occasion within a well-demarcated framework. On the Sabbath the Israelite enters the situation of repose in the model of God's own repose at the conclusion of the creation of the world described in Genesis 1:1–2:3. Then the Israelite household at rest recapitulates the celebration of God at the moment of the conclusion and perfection of creation. Then the Israelite household, like creation at sunset marking the end of the sixth day of creation, is sanctified: separated from the profane world and distinguished as God's domain. With all things in place and in order, at the sunset that marks the advent of the seventh day, the rest that marks the perfection of creation descends. The sanctification takes place through that very act of perfect repose which recapitulates the one celebrated at the climax of creation. Like God at the celebration of creation, now man achieves perfect, appropriate rest. That takes place when time, circumstance, but space too, come together. The advent of the Sabbath marks the time, the household, the space, and the conduct of home and family life, the circumstance.

Here, within the interiorities of the Israelite household, in the system of the halakhah, therefore, is where time counts, where we take the measure of space, and where the particularities of private conduct behind the household walls make all the difference. As the advent of the Sabbath, holy time, requires preparation in the temple, so the same time imposes upon the household a set of rules of sanctification. The Written Torah has set the stage. The Sabbath marks the celebration of creation's perfection (Genesis 2:1–3). Food for the day is to be prepared in advance (Exodus 16:22–26, 29–30). Fire is not to be kindled on that day, thus no cooking can take place (Exodus 34:2–3). Servile labor is not to be carried on on that day by the householder and his dependants, encompassing his chattel (Exodus 20:5–11, 23:13, 31:12–17, 34:21). The where matters as much as the when and the how. People are supposed to stay in their place: "Let each person remain in place, let no one leave his place on the seventh day" (Exodus 16:29–30), understanding by place the private domain of the household (subject to further clarification in due course).

Sages then make of the Sabbath the first and most important statement of their system, celebrating the stasis of creation, the perfection of the Creator's work, all evoked every time the word "Sabbath" resonated with the sounds of the beginnings, the melodies of the restoration. What the halakhah of the Oral Torah has to contribute to the topic, the Sabbath and its sanctification, emerges in the tractates of Shabbat and Erubin, the former devoted to all matters except remaining in place, the latter dedicated to the rule that each person is to remain in place. These represent some of the most profound and probing reflections of the entire corpus of the halakhah of the Oral Torah. The depths they plumb, the problems they probe – these remain to be exposed, first within the halakhah, then beneath its surface. A brief survey of the main points of the Mishnah's halakhah for the Sabbath, in the form of an outline, conveys the halakhic definition of how time is to be sanctified.

(a) Dimensions: space, time and the Sabbath

(i) SPACE

M. 1:1 [Acts of] transporting objects from one domain to another [which violate] the Sabbath (1) are two, which [indeed] are four [for one who is] inside, (2) and two which are four [for one who is] outside. How so? [If on the Sabbath] the beggar stands outside and the householder inside, [and] the beggar stuck his hand inside and put [a beggar's bowl] into the hand of the householder, or if he took [something] from inside it and brought it out, the beggar is liable, the householder is exempt. [If] the householder stuck his hand outside and put [something] into the hand of the beggar, or if he took [something] from it and brought it inside, the householder is liable, and the beggar is exempt. [If] the beggar stuck his hand inside, and the householder took [something] from it, or if [the householder] put something in it and he [the beggar] removed it – both of them are exempt. [If] the householder put his hand outside and the beggar took [something] from it, or if [the beggar] put something into it and [the householder] brought it back inside, both of them are exempt.

(ii) TIME

M. 1:2 A man should not sit down before the barber close to the afternoon [prayer], unless he has already prayed. Nor [at that time] should a man go into a bathhouse or into a tannery, nor to eat, nor to enter into judgment. But if they began, they do not break off [what they were doing]. They do break off [what they were doing] to pronounce the recitation of the *Shema*. But they do not break off [what they were doing] to say the Prayer.

M. 1:3 A tailor should not go out carrying his needle near nightfall, lest he forget and cross [a boundary]; nor a scribe with his pen. And [on the Sabbath] one should not search his clothes [for fleas], or read by the light of a lamp. Nonetheless they state: [On the Sabbath] a teacher sees [by the light of a lamp] where the children are reading, but he does not read.

M. 1:10 They do not roast meat, onions, and eggs, unless there is time for them to be roasted while it is still day. They do not put bread into an oven at dusk, nor cakes on the coals, unless there is time for them to form a crust [even] on the top surface while it is still day.

(b) Preparing for the Sabbath: light, food, clothing

(i) THE SABBATH LAMP

M. 2:1 With what do they kindle [the Sabbath light] and with what do they not kindle [it]? They do not kindle with (1) cedar fiber, (2) uncarded flax, (3) raw silk, (4) wick of bast, (5) wick of the desert, (6) or seaweed; or with (1) pitch, (2) wax, (3) castor oil, (4) oil [given to a priest as heave-offering which had become unclean and must therefore be] burned, (5) [grease from] the fat tail, or (6) tallow.

M. 2:7 Three things must a man state in his house on the eve of Sabbath at dusk: (1) "Have you tithed?" (2) "Have you prepared the symbolic meal of fusion [to unite distinct domains for purposes of carrying on the Sabbath]?" (3) "[Then] kindle the lamp [for the Sabbath]."

(ii) FOOD FOR THE SABBATH

M. 3:1 A double stove that [people] have heated with stubble or straw – they put cooked food on it. [But if they heated it] with peat or with wood, one may not put [anything] on it until he has swept it out, or until he has covered it with ashes.

M. 3:3 They do not put an egg beside a kettle [on the Sabbath] so that it will be cooked. And one should not crack it into [hot] wrappings. And one should not bury it in sand or in road dirt so that it will be roasted.

M. 3:6 [On the Sabbath] they do not put a utensil under a lamp to catch the oil. But if one put it there while it is still day, it is permitted. But they do not use any of that oil [on the Sabbath], since it is not something which was prepared [before the Sabbath for use on the Sabbath]. They carry a new lamp, but not an old one. They put a utensil under a lamp to catch the sparks. But [on the Sabbath] one may not put water into it, because he thereby puts out [the sparks].

(iii) ORNAMENTS FOR ANIMALS, CLOTHING FOR PERSONS

For animals:

M. 5:1 With what does a beast (Exodus 20:10) go out [on the Sabbath], and with what does it not go out? (1) A camel goes out with its curb, (2) a female camel with its nose ring, (3) a Libyan ass with its bridle, (4) and a horse with its chain. And all beasts which wear a chain go out with a chain and are led by a chain, and they sprinkle on the [chains if they become unclean] and immerse them in place [without removing them].

M. 5:3 And with what does [a beast] not go out? (1) A camel does not go out with a pad, nor (2) with forelegs bound together [or: hind legs bound together] or (3) with a hoof tied back to the shoulder. And so is the rule for all other beasts. One should not tie camels to one another and lead them. But one puts the ropes [of all of them] into his hand and leads them, so long as he does not twist [the ropes together].

For persons:

> M. 6:1 With what does a woman go out, and with what does she not go out? A woman should not go out with (1) woolen ribbons, (2) flaxen ribbons, or (3) with bands around her head (4) or with a headband, (5) head bangles, when they are not sewn on, (6) or with a hair-net, into the public domain. Nor [should she go out] (1) with a [tiara in the form of] a golden city, (2) a necklace, (3) nose rings, (4) a ring lacking a seal, or (5) a needle lacking a hole. But if she went out [wearing any one of these] she is not liable for a sin-offering.
>
> M. 6:2 A man should not go out with (1) a nail-studded sandal, (2) a single sandal if he has no wound on his foot, (3) tefillin, (4) an amulet when it is not by an expert, (5) a breastplate, (6) a helmet, or (7) with greaves. But if he went out [wearing any one of these], he is not liable to a sin-offering.

(iv) PROHIBITED ACTS OF LABOR ON THE SABBATH: NOT TRANSPORTING OBJECTS FROM ONE DOMAIN TO ANOTHER

The generative categories of prohibited acts of labor:

> M. 7:1 A governing principle did they state concerning the Sabbath: Whoever forgets the basic principle of the Sabbath and performs many acts of labor on many different Sabbath days is liable only for a single sin-offering. He who knows the principle of the Sabbath and performs many acts of labor on many different Sabbaths is liable for the violation of each and every Sabbath. He who knows that it is the Sabbath and performs many acts of labor on many different Sabbaths is liable for the violation of each and every generative category of labor. He who performs many acts of labor of a single type is liable only for a single sin-offering.
>
> M. 7:2 The generative categories of acts of labor [prohibited on the Sabbath] are forty less one: (1) he who sows, (2) ploughs, (3) reaps, (4) binds sheaves, (5) threshes, (6) winnows, (7) selects [fit from unfit produce or crops], (8) grinds, (9) sifts, (10) kneads, (11) bakes; (12) he who shears wool, (13) washes it, (14) beats it, (15) dyes it; (16) spins, (17) weaves, (18) makes two loops, (19) weaves two threads, (20) separates two threads; (21) ties, (22) unties, (23) sews two stitches, (24) tears in order to sew two stitches; (25) he who traps a deer, (26) slaughters it, (27) flays it, (28) salts it, (29) cures its hide, (30) scrapes it, and (31) cuts it up; (32) he who writes two letters, (33) erases two letters in order to write two letters; (34) he who builds, (35) tears down; (36) he who puts out a fire, (37) kindles a fire; (38) he who hits with a hammer; (39) he who transports an

object from one domain to another – lo, these are the forty generative acts of labor less one.

Domains and the prohibition of transporting objects from one domain to another:

M. 7:3 And a further governing rule did they state: Whatever is suitable for storage, which people generally store in such quantity as one has taken out on the Sabbath – he is liable to a sin-offering on its account. And whatever is not suitable for storage, which people generally do not store in such quantity as one has taken out on the Sabbath – only he is liable on its account who stores it away [and who then takes it out].

The prohibition of carrying on the sabbath across the lines of domains:

M. 10:3 He who takes [something] out, (1) whether in his right hand or in his left, (2) in his lap or (3) on his shoulder, is liable, for so is the manner of carrying [an object] by the children of Kohath (Numbers 7:9). [If he takes something out] (1) on the back of his hand, (2) on his foot, (3) in his mouth, (4) in his elbow, (5) in his ear, or (6) in his hair, (1) in his wallet with its mouth downward, (2) between his wallet and his cloak, (3) in the hem of his cloak, (4) in his shoe, (5) in his sandal, he is exempt [from liability for a sin-offering]. For he has not carried [the object] out the way people [generally] carry out [objects].
M. 10:4 He who intends to take out something before him, and it slipped behind him is exempt. [If he intended to carry it out] behind him and it slipped in front of him, he is liable. Truly did they say, A woman who wore drawers [and took something out in them], whether in front of her or behind her, is liable, for they are likely to be moved around.

Throwing objects from one domain to another:

M. 11:1 He who throws [an object] from private domain to public domain, [or] from public domain to private domain, is liable. [He who throws an object] from private domain to private domain, and public domain intervenes is exempt from penalty. How so? Two balconies opposite one another [extending] into the public domain – he who stretches out or throws [an object] from this one to that one is exempt. [If] both of them were [different private domains on the same side of the street and] at the same story, he who stretches [an object over] is liable, and he who throws from one to the other is exempt. For thus was the mode of labor of the Levites: Two wagons, one after the other, in the public domain – they stretch beams from this one to that one, but they do not throw [them from one to the other].

(v) PROHIBITED ACTS OF LABOR

What constitutes a whole act of labor:

M. 12:1 He who builds – how much does he build so as to be liable [on that count]? He who builds – in any measure at all. He who hews stone, hits with a hammer or adze, bores – in any measure at all is liable. This is the governing principle: Whoever on the Sabbath performs a forbidden act of labor and [the result of] his act of labor endures is liable.

M. 12:2 He who ploughs – in any measure whatsoever, he who (1) weeds, he who (2) cuts off dead leaves, and he who (3) prunes – in any measure whatsoever, is liable. He who gathers branches of wood – if [it is] to improve the field – in any measure at all; if [it is] for a fire – in a measure [of wood] sufficient to cook a small egg, [is liable]. He who gathers herbs if [it is] to improve the field – in any measure at all; if it is for cattle [to eat] – in the measure of a lamb's mouthful, [is liable].

Healing on the Sabbath:

M. 14:3 They do not eat Greek hyssop on the Sabbath, because it is not a food for healthy people. But one eats pennyroyal or drinks knot grass water. All sorts of foods a person eats [which serve for] healing, and all such drinks he may drink, except for palm tree water [purgative water] or a cup of root water, because they are [solely] for jaundice. But one may drink palm tree water [to quench] his thirst. And one anoints with root oil, [if it is] not for healing.

M. 14:4 He who has tooth problems may not suck vinegar through them. But he dunks [his bread] in the normal way, and if he is healed, he is healed. He who is concerned about his loins [which give him pain], he may not anoint them with wine or vinegar. But he anoints with oil – not with rose oil. Princes [on the Sabbath] anoint themselves with rose oil on their wounds, since it is their way to do so on ordinary days.

Knot-tying, clothing, and beds:

M. 15:1 On account of [tying] what sorts of knots [on the Sabbath] are [people] liable? (1) A camel driver's knot, and (2) a sailor's knot. And just as one is liable for tying them, so he is liable for untying them.

M. 15:2 You have knots on account of which they are not liable, like a camel driver's knot and a sailor's knot. A woman ties (1) the slit of her shift, (2) the strings of her hair-net and of her belt, (3) the thongs of a shoe or sandal, (4) [leather] bottles of wine or oil, and (5) a cover over meat. They tie a bucket with a belt but not with a rope.

(vi) ACTIONS THAT ARE PERMITTED ON THE SABBATH

Saving objects from a fire on the Sabbath:

M. 16:1 All Holy scriptures – do they save from fire, whether they read in them or do not read in them. And even though they are written in any language [besides Hebrew], [if they become useless] they require storage [and are not to be burned]. And on what account do they not read in [some of] them? Because of the neglect of the [proper study of the Torah in the] study house they save the case of the scroll with the scroll and the case of the phylacteries with the phylacteries, even though there is money in them. And where do they [take them to] save them? To a closed alley [which is not open as a thoroughfare and so is not public domain].

Handling objects on the Sabbath in private domain:

M. 17:1 All utensils are handled on the Sabbath, and their [detached] doors along with them, even though they were detached on the Sabbath. For they are not equivalent to doors of a house, for the [latter] are not prepared [in advance of the Sabbath to be used].

Circumcision on the Sabbath:

M. 18:3 And all things required for circumcision do they perform on the Sabbath.

Preparing food for man and beast:

M. 20:1 (1) On the festival they do not spread out a strainer, and (2) on the Sabbath they do not pour [wine] into one which is spread out. But on the festival they pour [wine] into one which is spread out.

Seemly and unseemly behavior on the Sabbath:

176

M. 23:1 A man [on the Sabbath] asks for jugs of wine or oil from his fellow, provided that he does not say to him, "Lend [them] to me." And so a woman [borrows] loaves of bread from her neighbor. And if one does not trust the other, he leaves his cloak with him and settles with him after the Sabbath. And so is the case on the eve of Passover in Jerusalem when that day coincides with the Sabbath: One leaves his cloak with him and takes his Passover lamb and settles with him after the festival.

M. 24:1 He who was overtaken by darkness on the road gives his purse to a gentile. If there is no gentile with him, he leaves it on an ass. [When] he reaches the outermost courtyard [of a town], he removes [from the ass] those utensils which may be handled on the Sabbath. And [as to] those [utensils] which are not to be handled on the Sabbath, he unloosens the ropes, and the bundles fall by themselves.

This brief survey of the Mishnah's laws provides a clear and firm structure of the halakhic Sabbath. That structure forms the very heart and soul of the Judaic life of piety, public and personal alike. From the specific rules we have examined, let us now turn to the generalizations instantiated by the rules. The advent of the Sabbath transforms creation, specifically reorganizing space and time and reordering the range of permissible activity. First comes the transformation of space that takes effect at sundown at the end of the sixth day and ends at sundown of the Sabbath day. At that time, for holy Israel, the entire world is divided into public domain and private domain, and what is located in the one may not be transported into the other. What is located in public domain may be transported only four cubits; that is, within the space occupied by a person's body. What is in private domain may be transported within the entire demarcated space of that domain. All public domain is deemed a single spatial entity, so too all private domain; thus one may transport objects from one private domain to another. The net effect of the transformation of space is to move nearly all permitted activity to private domain and to close off public domain for all but the most severely limited activities; people may not transport objects from one domain to the other, but they may transport objects within private domain, so the closure of public domain from most activity, and nearly all material or physical activity, comes in consequence of the division of space effected by sunset at the end of the sixth day of the week.

So when it comes to space, the advent of the Sabbath divides into distinct domains for all practical purposes what in secular time is deemed divided only as to ownership, but united as to utilization. Sacred time then intensifies the arrangements of space as public and private, imparting enormous consequence to the status of what is private. There, and only there, on the Sabbath, is life to be lived. The Sabbath assigns to private domain the focus of life in holy time: the household is where things take place then. When, presently, we realize that the household (private domain) is deemed analogous to the temple or tabernacle (God's household), forming a mirror image to the tabernacle, we shall understand the full meaning of the generative principle before us concerning space on the Sabbath.

Second comes the matter of time and how the advent of sacred time registers. Since the consequence of the demarcation on the Sabbath of all space into private and public domain effects, in particular, transporting objects from one space to the other, how time is differentiated will present no surprise. The effects concern private domain, the household. Specifically, what turns out to frame the halakhic issue is what objects may be handled or used, even in private domain, on the Sabbath. The advent of the Sabbath thus affects the organization of space and the utilization of tools and other objects, the furniture of the household within the designated territory of the household. The basic principle is simple. Objects may be handled only if they are designated in advance of the Sabbath for the purpose for which they will be utilized on the Sabbath. But if tools may be used for a purpose that is licit on the Sabbath, and if those tools are ordinarily used for that same purpose, they are deemed ready at hand and do not require reclassification; the accepted classification applies. What requires designation for Sabbath use in particular is any tool that may serve more than a single purpose, or that does not ordinarily serve the purpose for which it is wanted on the Sabbath. Designation for use on the Sabbath thus regularizes the irregular, but is not required for what is ordinarily used for the purpose for which it is wanted and is licitly utilized on the Sabbath.

The advent of sacred time calls into question the accessibility and use of the objects and tools of the world, but with a very particular purpose in mind. That purpose emerges when we note that if an object is ordinarily used for a purpose that is licit on the Sabbath, for example, for eating, it need not be designated for that purpose for use on the Sabbath. Since on the Sabbath it is used for its ordinary, and licit, purpose, that suffices. So the advent of the Sabbath requires that things licit for use on the Sabbath be used in the manner that is standard. If one wishes to use those things for a given purpose that is licit on the Sabbath, but that those objects do not ordinarily serve, one must designate those objects for that purpose in advance of the Sabbath; that is, regularize them. This rule covers whole, useful tools, but not broken ones or tools that will not serve their primary purpose.

The Sabbath then finds all useful tools and objects in their proper place; that may mean they may not be handled at all, since their ordinary function cannot be performed on the Sabbath; or it may mean they may be handled on the Sabbath exactly as they are handled every other day, the function being licit on the Sabbath; or it may mean they must be designated in advance of the Sabbath for licit utilization on the Sabbath. That third proviso covers utensils that serve more than a single function, or that do not ordinarily serve the function of licit utilization on the Sabbath that the householder wishes them to serve on this occasion. The advent of the Sabbath then requires that all tools and other things be regularized and ordered. The rule extends even to utilization of space, within the household, that is not ordinarily used for a (licit) purpose for which, on the Sabbath, it is needed. If guests visit, storage space used for food may be cleared away to accommodate them, the space being conceived as suitable for sitting even when not ordinarily used for that purpose. But one may not clear out a store room for that purpose. One may also make a path in a store-room so that one may move about there. One may handle objects that, in some way or another, can serve a licit purpose, in the theory that that purpose inheres. But what is not made ready for use may not be used on the Sabbath. So the advent of the Sabbath not only divides space into public and private, but also differentiates useful tools and objects into those that may or may not be handled within the household.

We come to the third generative problematics that is particular to the Sabbath. The effect upon activity that the advent of the Sabbath makes concerns constructive labor. I may state the generative problematic in a simple declarative sentence: In a normal way one may not carry out entirely on his own a completed act of constructive labor, which is to say, work that produces enduring results. That is what one is supposed to do in profane time. What is implicit in that simple statement proves profound and bears far-reaching implications. No prohibition impedes performing an act of labor in an other-than-normal way, for example, in a way that is unusual and thus takes account of the differentiation of time. Labor in a natural, not in an unnatural, manner is prohibited. But that is not all. A person is not forbidden to carry out an act of destruction, or an act of labor that produces no lasting consequences. Nor is part of an act of labor, not brought to conclusion, prohibited. Nor is it forbidden to perform part of an act of labor in partnership with another person who carries out the other requisite part. Nor does one incur culpability for performing an act of labor in several distinct parts, for example, over a protracted, differentiated period of time. The advent of the Sabbath prohibits activities carried out in ordinary time in a way deemed natural: acts that are complete, consequential, and in accordance with their accepted character.

The halakhah turns out to realize in detailed, concrete terms generalizations that sages locate in and derive from the story of creation. What qualities of Eden impress sages? With the halakhah as the vast corpus of facts, we focus upon two matters: (1) time and space, (2) time and activity. How is space demarcated at the specified time, and how is activity classified at that same time? The former works itself out in a discussion of where people may move on the Sabbath and how they may conduct themselves (carry things as they move). The latter finds its definition in the model of labor that is prohibited. With Eden as the model and the metaphor, we take a simple sighting on the matter. First, Adam and Eve are free to move in Eden where they wish, possessing all they contemplate. God has given it to them to enjoy. If Eden then belongs to God, he freely shares ownership with Adam and Eve. And – all the more so – the produce of Eden is ownerless. With the well-known exception, all the fruit is theirs for the taking.

Israel on the Sabbath in the Land like God on the Sabbath of Eden rests from the labor of creation. And that brings us to the question: What about that other principle of the Sabbath, the one set forth by the halakhah of Shabbat? The richly detailed halakhah of Shabbat defines the matter in a prolix, yet simple way. It is that on the Sabbath it is prohibited deliberately to carry out in a normal way a completed act of constructive labor, one that produces enduring results, one that carries out one's entire intention: the whole of what one planned one has accomplished, in exactly the proper manner. That definition takes into account the shank of the halakhah of Shabbat as set forth in the Mishnah-tractate, and the amplification and extension of matters in the Tosefta and the two Talmuds in no way revises the basic principles. Here there is a curious, if obvious, fact: it is not an act of labor that itself is prohibited (as the Ten Commandments in Exodus and Deuteronomy would have it), but an act of labor of a very particular definition.

No prohibition impedes performing an act of labor in an other-than-normal way. In theory, one may go out into the fields and plough, if he does so in some odd manner. He may build an entire house, so long as it collapses on the spot. The issue of activity on the Sabbath is therefore removed from the obvious context of work, conventionally defined. Now the activity that is forbidden is of a very particular sort, modeled in its indicative traits after a quite specific paradigm. A person is not forbidden to carry out an act of destruction, or an act of labor that produces no lasting consequences. He may start an act of labor if he does not complete it. He may accomplish an act of labor in some extraordinary manner. None of these acts of labor are forbidden, even though, done properly and with consequence, they represent massive violations of the halakhah. Nor is part of an act of labor that is not brought to conclusion prohibited. Nor is it forbidden to perform part of an act of labor in partnership with another person who carries out the other requisite part. Nor does one incur culpability for performing an act of labor in several distinct parts, for example, over a protracted, differentiated period of time. A person may not willingly carry out the entirety of an act of constructive labor from start to finish. The issue is not why not, since we know the answer: God has said not to do so. The question is: Whence the particular definition at hand?

Clearly, a definition of the act of labor that is prohibited on the Sabbath has taken over and recast the commonsense meaning of the commandment not to labor on the Sabbath. For considerations enter that recast matters from an absolute to a relative definition. One may tie a knot – but not one that stands. One may carry a package, but not in the usual manner. One may build a wall, only if it falls down. And, as I have stressed, one may do pretty much anything without penalty – if one did not intend matters as they actually happened. The metaphor of God in Eden, as sages have reflected on the story of Creation, yields the governing principles that define forbidden labor. What God did in the six days of creation provides the model.

The main principles involve the three preconditions. The act to be prohibited on the Sabbath must fully carry out the intention of the actor, as creation carried out God's intention. The act of labor must be carried out by a single actor, as God acted alone in creating the world. An act of labor is the like of one that is required in the building and maintenance of God's residence in this world, the tabernacle. The act of labor prohibited on the Sabbath involves two considerations. The act must be done in the ordinary way, just as scripture's account leaves in no doubt: God accomplished creation in the manner in which he accomplished his goals from creation onward, by an act of speech. And, weightier still, the forbidden act of labor is one that produces enduring consequences. God did not create only to destroy, but he created the enduring world. And it goes without saying that creation yielded the obvious consequences that the act was completely done in all ways, as God himself declared. The act was one of consequence, involving what was not negligible but what man and God alike deemed to make a difference. Sages would claim, therefore, that the activity that must cease on the Sabbath finds its definition in the model of those actions that God carried out in making the world.

To act like God on the Sabbath, the Israelite rests; he does not do what God did in creation. What then takes place inside the walls of the Israelite household when time takes over space and revises the conduct of ordinary affairs? On the Sabbath, in sanctified time, Israel goes home to Eden. Israel's Eden takes place in the household open to others, on the Sabbath, in acts that maintain life, share wealth, and desist from creation. The key words, therefore, are in the shift from the here and now of time in which one works like God, to the *then* and *there* when one desists from working, just as God did at the moment the world was finished, perfected, and sanctified. Israel gives up the situation of man in ordinary time and space, destructive, selfish, dissatisfied and doing. Then, on the Sabbath, and there, in the household, with each one in place, Israel enters the situation of God in that initial, that perfected and sanctified then and there of creation: the activity that consists in sustaining life, sharing dominion, and perfecting repose through acts of restraint and sufficiency. We now see a striking disproportion even in functionally comparable categories of religious law.

2 Islam: sacred time/pilgrimage

First, let us establish the foundations on which we compare the Sabbath with the pilgrimage. Like Judaism, Islam uses the lunar calendar; the Qur'an refers to the moon as the measurer of time, but it has no particular religious significance as such: "They ask you about the new moons. Say, 'They are a way of measuring for people and for the pilgrimage'" (Sura 2:190). The hours of the day are marked by the sun. The sun and the moon are considered, like all of creation, signs of God: "It was [God] who set the sun aglow and the moon alight and set stages for it so that you will know the number of years and reckoning. God has not created that except in truth. He set out signs for people who know" (Sura 10:6). "Whatever is in the heavens and whatever is on the earth glorifies God" (Sura 62:2). But there is no special ceremonial aspect to the celestial spheres themselves. Indeed, in order to prevent confusion of creation with the Creator – worshipping the sun or moon rather than God – Islam specifies that dawn prayer be performed just before sunrise; noon prayer after the sun reaches its apex; the afternoon prayer must be performed before sunset; and the evening prayer just after sunset. Prayer must not, according to hadith, be performed exactly at dawn, noon, or sunset.

Nor are there sacred seasons in Islam, as there are in Judaism. Fighting, except in self-defense, is forbidden in the months surrounding the annual fast and pilgrimage, and these four months are sometimes called sacred, but only insofar as they are reserved for sacred duties, not because the time itself is holy. The ninth month, Ramadan, is special in that it is the month of prescribed fasting, as we have seen. But, again, the special status of the month comes from its being the month during which the Qur'an was first revealed, not its cosmic or chronological positioning: "O Believers, fasting is [required] for you as it was for those before you, so that you may become righteous. . . . The month of Ramadan is that in which the Qur'an was sent down as guidance for humankind and clear proofs of guidance and discrimination" (Sura 2:184–86). The Qur'an also includes a chapter referring to the "night of power" or "destiny" (*leilat al-qadr*), which is said to be "better than a thousand months." During that night, angels and the Spirit descended, leaving peace until dawn (Sura 97:2–6). Although the month is not actually named, it is believed that was during Ramadan. Therefore, the Qur'an prescribes fasting during that month: "So whoever among you is present during this month, fast. But whoever is sick or on a journey, [fast] a number of other days" (Sura 2:186). Thus, even though the month commemorates special events, the fact that fasting is not required during the specified time for people who are sick or on a journey and that they can make up for it by fasting at a more convenient time indicates that it is the fasting that is the source of righteousness, not the time of year.

Among the purposes of prayer, five times every day, is the dedication of all efforts to God. The seminal notion in Islamic thought is tawhid: the oneness and unity of divinity, awareness of which is to be reflected in all human activity. Other creatures automatically reflect the Creator in that that they have no choice but to fulfill their form and function. Human beings must make the choice to fulfill God's will, and that takes continuous effort. The five daily prayers serve as constant reminders and correctives to ever-present distractions. In this sense, no moment is more sacred than any other. It is human effort to do the will of God, not the time of day or year, that is the focus of holiness in Islam.

Even the weekly day of communal prayer is no more holy than other days. As noted, there is no Sabbath as such in Islam. On Fridays, Muslims are expected to pray together in the mosque, just past midday. This was prescribed by the Qur'an in a chapter entitled "Congregation" (*jumu'ah*): "Believers, when the call for prayer on the day of congregation is made, hurry to the remembrance of God and leave business aside" (Sura 62:10). Before the Friday prayer begins, two sermons (or a two-part sermon) are generally agreed to be necessary, including uplifting sentiments and quotations from the Qur'an.

There is hadith material indicating that the day of congregational prayer is special. For example:

> Yahya related to me from Malik from Yazid ibn 'Abdullah ibn al-Had from Muhammad ibn Ibrahim ibn al-Harith at-Taymi from Abu Salama ibn 'Abd ar-Rahman ibn 'Awf that Abu Hurayra said, "I went to at-Tur (Mount Sinai) and met Ka'b al-Ahbar and sat with him. He related to me things from the Torah and I related to him things from the Messenger of Allah, may Allah bless him and grant him peace. Among the things I related to him was that the Messenger of Allah, may Allah bless him and grant him peace, said, "The best of days on which the sun rises is the day of Jumu'a. On it Adam was created, and on it he fell from the Garden. On it he was forgiven, and on it he died. On it the [last] Hour occurs, and every moving thing listens from morning till sunset in apprehension of the Hour except jinn and men. During it there is time when Allah gives to a Muslim slave standing in prayer whatever he asks for." Ka'b said, "That is one day in every year." I said, "No, every Jumu'a." Then Ka'b recited the Torah and said, "The Messenger of Allah has spoken the truth."[28]

There is some discussion that the special time of day may be the final moments of congregational prayer, but there is no unanimity on the subject. Although most Muslim countries now close government and business offices and schools on Fridays, Friday is different from other days only in that it is the day Muslims are supposed to pray together. Thus reminded of their ultimate goals, Muslims are advised by the Qur'an not to rush back to business and entertainment. Still, all the forms and conditions of prayer remain the same as for the midday prayer on any other day.

The month of the pilgrimage to Mecca (Hajj), however, is different. The month of pilgrimage is referred to in the Qur'an as the "sacred" or "holy" (*haram*) month, but the timing and the practice of pilgrimage are not innovations of Islam. The Ka'ba in Mecca had been a center of pilgrimage since time immemorial; it was the abode of the relics and symbols of a number of regional deities at the time of Prophet Muhammad. There was an annual period of truce during which regional peoples trekked to Mecca for trade, cultural exchange, and pilgrimage to the Ka'ba. What Prophet Muhammad did was cleanse the Ka'ba – a sanctuary in the center of Mecca – of its "idols" and dedicate it solely to "the [one] god," Allah. The annual period of truce and pilgrimage remained. As the Qur'an put it, "The months of the Hajj are well known" (Sura 2:198). But the pilgrimage itself was transformed. Not only was its goal a sanctuary dedicated to the one God, but the very rituals were made to commemorate the central event in monotheistic experience: the establishment of the covenant, the dedication of humanity to submission to the divine will. Mecca, of course, is the birthplace of Prophet Muhammad, but it is the presence of the Ka'ba that makes it an object of pilgrimage. The Ka'ba is believed to have been established by Ibrahim (Abraham) when he accompanied his son Isma'il (Ishmael) and Isma'il's mother Hagar to this spot. The Ka'ba at that time was dedicated to the one God and symbolized the commitment made by Ibrahim and demonstrated in his willingness to sacrifice Ishmael. It is the commemoration of that event, the renewal of the commitment to God's will, that sanctifies the time of the pilgrimage.

During the Hajj and within the confines of the Meccan sanctuary around the Ka'ba (the Haram), time and space are indeed considered sacred, but only under certain circumstances. As noted, the time for the Hajj is designated by a month of the same name: Dhu al-Hijja. Although people may make pilgrimages to Mecca at other times of the year (the "minor pilgrimage" or 'Umra), making the Hajj during the first two weeks of the month of Hajj is required of all Muslims at least once during their adult lives, provided they can afford it and are physically able to make the trip: "And complete the Hajj and the 'Umra for the sake of God: but if you are kept, then offer whatever is easily available. . . . And whoever among you is sick or has a head injury, an offering either by fasting or charity or sacrifice" (Sura 2:197). This requirement was reflected in Islamic law from the earliest times: "[Shafi'i said]: God imposed the duty of al-hajj (pilgrimage) on all who can perform it. It has been related from the Prophet that the means (*al-sabil*) consist of the necessary provisions and transport (i.e., donkey or camel)." The pilgrimage, therefore, is a Pillar of Islam, meaning an obligation incumbent upon everyone to perform.

Every aspect of the pilgrimage is stipulated by law so that it will be sanctified, beginning long before arrival in Mecca:

And he [the prophet] specified the time of Pilgrimage, how to pronounce the formula of fulfilling [the duty], and what is decreed [as

184

recommended acts], and what should be avoided in the wearing of garments and the use of perfumes as well as other procedural matters [such as the halts] at the [sanctuary] of 'Arafa and the [passing of the night at] Muzdalifa, and the throwing [of the stones at Mina], the shaving [of the head], the circumambulation [of the Ka'ba] and other matters.[29]

In Malik ibn Anas's *Al-Muwatta,* prescriptions for performance of the Hajj occupy one of the longest sections.

The preparations and procedures for performing the pilgrimage make it clear that one is leaving the ordinary level of existence to enter temporarily an entirely different one. That condition is known as *ihram*, a state of ritual purity or consecration. One must make a will, as in readiness for death, make provisions for those left behind, and pay all debts. Even the money saved for the trip should be symbolically purified, by giving an equal amount in charity.

One must make a clear intention to perform the Hajj and enter the state of ihram, and begin the final preparation for the Hajj, actual and ritual bathing (*ghusl*). The ghusl is accompanied by cutting the hair (including the moustache) and clipping fingernails, since these tasks will not be done again at least until after the first portion of the pilgrimage ritual is completed. From the time of bathing, the pilgrim chants a special prayer (the *talbiyya*), loosely translated as "At your service, my God, at your service." The talbiyya continues: "At your service. You are without partners. At your service. Praise and blessing to you, and sovereignty." (In some schools the talbiyya begins at the time travel is begun. There is disagreement among the schools of law regarding the precise order of the ghusl, declaring intention, reciting the talbiyya, commencing travel, and commencement of the state of purity; they generally agree, however, that all these components are necessary.) The talbiyya is said aloud; men are actually supposed to raise their voices, although "[w]omen do not have to raise their voices when they are doing the talbiya, and a woman should only speak loudly enough to hear herself."[30]

The talbiyya indicates not only that the intention of the pilgrim to perform the Hajj has been declared, but the fact that s/he is entering ihram. This indicates, again, that although the sanctuary housing the sacred shrine, the Ka'ba, is the geographic goal of the pilgrimage, the purity and sacredness associated with this place are actually a function of the ihram of the pilgrims, and that ihram can begin before one physically enters the Haram:

Malik was asked whether one of the people of Makka could go into ihram to do 'umra (the "lesser" pilgrimage) in the centre of Makka, and he said, "No. He should go outside the Haram and go into ihram there."[31]

Similarly, the rule that only Muslims may enter the Haram is well known, but in fact it is not the geographic place that is inaccessible to non-Muslims; it is ihram. This condition of purity, into which Muslims enter for pilgrimage, is the privilege of Muslims.

Yet physical presence in Mecca is also an essential part of the ihram required for Hajj. The point is made in discussions concerning the permission for people who cannot make the pilgrimage to send animals for sacrifice along with pilgrims:

> Yahya related to me from Malik that Yahya ibn Sa'id said, "I asked 'Amra bint 'Abd ar-Rahman if there was anything that was haram [forbidden] for someone who sent a sacrificial animal (to Makka) but did not go there himself, and she told me that she had heard 'A'isha say, 'It is only someone who goes into ihram for hajj and begins saying the talbiya for whom things are haram.'"[32]

In other words, neither the desire nor the partial or vicarious participation in the events of the Hajj is sufficient to qualify one as a pilgrim. Not only is place but also time of utmost importance for the Hajj. One may make a pilgrimage to Mecca at any time, but only during Dhu al-Hijja (the month of pilgrimage) is the religious duty fulfilled. Still, like the sacredness of the location, the sacredness of the time is a function of the condition of the pilgrims – ihram – and their declared intention to fulfill the will of God, commemorating the events associated with the initial establishment of the covenant by Abraham.

Because of the care taken in entering ihram, the precise location of entering the state for people from various locations is specified:

> Yahya related to me from Malik from Nafi' from 'Abdullah ibn 'Umar that the Messenger of Allah, may Allah bless him and grant him peace, said, "The People of Madina should enter ihram at Dhu'l-Hulayfa, the people of Syria should do so at al-Juhfa, and the people of Najd should do so at Qarn."
>
> 'Abdullah ibn 'Umar added, "I have heard that the Messenger of Allah, may Allah bless him and grant him peace, said, 'The people of Yemen should enter ihram at Yalamlam.'"[33]

These specifications have been extended to include all pilgrims. In general, all pilgrims from Syria (which now includes the states of Syria, Lebanon, Israel, Palestine, and Jordan) enter at Dhu'l-Hulayfa (Masjid al-Shajarah); North Africans enter at al-Juhfa; and from Iraq people enter ihram at al-Aqiq. The Sunni schools allow pilgrims to enter ihram before the designated spots, provided the precise requirements of ihram are maintained.

At the entry points, pilgrims put on special clothes (if they have not done so already), also called ihram and symbolizing the state of purity which pilgrims have entered. The clothes must be unadulterated by dyes or perfumes, simple, and unadorned. That includes wearing sandals rather than shoes: "Yahya related to me from Malik from ʿAbdullah ibn Dinar that ʿAbdullah ibn ʿUmar said, 'The Messenger of Allah, may Allah bless him and grant him peace, forbade anyone in ihram to wear a garment which had been dyed with saffron or yellow dye, and said, "Anyone who cannot find sandals can wear leather socks, but he should cut them off below the ankles."'"[34] The prohibition of the use of saffron or yellow dye was soon extended to the use of all dyes. The requirement for simple clothes included the prohibition of stitched clothing, and was standardized as a two-piece white garment for men (a waist cloth and a cloak), and similarly simple clothes for women, but covering the entire body. Adornments and perfume are also proscribed. "Yahya related to me from Malik from Nafiʿ from Aslam, the mawla of ʿUmar ibn al-Khattab, that ʿUmar ibn al-Khattab noticed the smell of perfume while he was at ash-Shajara, and he asked, 'Who is this smell of perfume coming from?' Muʿawiya ibn Abi Sufyan answered, 'From me, Amir al-Muminin.' ʿUmar said, 'From you? By the life of Allah!' Muʿawiya explained, 'Umm Habiba perfumed me, Amir al-Muminin.' ʿUmar then said, 'You must go back and wash it off.'"[35] Even looking into a mirror is prohibited.

Men must also remove any head covering so that no rank is signified; all are equal in ihram. Women, however, are allowed to veil in most schools, although their faces should be visible.

No hunting is allowed during the Hajj, but most schools allow pilgrims to kill animals that "trespass," such as crows, kites, scorpions, rats and mice, and wild dogs. Imam Malik declared that

> any animals that wounded, attacked or terrorized men, such as lions, leopards, cheetahs and wolves, were counted as wild dogs. However, someone who was in ihram should not kill beasts of prey that did not attack [people], such as hyenas, foxes, cats and anything else like them, and if he did then he had to pay a forfeit for it.[36]

Nor are pilgrims allowed to engage in agricultural activities, such as uprooting trees or cutting down anything that has grown naturally. Such endeavors would distract the pilgrim from her/his purpose. Similarly, it is not permissible to arrange or contract marriage or engagement during Hajj. Important as these activities are to human life, the pilgrim's sole attention should be focused on the pilgrimage rituals themselves. The prohibition of sexual arousal and intercourse during the pilgrimage is a function of rules for ihram; in Islamic law sexual activity and contact with fluids associated with sexual arousal violate purity. If a pilgrim engages in sex before the first exit from ihram, s/he must conclude the pilgrimage, but will not have fulfilled the obligation for performing the Hajj. (If it is after the first exit from ihram, the pilgrimage is still valid but the offender must sacrifice a camel or sheep.)

From the moment they see the Ka'ba, the cubically shaped sanctuary which is the destination of the Hajj, pilgrims exclaim, "God is great. There is no god but God."

The rituals of the Hajj are highly elaborate; there are requirements and recommendations for virtually every thought, word, and deed, with minor variations among the schools and for various kinds of pilgrimage. The outline of the required pilgrimage is as follows. Pilgrims begin by walking around the Ka'ba, counter-clockwise, seven times, paying particular attention to the black stone embedded in a corner of the building and believed to have been laid by Ibrahim. This circumambulation is called *tawaf*, and is in imitation of the practice of Prophet Muhammad. If possible, pilgrims touch or kiss the stone, again imitating the Prophet's example:

> Yahya related to me from Malik from Hisham ibn 'Urwa from his father that 'Umar ibn al-Khattab said to the corner of the Black Stone while he was doing tawaf of the House [the Ka'ba], "You are only a stone, and if I had not seen the Messenger of Allah, may Allah bless him and grant him peace, kiss you, I would not do so." Then he kissed it.[37]

Those who are not close enough to touch the stone generally reach toward it and recite the talbiyya.

Two cycles of prayer are then recited in the direction of a stone marking a spot where Ibraham is believed to have prayed. Pilgrims then go back and forth seven times between two hills (Safa and Marwa), between which Hagar is said to have run searching for water for her son Isma'il. This is called "the sa'y". Most people walk half the distance and run the other half, again following the reported example of Prophet Muhammad:

> Yahya related to me from Malik from Jafar ibn Muhammad from his father from Jabir ibn 'Abdullah that the Messenger of Allah, may Allah bless him and grant him peace, walked when he came down from Safa and Marwa and then, when he reached the middle of the valley, he broke into a light run until he had left it.[38]

Pilgrims may then get a haircut (the schools represent various opinions on the amount of hair it is necessary to cut) and exit the state of ihram briefly, but those who do must offer a special sacrifice. After a sermon reminding them of their duties, pilgrims proceed to the Plain of 'Arafat, a few miles from Mecca. There, on the ninth day of the Hajj, they stand (or "halt;" this part of the ritual is called the halting, *wuquf*) from daybreak or noon until sunset or beyond, depending upon the school, and meditate prayerfully on

Ibrahim's act of submission. Pilgrims then go to Muzdalifa nearby, according to the Qur'an: "When you pour forth from 'Arafat, then remember God in al-Mash'ar al-Haram [at Muzdalifa], remembering him as he has guided you" (Sura 2:199). There they offer evening and night prayer together, and spend the night. They also collect a number of small stones to throw at pillars symbolizing the devil's temptation of Abraham to abandon God's will. They will throw the stones at the pillars at Mina on the morning of the tenth day, the day of sacrifice, and several more times during the next two or three days, reciting the phrases, "God is greater" ("Allahu akbar," the *takbir*) and "Glory to God" ("Subhan Allah," the *tasbih*).

The tenth day begins the feast of the sacrifice, when pilgrims sacrifice an animal, reenacting the act of Ibrahim when he demonstrated his submission to God through his willingness to sacrifice his son. This is celebrated throughout the Muslim world as *'id al-adha*, the feast of the sacrifice; it is the greatest holiday in the Islamic calendar. The sacrificial animals must be healthy and sound, and either cows, camels, sheep or goats, all of a minimum age (i.e., not babies) but not old, and must be killed according to specific procedures, including the draining of all their blood. The flesh becomes part of a great feast, but it must be shared with neighbors and the poor, in accordance with the Qur'an:

> And to every people we appointed rites of sacrifice, that they might mention the name of God over animals like cows that he has provided for them. For your god is one God, so submit to him and give good tidings and be humble. . . . And among the signs of God we have appointed for you sacrifical animals. In them there is good for you. So mention the name of God over them as they stand tied up in lines. And when they fall down on their sides, eat of them and feed whoever is poor and who is in need. We have subjected them to you so you may be grateful. Their flesh does not reach God nor their blood but your righteousness reaches God.
>
> (Sura 22:35–38)

Pilgrims then get a haircut, often a full shaving for males and a trim for women, and again exit ihram. Following three days of the feast, pilgrims return to the Ka'ba and walk around it seven more times, and do the two cycles of prayer, after which they are then relieved of all the prohibitions of ihram, including sex. Those who temporarily exited ihram earlier now do the sa'y again. Many pilgrims then go back to Mina, spend the night, and then stone the pillars three more times. Returning to Mecca, pilgrims perform the final circumambulation of the Ka'ba which marks the end of the pilgrimage ritual.

There is, no doubt, an ultimate aspect to the state of ihram, as is evidenced by the preparations necessary to enter it. As on the Judaic Sabbath, the condition achieved is similar to that of human beings before they fell from divine grace through disobedience in Eden. They are pure, ready to meet their maker. Their condition becomes like that of other creatures, those who unquestioningly perform the will of God, fulfilling the purpose of their creation. But the time and place are not so much the focus of the pilgrimage ritual as is the condition of purity and demonstration of willingness to do the will of God – in commemoration of the deeds of Ibrahim – symbolized in the sacrificial slaughtering. This points up a significant difference between the Judaic sacred time/space of the Sabbath and the Muslim sacred time/space of the pilgrimage. The sacred state of the former is likened to the sacred condition in Eden; that, in itself, is the goal. The sacred state in the Muslim pilgrimage is one of readiness for further action. In the Muslim world view, human beings have been deputized to carry out the will of God on earth: to create a just society. Carrying out that will requires ongoing commitment, and renewal of that commitment is the goal of the Hajj. The expectation is that, upon completion of the pilgrimage, people will return to their daily lives with renewed courage to "extend every effort in the way of God."

D Conclusions

Will the Islamic faithful concur that the pilgrimage compares with the Sabbath, and will the Judaic faithful recognize the Sabbath in the pilgrimage? It is not very likely. Yet we have shown that the two quite distinct religious institutions address the same questions of the interplay of the life of the faithful with the movement of heavenly bodies. The matter of proportions, important at the beginning of this chapter, loses consequence, and we find ourselves wondering how much insight is yielded by the labor of comparison and contrast. We have therefore to conclude that while we may compare the laws on the same subject set forth by each system respectively, the upshot of the comparison is to underscore difference, not commonality. When it comes to disproportions, the contrast highlights how one religion attaches enormous consequence to what the other deems null, and that difference requires explanation in its own terms. In the Epilogue, we address this question head-on. But first comes the matter of unique categories. How can we compare and contrast religions that at critical components of their structures bear nothing in common at all? What is there to be learned about a common humanity, a shared human condition, brought into being by monotheism, when belief in one and the same, unique God produces behavior so remarkable for its diversity? Islam, Judaism, and Christianity all confront that dilemma when they take cognizance of one another and begin to wonder.

7

UNIQUE CATEGORIES

A The unique category

One of the difficulties in one religion's understanding of the other emerges in this chapter, where we deal with ideas and experiences in the one religion that have no counterpart in the other. Lacking an interior analogy upon which to draw in making sense of the other, each religion finds itself baffled by matters critical to the world construction of its counterpart. We do not point to the unique categories as insuperable obstacles in the nurture of reasonable discourse between the two faiths, for in the great age of Islamic and Judaic philosophy and theology, in the Middle Ages, Islam and Judaism found themselves quite able to conduct civil and reasonable debate. But we do find in these categories consequential examples of why interfaith dialogue may yield only confusion.

That is because we come now to Islam's and Judaism's indicative categories of law. These turn out to be unique, each without parallel in the category formation of the other. These unique categories tell us what is distinctive about each religion. In previous chapters we have shown significant congruence between Judaic and Islamic law in structure and procedures. We have also discussed areas of relative incongruity, where each tradition treats the same subjects as the other, but presents them in different ways or with varying degrees of emphasis. Thus each religion offers to the other categories that are comparable to those of the other, and the one may understand the other, if not in detail, then at least in general terms: this is not exactly like that, but it is sufficiently similar to make sense in the context of the counterpart party to dialogue. We may, for instance, find ideas or practices that function, each in its own structure, in a manner similar to those of the other. At the point at which each religious tradition speaks of unique matters, however, the one tradition proves utterly inconsistent with the other.

What are some of these unique categories? For Judaism, one such category without a counterpart in Islam speaks of the relations of a specific, limited community in the model of God's relation with Moses; another involves the formation of the Israelite man in the image and likeness of God as revealed to "our rabbi," Moses. We shall discuss these under the rubrics "Land of Israel" or "enlandisement," and "The Sage and Torah Study." For Islam, unique categories deal with human beings delegated to create a universal society, equally subject to divine law, with divinely inspired law providing legitimacy. These will be discussed under the rubrics "Jihad" and "Khilafat and Legal Scholars." In these areas, each tradition defines for itself categories of law – norms of behavior that realize norms of belief – with no counterpart whatsoever in the system of the other. We will also see that the rationale for these unique categories is reflected in the two religions' respective conceptions of history.

While we have confined our treatment to classical sources, we are now discussing matters of acutely contemporary concern, and it is important to underscore that we do not propose to explain political conflict by appeal to religious difference. Let us explain what we can, and cannot accomplish in the comparison of religions that, in a worldly framework in specific places and for secular reasons now enter into hostilities with one another. With each religion focused for its own reasons upon its particular concerns, dialogue between the two proves difficult. And in a world in which, for political reasons, Islam and Judaism intersect under circumstances not favorable to interfaith dialogue of a philosophical and theological character, the result is uncomprehending dismissal of the other. The other makes no sense. So we turn to the conflict of categories created when each party finds the other beyond all rationality, because the one side speaks of matters, values things, for which the other has no vocabulary and bears no appreciation.

For, as we shall now see, where Judaism identifies categories unique to itself and for theological reasons develops those categories within its own logic and rationality, Islam has not the resources to grasp why those categories matter or what they entail. Thus both Islam and Judaism must find exceedingly difficult the task of understanding even the theological foundations of the political conflict in the secular world. So too, where Islam frames its theory of the meaning and end of human history, the tasks assigned by God to Muslim faith, it takes up a position in conflict with Judaism (and Christianity, as a matter of fact) that is not to be resolved by appeal to considerations which Judaism (or Christianity) is able to find self-evidently reasonable. No shared rationality allows the one side to make sense, in its terms, of the points of difference with the other.

We do not suggest that religious practice or theological conviction lays the foundations of the conflict between Jews and Arabs. The secular and the political define the terms of today's headlines. But what we can show is that the respective religions do not contribute to the resolution of conflict and may, for reasons hardly generated by politics, vastly complicate the political relationships between Jews and Arabs. That fact makes all the more weighty the record of amity and even religious understanding written at some times and places past and present, contemporary Turkey and Morocco, but also contemporary Britain and the USA, representing the hopeful side of the relationship. So amity can be attained, but let us now consider the theological-legal obstacles.

What is at stake in the task at hand? In identifying categories unique to the one religion or the other, we can clarify some of the bases of mutual incomprehension. In the everyday world of the present, the two religions conflict in specific ways. As citizens of the contemporary world order and as scholars, we owe an account of how in concrete ways comparable category formations prove incompatible. Here we make our contribution to understanding why communication in religious terms between the two religions is so difficult: each party assumes it understands the other, while in fact neither grasps the rationality of the other. That is because the one talks in its language about its concerns, and the other draws upon its profound resources of faith and theology to set forth its own message to its own believers. The result is that neither party grasps what the other is saying. In the conviction of the Enlightenment that learning enlightens and yields mutual understanding to mitigate and even overcome difference, we address the acute contemporary crisis in the meeting of Islam and Judaism. An issue of politics – the relationship between the State of Israel and the Muslim world – has enveloped theological convictions of a profound and other-worldly character. These concern the meaning of enlandisement, specifically, the point at which, in the theology and religion of Judaism, particular places are identified as holy. Where God is to be found, where God takes place – that is at issue in enlandisement. In the case of Islam, the issue is simply that God is to be found everywhere – in any land – where Islamic law prevails and that, for the benefit of all humanity, Islam envisions the entire world ideally subject to God through divinely inspired law.

That brings us to the contrasting categories, Land of Israel and jihad – the most distinctive categories unique to the traditions under discussion. What we shall see is that while both Islam and Judaism concur that certain places are made holy by God's relationship to those places, what the one party means scarcely corresponds with the statement and intent of the other. So even when both speak of exactly the same place, Jerusalem, using much the same language, they turn out to talk past one another. Nothing that academic learning contributes can provide a shared language or acceptance of the other's position, but pointing out the categorical differences involved in the warring parties' use of theological language may help to clarify what is at stake in the statements of each in this political dispute.

B Enlandisement (Judaism)

Judaism encompasses a religious system set forth in the Torah, written and oral. Zionism is a national political movement. But they intersect at the critical point, the importance accorded by both to a specific territory: (1) the

Land of Israel, the Torah's promised land, and (2) the State of Israel, the goal of Zionism. In Judaism as distinct from Zionism, the Land of Israel forms a critical venue and occasion of theological expression. It is therefore all too easy to confuse the enlandised character of classical Judaism – its insistence upon the special holiness of a particular territory – with the politics of the nation-state, the state of Israel. But in fact, the Land of Israel is valued within the documents of the Torah for considerations that do not operate in Zionism, and Zionism endows the Land of Israel with importance that scarcely pertains to the Torah. So, though it requires great effort, let us keep separate the enlandised religion, Judaism, from the land-focused nationalism, Zionism, and take up only the former and its statements about the Land of Israel. This is because, in order to understand the enlandised character of the religion Judaism, we have to put aside for the moment the other, and competing, explanation of the relationship of the Jews to the territory known as Palestine or the State of Israel, the secular, Zionist one.[1]

Let us expand on this point, because it is the source of much confusion. The religion, Judaism, views the Jews as Israel, a holy people called into being at Sinai and defined by the Torah revealed there; the secular national movement, Zionism, views the Jews as one people, that ought to form a political entity and which realized that aspiration in the founding of the State of Israel in the Land of Israel. While comparable in detail, the two conceptions of what the Jews are – a people called into existence by God at Sinai to receive the Torah and live by it, or a people formed by a common history and destiny and linked to a particular territory by tradition and sentiment – should not be confused. Each bears within itself its own logic, and the statements of the one, even though they coincide with those of the other, make sense only in context, whether theological for Judaism, the religion or political for Zionism, the political movement. Here we want to understand why the Land of Israel takes so critical a role in the religion Judaism.

Then why does a particular territory take so critical a role in Classical Judaism as set forth by the dual Torah? It is not because of miracles which happened in that place; that is, as ground made holy by events. The Land of Israel stands for something that transcends history and speaks to eternity. How is that so? We find the answer in the context in the encompassing and coherent theological system that nourishes classical Judaism. Judaism accounts for creation and humankind from beginning to end by appealing to the Hebrew scriptures (the written Torah) from Genesis forward. There, like Christianity and Islam still later, Judaism encounters God's account of who Man is: the story of Eden and the fall. And as Christianity appeals to Jesus as the Last Adam, come to repair the damage brought about by the first, so Judaism seeks to restore Eden and to put Adam and Eve back into Paradise. This it does by treating Israel, the people, as God's candidates for those who will love God and carry out his will, as Adam and Eve did not; and by finding the Land of Israel, fully permeated by God's will in the Torah, as God's choice for the renewed Eden. That account of Israel as Adam's successor, the Land as the stead of Eden, carries us far beyond the mundane realities of contemporary politics and wars.

So classical Judaism set forth a system that treats the holy people of Israel as counterpart but ultimately opposite to Adam. Adam lived in Eden but rebelled against God and was driven out. Israel lived in the Land of Israel and for a brief moment, upon entry, Israel recapitulated Eden. But as the Torah (scripture) says in the authorized history from Genesis through Kings, Israel rebelled against God and was driven out. But what distinguishes Israel from Adam is that Israel possessed the Torah, which held the power to transform the heart of man and so turn man from rebellion to loving submission. And when the Israelite man, regenerate in the Torah, fully conformed to the Torah, then Israel would recover its Eden, the Land of Israel.

This account of matters is not merely implicit in the Written Torah but is made explicit in the Oral Torah. That statement is made in so many words. Here, the Land of Israel to Israel is like Eden to Adam, and the story of the two are the same, with the difference that Israel, driven from the Land, can return:

1. A. R. Abbahu in the name of R. Yosé bar Haninah commenced [discourse by citing this verse]: "'But they are like a man, they have transgressed the covenant. There they dealt treacherously against me' (Hosea 6:7).

   B. "They are like a man, specifically, this refers to the first man [Adam]. [We shall now compare the story of the first man in Eden with the story of Israel in its land.]

   C. "Said the Holy One, blessed be He, 'In the case of the first man, I brought him into the garden of Eden, I commanded him, he violated my commandment, I judged him to be sent away and driven out, but I mourned for him, saying "How..."' [which begins the book of Lamentations, hence stands for a lament, but which is also written with the consonants that also yield, Where are you].

   D. "'I brought him into the garden of Eden,' as it is written, 'And the Lord God took the man and put him into the garden of Eden' (Genesis 2:15).

   E. "'I commanded him,' as it is written, 'And the Lord God commanded . . .' (Genesis 2:16).

   F. "'And he violated my commandment,' as it is written, 'Did you eat from the tree concerning which I commanded you' (Genesis 3:11).

   G. "'I judged him to be sent away,' as it is written, 'And the Lord God sent him from the garden of Eden' (Genesis 3:23).

   H. "'And I judged him to be driven out.' 'And he drove out the man' (Genesis 3:24).

I. "'But I mourned for him, saying, How. . . .' And He said to him, 'Where are you' (Genesis 3:9), and the word for 'where are you' is written, 'How. . . .'

J. "'So too in the case of his descendants, [God continues to speak,] I brought them into the Land of Israel, I commanded them, they violated my commandment, I judged them to be sent out and driven away but I mourned for them, saying, How. . . .'

K. "'I brought them into the Land of Israel:' 'And I brought you into the land of Carmel' (Jeremiah 2:7).

L. "'I commanded them:' 'And you, command the children of Israel' (Exodus 27:20). 'Command the children of Israel' (Leviticus 24:2).

M. "'They violated my commandment:' 'And all Israel have violated your Torah' (Daniel 9:11).

N. "'I judged them to be sent out:' 'Send them away, out of my sight and let them go forth' (Jeremiah 15:1).

O. "'. . . and driven away:' 'From my house I shall drive them' (Hosea 9:15).

P. "'But I mourned for them, saying, How. . . :' 'How lonely sits the city [that was full of people! How like a widow has she become, she that was great among the nations! She that was a princess among the cities has become a vassal. She weeps bitterly in the night, tears on her cheeks, among all her lovers she has none to comfort her; all her friends have dealt treacherously with her, they have become her enemies]' (Lamentations 1:1–2)."

(Lamentations Rabbati IV.I.1)

Israel represents the new Adam, God's way of correcting the errors of the initial creation. The Land of Israel stands for the new Eden. Just as Adam entered a perfect world but lost it, so Israel was given a perfect world but lost it. The difference, however, is that Israel has what Adam did not have, which is the Torah, a point that does not enter here except by indirection. The upshot is that the enlandisement of Judaism, involving as it does the enchantment of the Land of Israel, takes its place, makes sense, only in the context of the Torah's theory of who is man and what God wants from man, which is man's willing submission to God's will, made known in the Torah.

The restoration of Israel to the Land then forms a chapter in the story of the redemption of all of mankind. The last things are to be known from the first. In the just plan of creation man was meant to live in Eden, and Israel in the Land of Israel in time without end. The restoration to the Land will bring about that long and tragically postponed perfection of the world order, sealing the demonstration of the justice of God's plan for creation. Risen from the dead, having atoned through death, man will be judged in accord with his deeds. Israel for its part, when it repents and conforms its will to God's, recovers its Eden.

So the consequences of rebellion and sin having been overcome, the struggle of man's will and God's word having been resolved, God's original plan will be realized at the last. The simple, global logic of the system, with its focus on the world order of justice established by God but disrupted by man, leads inexorably to this eschatology of restoration, the restoration of balance, order, proportion – eternity. Holy Israel, the people defined theologically and not politically, then assembles at prayer and expresses the hope that God at the end of days, will call all humanity to his worship, as, even now, he has called Holy Israel. Then everyone will acknowledge the sovereignty of the one and only God and accept his dominion.

In the theology of Judaism, the stakes prove cosmic. Death does not mark the end of individual human life, nor exile the last stop in the journey of Holy Israel. Israelites will live in the age or the world to come, all Israel in the Land of Israel; and Israel will comprehend all who know the one true God. The restoration of world order that completes the demonstration of God's justice encompasses both private life and the domain of all Israel. For both restorationist theology provides eternal life; to be Israel means to live. So far as the individual is concerned, beyond the grave, at a determinate moment, Man (1) rises from the grave in resurrection, (2) is judged, and (3) enjoys the world to come. For the entirety of Israel, congruently: all Israel participates in the resurrection, which takes place in the Land of Israel, and enters the world to come.

The priority of the Land of Israel is aligned with the conception of the resurrection of the dead, and the result is that the latter must take place in the designated holy space. The same position is taken in the following composite:

III.17 A. Said R. Eleazar, "The dead that are abroad will not come back to life: 'And I will set glory in the land of the living' (Ezekiel 26:20) – the dead buried in the land where I have my desire will live, but the dead of the land in which I have no desire won't live."

　　　 B. Objected R. Abba bar Mammal, "'Your dead shall live, my dead bodies shall arise' (Isaiah 26:19) – doesn't 'your dead shall live' mean, they will live among the dead that are in the Land of Israel, and doesn't 'my dead bodies shall arise' mean, to the dead outside of the Land; and doesn't 'and I will give glory in the Land of Israel' refer to Nebuchadnezzar, concerning whom the All-Merciful has said, 'I will bring against them a king who is as swift as a stag'?"

　　　 C. He said to him, "My lord, I expound another verse of scripture: 'He who gives breath to the people upon it, and spirit to them that walk therein' (Isaiah 42:5)."

　　　 D. But isn't it written, "My dead bodies shall arise"?

　　　 E. That refers to abortions.

The same view is expressed in a different way:

III.18 A. "And spirit to them that walk therein":
      B. Said R. Jeremiah bar Abbah said R. Yohanan, "Whoever walks four cubits in the Land of Israel is certain that he will belong to the world to come."

The problem finds its now-familiar solution:

III.19 A. Then according to R. Eleazar, won't the righteous who are outside of the Land live [at the end of time]?
      B. Said R. Ilaa, "It will come about through rolling [to the Land]."
      C. Objected R. Abba Sala the Elder, "Won't the rolling hurt the righteous?"
      D. Said Abbayye, "Underground passages will be made for them."
                (Bavli-tractate Ketubot 13:11 III.16FF./111A)

So too the Land of Israel is where one will want to be buried, and that fully accords with the system's conception of the special sanctity of the Land of Israel when it is occupied by Israel:

A. He would say, "Whoever is buried in other lands is as though he were buried in Babylonia. Whoever is buried in Babylonia is as if he were buried in the Land of Israel. Whoever is buried in the Land of Israel is as if he were buried under the altar.
B. "For the whole of the Land of Israel is suitable as a location for the altar.
C. "And whoever is buried under the altar is as if he were buried under the throne of glory.
D. "As it is said, You throne of glory, on high from the beginning, you place of our sanctuary (Jeremiah 17:12)."
                (The Fathers According to Rabbi Nathan XXVI:III:.1)

The corollary of the doctrine that the dead will be raised at the last judgment, which will take place in the Land of Israel, is that one is best off being buried in the Land of Israel. The righteous who are buried abroad will be brought back there for resurrection. Once the matters of the priority of the Land and the last judgment are juxtaposed, the doctrines set forth here become predictable. The enlandisement of Judaism takes place within the fundamental doctrine of man, his fall from Eden and restoration to the condition of Paradise, through the eschatological drama played out by the holy people of Israel – the people defined as that sector of humanity that knows God as one and unique – in the Holy Land, the counterpart to Eden that is the Land of Israel. That is what the classical statement of Judaism means when it speaks of Israel and of the Land of Israel: a society sanctified by God through the Torah, a territory that is transcendent over ordinary space.

C Jerusalem and the lack of enlandisement in Islam

Enlandisement is unique to Judaism, with no counterpart in Islam. This fact is illustrated by the centrality of Jerusalem in classical Judaism, and its relatively limited importance in Islam. In classical Judaism, Jerusalem is represented as the highest point, the location of the temple where God is served through the sacrifices daily, weekly, monthly, and at appointed times; these atone for sin and propitiate God. The destruction of Jerusalem in 586 CE, its restoration under Holy Israel's nurture three generations later, its destruction in 70 CE — these represent cosmic events, not merely this-worldly happenings. Just as the Land possesses theological meaning, vastly transcending issues of geography and politics, so does the Holy City.

By contrast, Islamic law has very little to say about Jerusalem. When the early texts do mention it, it is usually by way of examples of *naskh*, abrogation of later earlier texts by later texts. In discussing the possibility of abrogation under various circumstances, as we saw in Chapter 3, al-Shafi'i was asked if it was possible that a hadith report had been abrogated but that the abrogating report had not been transmitted. Al-Shafi'i replied:

> That is impossible. For how could the transmitted sunna be possibly abrogated while the one which is binding was abandoned? Were this permissible the whole sunna might be abandoned by men, for they would [then] say: "Perhaps it was abrogated." No duty has ever been abrogated unless it was replaced by another. The abrogation of qibla [i.e., prayer in the direction] of Jerusalem by another [in the direction of] the Ka'ba [in Mecca] is a case in point. For whatever has been abrogated in the Book or in the sunna must have been [replaced by] something else.[2]

Again:

> God has commanded the Apostle to turn in the direction of Jerusalem in prayer. Before this direction was abrogated it was not permitted to turn in any other direction. But it was abrogated and [the Apostle] was ordered to turn in the direction of the [Sacred] House [of Mecca]: It became unlawful in accordance with the textual command to turn either in the direction of Jerusalem or to any other direction than that of the Sacred House.
>
> . . . Each [direction] was valid in its time: The turning toward Jerusalem — when God ordered His Prophet to turn to it — was obligatory; but after it was abrogated it became obligatory to turn

only toward the Sacred house, and no other direction is permitted by law, except in the event of fear [of danger] or in a supererogatory prayer in travel as indicated in the Book and the sunna.[3]

Hadith literature offers some reports on the merit of prayer in the mosque of Jerusalem and the permissibility of making lesser (or supererogatory) pilgrimage ('umra) only to the mosques of Mecca, Medina, and Jerusalem. The Jerusalem mosque is undoubtedly sacred in Islam. But there is no sacralization of the city as a whole, or of its land. Indeed, as we saw in the case of the Hajj (the required pilgrimage), even the sacredness of Mecca is a matter of the condition of purity (ihram) of the believer in preparation for commemorating the establishment of the covenant, rather than an attribute inherent to the time or place of pilgrimage. The Qur'an ultimately settles the issue by saying that the direction of prayer is not the source of holiness:

> It is not piety that you turn your faces to the East or the West. Pious is one who believes in God and the Last Day, the angels, the Book, and the prophets, and spends for love of Him on relatives, orphans, poor people, travellers, the needy, and for captives, performs the prayer, and gives charity; and the one who keeps promises, is patient in poverty and hardship and conflict. It is these who are truthful and pious.
>
> (Sura 2:178)

Mecca is the place of required pilgrimage in Islam because of its special status as the place where Abraham established a sanctuary to commemorate the covenant or pact to submit to divine will. But the covenant was not between Abraham and God alone; Abraham spoke for all human beings, at least potentially; the covenant was God's promise of eternal reward for those who submit to the divine will. Nor was the covenant limited to Abraham's family. The Qur'an addresses this question specifically when recounting the establishment of the covenant: "And they say no one will enter Paradise unless he is a Jew or a Christian. These are their wishes. Say, 'Show your proof if you are truthful.' No, whoever submits his will to God and does good will have his reward with his Lord" (Sura 2:112–13). To emphasize that the covenant is not limited to a specific group, as was noted above, the Qur'an continues:

> People of Israel, remember my blessing to you and that I preferred you over all. And beware the day that no one will redeem anything for another. . . . And when his Lord tested Abraham with certain words and he fulfilled them, He said, "I will make you a leader of people." [Abraham] said, "And my offspring?" And He said, "My covenant does not extend to the oppressors."
>
> (Sura 2:123–25)

Similarly, wherever the covenant was established and renewed, whether Sinai or Mecca, as Islamic teaching it was not concerned with a specific piece of land. The Qur'an says, "To God belongs the East and the West, so wherever you turn, there will be the face to God. Indeed, God is bountiful and all knowing" (Sura 2:116). The land of God is therefore, like the people of God, potentially universal. Wherever Islamic law prevails, this is the land of God. As we saw in Chapter 3, Islamic law refers to dar al-Islam, the abode of Islam, those areas where Islamic law prevails. Other lands were referred to as the dar al-'ahd, "abode of treaty," dar al-sulh, "abode of truce," or dar al-harb, the "abode of war." Indeed, "dar al-Islam" became the most common designation of the Muslim community among the classical legal scholars.[4] Dar al-'ahd and dar al-sulh are both regions whose leaders have agreed to pay the Muslim leaders a certain tax and to protect the rights of any Muslims and/or their allies who dwell there, but who otherwise maintain their autonomy, including their own legal systems. Dar al-harb includes those regions whose leaders have made no such agreement and where, therefore, Muslims and their allies, unprotected by law, are technically under threat. The goal envisioned by the classical sources of Islamic law is for all people to be protected from error, and the inevitable punishment resulting from it, by submitting to God's will as expressed in Islamic law. The counterpart to the Land of Israel in Islamic law, then, is not another piece of land, but the category concerning the means by which the will of God is to be made universal.

D Jihad (Islam)

Since the Land of Israel in classical Judaism is treated as comparable to Eden, and since it is there that the dead will be raised for eternal life, we may say that the Land of Israel plays a critical role in the eschatology, the theory of the Last Things, of Judaism. Islam has no counterpart, no specific this-worldly locale where the Last Things play themselves out. Yet we are treating jihad in this chapter, parallel with the Land of Israel for Judaism because it is not only a category with no counterpart in Judaism, but in this uniqueness, like the uniqueness of enlandisement in Judaism, it makes clear what ultimately distinguishes Islam as a religion.

In Islam the reward for submitting to God's will is eternal life. Like Jews, Muslims are required to submit to the divine will in order to achieve their eternal reward, but there is no guarantee of an earthly, much less a land-based, reward – although the possibility is not denied. Furthermore, Muslims believe that the divine will has been clearly revealed. The word "islam" means "submission," as we have seen, and it is assumed that it is to the will of God that submission is to be made. Yet while both Judaism and Islam institutionalize the divine will in their legal codes, in Islam the legal code is recognized as a human construct and therefore fallible and open to revision.

"Shari'a," the term often used for Islamic law, is described as eternal and immutable. Shari'ah, "the way," however, actually refers to God's will for humanity. As such, it is indeed eternal and immutable. The term for the actual codes of law, as noted in Chapter 2, is fiqh, which refers to knowledge or human understanding of, and efforts to apply, the divine will to specific circumstances. Accordingly, while God's will is eternal and changeless, and the ultimate goal of humanity is to submit to it, part of the struggle to do so is the effort to understand and implement it properly.

It is conceivable in Islam, in other words, that one could follow Islamic legal codes to the letter in a given time and place, and still not be fulfilling the will of God. This is because the codes themselves are not considered to be the final word. The Qur'an, in fact, leaves the struggle to do the will of God open ended. It describes itself as "guidance for people" (hudan li'l-nas). It gives a number of specific rules, as have been noted; prohibitions against murder, theft, drunkenness, and gambling, for example, are clear, and circumstances under which such rules would be abrogated are inconceivable. However, the majority of the Qur'an's guidance is of a more general nature. Requirements of generosity, mercy, and kindness, for example, and prohibitions against exploitation of the weak, cruelty, and oppression must be revisited on a regular basis.

What is considered mercy in one context may turn out to be exploitation of the weak in another. As we noted in Chapter 6, for instance, classical Islamic legal codes specified what they considered to be fair treatment of slaves. In the contemporary period, however, it is unanimously agreed that slavery of any form is unjust. This does not mean that contemporary legal thought judges early Muslims to have been unfair. On the contrary, commentators concur that in the circumstances in which early fiqh developed, the regulations safeguarded those who found themselves in the position of slaves. This reflects the fact that Islamic law is not a closed system; as discussed in Chapter 3, one of the sources of legislation is ijtihad, the effort to understand revealed sources in light of, and for application in, circumstances which may have changed from those eliciting earlier applications.

This brings us to the much-misunderstood category of jihad, which has been treated as a secular and political matter, when in fact it is the key to Islamic piety: the ongoing struggle to fulfill the will of God. Ijtihad, the effort to understand and articulate specific ways to fulfill the will of God, is a kind of jihad; the two terms come from the same root, which means "to give utmost effort." Noted Pakistani scholar Fazlur Rahman says:

> The intellectual endeavor or jihad, including the intellectual elements of both the moments – past and present – is technically ijtihad, which means "the effort to understand the meaning of a relevant text or precedent in the past, containing a rule, and to alter that rule by

extending or restricting or otherwise modifying it in such a manner that a new situation can be subsumed under it by a new solution.[5]

The Qur'an is considered complete; it is the final word of God and sufficient, along with the clarifications provided by hadith literature, to guide believers to fulfillment of the will of God. But what it calls for is not mere conformity with a closed or limited set of instructions. By its very nature it poses a challenge for human beings to find ever more effective ways to create the society it envisions. Every effort extended in such endeavor is called jihad, according to the contemporary understanding expressed by Fazlur Rahman.

There is support for this view in the Qur'an. "O you who believe, shall I point out a bargain that will save you from a painful punishment? Believe in God and His messenger and strive [do jihad] in the path of God with your possessions and your persons. That is better for you if you have knowledge" (Sura 61:11–12). It seems clear especially in the early verses, those revealed before the emigration from Mecca to Medina, that the emphasis is on jihad by means other than warfare. For example, the root of jihad is used to refer to efforts to remain steadfast in monotheism despite efforts of others to persuade one otherwise. The theme of spiritual jihad, in the sense of controlling one's wayward desires, also became popular in oral literature. It is reflected in the popularly quoted hadith according to which Prophet Muhammad, upon returning from a battle, said that now that the lesser jihad was complete, he could continue with the greater jihad of non-military struggle. This same spirit is reflected in discussions in later centuries of four kinds of jihad: by the heart, the tongue, the hands, and – only lastly – by the sword.[6]

The classical legal sources make some reference to non-military jihad. For example, Malik's *al-Muwatta* includes the following in his discussion of jihad:

> Yahya related to me from Malik from Zayd ibn Aslam from Abu Salih as-Samman from Abu Hurayra that the Messenger of Allah, may Allah bless him and grant him peace, said, "Horses are a reward for one man, a protection for another, a burden for another. The one for whom they are a reward is the one who dedicates them for use in the way of Allah, and tethers them in a meadow or grassland. Whatever the horse enjoys of the grassland or meadow in the length of its tether are good deeds for him. If it breaks its tether and goes over a hillock or two, its tracks and droppings are good deeds for him. If it crosses a river and drinks from it while he did not mean to allow it to drink it, that counts as good deeds for him, and the horse is a reward for him. Another man uses his horse to gain self reliance and upstandingness and does not forget Allah's right on their necks and backs. Horses are a protection for him. Another man uses them out of

pride to show them off and in hostility to the people of Islam. They are a burden on that man.

The Messenger of Allah, may Allah bless him and grant him peace, was asked about donkeys, and he said, "Nothing has been revealed to me about them except this single all-inclusive [verse]: 'Whoever does an atom of good will see it, and whoever does an atom of evil will see it'."

(Sura 99:7–8)

In other words, efforts will be judged according to their intent and effect. Apparently, Malik believed that all such efforts fall into the category of jihad. The section continues:

> Yahya related to me from Malik that Yahya ibn Sa'id said, "'Ubayda ibn al-Walik ibn 'Ubada ibn as-Samit informed me from his father that his grandfather ['Ubada] said, 'We made a contract with the Messenger of Allah, may Allah bless him and grant him peace, to hear and obey in ease and hardship, enthusiasm and reluctance, and not to dispute with people in authority and to speak to establish the truth wherever we were without worrying about criticism.'"

Steadfastness in adversity, then, as well as honesty even in the face of harsh reaction, likewise fall into the category of jihad. Malik also includes patience and faith in times of fear in his discussion of jihad:

> Yahya related to me from Malik that Zayd ibn Aslam had said that 'Ubayda ibn al-Jarrah had written to 'Umar ibn al-Khattab mentioning to him a great array of Byzantine troops and the anxiety they were causing him. 'Umar ibn al-Khattab wrote in reply to him, "Whatever hardship befalls a believing slave, Allah will make an opening for him after it, and a hardship will not overcome two eases. Allah the Exalted says in His Book, 'O you who trust, be patient, and vie in patience! Be steadfast and fear Allah, perhaps you will profit.'"

(Sura 3:200)[7]

Thus, any earnest effort to do the right thing, to obey the commandments of God and duly established authority, to be honest and establish true belief, or simply to maintain faith in times of stress is considered jihad by Malik. Nevertheless, given that there is little legislation possible concerning people's ongoing struggle to do the will of God, the greatest attention to jihad in classical legal sources is given to military jihad. Malik's chapter on jihad is one of the shortest in his compendium, but it opens with a report of the necessity of jihad:

Yahya related to me from Malik from Abu'z-Zinad from al-A'raj from Abu Hurayra that the Messenger of Allah, may Allah bless him and grant him peace, said, "Someone who does jihad in the way of Allah is like someone who fasts and prays constantly and does not slacken from his prayer and fasting until he returns."

Here it is clear that the reference is to military jihad, especially in the succeeding discussion of the merits of martyrdom, a topic to which he will return:

[A]nd "Allah guarantees either the Garden or a safe return to his home with whatever he has obtained of reward or booty for the one who does jihad in His way, if it is solely jihad and trust in his promise that brings him out of his house."

Yahya related to me from 'Abdullah ibn 'Abd ar-Rahman ibn Ma'mar al-Ansari that 'Ata' ibn Yasar said that the Messenger of Allah, may Allah bless him and grant him peace, "Shall I tell you who has the best degree among people? A man who takes the rein of his horse to do jihad in the way of Allah. Shall I tell you who has the best degree among people after him? A man who lives alone with a few sheep, performs the prayer, pays the [alms tax], and worships Allah without associating anything with Him."[8]

The rest of Malik's chapter on jihad focuses entirely on regulations concerning military jihad. For example, it is forbidden to carry a copy of the Qur'an in enemy territory lest it fall into unfriendly hands. If someone wants to go on military campaign and his parents disapprove, he should obey them and delay going on campaign for a year. A great deal of attention is paid to disposition of the spoils of war. It is assumed, according to tradition, that one-fifth of the spoils go to the Muslim leader for administrative purposes, but the rest is distributed among the warriors, with a double (or triple) share for warriors fighting on horseback. If there are not enough camels to distribute equally among the participants in the jihad, then they can substitute ten sheep for one camel. If a paid laborer participates in the battle he should get a share of the booty, but only free men present at the battle receive a share. Participants in the battle may eat as much as they like of the food they find before having to divide it up as spoils.

If while distributing spoils it is noticed that some of it actually belongs to a Muslim, having been plundered by the now defeated enemy, then that property must be returned to its owner before distribution of booty. But if the distribution takes place before rightful ownership is recognized, it is too late. "Whatever has already been distributed is not returned to anyone."[9] An exception is made in the case of an umm walad, i.e., a slave woman who had been impregnated by her Muslim owner. Ordinarily, women and children captured in battle are made slaves for Muslims, but if the umm walad had been captured by the enemies from a Muslim, then the leader of the community or the father of child should pay the appropriate ransom. The personal effects of the slain enemies go to the Muslim warriors who can prove they actually did the killing, provided permission is given by the Muslim leader. Otherwise, the personal effects become part of the booty to be distributed equally among the warriors.

As noted, a good deal of Malik's treatment of military jihad deals with the fact that those who die on campaign become martyrs and are thus rewarded in the afterlife. So powerful a stimulus to jihad is the promise of bountiful eternal reward that Malik relates that the Prophet himself wished to become a martyr:

> Yahya related to me from Malik from Abu'z-Zinad from al-Aʿraj from Abu Hurayra that the Messenger of Allah, may Allah bless him and grant him peace, said, "By He in whose hand my self is! I would like to fight in the way of Allah and be killed, then be brought to life again so I could be killed, and then be brought to life again so I could be killed."
>
> Abu Hurayra said three times, "I testify to it by Allah!"[10]

Further impetus is given in a report about God's delight in martyrs' sacrifices: "Allah laughs at two men. One of them kills the other, but each of them will enter the Garden; one fights in the way of Allah and is killed, then Allah turns (in forgiveness) to the killer, so he fights (in the way of Allah) and also becomes a martyr."[11] Malik relates further that martyrdom is so glorious that on the last day martyrs' wounds will bleed again, but this time the blood will smell of musk. At death, all martyrs' faults will be forgiven, although their debts will remain outstanding. Martyrs need not even be washed or prayed over at death; they are to be buried where they fall.

Therefore, although jihad is any strenuous exertion to do the will of God, including spreading what is considered to be true belief, military jihad receives the most attention in classical sources because of the necessity of specific legislation about the topic. In addition to the basic issues covered by Malik above, two further areas of jihad legislation must be examined for a full understanding of the subject. First, military jihad is not a duty for all Muslims. It falls into a category of duties known as *kifaya*, which means that the duty is collective; provided a sufficient number of community members undertake the duty so that the job is done, others are excused the duty.

The status of the duty of jihad, in fact, is the gist of al-Shafiʿi's treatment of the subject, which comes in the context of his discussion of legal knowledge. As we saw in Chapter 3, he says that there are two kinds of legal knowledge. First, knowledge of the requirements for daily prayers, fasting, pilgrimage, and alms tax, and the prohibition of such things as usury, adultery, murder, theft, and intoxicants is required of all people. It is found in the Qur'an and basic Islamic practice; it is therefore unacceptable for any adult Muslim to be ignorant of it. The second kind, however, is more complex, derived not necessarily from specific texts but from analogical reasoning based on texts, and therefore subject to differing interpretations. Not all people are capable of this level of knowledge. Al-Shafi'i does not imply that this kind of knowledge is rare because it takes a rare intelligence, however, but because it takes a great deal of study, making it impractical for everyone in the community to engage in its pursuit. Not everyone can make a full-time job of legal knowledge. Instead, he says that the pursuit of advanced legal knowledge, like other kifaya duties, is supererogatory. It merits reward but, provided enough people engage in it to assure that the task is accomplished, those who do not are excused of the duty. That is, those who do not perform kifaya duties are not punished: "The public is incapable of knowing this kind of knowledge, nor can all specialists obtain it. But those who do obtain it should not all neglect it. If some can obtain it, the others are relieved of the duty [of obtaining it]; but those who do obtain it will be rewarded."[12]

When pressed for a textual basis for this distinction, al-Shafi'i cited the example of jihad:

God has imposed the [duty of] jihad as laid down in His Book and uttered by His Prophet's tongue. He stressed the calling [of men to fulfill] the jihad [duty] as follows:

God has bought from the believers their selves and their possessions against [the gift of] Paradise. They fight in the way of God; they kill, and are killed; that is a promise binding upon God in the Torah and Gospel and the Qur'an; and who fulfills his covenant better than God? So rejoice in the bargain you have made with Him. That is the mighty triumph. [Sura 9:112]

And He said:

Fight the polytheists totally as they fight you totally; and know that God is with the God-fearing. [Sura 9:36]

And He said:

Slay the polytheists wherever you find them, and take them, and confine them, and lie in ambush for them everywhere. But if they repent and perform the prayer and pay the zakat, then set them free. God is All-forgiving, All-compassionate. [Sura 9:5]

And He said:

> Fight those who do not believe in God nor in the Last Day, who do not forbid what God and His Apostle have made forbidden, and who do not practice the religion of truth, of those who have been given the Book, until they pay the jizya out of hand and have been humbled. [Sura 9:29]

With these scriptural quotes, al-Shafi'i believes he has demonstrated the fact that military jihad is a duty. He then quotes hadith material which indicates that military jihad is a duty incumbent upon all Muslims:

> 'Abd al-'Aziz b. Muhammad al-Darawardi told us from Muhammad b. 'Amr b. 'Alqama from Abu Salama [b. 'Abd al-Rahman] from Abu Hurayra, who said that the Apostle of God said:

> > I shall continue to fight the unbelievers until they say: "There is no god but God;" if they make this pronouncement they shall be secured their blood and property, unless taken for its price, and their reward shall be given by God.

> And God, glorified be His praise, said:

> > O believers, what is the matter with you, that when it is said to you, "Go forth in the way of God," you sink down to the ground? Are you so content with this present life as to neglect the Hereafter? The enjoyment of this life is little in comparison with the Hereafter. If you do not go forth, He will inflict upon you a painful punishment, and instead of you He will substitute another people; and you will not hurt Him at all, for God is powerful over everything. [Sura 9:38–39]

> And He said:

> > Go forth, light and heavy! Struggle in God's way with your possessions and yourselves! That is better for you, did you but know. [Sura 9:41]

Al-Shafi'i draws the obvious conclusion from these quotes:

> [Shafi'i] said: These communications mean that the jihad, and rising up in arms in particular, is obligatory for the able-bodied [believers], exempting no one, just as prayer, pilgrimage and [payment of] alms are performed, and no person is permitted to perform the duty for another, since performance by one will not fulfill the duty for another.

But he then returns to his earlier position, claiming that the duty is collective, not individual:

They also mean that the duty of [jihad] is a collective (kifaya) duty different from that of prayer: Those who perform it in the war against polytheists will fulfill the duty and receive the supererogatory merit, thereby preventing those who have stayed behind from falling into error.

In an effort to reconcile the two seemingly irreconcilable positions – that military jihad is required of all able-bodied Muslims and that it is a collective duty which must be carried out only by enough people to do the job – al-Shafi'i concludes that while military jihad is indeed a collective rather than individual duty, meaning that those who do not engage in it will not be punished, God nevertheless "prefers" those who do engage in it:

> But God has not put the two [categories of men] on an equal footing, for He said:
>
>> Such believers who sit at home – unless they have an injury – are not the equals of those who fight in the path of God with their possessions and their selves. God has given precedence to those who fight with their possessions and their selves over those who sit at home. God has promised the best of things to both, and He has preferred those who fight over those who sit at home by [granting them] a mighty reward.
>>
>> (Sura 4:97)

Al-Shafi'i cannot restrain himself from concluding that this verse means that military jihad is an individual duty: "The literal meaning of this communication is that the duty is obligatory on all men." But when his interlocutor asks, "Where is the proof for your opinion that if some people perform the duty, the others would be relieved of punishment?" al-Shafi'i has to admit that he has already cited the relevant verse: "God said, 'Yet to each God has promised the best of things.'"

> Thus God has promised "the best of things" for those who stayed behind and could not go to the jihad, although he clearly specified his preference for those who went to the jihad over those who stayed at home. If those who stayed at home were in error, while others were fighting, they would be committing a sin, unless God forgives them, rather than receiving "the best of things."

If al-Shafi'i appears to be struggling still with his apparent desire to characterize military jihad as a duty incumbent upon all Muslims, he is nevertheless forced to cite a definitive proof when asked one more time about the issue:

[His interlocutor] asked: Is there any other [proof]?
[Shafi'i] replied: Yes, God said:

> It is not for the believers to go forth all together, but why should
> not a party of every section of them go forth, to become learned
> in religion, and to warn their people when they return to them,
> perhaps they will be aware.
>
> (Sura 9:123)

> [When] the Apostle went to battle he was accompanied by some of
> his companions while others stayed at home; for 'Ali b. Abi Talib
> stayed at home during the battle of Tabuk. Nor did God ordain that
> all Muslims were under obligation to go to battle, for He said: "Why
> should not a party of every section of them go forth?" So He made it
> known that going into battle was obligatory on some, not on all,
> [just] as knowledge of the law is not obligatory on all but on some,
> save the fundamental duties which should be known to all men. But
> God knows best.
>
> Shafi'i said: In like manner are other duties, the fulfillment of
> which is intended to be collective; whenever they are performed by
> some Muslims collectively, those who do not perform them will not
> fall into error.[13]

As latter jurists grappled with the issue, it was generally determined that
military jihad is a communal duty, under the control of the state. For
example, eleventh-century Shafi'i jurist al-Mawardi specified in his
exposition on Islamic government (*Al-Ahkam al-Sultaniyya*) that only the
head of state can declare jihad. To defend Islamic lands "and protect them
from intrusion so that people may earn their livelihood and travel without
danger," to protect the borders by maintaining adequate fortresses "so that
the enemy may not take them by surprise, commit profanation there, or shed
blood, either of a Muslim or an ally," and to spread Islam and wage military
jihad against those who refuse either to become Muslims or enter alliances
with Muslims are among the government's major responsibilities.[14] Only in
cases of sudden attack does military jihad become a duty incumbent upon
every able-bodied Muslim.

Thus, just as it has been noted that contemporary political use of Judaic
religious themes must not be confused with their meaning in the classical
texts, so is the case of contemporary political use of the term "jihad." Not
only is military jihad only one aspect of the term's overall meaning, but
even military jihad is a duty of only "a section" of the community, and is
surrounded by a number of significant restrictions.

For example, from the very earliest times, killing women and children has
been prohibited. Malik's *al-Muwatta* relates the following tradition:

The Messenger of Allah, may Allah bless him and grant him peace, forbade those who fought Ibn Abi Huqayq (a treacherous Jew from Madina) to kill women and children. He said that one of the men fighting reported that the wife of Ibn Abi Huqayq began screaming and he repeatedly raised his sword against her. Then he would remember the prohibition of the Messenger of Allah, may Allah bless him and grant him peace, so he would stop. Had it not been for that, we would have been rid of her.[15]

This prohibition is repeated wherever the conduct of war is discussed, along with prohibitions against destruction of natural resources, inhabited homes, animals, and property. Malik relates a hadith from Abu Bakr (the first caliph):

I advise you ten things: Do not kill women or children or an aged, infirm person. Do not cut down fruit-bearing trees. Do not destroy an inhabited place. Do not slaughter sheep or camels except for food. Do not burn bees and do not scatter them. Do not steal from the booty, and do not be cowardly.

Tenth-century Maliki jurist al-Qayrawani also proscribes the killing of monks and rabbis, unless they have taken part in the fighting.[16]

Malik quotes another hadith which adds: "Do not mutilate." This is generally seen as a rejection of the pre-Islamic practice of mutilating the corpses of fallen enemies in order to make an example of them. After the wife of the leader of the Meccan troops mutilated the corpse of Prophet Muhammad's uncle Hamza in the famous Battle of Uhud (625 CE), the practice was proscribed. Again, this passage ends by stressing "and do not kill children."[17]

Combatants are also required to honor their promises of safety in battle:

Yahya related to me from Malik from a man of Kufa that 'Umar ibn al-Khattab wrote to a commander of an army which he had sent out, "I have heard that it is the habit of some of your men to chase an unbeliever till he takes refuge in a high place. Then one man tells him in [his own language] not to be afraid, and when he comes up to him, he kills him. By He in whose hand my self is, if I knew someone who had done that, I would strike off his head."

Although it is suggested that this is not a reliable hadith and therefore not universally practiced, Malik goes on to claim that a promise of safe conduct in wartime made by gesture has the same status as one made verbally, and that "as far as I am concerned, gesture has the same status as speech. I have heard that ʿAbdullah ibn ʿAbbas said, 'There is no people who betray a pledge, but that Allah gives their enemies power over them."[18] Al-Qayrawani considered the honoring of safe conduct promises so important that he included those given by women and minors as valid.[19]

Perhaps most importantly, the purpose of military jihad is to spread what is considered to be true religion. It is not permitted to declare war simply for the appropriation of property, for example. For that reason, Muslims were not permitted to claim the land of those defeated in war. Malik makes an exception in the case of intransigent enemies, those who refuse to sign a treaty:

> Malik was asked whether he thought that when an imam had accepted [tax] from a people and they gave it, the land of any of those who surrendered belongs to the Muslims. Malik said, "That varies. As for the people who make a treaty – those of them who surrender are entitled to their land and property. As for the people of force who are taken by force – if one of them surrenders, his land and property belong to the Muslims because the people of force are overcome in their towns, and this becomes booty for the Muslims. As for the people with a treaty, their property and lives are protected by the treaty they made. Only the terms of the treaty are demanded of them."[20]

Nor was warfare to be used for personal aggrandizement. As we saw above, the spoils of jihad were to be shared among the community.

The Qurʾan makes it clear that warfare can be used in self-defense:

> And fight in the way of God against those who fight against you, but do not transgress. Surely, God does not love those who transgress. And kill them wherever you find them and drive them out from where they have driven you out; for persecution is worse than killing. Do not fight them near the sacred mosque unless they fight you there. But if they fight you, then fight them. That is the punishment of non-believers.
>
> (Sura 2:191–92)

Similarly:

> Permission is given [to fight] to those against whom war is made, because they have been wronged, and God has power to help them. Those who have been driven from their homes unfairly only because they say, "Our lord is God," and if God did not defend some people with some others, then monasteries and churches and prayer halls

212

and mosques, where the name of God is remembered, would have been destroyed.

(Sura 22:40–42)

But Muslims are told then that if the oppressors cease their aggression, then the fighting must stop: "But if they desist, then surely God is forgiving and merciful" (Sura 2:193). Again, the Qur'an reminds people of the purpose of the fighting: "And fight them until there is no persecution, and religion is for God. But if they desist, then no hostility except against the oppressors" (Sura 2:194).

Nevertheless, military jihad is not strictly a defensive operation. It is a function of Islam's overall goal, which is to make sure that all people submit to the will of God. This requires that false belief we wiped out. According to the Qur'an:

But who could be more oppressive than one who lies against God while being called to submission? God does not guide the oppressive. They desire to put out the light of God with their mouths but God will perfect his light, even if the non-believers hate. He is the one who has sent His messenger with guidance and the religion of truth to cause it to prevail over all religion, even if the polytheists hate.

(Sura 61:28)

For that reason, military jihad can be used not only in self-defense but to spread that Islamic belief and practice.

People cannot be forced to become Muslim. The Qur'an states, "There is no compulsion in religion. Right has become distinct from wrong, so whoever does not believe in idols and believes in God has grasped a strong handle that cannot be broken" (Sura 2:257). The Qur'an categorizes all monotheists as believers; they are part of the Islamic community under Islamic law, assuming the status of protected peoples. People who reject belief in God, however, must be called to join Islam. If they reject the call, and refuse to sign an agreement with Muslims, then military jihad is the final recourse. As the Qur'an puts it:

And a proclamation from God and His messenger to the people on the day of the greater pilgrimage that God and His messenger are free of the idolaters. So if you repent, it will be better for you. But if you turn away, know that you cannot frustrate God. And give good news to the idolaters and those with whom you have made an agreement and who have not failed you in anything or given help to anyone against you. Fulfill the treaty with them to its limit. Truly, God loves the righteous. And when the months during which fighting is forbidden have passed, kill the idolaters wherever you find them and take them and imprison them and lie in wait for them at every place of ambush. But if they repent and perform the prayer and pay the charity tax, then let them go their way. God is forgiving and merciful.

(Sura 9:3–5)

This verse reveals the final requirement for legitimate military jihad. In accordance with its purpose – to spread true belief – it must be preceded by the invitation to join the Muslim community, whether through conversion or treaty. We have seen above references to "being called to submission" and the command to Muslims to "give good news" – i.e., of religious truth. In another version of the hadith report concerning behavior in wartime, Muslim relates:

When you meet your enemies who are polytheists, invite them to three courses of action. If they respond to any one of these, you also accept it and withhold yourself from doing them any harm. Invite them to (accept) islam; if they respond to you, accept it from them and desist from fighting against them. Then invite them to migrate from their lands to the land of [those who emigrated from Mecca with Prophet Muhammad – i.e., Medina] and inform them that, if they do so, they shall have all the privileges and obligations of the [emigres]. If they refuse to migrate, tell them that they will have the status of Bedouin Muslims and will be subjected to the Commands of Allah like other Muslims, but they will not get any share of the spoils of war or [the wealth surrendered by those who choose not to fight] except when they actually fight with the Muslims (against the disbelievers). If they refuse to accept Islam, demand from them the [tax paid instead of the alms tax paid by Muslims]. If they agree to pay, accept it from them and hold off your hands. If they refuse to pay the tax, seek Allah's help and fight them.[21]

Therefore, although there are reports that Prophet Muhammad led surprise raids, it is considered praiseworthy to engage in military jihad only after efforts to transform the unbelievers into Muslims or, at least, to accept Muslim sovereignty and protection through treaty. The great Hanafi jurist al-Shaybani also described the call to Islam, as did his commentator al-Sarakhsi (comments in square brackets):

When the Muslims encounter polytheists whom Islam has never reached before, it is not necessary to fight them, until they have been called to accept Islam. [According to God's Word, exalted be He: "We used not to chastise, until We have sent a messenger" (17:15).

214

And this the Prophet advised the commanders of his armies, saying, "Call them first to the testimonial that there is no god but God," for they often think that we attack them in greed for their possessions and to carry off their women and children, whereas if they knew that we attack them in service to God, they might respond without any necessity for fighting. In expounding Islam to them, they should be called to the path of God with wisdom and kindly exhortation, at least in the beginning.][22]

As noted in Chapter 5, Shafi'i jurist al-Mawardi held that one of the duties of the head of state is to wage jihad but, again, only "against those who, after having been invited to accept Islam, persist in rejecting it, until they either become Muslim or enter the Pact [dhimma] so that God's truth may prevail over every religion."[23] (It should be noted that the offer of the pact of protection in alliance with the Muslim community was available only to "people of the Book" – those to whom it was believed God had already sent a proper messenger. From those without a recognized belief system – such as the Arab polytheists – and for those who had received Islam and then rejected it, in the words of al-Shaybani, "nothing may be accepted except Islam or the sword.")[24]

It is clear, then, that jihad is a function of Islam's perception of itself as a potentially universal community. In stark contrast to Judaism's self-perception as a limited community of people chosen by God to live in accordance with the Torah, the classical presentation of jihad clearly demonstrates the Muslim community is considered to be utterly inclusive, its goal being to encompass all humanity. What is more, in contrast to Judaism's prayer that at the end of time all humanity will be called to join in God's community, in Islam, the inclusion of all humanity in the promise of the covenant is a this-worldly goal. Jihad is the means to achieve that end.

E The sage and Torah study in Judaism

Related to the centrality of law in determining the land or "dar" al-Islam is the role of legal scholars in establishing a legitimately Islamic government. The role of religious scholars in Judaism is very different. In Judaism the sages of the Torah carry forward the revelation of the Torah of Sinai, through their processes of reasoning joining into dialogue with God, who reasons in the same ways about the same matters. That accords to Torah learning a sanctity that legal study in Islam does not possess. The counterpart to Muhammad as prophet of the one true God is obviously Moses. But in classical Judaism, Moses is treated as not unique but exemplary; he defines the character and virtues, the responsibilities and modes of conduct, of all persons of his class, which is to say, sages or rabbis. He is called "Moses, our rabbi," that is to say, Moses the model of the rabbi. But all those who adhere to that model are like him and belong in his class. He is not unique in Judaism in the way that Muhammed is unique in Islam. In Islam, Prophet Muhammad unquestionably establishes a model of behavior to be emulated. As we saw in Chapter 2, that is one of the premises upon which the Sunna was established. But in his prophetic role he was unique. This is not the case with Moses in Judaism. A key indicator to the place of Moses in Judaism comes from the Passover narrative, the Haggadah read at the family celebration of God's bringing about the exodus of ancient Israel from Egypt: Moses is never mentioned.

Where Moses serves, it is to exemplify the process that turns an ordinary Israelite into a disciple of sages, just as Moses was disciple of God, in the language of tractate Abot 1:1: "Moses received Torah from Sinai." The way in which the Torah was received and handed on at Sinai, received from God, handed on to Joshua — the verbs in Hebrew, QBL and MSR, yield Qabbalah and Masoret, both bearing the sense of "tradition" — is the way in which the Torah is received and handed on even today. This is stated in so many words in the following account:

A. *Our rabbis have taught on Tannaite authority:*
B. What is the order of Mishnah teaching? Moses learned it from the mouth of the All-Powerful. Aaron came in, and Moses repeated his chapter to him and Aaron went forth and sat at the left hand of Moses. His sons came in and Moses repeated their chapter to them, and his sons went forth. Eleazar sat at the right of Moses, and Itamar at the left of Aaron.
D. Then the elders entered, and Moses repeated for them their Mishnah chapter. The elders went out. Then the whole people came in, and Moses repeated for them their Mishnah chapter. So it came about that Aaron repeated the lesson four times, his sons three times, the elders two times, and all the people once.
E. Then Moses went out, and Aaron repeated his chapter for them. Aaron went out. His sons repeated their chapter. His sons went out. The elders repeated their chapter. So it turned out that everybody repeated the same chapter four times.
F. On this basis said R. Eliezer, "A person is liable to repeat the lesson for his disciple four times. And it is an argument a fortiori: If Aaron, who studied from Moses himself, and Moses from the Almighty — so in the case of a common person who is studying with a common person, all the more so!"
G. R. Aqiba says, "How on the basis of scripture do we know that a person is obligated to repeat a lesson for his disciple until he learns it [however many times that takes]? As it is said, 'And you teach it to the children of Israel' (Deuteronomy 31:19). And how do we know that that is until it will be well ordered in their mouth? 'Put it in their mouths' (Deuteronomy 31:19). And how on the basis of scripture do we know that he is

liable to explain the various aspects of the matter? 'Now these are the ordinances which you shall put before them' (Exodus 31:1)."

(Talmud of Babylonia Tractate Erubin B. 5:1/I.43/54B)

The way God handed on the Torah to Moses, through a process of oral formulation and oral transmission in memory, defines exactly how to the present day the sage is supposed to hand on the Torah to his disciples. In this process of tradition, Moses relates to God as the disciples to the master.

The question arises: What about the prophets, to whom God speaks directly, and who set forth God's words not out of a process of tradition but in direct quotation? Sages stand higher than prophets; after the destruction of the temple, prophecy became vested in the sages:

II.4 A. Said R. Abdimi of Haifa, "From the day on which the house of the sanctuary was destroyed, prophecy was taken away from prophets and given over to sages."

B. So are sages not also prophets?

C. This is the sense of the statement: Even though it was taken from the prophets, it was not taken from sages.

D. Said Amemar, "And a sage is superior to a prophet: 'And a prophet has a heart of wisdom' (Psalms 90:12). Who is compared to whom? Lo, the lesser is compared to the greater."

E. Said Abbayye, "You may know that [sages retain the power of prophecy,] for if an eminent authority makes a statement, it may then be stated in the name of some other eminent authority [who can have gotten it only by prophecy]."

F. Said Raba, "So what's the problem? Maybe both were born under the same star."

G. Rather, said Raba, "You may know that that is so, for an eminent authority may say something, and then the same thing may be reported [12B] in the name of R. Aqiba bar Joseph."

H. Said R. Ashi, "So what's the problem? Maybe as to this particular matter both were born under the same star."

I. Rather, said R. Ashi, "You may know that it is the case, because an eminent authority may say something, and then the same thing may be reported as a law revealed by God to Moses at Mount Sinai."

J. But perhaps the sage just makes a good guess [literally: is no better than a blind man groping about to a window]?

K. But doesn't the sage give a reason for what he says [so it cannot be merely a good guess]!

(Talmud of Babylonia Tractate Baba Batra 1:6 II.4/12a–b)

The work of hierarchization is conducted tangentially, the inquiry focusing to begin with upon the fate of prophecy. That the sages are superior to the prophet is demonstrated by the sages' access to prophecy, though in the medium of acute logic (divining the logic that compelled an authority to take the position that he did). So what the sage possesses which the prophet lacks is the power of analysis, and reason carries man into the mind of God.

Framed by a generative myth of such a character, the law for its part embodies the theological norm in a variety of concrete rulings on practical matters. Here is a concrete case in which the theological principle that Torah study brings the disciple into the world to come is embodied in an everyday transaction:

A. [If one has to choose between seeking] what he has lost and what his father has lost,
B. his own takes precedence.
C. [If he has to choose between seeking] what he has lost and what his master has lost,
D. his own takes precedence.
E. [If he has to choose between seeking] what his father has lost and what his master has lost, that of his master takes precedence.
G. For his father brought him into this world.
H. But his master, who has taught him wisdom, will bring him into the life of the world to come.
I. But if his father is a sage, that of his father takes precedence.
J. [If] his father and his master were carrying heavy burdens, he removes that of his master, and afterward removes that of his father.
K. [If] his father and his master were taken captive,
L. he ransoms his master, and afterward he ransoms his father.
M. But if his father is a sage, he ransoms his father, and afterward he ransoms his master.

(Mishnah-tractate Baba Mesia 2:11)

Given the indicative trait of the Mishnah – its sustained preoccupation with hierarchical classification – we hardly find surprising the formulation of matters in a problem of hierarchization. The master takes priority over the father.

The halakhah goes still further in its formulation of the Torah myth in concrete terms. In the hierarchical society conceived by the law of Judaism, the priests occupied the apex, followed by Levites, Israelites, and the under-castes. But a mamzer who was a disciple of a sage takes precedence over a high priest who was ignorant of the Torah (called "an am haares"). In the present case sages wish to prove that hierarchization governs the social order, with the several castes related to one another in descending order:

Mishnah-tractate Horayot 3:5, and Tosefta-tractate Horayot 2:8:
A. A priest takes precedence over a Levite, a Levite over an Israelite, an Israelite over a mamzer [a person whose parents may not legally ever

marry, e.g., brother and sister], a mamzer over a Netin [a descendant of the caste of Temple servants], a Netin over a proselyte, a proselyte over a freed slave.

B. Under what circumstances?

C. When all of them are equivalent.

The initial hierarchization having been established out of self-evident facts, the variable is introduced involving the Torah, so making the point that the Torah violates natural hierarchies in favor of God's choice:

D. But if the mamzer was a disciple of a sage and a high priest was an am haares [in context: ignorant of the Torah], the mamzer who is a disciple of a sage takes precedence over a high priest who is an am haares.

(Mishnah-tractate Horayot 3:8)

We now turn to the complementary compilation of laws, the Tosefta, which contains citations and glosses of the Mishnah's rules as well as free-standing statements:

E. A sage takes precedence over a king; a king takes precedence over a high priest; a high priest takes precedence over a prophet; a prophet takes precedence over a priest anointed for war; a priest anointed for war takes precedence over the head of a priestly watch; the head of a priestly watch takes precedence over the head of a household [of priests]; the head of a household of priests takes precedence over the superintendent of the cashiers; the superintendent of the cashiers takes precedence over the Temple treasurer; the Temple treasurer takes precedence over an ordinary priest; an ordinary.

(Tosefta-tractate Horayot 2:10F–H)

F. A priest takes precedence over a Levite; a Levite takes precedence over an Israelite; an Israelite takes precedence over a mamzer; a mamzer takes precedence over a Netin; a Netin takes precedence over a proselyte; a proselyte takes precedence over a freed slave. Under what circumstances? When all of them are equivalent. But if the mamzer was a disciple of a sage, and a high priest was an ignoramus, the mamzer who is the disciple of a sage takes precedence over a high priest who is an ignoramus.

Matters having been set forth, the Tosefta makes its comment, and it is a harsh one:

G. A sage takes precedence over a king.

H. For if a sage dies, we have none who is like him.

I. [If] a king dies, any Israelite is suitable to mount the throne.

(Tosefta 2:8)

From sages, the Tosefta's formulation turns to the hierarchy of holy classes in Israel: priests, prophets, messianic priests (anointed ones):

J. [A high priest anointed with oil takes precedence over one dedicated through many garments.]

K. A prophet takes precedence over the high priest anointed for battle,

L. and the high priest anointed for battle takes precedence over the prefect,

M. and the prefect takes precedence over the head of the weekly course [of the priests, who take care of the cult in a given week],

N. and the head of the priestly course takes precedence over the superintendent of the cashiers,

O. and the superintendent of the cashiers takes precedence over the treasurer.

P. And the treasurer takes precedence over an ordinary priest.

Q. And an ordinary priest takes precedence over a Levite.

(Tosefta-Horayot 2:10A–I)

In a well-ordered system, the same principles that govern classes of persons must pertain to classes of objects, that is, the comparison and contrast of the indicative traits. Here we find ourselves at the very heart of the legal system, the point at which the reversals take place. Just as a man takes a higher status than a woman, but a woman who practices self-sacrificial charity is valued by heaven above even a sage, so here too, however high the genealogy, mastery of the Torah takes priority, placing the outcaste on to the pinnacle of the social ladder.

The final statement of the same matter – the ultimate priority of Torah learning over all else – assigns to study of the Torah a higher value than practice of the commandments:

I.2 A. Once R. Tarfon and the elders were reclining at a banquet in the upper room of the house of Nitezeh in Lud. This question was raised for them: "Is study greater or is action greater?"

B. R. Tarfon responded: "Action is greater."

C. R. Aqiba responded: "Study is greater."

D. All responded, saying, "Study is greater, for study brings about action."

(Talmud of Babylonia Tractate Qiddushin 1:10E–G I.2/40b)

I.3 A. *It has been taught on Tannaite authority:*

B. R. Yosé says, "Great is study, for it preceded the commandment to separate dough-offering by forty years, the commandments governing priestly rations and tithes by fifty-four years, the commandments covering remission of debts by sixty-one years, the commandment concerning the Jubilee Year by one hundred and three years." [Freedman: The Torah was given to Israel two months after the

Exodus from Egypt, but liability to dough-offering came into force forty years later, and so throughout.]

E. And just as study of the Torah came prior to the actual practice of it, so judgment on that account takes precedence over judgment concerning practice of the Torah.

G. And just as judgment concerning study takes priority over judgment concerning practice, so, too, the reward for studying the Torah takes priority over the reward for practice: "And he gave them the lands and nations, and they took the labor of the people in possession, that they might keep his statutes and observe his laws" (Psalms 105:44–45).

(Talmud of Babylonia Tractate Qiddushin 1:10Een;G I.2/40b)

That the higher value assigned to Torah study produced practical results emerges in the statements of priorities set forth above. Faced with actual decisions in the workaday world, the disciple of the sage had rules to guide his judgment. The rules extend deep into the life of the academy, with rituals guiding conduct in the presence of the sage:

B. When the patriarch enters, everyone rises and does not sit down until he says to them, "Sit down."

C. And when the head of the court enters, they set up for him two rows, one on one side, one on the other side, through which he goes, and he sits down in his place.

D. When a sage who comes in, one rises as another sits down, until he comes in and sits down in his place.

E. Younger sages and disciples of sages, when the public requires their services, even step over the heads of the people.

F. And even though they have said, "It is no praise for a disciple of a sage to come in last," if he went out for need, he comes back and sits down in his place.

G. Younger sages and disciples of sages, when they have a capacity to understand, turn toward their fathers [on the court], with their backs toward the people. When they do not have the wit to understand, they enter and take their seats before their fathers, facing the people.

(Tosefta-Tractate Sanhedrin 7:8–9)

The disciple is required to defer to the master and may not give decisions in the presence of the master. Certainly rules that confer special status upon a given class of religious authorities present no surprises; they are common among most religions. What is particular to Judaism is the mythic foundation: the sage embodies Israel's relationship with God just as Moses did at Sinai, and the sage in the model of Moses, who for his part learned the Torah from God, comes as close to God as man can. It follows that through study of the Torah man meets God, and it is in the synagogue and schoolhouse that God takes up residence on earth. This is stated in so many words in the following:

A. "And it came to pass in the days of Ahaz" (Isaiah 7:1).
B. What was the misfortune that took place at that time?
C. "The Syrians on the east and the Philistines on the west [devour Israel with open mouth]" (Isaiah 9:12).
D. The matter [the position of Israel] may be compared to a king who handed over his son to a tutor, who hated [the son]. The tutor thought, "If I kill him now, I shall turn out to be liable to the death penalty before the king. So what I'll do is take away his wet nurse, and he will die on his own."
E. So thought Ahaz, "If there are no kids, there will be no he-goats. If there are no he-goats, there will be no flock. If there is no flock, there will be no shepherd. If there is no shepherd, there will be no world."
F. So did Ahaz plan, "If there are no children, there will be no disciples; if there are no disciples, there will be no sages; if there are no sages, there will be no Torah; if there is no Torah, there will be no synagogues and schools; if there are no synagogues and schools, then the Holy One, blessed be he, will not allow his Presence to come to rest in the world."
G. What did he do? He went and locked the synagogues and schools.
H. That is in line with the following verse of scripture: "Bind up the testimony, seal the Torah [teaching] among my disciples" (Isiah 8:16).

(Leviticus Rabbah XI:VII.3)

The laws turn out to articulate in gestures and acts of restraint the theological conviction, animating all else, that in the Torah man meets God.

F Khilafah and the legal scholars in Islam

The study of law is central in Islam as well, but not because one "meets God" in it.[25] In the Sunni Islamic conception, the study of law is paramount because it is through the law that God's will is expressed, understood, and implemented. In other words, it is through the law that *islam* – submission to the divine will – is achieved, and that, as we have seen, is the purpose of human existence. Human beings, in accepting the "trust" (*amana*) offered by God at creation, became God's vicegerents or vicars (*khulafa'*, sing. *khalifah*):

> We offered the trust to the heavens and the earth and the mountains, but they refused to bear it and were afraid of it. But the human accepted it, [despite] his sinfulness and foolishness, that God may chastise hypocritical men and women, idolatrous men and women,

and turn to the believing men and women. God is forgiving and merciful.

(Sura 33:73–74)

We destroyed the generations before you when they did wrong and clear signs came to them with their messengers but they would not believe. This is how we compensate the evildoers. Then we made you viceroys [*khala'if*; sing. *khalifah* or caliph, vicar, delegate] on earth after them so we might see how you would do.

(Sura 10:14–15)

It is in the position of God's vicars or delegates that human beings reach fulfillment. Their task is to universalize the religion of submission to the divine will, which means making Islamic law prevail over the earth. (As we have seen, "People of the Book" – those communities which have established law based on revelation, such as Jews and Christians, are allowed to maintain their own religious and legal systems under Islamic rule.) It has been noted that the abode of Islam is wherever Islamic law is established. It has also been noted (Chapters 4 and 5) that God's eternal will, the Shari'a, must be made practical in codes of law (fiqh). It is human beings' task to articulate and implement the law. The study of Islamic law, therefore, is called the "queen" of Islamic sciences.

Successors to the position of community leadership after the death of Prophet Muhammad (632 CE) were initially called commanders of the faithful, but as the empire spread and the administration became more complex, they came to be called caliphs. But they were not considered inheritors of the Prophet's religious position. In fact, it was asserted specifically that prophecy ended with Muhammad. The Qur'an says, "Muhammad is not the father of any of your men, but the messenger of God and the seal of the prophets. And God has knowledge of everything" (Sura 33:41). This is a key verse, taken to mean that after Muhammad, no further prophecy is necessary. God's will has been fully and ultimately revealed, sufficiently for all people for all time. As early twentieth-century scholar Muhammad 'Abduh put it: "Muhammad's prophethood brought prophecy to an end. His message terminated the work of messengers, as the Book affirms and the authentic tradition corroborates."[26] Instead, those with the title caliph were merely executive authorities. The primary responsibility for influencing the life of the community was in the hands of legal scholars, the legislative and judicial branch of Islamic authority.

This remained implicit in the early days of Islam. It was not until the full development of the legal schools under the 'Abbasids (beginning in 750 CE) that the role of legal scholars was explicated in legal texts. Then, as legal historian N.J. Coulson put it, "The legal scholars were publicly recognized as the architects of an Islamic scheme of state and society which the 'Abbasids had pledged themselves to build."[27] The first comprehensive articulation of the Islamic theory of state was that produced by Shafi'i jurist al-Mawardi (d. 1058 CE).[28] According to al-Mawardi, the office of the caliphate was established in order to continue the work of the Prophet in his capacity as defender of Islam and in worldly governance.[29] Reason tells us, as noted, that "without rulers men would live in anarchy and heedlessness like benighted savages." Revelation tells us that we must "obey God, the Messenger, and those in authority among you" (Sura 4:62). Furthermore, there is a hadith report that the Prophet said, "Other rulers after me will rule over you, the pious according to his piety, the wicked according to his wickedness. Hear them and obey in all that accords with the truth. If they do good, it will count for you and for them. If they do evil, it will count for you and against them." There must be a caliph, says al-Mawardi, a chief executive of the community. As we saw, if no one is in the position of caliph, then the community must come up with a group of candidates eligible for the position and a group of electors to choose from among the candidates.

The ideal candidate for caliph was considered to be the legal scholar, according to Shafi'i scholar al-Juwayni (d. 1085 CE). The caliph should be well enough trained to be able to practice ijtihad. But the caliph could be a *muqallid* (follower of legal precedents or imitator, rather than an independent thinker), so long as he consulted the religious scholars.[30] In other words, the real authority in the Islamic state was the law; even the caliph was subject to it and derived legitimacy from it.

In fact, recognizing that the chief executive of the Islamic community, after the period of the Prophet and his immediate successors, was unlikely to be chosen from among legal scholars, al-Mawardi lists the duties of the caliph as strictly executive.[31] As we saw in Chapter 5, his primary task is to ensure that the established principles of religion are safeguarded (article 1), and that legal judgments and penalties are enforced (articles 2 and 4). Other than the requirement that the caliph pay attention to his work and not delegate it irresponsibly, the rest of his duties fall into one of three categories: defense, treasury, or executive. He is to defend the community from attack (article 3), maintain frontier defenses (article 5), and wage military jihad against those who refuse to either become Muslims or enter into treaty with Muslims (article 6); regarding fiduciary responsibility, he is to collect both the charity payments required of all Muslims to be spent on the needs of the community at large and the legitimate spoils of wars (article 7), fairly determine and pay salaries from the treasury (article 8), and make sure that those whom he appoints handle treasury moneys honestly (article 9). In no case is the caliph granted legislative or judicial authority.

Again, the defining paradigm of Islamic political thought is that Islamic law is the ultimate source of political authority. Fourteenth-century Hanbali scholar Ibn Taymiyya expressed the same idea when he claimed that the identifying feature of an Islamic society is not the character of the leader but the people's responsiveness to Shari'a.[32] In his treatise on the authority of the founders of the four Sunni schools of law, Ibn Taymiyya reminded readers of the Qur'anic injunction to obey God, the Prophet, and those in authority in the community. He then identified "those in authority among you" as the religious scholars.[33] Legal scholarship is therefore the backbone of the Islamic community; it is the highest calling. Studying the law is not so much the personal experience of "meeting God" as assuming responsibility in the command to make all religion the religion of God; it is taking leadership in the struggle – jihad – to universalize Islam.

G History, time, and paradigm in Judaism

History, in the Judaic view, consists of a sequence of one-time events, each of them singular, all of them meaningful. These events move from a beginning somewhere to an end at a pre-ordained goal. History moves toward the eschaton, the end of history. The teleology of Israel's life finds its definition in eschatological fulfillment. Eschatology therefore constitutes not a choice *within* teleology, but the definition *of* teleology. That is to say, a theory of the goal and purpose of things (teleology) is shaped solely by appeal to the account of the end of time (eschatology). History viewed in this way then sits enthroned as the queen of theological science. Events do not conform to patterns, they *form* patterns. What happens matters because events bear meaning, constitute history.

By "history" we mean not merely events, but how events are so organized and narrated as to teach (for them, theological, for us, religio-historical or social) lessons, reveal patterns, tell us what we must do and why, what will happen to us tomorrow. Legal systems that undertake to define the social order have therefore to create laws that will realize in the everyday the lessons that history is supposed to teach. That explains why Judaic and Islamic legal sources encompass historical events and each system makes use of history to set forth an important part of its encompassing statement.

How the legal system of Judaism sets forth modes of regulating history, organizing its events into intelligible patterns, recapitulating in rules of public conduct the principal myths and symbols that make the past usable, leads us into the examination of silences as much as of speech. For the Judaic legal system described, unlike the Islamic system – as we shall see below, demonstrates a powerful bias in favor of the continuing present tense; the past forms a principal part of the present, the present of the past as well. So events are commemorated, the mode of celebration being subject to ample legal definition, but the commemoration serves to establish in the here and now a long-ago event and its meaning. Creation, which we encountered in Chapter 6, does not constitute an event in historical time – a long-ago past, a one-time happening in a linear sequence of such happenings crossing the barrier between past and present – but a moment in the week at which a different mode of being takes over. The past therefore contributes to the present not moments to remember but experiences to recapitulate, and the law defines how that re-experiencing is to take place. In Islam, by contrast, the legal system is distinctly oriented toward the future, an ongoing struggle to spread Islam to all human beings.

Before turning to the two legal systems, let us ask how each religious system in its classical statement deals with history, and that means how the founding events of the religions are mediated to the later generations. The answer to that question emerges in the way in which the Written Torah, on the Judaic side, and the Qur'an, on the Islamic side, are read: as one-time historical events, or as eternal patterns, paradigms, for the emulation of the faithful.

For Judaism, the sages of the Torah insisted that, in the narrative of scripture, considerations of temporal sequence play no role in the Torah. What sages meant was that the Torah does not narrate history in the ordinary order: "This came first, then that happened, and finally the other thing took place – and this is what it all means." Rather, events are ordered in accordance with some other logic than a narrative-teleological one, a logic that responded to the meaning and proportion and consequence of events, not the order in which they took place. For us, used as we are to seeing the past as a sequence of one-time and unique events, this concept is difficult to grasp. But if we recall that when we think about events in nature, what matters is not what is unique but what is routine, what we seek is the rule and not the exception, then the interest in something other than the sequence of moments will prove to be more rational. In the following reading of Exodus 15, sages undertake to prove that the actual sequence of events does not govern the ordering of the Torah's statement:

1. A. "The enemy said, ['I will pursue, I will overtake, I will divide the spoil, my desire shall have its fill of them. I will draw my sword, my hand shall destroy them]:'"
   B. This [statement was made] at the outset of the sequence of events, and why then was it stated here?
   C. It is because considerations of temporal sequence play no role in the Torah.
2. A. Along these same lines: "And it came to pass on the eighth day that Moses called" (Leviticus 9:1).
   B. This [statement was made] at the outset of the sequence of events, and why then was it stated here?
   C. It is because considerations of temporal sequence play no role in the Torah.
3. A. Along these same lines: "In the year that king Uzziah died" (Isaiah 6:1).
   B. This [statement was made] at the outset of the sequence of events, and why then was it stated here?

226

C. It is because considerations of temporal sequence play no role in the Torah.

4. A. Along these same lines: "Son of man, stand on your feet" (Ezekiel 2:1).

B. Some say, "Son of man, put forth a riddle" (Ezekiel 17:2).

C. This [statement was made] at the outset of the sequence of events, and why then was it stated here?

D. It is because considerations of temporal sequence play no role in the Torah.

5. A. Along these same lines: "Go and cry in the ears of Jerusalem" (Jeremiah 2:2).

B. This [statement was made] at the outset of the sequence of events, and why then was it stated here?

C. It is because considerations of temporal sequence play no role in the Torah.

6. A. Along these same lines: "Israel was a luxuriant vine" (Hosea 10:1).

B. This [statement was made] at the outset of the sequence of events, and why then was it stated here?

C. It is because considerations of temporal sequence play no role in the Torah.

7. A. Along these same lines: "I, Qoheleth, have been king over Israel in Jerusalem" (Qoheleth 1:12).

B. This [statement was made] at the outset of the sequence of events, and why then was it stated here?

C. It is because considerations of temporal sequence play no role in the Torah.

(Mekhilta XXXII:I.1–7)

The atemporality of scripture's narrative is further illustrated:

A. R. Yosé the Galilean says, "When the Israelites went into the sea, Mount Moriah had already been uprooted from its place, with the altar of Isaac that was built on it, and with the array of wood on it, and Isaac was as if bound and set on the altar, and Abraham as though his hand were stretched out, having taken the knife to sacrifice his son.

B. "Said the Omnipresent to Moses, 'Moses, my children are in trouble, with the sea shutting the way before and the enemy pursuing, and you are standing and protracting your prayer!'

C. "Moses said to him, 'And what am I supposed to do?'

D. "He said to him, 'Lift up your rod [and stretch out your hand over the sea and divide it, that the people of Israel may go on dry ground through the sea].'

E. "'You should now exalt, give glory, and praise, and break out in songs of praise, exaltation, laudation and glorification of the One who possesses war.' "

(Mekhilta XXII:I.24)

When two events that, in historical thinking, are unique and are represented as coinciding, we meet a kind of thinking that is ahistorical. The only way to validate the striking proposition that temporal considerations do not affect the narrative of scripture, which pays no attention to the order in which events took place, is through examples of atemporality. The examples of the first composition show that the Torah cites later in its narrative what in fact took place earlier, and these shifts validate the claim made at the outset. The second composition makes the same point in a very different way, by claiming that the binding of Isaac was taking place at the very moment when Israel was tested at the sea. The events then correspond and take place in the same indeterminate moment. It is in a system of thought that aims at uncovering the patterns underlying history, at discovering the inner logic of humanity's life, that people impose eternity on time, as we see them doing here.

Through the medium of law, rabbinic Judaism lays down its theology of history. The framers of the Mishnah, in particular, present us with a kind of historical thinking quite different from the one that they, along with all Israel, had inherited in scripture. In scripture what happens is singular, therefore an event to be noted, and points toward lessons to be drawn for where things are heading and why. With such views in mind, people ought – we should anticipate – to write history as a means of making their religious statement. But the classical writings of rabbinic Judaism do not encompass history writing at all; that is because here we have a Judaism that does not appeal to history as a sequence of one-time events, each of which bears meaning on its own. What the Mishnah has to say about history is quite different, and consequently the Mishnah and the halakhic system built upon it do not conform in any way to the scriptural pattern of representing, and sorting out, events: history, myth, apocalypse.

We start with the negative side: what we do not find, for the first difference appears right at the surface. scripture places its halakhah into a narrative setting, the revelation at Sinai, God's conversations with Moses, Moses's recapitulation, in Deuteronomy, of the lessons of the Torah. But the Mishnah contains no sustained narrative whatsoever, very few tales, and no large-scale conception of history. Scripture organizes its system through narrative. The halakhic statement of the Mishnah and continuator documents organizes its system in non-historical and socially unspecific terms. That is to say, there is no effort to set into a historical context, for example, a particular time, place, a circumstance defined by important events, any of the laws of the Mishnah. The Mishnah's system is set forth out of all historical framework. That is a medium for the presentation of a system that has no precedent in prior

228

systems of Judaism or in prior kinds of Judaic literature. The law codes of Exodus and Deuteronomy, for example, are set forth in a narrative framework, and the priestly code of Leviticus, for its part, appeals to God's revelation to Moses and Aaron, at specific times and places. In the Mishnah we have neither narrative nor setting for the representation of law.

Now to the positive side, which brings us to the law and how it serves to encase history within a framework of imposed order and structure. Instead of narrative which, as in Exodus, spills over into case law, the Mishnah gives a description of how things are done in general and universally, that is, descriptive laws. Instead of reflection on the meaning and end of history, its halakhah constructs a world in which history plays little part. Instead of narratives full of didactic meaning, the Mishnah's authorship, as we shall see below, provides lists of events so as to expose the traits that they share and thus the rules to which they conform. And that, as we learned in Chapter 3, is how the law is spun out. The definitive components of a historical-eschatological system of Judaism – a description of events as one-time happenings, analysis of the meaning and end of events, and interpretation of the end and future of singular events – none of these commonplace constituents of historical thinking finds a place in the Mishnah's system of Judaism. So the Mishnah finds no precedent in prior Israelite writings for its mode of dealing with things that happen. The Mishnah's way of identifying happenings as consequential and describing them, its way of analyzing those events it chooses as bearing meaning, its interpretation of the future to which significant events point – all those in context were unique. In form the Mishnah represents its system outside of all historical framework.

Yet to say that the Mishnah's halakhic system is ahistorical could not be more wrong. The Mishnah through the halakhah presents a different kind of theory and theology of history. Its authorship revises the inherited conception of history and reshapes that conception to fit into its own system. When we consider the power of the biblical myth, the force of its eschatological and messianic interpretation of history, the effect of apocalypse, we must find astonishing the capacity of the Mishnah's framers to think in a different way about the same things. Within the law of Judaism, some events contain richer lessons than others; the destruction of the Temple of Jerusalem teaches more than a crop failure, being kidnapped into slavery more than stubbing one's toe. Furthermore, lessons taught by events – "history" in the didactic sense – follow a progression from trivial and private to consequential and public.

The framers of the Mishnah's halakhah explicitly refer to very few events, treating those they do mention within a focus quite separate from what happened: the unfolding of the events themselves. That is why they rarely create or use narratives. More probative still, historical events do not supply organizing categories or taxonomic classifications. We find no tractate devoted to the destruction of the temple, no complete chapter detailing the events of Bar Kokhba, nor even a sustained celebration of the events of the sages' own historical life. No category formation of the law deals with only one enormous event, even the destruction of the temple. Nor are sages given systematic biographies of any kind comparable to the Gospels. When things that have happened are mentioned, it is neither in order to narrate, nor to interpret and draw lessons from, the event. It is either to illustrate a point of law or to pose a problem of the law — always *en passant*, never in a pointed way. So when sages refer to what has happened, this is casual and tangential to the main thrust of discourse.

Where the Mishnah provides little tales or narratives, moreover, they more often treat how things in the cult are done in general than what, in particular, happened on any one day. It is sufficient to refer casually to well-known incidents. Narrative, in the Mishnah's limited rhetorical repertoire, is reserved for the narrow framework of what priests and others do on recurrent occasions and around the temple. In all, that staple of history, stories about dramatic events and important deeds, in the minds of the Mishnah's juris-prudents provide little nourishment. Events, if they appear at all, are treated as trivial. They may be well known, but are consequential in some way other than is revealed in the detailed account of what actually happened. Let me now show some of the principal texts that contain and convey this other conception of how events become history and how history teaches lessons.

How, in concrete terms, does the halakhah encompass history? Since the greatest event in the century-and-a-half, from *c.* 50 to *c.* 200, in which the Mishnah's materials came into being, was the destruction of the temple in 70, we must expect the Mishnah's treatment of that incident to illustrate the document's larger theory of history: what is important and unimportant about what happens. Although the sages surely mourned for the destruction and loss of Israel's principal mode of worship, and certainly recorded the event of the ninth of Ab in the year 70, they did so in their characteristic way: they listed the event as an item in a catalogue of incidents that are similar to one another and so demand the same response. But then the destruction no longer appears as a unique event. It is absorbed into a pattern of similar disasters, all exhibiting similar taxonomic traits, events to which the people, now well schooled in tragedy, know full well the appropriate response. So it is in demonstrating regularity that sages reveal their way of coping. Then the uniqueness of the event fades away, its mundane character is emphasized. The power of taxonomy in imposing order upon chaos once more does its healing work. The consequence was reassurance that historical events obeyed discoverable laws. Israel's ongoing life would override disrup-tive, one-time happenings. So catalogs of events, as much as lists of species of melons, served as a brilliant apologetic by providing reassurance that nothing lies beyond the range and power of ordering system and stabilizing pattern. Here is a way in which the irregular was made regular and orderly, subject to rules:

4:6 A. Five events took place for our fathers on the seventeenth of Tammuz, and five on the ninth of Ab.

B. On the seventeenth of Tammuz
(1) the tablets [of the Torah] were broken,
(2) the daily whole offering was cancelled,
(3) the city wall was breached,
(4) Apostemos burned the Torah, and
(5) he set up an idol in the Temple.

C. On the ninth of Ab
(1) the decree was made against our forefathers that they should not enter the land,
(2) the first Temple,
(3) the second [Temple] were destroyed,
(4) Betar was taken,
(5) the city was ploughed up [after the war of Hadrian].

D. When Ab comes, rejoicing diminishes.

(Mishnah-tractate Taanit 4:6)

4:7 A. In the week in which the ninth of Ab occurs it is prohibited to get a haircut and to wash one's clothes.

B. But on Thursday of that week these are permitted,

C. because of the honor due to the Sabbath.

D. On the eve of the ninth of Ab a person should not eat two prepared dishes, nor should one eat meat or drink wine.

E. Rabban Simeon b. Gamaliel says, "He should make some change from ordinary procedures."

F. R. Judah declares people obligated to turn over beds.

G. But sages did not concur with him.

(Mishnah-tractate Taanit 4:7)

The stunning calamities cataloged at 4:6 form groups, reveal common traits, and so are subject to classification. Then the laws provide regular rules for responding to, coping with, these untimely catastrophes, all (fortuitously) in a single classification. So the raw materials of history are absorbed into the ahistorical, supernatural system of the Mishnah. The process of absorption and regularization of the unique and one-time moment is illustrated in the passage at hand.

The law takes over and recasts the history of the Temple of Jerusalem and the cult centers that preceded it over time. Here the law provides a still more striking example of the reordering of one-time events into all-time patterns. It derives from the effort to put together in a coherent way the rather haphazard history of the cult inherited from scripture, with sacrifices made here and there and finally in Jerusalem. Now, the entire history of the cult, so critical in the larger system created by the Mishnah's lawyers, produced a patterned and therefore sensible and intelligible picture. As is clear, everything that happened turned out to be susceptible to classification once the taxonomic traits were specified. An exercise, sorting out periods and their characteristics, took the place of narrative, to explain things in its own way: first this, then that, and, in consequence, the other. So in the neutral turf of holy ground, as much as in the trembling earth of the temple mount, everything was absorbed into one thing, all classified in its proper place and by its appropriate rule. Indeed, so far as the lawyers proposed to write history at all, they wrote it into their picture of the long tale of the way in which Israel served God: the places in which the sacrificial labor was carried on, the people who did it, the places in which the priests ate the meat left over after God's portion was set aside and burnt.

This "historical" account forthwith generated precisely that problem of locating the regular and orderly which the philosophers loved to investigate: the intersection of conflicting but equally correct taxonomic rules, as we see at 14:9, below. The passage that follows is therefore history, insofar as the Mishnah's creators proposed to write history: the reduction of events to rules forming compositions of regularity, therefore meaning.

I A. Before the tabernacle was set up, (1) the high places were permitted, and (2) [the sacrificial] service [was done by] the first born [Numbers 3:12–13, 8:16–18].

  B. When the tabernacle was set up, (1) the high places were prohibited, and (2) the [sacrificial] service [was done by] priests.

  C. Most Holy Things were eaten within the veils, Lesser Holy Things [were eaten] throughout the camp of Israel.

(Mishnah-tractate Zebahim 14:4)

II A. They came to Gilgal.

  B. The high places were prohibited.

  C. Most Holy Things were eaten within the veils, Lesser Holy Things, anywhere.

(Mishnah-tractate Zebahim 14:5)

III A. They came to Shiloh.

  B. The high places were prohibited.

  C. (1) There was no roof-beam there, but below was a house of stone, and hangings above it, and (2) it was "the resting place" [Deuteronomy 12:9].

  D. Most Holy Things were eaten within the veils, Lesser Holy Things and second-tithe [were eaten] in any place within sight [of Shiloh].

(Mishnah-tractate Zebahim 14:6)

IV A. They came to Nob and Gibeon.

B. The high places were permitted.

C. Most Holy Things were eaten within the veils, Lesser Holy Things, in all the towns of Israel.

(Mishnah-tractate Zebahim 14:7)

V A. They came to Jerusalem.

B. The high places were prohibited.

C. And they never again were permitted.

D. And it was "the inheritance" [Deuteronomy 12:9].

E. Most Holy Things were eaten within the veils, Lesser Holy Things and second-tithe within the wall.

(Mishnah-tractate Zebahim 14:8)

A. All the Holy Things which one sanctified at the time of the prohibition of the high places and offered at the time of the prohibition of high places
outside –

B. lo, these are subject to the transgression of a positive commandment and a negative commandment, and they are liable on their account to extirpation [for sacrificing outside the designated place, Leviticus 17:8–9, M. 13:1A].

C. [If] one sanctified them at the time of the permission of high places and offered them up at the time of the prohibition of high places,

D. lo, these are subject to transgression of a positive commandment and to a negative commandment, but they are not liable on their account to extirpation [since if the offerings had been sacrificed when they were sanctified, there should have been no violation].

E. [If] one sanctified them at the time of the prohibition of high places and offered them up at the time of the permission of high places,

F. lo, these are subject to transgression of a positive commandment, but they are not subject to a negative commandment at all.

(Mishnah-tractate Zebahim 14:9)

The upshot is to cover all sorts of circumstances within a single well-composed pattern. This is easy to represent by simple symbols. We deal with two circumstances and two sets of actions: the circumstance of the prohibition of high places (−), and that of their permission (+), and the act of sanctification of a sacrifice (A) and offering it up (B), as follows:

$$A: - A - B = \text{negative, positive, extirpation}$$
$$C: + A + B = \text{negative, positive}$$
$$E: - A + B = \text{positive only.}$$

We cannot have +A +B, since there is no reason to prohibit or to punish the one who sanctifies and offers up a sacrifice on a high place when it is permitted to do so! Accordingly, all possible cases are dealt with. In the first case, both sanctification and offering up take place at the time that prohibition of high places applies. There is transgression of a positive commandment and a negative commandment. The negative is Deuteronomy 12:13, the positive, Deuteronomy 12:14. *Take heed that you do not offer your burnt-offerings at every place that you see; but at the place which the Lord will choose in one of your tribes, there you shall offer your burnt-offerings. . . .* The mixtures, C and E, then go over the same ground. If sanctification takes place when it is permitted to sanctify animals for use in high places, but the offering up takes place when it is not allowed to do so (for example, the former for 14:4, the latter, 14:6), extirpation does not apply (Leviticus 17:5–7).

In the continuation, the rule making out of the raw materials of disorderly history continues unabated.

A. These are the Holy Things offered in the tabernacle [of Gilgal, Nob, and Gibeon]:

B. Holy Things which were sanctified for the tabernacle.

C. Offerings of the congregation are offered in the tabernacle.

D. Offerings of the individual [are offered] on a high place.

E. Offerings of the individual which were sanctified for the tabernacle are to be offered in the tabernacle.

F. And if one offered them up on a high place, he is free.

G. What is the difference between the high place of an individual and the high place of the community?

H. (1) Laying on of hands, and (2) slaughtering at the north [of the altar], and (3) placing [of the blood] round about [the altar], and (4) waving, and (5) bring near.

I. R. Judah says, "there is no meal-offering on a high place [but there is in the tabernacle]" –

J. and (1) the priestly service, and (2) the wearing of garments of ministry, and (3) the use of utensils of ministry, and (4) the sweet-smelling savor and (5) the dividing line for the [tossing of various kinds of] blood, and (6) the rule concerning the washing of hands and feet.

K. But the matters of time, and remnant, and uncleanness are applicable both here and there [by contrast to 14:3F–I].

(Mishnah-tractate Zebahim 14:10)

Let us rapidly review the exposition of the law. When 14:4–8 refer to a high place which was permitted, and also to the presence of veils, it is assumed that there were both a tabernacle (hence the veils) and also high places. This must mean Gilgal (14:5) and Nob and Gibeon (14:7). Now the issue is, if there are both a tabernacle and high places, which sorts of offerings belong to which kind of altar? It follows that the pericope treats the situations specified at 14:5, 7, a secondary expansion. A is answered by B. C–F go on to work out their own interests, and cannot be constructed to answer A, because they specify *they are offered in the tabernacle* as a complete apodosis, which A does not require and B clearly does not want. B tells us that even though it is permitted to offer a sacrifice on a high place, a sacrifice which is set aside for the tabernacle (obviously) is to be offered there. Then C–F work the matter out. C and D are clear as stated. Holy things which are sanctified for the tabernacle are offerings of the congregation (C). It is taken for granted that they are meant for the tabernacle, even when not so designated as specified (B). Individuals' sacrifices are assumed to be for high places unless specified otherwise (D). Obviously, if they are sanctified for the tabernacle (E), they are sacrificed there. But there is no reason to inflict liability if they are offered on a high place (F). The whole is carefully worked out, leaving no unanswered questions.

G then asks what difference there is between the high place which serves an individual, and "the high place" – the tabernacle – which serves the congregation, that is, the ones at Gilgal, Nob, and Gibeon. H specifies five items, J six more, and Judah brings the list up to twelve. K completes the matter. *Time* refers to the improper intention to the flesh or burn the sacrificial parts after the appropriate time, thus *refuse*. The word choice is unexpected. The inclusion of Mishnah-tractate Zebahim 14:9, structurally matching Mishnah-tractate Taanit 4:7, shows us the goal of the historical composition. It is to set forth rules that intersect and produce confusion, so that we may sort out confusion and make sense of all the data. The upshot may now be stated briefly: the authorship at hand had the option of narrative, but chose the way of philosophy: generalization through classification, comparison and contrast.

The Mishnah absorbs into its encompassing system of halakhah all events, small and large. With what happens the sages accomplish in constructing their legal system what they do with everything else: a vast labor of taxonomy, an immense construction of the order and rules governing the classification of everything on earth and in heaven. The disruptive character of history – one-time events of ineluctable significance – scarcely impresses the philosophers. They find no difficulty in showing that what appears unique and beyond classification has in fact happened before and so falls within the range of trustworthy rules and known procedures. Once history's components, one-time events, lose their distinctiveness, then history as a didactic intellectual construct, as a source of lessons and rules, also loses all pertinence.

So lessons and rules come from sorting out items and classifying them; that is, from the procedures and modes of thought of the philosopher seeking regularity. To this labor of taxonomy, the historian's way of selecting data and arranging them into patterns of meaning to teach lessons proves inconsequential. One-time events are not what matters. The world is composed of nature and supernature. The repetitious laws that count are those to be discovered in heaven and, in heaven's creation and counterpart, on earth. Keep those laws and things will work out. Break them, and the result is predictable: calamity of whatever sort will supervene in accordance with the rules. But just because it is predictable, a catastrophic happening testifies to what has always been and must always be, in accordance with reliable rules and within categories already discovered and well explained. The legal system takes as its task an explanation of how things are.

G History in Islam

In Islam, the question of history is more complex than it is in Judaism. As discussed in Chapter 2, the Qur'an includes countless historic references that clearly pertain to concrete, specific persons and events, not merely exemplifications in concrete terms of timeless virtues. The book itself is essentially historic on several levels. First, the Qur'an's claim to authenticity is given its context in the history of monotheism. It claims to be the culmination of the monotheistic tradition, Judaism and Christianity having come before it and the human race thus being prepared to recognize its truth. The Qur'an is convinced that those familiar with the Torah and the Gospels will recognize its validity. Furthermore, its teachings are based on lessons of history. Yet as also noted in Chapter 2, the Qur'an is unconcerned with chronology in its historical allusions. As in Judaism, its primary concern in relating the stories, with which it clearly considers its audience to be familiar, is to teach moral lessons. Also like Judaic scriptures, the Qur'an points out patterns, not just cosmic patterns but the divine pattern. In fact, it refers to the *sunna* of God, God's way of acting. In particular, it points out repeatedly that God favors those who submit to the divine will – who "do good and prevent evil" – and punishes those who do not, regardless of the time or place in which they live.

> If the hypocrites and those in whose hearts is disease and those who cause commotion in the duty do not stop, we will indeed encourage you against them and they will not be your neighbors except for a short time.
> Cursed, wherever they are found they will be seized and destroyed.
> This is the sunna of God with those who have come before and you will never find change in the sunna of God.
>
> (Sura 33:61–62)

The names of numerous prophets familiar to Jews and Christians, as well as some unknown to those groups are used repeatedly, along with references to the fates of their communities. The stories, told in brief episodes, are recounted specifically to demonstrate the truth of the Qur'an's teachings.

Lessons are to be learned from the earlier communities. Regardless of the specific details of their history, each community had received a prophet and each had somehow turned away from his teachings. As a result, each community had fallen either into oblivion or – as in the case of the Jews and Christians at the time of Prophet Muhammad – into weakness and disarray.

On the other hand, the Qur'an also sets the Islamic community on a distinctly future-oriented path. Having recounted God's way of dealing with people, the numerous failures of earlier societies, the Qur'an addresses its readers as "the best nation ever brought forth to people, commanding good and forbidding evil, and believing in God" (Sura 3:106). The failures of earlier communities are now to be corrected. This new community, being constituted by the Qur'an's teaching, is described as the *ummat al-wasit*, the "median community," the one that does not go to the extremes of the earlier communities, the one that is concerned with neither worldly affairs nor the afterlife, the one that will finally make the true religion of God paramount in all creation. The community has inherited the amana, the trust, the duty to fulfill the covenant by establishing a universal, just society. They are witnesses to the last prophet, the "seal" of prophets, the ultimate message to all humanity. They are enjoined to extend every effort in the struggle to make God's will prevail. As Majid Khadduri expressed it:

> The [Islamic community] was therefore potentially capable of embodying the whole of mankind, and the Islamic state, whether it engulfed the whole of the [community] or only a part, was the instrument which would achieve the ultimate religious objective. . . . The ultimate objective of Islam was to establish peace and order in accordance with Islamic justice within the territory brought under the pale of its public order, and to expand the area of the validity of that order to include the whole world.[34]

This, then, is history in the making. Every aspect of Islamic law is focused on fulfilling that mission. We saw in Chapter 3 that a major feature of Islamic law is ijtihad, the application of human reason to revealed sources for the purpose of creating positive law. Ijtihad reflects the very fluid and future-oriented nature of Islamic law. The sources themselves remain eternal and unchanging, but human efforts to understand and implement the teachings of the sources are not perfect. Even if they were, given the Islamic mission, the circumstances in which the law will be applied vary. The law must therefore remain flexible enough to accommodate change. As Wael Hallaq put it, "The primary objective of legal theory . . . was to lay down a coherent system of principles through which a qualified jurist could extract rulings for novel cases."[35] Unquestionably, controversy arose over the extent to which ijtihad could be exercised and the qualifications necessary to practice it. Nevertheless, the importance of ijtihad as the vehicle for creating the legislation necessary to define any and all society as Islamic remains central to Islamic thought.[36]

We also saw, in Chapter 6, that whereas Judaism stresses sacred time as a return to a mythical past, Islam's sacred time – during the pilgrimage, for example – is designed to strengthen the believers in their continued struggle for fulfillment of the Islamic mission. In Judaism, the Sabbath takes the community back to the mythic time of Eden, a timeless perfection. In telling contrast, Islam's notion of Eden is part of the historic struggle of human beings against chaos. The more important part of the story takes place before creation, in the primeval period during which God contemplated creation and then charged humanity with the "trust" which is the Islamic mission: human beings were designated God's viceroys in creation, delegated to bring all humanity to submission to the one God.

Finally, we saw that the most distinctive category unique to Islam is jihad. With no conceivable counterpart in Judaism, jihad distinguishes Islam as the religion, in its own perception, historically destined to reign over all religions. For that reason, historiography is a highly developed discipline in Islam, and was so even in Islam's formative stages. Among Islam's greatest scholars are its historians, whose task it was to track the advance of Islam across the globe. Many of the early Islamic historians were in fact religious scholars. Sir Hamilton A. R. Gibb, in commenting on the unique historical consciousness of the early Islamic community, observes that understandable pride in their extensive conquests could have motivated early Islamic historiography. But he believes the fact that

> the collectors of the historical tradition were almost exclusively theologians and *muhaddiths* [collectors of hadith reports] suggest[s] that a deeper reason existed. For in the theological view history was the manifestation of a divine plan for the government of mankind; and while the historical outlook of the earlier generations might be limited to tracing it through the succession of prophets which culminated in Muhammad, all Islamic schools were agreed that it did not end there. In the Sunni doctrine, it was the Islamic community, the *ummat Allah*, with which the continuation of the divine plan on earth was bound up; consequently the study of its history was a necessary supplement to the study of the divine revelation in [Qur'an] and *hadith*.[37]

Chronicling the victories of the Muslim armies, therefore, was chronicling the fulfillment of the divine command. Earliest Islamic historiography began with accounts of the life of the Prophet, found in the hadith traditions. These included his military engagements, the maghazi. Eventually, a full-scale biography of the Prophet (*sira*) was compiled, that of Ibn Ishaq (d. 768 CE), which began at creation, tracing the history of prophets through Muhammad, all the way to his death. This pattern of tracing the history of the Muslim community, beginning with creation, became standard in Islamic historiography, and clearly reveals the community's universalist self-perception. The Muslim community is "the best of all communities" to take up the responsibility to fulfill the divine will, the covenant. Its history is the culmination of human history. Gibb notes that the "Universal History" paradigm, which developed in the third century of Islam, is "a summary of world history on a larger or smaller scale by way of introduction to Islamic history proper."[38] Implicit in this paradigm was the equation of history with the spread of the Islamic empire. The tradition of compiling maghazi reports thus continued, and came to include the military expeditions of his successors as well. One of the best examples is Ahmad ibn Yahya al-Baladhuri's (d. 892 CE) *Opening Up of the Lands*. The culmination of this early phase of Islamic historiography was the voluminous work of Muhammad ibn Jarir al-Tabari (d. 923 CE), *History of the Prophets and Kings*. It is significant that al-Tabari's training was as a hadith compiler; his *History*, according to Gibb, was meant as a supplement to his earlier commentary on the Qur'an.

The Islamic conception of history, therefore, while not a legal category, reflects the unique characteristics of Islamic law. It is predicated on religious beliefs that define the Islamic community as one charged with the responsibility of making Islam – submission to the will of the one God that human beings live in a pious and just society – universal. No individual can expect to accomplish that task entirely but divine judgment will be based on the extent to which one participated in efforts to do so. It would be difficult to find two more different constructions of the past than those put forth by Judaism and Islam in their respective classical statements!

So have we demonstrated only the utter incompatibility of Islam and Judaism, not only their differences but their complete incapacity to comprehend, each within its resources of rationality, the character of the other? Now that we have followed the fault-line that separates the two monotheisms of law, we have to ask: What have we learned about them from the process of comparison and contrast through law? We turn to that final question in the Epilogue.

8

EPILOGUE

The consequences of comparison

A Comparisons up close

What in retrospect has validated this exercise in comparative religions? Systematic comparison of the legal structures and categories of classical Judaism and Islam reveals remarkable similarities between the two religions. Each relies on written and oral texts which are believed to express the will or mind of God. The written texts were verbally revealed through prophets, while the oral texts contain material whose meaning, if not its exact words, is accorded the status of revelation because of its continuity with the sources of direct (verbal) revelation. Both religions therefore perceive themselves as historically continuous communities, directly linked through revelation and divine intervention to the original community of the divine covenant. Islam's legal sciences display greater literacy than do those of Judaism. We do not have to abstract from practical cases the scholars' mode of reasoning as we do in Judaism; Islam's science of *usul al-fiqh* articulates its hermeneutical principles, including analogical reasoning and consensus. More highly developed literacy also accounts for greater emphasis on learning and intellectual prowess as criteria for entering the ranks of legal scholars in classical Islam than in Judaism. Judaism's reliance on charismatic authority is characteristic of oral societies. Nevertheless, the nature and purpose of the court system in Judaism is virtually identical to that in Islam. In both cases, the courts are staffed by people who are thoroughly grounded in religious law and have jurisdiction over all aspects of life, and their purpose is to adjudicate divinely inspired law.

The similarity between Judaism and Islam is also revealed in a comparison of the actual categories constructed in the two traditions. Each legislates extensively concerning the individual's and the community's relationship with God. Laws about the details of prayer, both private and public; fasting, both individually and communally; and ablutions, are essential parts of both legal systems. Judaism and Islam both consider family matters – betrothal, marriage, divorce, and inheritance – to be important legal matters. Charity is also a matter of legal concern in both systems, as are commercial relations.

240

Both systems include as well in their discussion acts that are not necessarily enforceable but are highly recommended as pleasing to God, and others that are not necessarily punishable but are discouraged. The legal systems of Judaism and Islam, in other words, encompass all aspects of life, reflecting the shared view that there is nothing in human life beyond the scope of divine concern.

But the differences also impress us, both minor and major ones. The two legal systems, first of all, share some categories which they treat in different ways. Judaic law, for example, includes highly detailed legislation about the temple and sacrifice, while Islam has no temple and legislates sparingly on animal sacrifice. On the other hand, Islamic legal sources contain detailed laws about slavery, while the Judaic sources deal with the issue only in passing. Of far greater significance, Judaic sources treat the Sabbath and sacred time in exacting detail. By contrast, Islam requires people to pray communally once a week, and the time of prayer is determined by the position of the sun, but neither the time nor day of the week is considered sacred as such. It is the act of prayer that is considered pleasing to God. On the other hand, the Islamic calendar sets out two months for holy activities: during the month of Ramadan Muslims are required to fast during daylight hours, and at least once in a lifetime Muslims are required, if possible, to make the pilgrimage to Mecca during Dhu al-Hijja. Although some would consider these months themselves as sacred, the classical texts make it clear that it is the activity of the believers during these periods that sanctifies the time.

But there is more. We focused particularly on the month of the pilgrimage, the subject of legislation to the minutest detail in Islam's classical sources. There we find a significant correlation with the patterns of the Judaic Sabbath, in that the rituals involved commemorate deeds associated with the establishment of God's special relationship with the community of believers. On the Judaic Sabbath, families re-create in their homes the time before the departure from Eden, when God was pleased with humanity. During the Muslim pilgrimage, believers enter a state of purity and re-enact deeds associated with Abraham's establishment of the covenant with humankind. Yet there are important differences between the two notions of sacred time as well. As noted, for Muslims the time of the pilgrimage, like the time of the Ramadan fast, is made holy by people's performing acts pleasing to God. It would be difficult to argue that the times themselves are inherently sacred, given Islam's overwhelming emphasis on the centrality of good deeds as determinants of piety. As the much-quoted Qur'anic verse has it,

It is not piety that you turn your faces to the East or the West. Pious is the one who believes in God and the Last Day, the angels, the Book, and the prophets, and spends for love of Him on relatives and

241

orphans, poor people, travellers, the needy, and for captives, performs the prayer, and gives charity; and the one who keeps promises, is patient in poverty, hardship and conflict. It is these who are truthful and pious.

(Sura 2:178)

More telling, perhaps, is the difference between the Judaic perception of re-creating a sacred time and the Muslim perception of commemorating or re-enacting sacred deeds. The Judaic Sabbath re-establishes the idyllic time in Eden when human beings lived in accordance with God's will. It was a time of equilibrium in the life of God's creatures; human beings wanted for nothing. The Muslim pilgrimage, by contrast, reminds believers of a covenant yet unfulfilled. The enormous spiritual energy derived from the pilgrimage – like that of the month-long fast – is meant to carry over into everyday life. It serves to motivate and strengthen believers for the task ahead of them. That task – fulfilling the trust human beings took upon themselves as God's deputies, to make all religion God's religion, to "do good and prevent evil," to re-create in society the equality which all humans share in the eyes of God – is the focus of every aspect of Islamic thought and practice. The pilgrimage, as the culmination of the Islamic year, allows believers a respite from their daily struggle; bringing them to intense mindfulness of the divine, they are relieved temporarily of the burden of self-concern. Yet its rituals constantly remind believers of the struggle that lies ahead. Believers re-enter daily life with renewed commitment to expend every effort "in the way of God."

These disproportions point to a uniqueness in each tradition made even more explicit in the categories they do not share with the other. In the chapter dealing with that subject we identified categories that occur in either the Judaic or the Islamic legal sources but not in both. Judaic treatment of the Land of Israel, "enlandisement," has no counterpart in Islam, while Islam's jihad is nowhere to be found in Judaic law. In the Judaic perception, God chose the people of Israel to live according to His will, expressed in the Torah. (We noted the importance of distinguishing between this notion of "holy Israel" – the people who live according to the Torah – from the citizens of the contemporary state of Israel.) This community lived in the Land of Israel at one time, but because of disobedience, they were driven out. The community, Holy Israel, is promised new life in the Land of Israel in return for living according to God's will as expressed in the Torah. But that reward is envisioned after the final judgment, repentance, and resurrection. The prayer of the people of Israel is that God will ultimately call all humanity to perfection through submission to divine sovereignty. The notion of enlandisement in the classics of Judaism, then, means that the faithful will be resurrected in the Land of Israel. That is why, even now, pious Jews choose to be buried in the Holy Land. The special relationship of Holy Israel to the

Land of Israel, then, is part of an eschatology in which, as a reward for having transformed their world through living according to divine law, God calls all humanity to a new Eden. The believers having shown themselves worthy, God will transform the world into a realm of peace and justice.

In the Islamic conception, by contrast, the task of creating peace and justice is a this-worldly one. There is undoubtedly a strong strain of fatalism in popular Islam and, as in Judaism, many believe that the final era of cosmic order will be ushered in by a messiah, though there is no mention of such a figure in the Qur'an. Nevertheless, the overall spirit of Islamic teaching is essentially activist. Each individual must contribute to the greatest extent possible to the establishment of a peaceful and just society. "Enjoin good and forbid evil" is the Qur'anic refrain expressing this motif, and jihad is the legal category encompassing its enforceable aspects. As noted, jihad is both a personal and a communal responsibility. No individual is expected to be able to achieve the goal of social justice single-handedly, yet each must participate to the extent of her/his capabilities and as the situation demands. Jihad on the individual level therefore includes all the personal efforts one extends in the struggle to be a responsible and contributing member of a God-fearing society. On the communal level, in time of war, a sufficient number of people must participate in order to make the effort successful; in cases of external attack, all able-bodied believers are expected to join the effort to defend the community. Whether personal or communal, however, the goal of jihad is to bring all the world to submission to God.

As in the Judaic prayer, Muslims foresee a world in which everyone is called to eternal life through God. But in Islam, that call is not put off until the eschaton or left to further divine intervention. In keeping with the belief that Muhammad is the last, the "seal" of the prophets, the call to Islam is the duty of believers themselves. Although the Qur'an forbids coercion in matters of religion, Islamic law requires that Muslims call all others to true religion, meaning monotheism. Those who already believe in one God – Jews, Christians, and Sabeans, according to the Qur'an (Sura 5:70) – are accepted as "People of the Book," sufficiently guided by their own scriptures to be able to please God. Other communities, such as Zoroastrians and Hindus, have at times been included in that category. Islamic political law also allows for treaties with non-believers for specific reasons, such as that the group's strength threatens to overpower the Muslims. But such treaties must ensure justice for those bound by them. For example, the Hanafi jurist al-Shaybani holds that it is not lawful to make a treaty with a non-believer that allows him to treat his people cruelly – for example, beheading and crucifying them.[1] Furthermore, such treaties are only temporary, designed not to exceed a period of ten years. The responsibility to call all people to Islam remains, in the sincere belief that the peace and justice promised by God for all humanity can only be achieved through submission to Islamic law. The Qur'an allows that God guides whomever he will; it is not possible for human beings to understand why some people accept divine sovereignty and others reject it in favor of instability and injustice. Nevertheless, all believers share the responsibility not only of making sure that they themselves follow the law of God but of calling all humanity to follow suit.

The juxtaposition of enlandisement and jihad, then, highlights a paradigmatic difference between Judaism and Islam. The two share an ultimate vision, an eschaton in which all human beings live in blissful equanimity with their creator, having been called to submit to divine sovereignty or suffer eternal perdition. The difference between the two lies in the question of the role of the believers in bringing about that state of affairs. The classics of Judaism reveal an eschatology in which the active participant in establishing the state of peace and justice is God, working through the Messiah; the role of the believers is to make themselves worthy to enjoy it. In the classics of Islam, the believers themselves are called upon to actively participate in transforming the world into an abode of peace and justice. God has made the path to perfection clear through revelation, and it is the believers' responsibility, as God's vicegerents, to bring all humanity to Islam, "the straight path."

This difference in perception of the role of the believer is reflected in differing views on two other category formations. In Judaism, the scholar meets God in the Torah. Moses is regarded as a model and an exemplar in the Judaic classics, but he is not considered to be a prophet. His exemplary role is as teacher of the law. In fact, the study of law, its formulation and oral transmission, is of such paramount importance in Judaism that legal scholars are elevated above the status even of prophets. They are holy sages, carrying on the work of prophets, which ended with the destruction of Jerusalem. But sages do not merely transmit the law, as did the prophets. Through their power of analysis, they gain access to the very mind of God. Studying the law, then, is a theological encounter and, as such, an end in itself. Indeed, studying the law is more highly valued than even practicing the commandments; understanding takes precedence over simple observance.

In Islam, as the name suggests, nothing takes precedence over carrying out the will of God. The study of law is a means toward the overall end: understanding how to implement the will of God. Because of the universal mission of Islam, the classical legal sources recognize that the law must remain flexible. For that reason, in addition to the written scripture, the oral tradition, and the consensus of scholars, ijtihad is included as a source of law. Ijtihad is the procedure that allows Islamic law to be suitable in every time and place. Even the founders of the four official Sunni schools of law, according to fourteenth-century Hanbali jurist Ibn Taymiyya, admonished people not to follow their judgments blindly but, after studying the entire corpus of Islamic law, to return to the Qur'an and Sunna in order to determine the most appropriate ruling in a given case.[2] The study and articulation of Islamic law, then, is an ongoing and dynamic activity, in keeping with the dynamic nature of an expanding and potentially universal society. As we have seen, all people are to be called to Islam, and Islam is essentially submitting to the divine will as expressed in law. Thus, law provides the essential component of Islamic society, that which distinguishes a society as Islamic. So important is the law in Islam that some schools even consider its study to be a religious requirement. In any case, the study of law is a communal duty; enough people must engage in it for the goal to be achieved. That goal, again – establishing a just social order in accordance with the will of God – is the reason for studying law in Islam. In the classical sources of Sunni Islam, then, the study of law – unlike its counterpart in Judaism – is not an end in itself. It is a means to the goal of implementing the will of God.

The paradigmatic difference in the Judaic and Islamic perceptions of the role of human beings in the divine plan, as expressed in their classical legal sources, is also evident in the two traditions' differing views of history. We noted that both religions use historical events as pedagogical tools; what happened in the past teaches lessons for the present and the future. We have also seen that both Judaism and Islam regard history as a continuous, linear chain of events proceeding from creation to the present and eventually to the end of time as we know it. However, we saw that the Judaic legal system, with its emphasis on sacred time and eternal patterns, is essentially focused on the continuing present. The mode of celebrating the Sabbath, for example, extensively detailed in legal sources, seeks to re-establish a past event in the present. The relationship between God and Holy Israel is not merely commemorated in the weekly Sabbath rituals but is actually re-created. The elaborate legislation surrounding the day is meant to allow believers to re-experience the ideal relationship between God and the people whose needs he fulfilled. Creation, therefore, in the classical sources of Judaism, is not a one-time historical event but an eternal pattern, to be recapitulated on a regular basis. Eternal patterns are the focus of legal treatment of other past events as well. The law seeks to express, eternally and therefore timelessly, God's relationship to humanity as exhibited in timeless patterns.

The Islamic conception of history, as we saw, is essentially forward-looking. It envisions a time when all humanity will be subject to divine law. It therefore establishes a system of duties, personal and communal, designed to strengthen Muslims in their commitment to creating God's society on earth as well as to expand that society. All Muslims must commit themselves to monotheism and the message of Prophet Muhammad, renew that commitment repeatedly every day, contribute to the support of the needy and efforts to expand the Islamic community, fast during the month of Ramadan, and perform the ritual pilgrimage to Mecca for the sake of spiritual renewal. But the spiritual strength derived from these "pillars" is directed toward personal submission to the divine will and, at the same time, calling others to follow suit. Thus, Islamic law adds communal duties of jihad and, in the view of some, the study of law. These communal duties are not required of all individuals but are highly recommended supererogatory undertakings

245

required of enough people to ensure that the law of God prevails. The goal of universalizing *islam*, ever present in the sources and codes of Islamic law, is inevitably future oriented. That forward view is evident in Islam's highly developed historiography. The writing of history was, as we saw, closely associated with Islamic religious sciences. A common paradigm was the "universal" or "world" history, beginning with creation and ending with the most recent expansions of Islamic jurisdiction. Confidence in the inevitability of ultimate victory is apparent; the eternal lessons of the past demonstrated unquestionably that oppressors fail.

Overall, the comparison of classical formulations of Judaic and Islamic law reveal religions which envision the transformation of the world from chaos and oppression to peace and justice. The difference is that, for Judaism, that transformation will be a reward for Holy Israel's obedience to the Torah. At the end of time, all humanity will be called to share in the reward for Holy Israel's submission to the will of God. In Islam, the world will be transformed through human efforts; God will reward with eternal life all those who contribute to the effort to re-create in society the equality which in his eyes all human beings share. If we did not know the historical fact that Islam is a world-conquering religion, with vast successes in its history, and that Judaism is a world-imagining religion, with a record of defeat to consider, from the theological differences we have examined, we might well have come up with that very characterization of each. Our picture emerges of religions that compare but that are concentric only in modest measure. But that distorts an underlying reality of commonality, at which point we choose to conclude.

B Judaism and Islam: companions in the context of world religions

We have spent these pages comparing Judaism and Islam through law, because, as religions of law, they present many suitable cases for comparison. But we have then underscored their differences. The reason that Judaism and Islam seen up close look so different is that, in the correct perspective, they look so much alike. Because they bear so much in common, we are able to compare them – and then to perceive the striking contrasts. We conclude that Judaism and Islam are not identical twins, they are fraternal twins. The differences take on weight, because the similarities so impress.

Consider the points on which they concur. First and most important, there is one and only one God, Creator of heaven and earth. That conviction, fundamental to all else, separates Judaism and Islam, along with Christianity, from all other religions known to humanity, past and present. Not only so but, they agree, it is the one God whom humanity knows because of God's self-manifestation to prophets, beginning with Abraham. So they agree not only that there is one unique God, but also that there is a single story to be told about Him. And yet there is more. They concur in calling God "the all-merciful," and they share the faith that God passionately loves Man. That unique God created heaven and earth and rules the lives of human beings, pursuing justice, governing with mercy, demanding the submission to his will of all the faithful. So theologically, Judaism and Islam agree on basics. When Muslims write in Hebrew or Judaists in Arabic, much of what they write sounds native to the faithful of the other religion. And that is hardly surprising, since both religions insist there is only one God, and the logic of the position of each requires assent that they speak of one and the same God.

Second, Judaism and Islam agree that politics, culture, the social order – the whole of humanity's existence must respond to, be shaped by, God's revealed will. The pages of this book have underscored the structural comparability of Judaism and Islam. They concur that religion is public, not personal alone; religion defines shared and common responsibilities and cannot be treated as something essentially private. Indeed, both religions maintain that religion takes the critical, indeed the definitive position in the formation of the social order. Politics, culture, the life of imagination and of action – every chapter of life, both personal and public, responds to God's will.

Third, it follows for both religions that law, the norms of society, the rules for conduct of both public and private life – these define the consequential dimensions of the holy way of life. Law tells the faithful when to pray and how to pray, and neither Judaism nor Islam would assign prayer to individual option alone, though both concur that the faithful speak to God not only with the community but on their own. God's law, the prophet's instructions – these frame the realm of politics and war, economics and the conduct of affairs, home and family alike.

Why should the two religions concur on so many fundamental propositions concerning the form that religion should take in the here and now of ordinary life? It is because of the character of the revelation – Torah, Qur'an – that each means to realize in the social order. When Moses came down from Sinai bearing the Torah, he did not report about a personal experience of encounter, but set forth commandments and laws for the people down below. And that people is not to be confused with a secular ethnic group, because the revelation of the Torah identified as God's people those whom God had freed from slavery and to whom He entrusted the Torah. When Muhammad recited the Qur'an, he was instructed to disclose the revelation to others and to form of them a community to realize in the here and the now the words which God had spoken. Not only so, but both Holy Israel (not to be confused with the contemporary State of Israel) and the community of Islam forthwith undertook tasks in history, political enterprises. They created what they conceived to be godly states, enforced divine law among men, and took responsibility, before God, for the human condition.

Some would draw the comparison in more secular terms. They might

247

appeal to geographical determinism, for instance, finding in the common trait of groups of people resident in the desert – Israel in Sinai, Muhammad and the first Muslims in Arabia – a reason for the severe monotheism, the intense legalism, characteristic of both religions. Quite how and why this and kindred secular explanations accomplish their tasks we do not claim to grasp. While this-worldly explanations, deriving from historical and social circumstance, may serve, in our view we do well to consider the configuration of the theology that animates each religion as well.

Why, then, the stress on culture and politics as arenas for godly living and pious activity? It is because the two religions share a single perspective upon knowledge of God: it is not only immediate and acutely present tense, it is also inherited and preserved out of the past. Both Islam and Judaism offer humanity knowledge of God in books, encounter through traditions out of the past the record of God's self-manifestation to humanity at one time that pertains to all times to come. If, in Judaism, you wish to meet God, you not only say prayers or engage in acts of piety, but you open the Torah and contemplate the record of God's meeting with Abraham, Isaac, Jacob, Moses, and the other prophets. The Torah records God's encounter with humanity through the prophets and, we realize, the sages of the Oral Torah as well. The Torah offers knowledge of God of a specific, very particular character: these words, these commandments. And Islam concurs. In Islam, along these same lines, the Qur'an records the exact words that God chose to make his person and his will known through Prophet Muhammad. What have culture and politics to do with meeting God in books?

As soon as we ask this question, the answer presents itself. Books are artifacts of culture. They require readers, meaning enduring media of formulation and transmission – whether schools and teachers or inchoate and intangible media of child-raising patterns, family constructions, implicit expectations, and the other enduring means by which culture transmits itself. And culture spills over into politics – the science that tells us who legitimately does what to whom, or, in more elegant language, the science of social power. The religious cultures of the Torah and the Qur'an secure a long future for themselves within culture, and therefore through the instrumentalities of collective and public action, and that is a policy natural to the conviction that God, though everywhere and always accessible to prayer, picks and chooses to whom He will speak. Judaism and Islam tell the story of God's particular revelation, at a singular moment, a moment in time, to specific persons, Moses and Muhammad, for Holy Israel and Islam, respectively. And once the definitive revelation has gone forth, generations to come take up the task, which by definition devolves upon society and its culture of continuity, of preserving and transmitting the tradition that embodies the religious encounter of the ages. As between geographical determinism and an explanation that appeals to the substance of theology, we find in the propositions of the faith a more plausible explanation of the character of the culture and politics that the faith generates. What people do together expresses what they believe, both severally and jointly.

So to account for the shared traits of public, cultural policy that they exhibit in common, what characterizes both Judaism and Islam is the conviction that God reaches out to mankind. Each in its own terms maintains that the religious encounter of the holy men and women of the past endures as the record of how human beings know God and what we know about God. That then distinguishes those two religions (and the other book religions that concur, for example, Christianity) from the religions that afford the encounter with God through acute, contemporary experience alone or principally. Those religions do not concur that the faithful find God in books, in the record of God's encounter with prophets or sages of old. The faithful undertake the quest for God through direct encounter in the here and now, there alone. Then the holy books, if any, preserve the experience of prior seekers, but they do not make accessible that experience in the way in which for Judaism and for Islam the Torah and the Qur'an do.

Judaism and Islam stand for the continuity of religious experience from the remote past to the acutely present moment, and, it follows, they also value the institutions of continuity, the forces for the continuation of the tradition of old, represented by politics and by culture. For Judaism and Islam the past possesses authority because it makes available what, for most, is accessible only in the record of the prophets and their teachings. If Moses or Muhammad set the standard, then what is the community of the faithful to do if not try to meet that ever-present standard? And while, everyone assumes, prayer and piety and even the mystic quest afford direct and immediate encounter with, even knowledge of, God, Moses or Muhammad has already set down the results to anticipate, the outcome to expect, in that present-tense moment. So Judaism and Islam define themselves as religions of culture and society by reason of the theological convictions that animate each. Then, for both, the priority of the prophet forms the criterion of truth. And God's revelation to the prophet – the Torah, the Qur'an, respectively – takes priority over all subsequent revelations and stands in judgment upon them. That is why, while the latter-day generations may and do meet God, for example, in prayer, in direct personal encounter, or in intellectual pursuits yielding learning and poetry, none anticipates that God will change his mind. All later revelations link themselves to and are judged as authentic by the criterion of the original one.

How do these observations allow us to situate the companion religions, Judaism and Islam, within the larger realm of religion? Christianity comes first. If we consider only the classical phase in the history of Christianity as we have the classical phases of Judaism – the Written Torah and the writings of the Oral Torah of the first six centuries of the Common Era – and of Islam – the Qur'an and the first three hundred years of Muslim theology and jurisprudence, what do we consider? The counterpart is the New Testament

249

and the writings of the Church Fathers to Nicea, 325 CE, the centuries before Christianity became licit, then the official religion of the Roman Empire. In the Gospels and the Letters of Paul, in the writings of the Catholic fathers of the early centuries, we look in vain for the conception of Christ as King in a this-worldly sense or of Christ as the source of culture. The Syriac Church Father, Aphrahat, for example, called the Christians "the people that is no people," or "the people that is of the peoples." The conception that animates Islam and Judaism at their very foundations, that to accomplish his goals God calls into being not only a community of the faithful but a godly state, scarcely matches the notion of rendering to Caesar what is his. And while Islam and Judaism from their roots set forth doctrines that constituted an economics, so proposing to manage the rational utilization of scarce resources in accord with God's, not man's, rationality, Christianity took well over a thousand years to put forth a counterpart.

Thus Islam and Judaism worked out by their theological nature what Christianity would bring forth only with much difficulty and distress, which is the notion of the Christian Empire. And, by the time that it did, Judaism would find necessary a complete revision of its conceptions of politics and culture, "Israel" as a theological political entity having lost all foundation in everyday reality with the end of the Jews' autonomy as a nation in any political sense. Then, for centuries to come, the contending empires, the one in the name of Islam, the other of Christianity, would work out on battle-fields of Spain and France, the Balkans and the Middle East, and ultimately even India and eastward, their agreement concerning God's politics, and their difference as to the details thereof.

The three monotheist religions, Judaism, Islam, and Christianity, differentiate themselves from all other religions not only in telling intertwined stories — first Judaism's, then Christianity's, then Islam's, in sequence — but also in their resort to the media of culture and politics for the telling. They distinguish themselves, also, from those religions that lay stress on the immediate and direct encounter with God, the accessibility of God through quotidian revelation, in preference to the priority afforded the initial, definitive encounter. So we should have to differentiate by appeal to the criteria of not only theological conviction but also religious experience: what is deemed possible, what is held normative. And, it goes without saying, those religions that deem the religious activity to be essentially personal will take leave of the ones at hand, and the religions that find possible the differentiation of religion from other chapters of culture will set forth very different policies of public life from the monotheist ones. It would carry us far afield to examine the classes of religions and their categorization that our recognition of the shared traits of Judaism and Islam might yield. One reasonably illuminating comparison, such as we claim to have set forth above, affords a perspective upon the comparison and contrast of many other, comparable phenomena.

But if we had to choose a single point of differentiation between Judaism and Islam, on the one side, and other religions, including Christianity, on the other, what would it be? We find the most telling common characteristic of Judaism and Islam to be the ambiguity of their reading of the category "religion." Both differentiate only with great difficulty between religion and culture, religion and politics. In that regard, they part company from Christianity, with its successive heritage of separation from politics and integration with the empire. Whether in consequence of its historical experience or for less tangible reasons, Christianity could distinguish "church" from "state," in ways in which Judaism could, and cannot, between "synagogue" or more aptly, "Torah" and state, or Islam, "mosque," and state. And yet both recognize the autonomous working of God not only within culture but through culture, producing a theological consciousness with only limited analogues in other religions integrated as they are with culture and politics.

That is to say, even though the Hebrew of the Torah, oral and written, and the Arabic of the Qur'an yield no word for "religion" as such, both Judaism and Islam can discourse about "religion," speaking not of politics or culture but of a clearly differentiated body of human experience of and aspiration to God. It is that ambiguous middle ground which those two religions occupy, not all by themselves, but not with many others. Whether philosophical traditions with supernatural or mythic overtones such as flourish in India and China compare remains for others to say. To us, India and China yield no close analogues when it comes to the interplay of religion, viewed as a distinct phenomenon, culture, and politics, to the definitive traits of Islam and Judaism.

We conclude with this morning's news: Christianity has found several, quite authentic modes of mediation between State and Church, Christ and culture, in the encounter with the secular world order. Whether the Catholic, the Protestant, or the Orthodox settlement, the principal media of Christianity know how to engage with our modern condition in both politics and culture. Christianity can concede that there is such a thing as religion, distinct from culture, separate from the social order. Within the religious world of Hindu India or Buddhist Southeast Asia or Shinto Japan, so far as we deal with religion and not philosophy, religion and not ethnicity transmuted into nationalism, we look in vain for a counterpart engagement. Religious activities go forward in timeless rhythm, and philosophical reflection carries on unimpeded, the two rarely flowing together in a single stream of thought and experience.

In their contemporary formulations of the classical revelation and convictions pertaining thereto, even with their respective heritage of theological and systematic thought, today Judaism and Islam find difficult the isolation of religion from culture and society, the definition of religion apart from the social order. It is principally in Islam and in Judaism that we encounter the struggle, yet to be resolved, between the essentially secular world of politics and culture and the enduringly religious world of politics and culture that the modern world presents as the critical issue confronting the two kindred faiths. In the yeshivas of Benei Beraq and in the madrasas of Qum, sages and legists, in the name of the one and only God, continue to puzzle over the confusions of the contemporary world, where the religious and the secular viewpoint compete, serially, in the same country, in the same city, in the same household, in the same soul. God reveals how he wants the social order to take shape and the individual life to unfold, so to speak of religion is to divide the indivisible.

But enough of the world, even near at hand, knows and cares nothing of the revealed will of God to call into question anyone's certainty of the unity of society, politics, culture, and revelation. So even in the very citadels of the faithful, the conception of "religion" in its own terms and framework – as distinct from culture, separate from politics, autonomous of society – finds its position. The Christian resolution of the conflict has played itself out. Everyone knows the several options which Christianity has worked out for itself; and they do work. The world still waits for Judaism, principally in the State of Israel but also in the main centers elsewhere where the faith is practiced in sizable numbers, and Islam worldwide, to show the alternative to the Christian settlement. If the conditions of modern times permit a third way, between self-isolation and a latitudinarian, ever-compromising integration, Islam and Judaism promise to identify it. Formidable intellectual tasks of public policy in the theological idiom confront the framers of contemporary Judaism and Islam respectively. The test of that original, eternal moment of revelation for both comes tomorrow, not yesterday.

But how matters will work themselves out is not for us to say: God decides, as both Judaism and Islam concur, along with Christianity. Perhaps in the twenty-first (Christian) century, the occasion will arise for a meeting of our rabbi Moses, Muhammad the prophet and seal of prophecy, and Jesus Christ. We hope that, in some modest measure, we have helped people imagine what, at such a meeting, the embodiments of the religion that, all concur, commenced with God's call to Abraham, Judaic, Christian, and Muslim faithful might try to discuss in common.

NOTES

1 COMPARING ISLAM AND JUDAISM

1 The work on comparative theology of formative Christianity and Judaism is contained in the following books by Bruce D. Chilton and Jacob Neusner: *Common Heritage, Diverse Dispositions. Judaic and Christian Classics Doctrinally Compared* (London: Routledge, 1988); *Judaism in the New Testament. Practices and Beliefs* (London: Routledge, 1995); *Types of Authority in Formative Christianity and Judaism. Institutional, Charismatic, and Intellectual* (London: Routledge, 1999); *The Intellectual Foundations of Christian and Jewish Discourse: The Philosophy of Religious Argument* (London: Routledge, 1997); *Christianity and Judaism: The Formative Categories. I. Revelation. The Torah and the Bible* (Philadelphia: Trinity Press International, 1995); *Christianity and Judaism: The Formative Categories. II. The Body of Faith: Israel and Church* (Philadelphia: Trinity Press International, 1997); *Christianity and Judaism: The Formative Categories. III. God in the World* (Philadelphia: Trinity Press International, 1997); *Judaeo-Christian Debates. Communion with God, the Kingdom of God, the Mystery of the Messiah* (Minneapolis: Fortress Press, 1998).
2 Some basic points are made in J. Neusner, *First Principles of Systemic Analysis. The Case of Judaism in the History of Religion* (Lanham: University Press of America, 1988) ("Studies in Judaism" series).
3 Marshall Sahlins, *How "Natives" Think* (Chicago: The University of Chicago Press, 1994), p. 163, citing Michel Foucault, *The Order of Things* (New York: Vintage Books, 1973), p. xv. That the entire conceit is Borges's own invention is clear.

2 DOCUMENTS OF JUDAISM AND ISLAM

1 That is to say, the community of Judaism. By "the Jewish People" in pre-modern times, people ordinarily understood "those that practice the religion, Judaism." The conception that a person or community of persons could be Jewish but not Judaic, that is, ethnically or culturally Jewish but not religiously Judaic, and that ethnicity or nationality could be separated from religion, is particularly modern and European. In these pages, "Jewish people" and "people of Judaism" or "people of Israel" all refer to the same social entity, comparable in its theological self-definition to the abode of Islam. At no point does "Israel" here refer either to the geographical entity, the Land of Israel, or to the political State of Israel. When the Jewish state is under discussion, it is always identified as "the State of Israel." Otherwise "Israel" stands for the holy people of whom the Torah speaks; that is to say, a theological, not a political, category.

253

2 For an account of the canonization of the Qurʾanic text, see Arthur Jeffery, *Materials for the History of the Text of the Koran* (Leyden: E.J. Brill, 1937). The text of the Qurʾan was not finally established until the early tenth century, some 200 years following the prophet's death, when vowels were indicated and diacriticals were added, at which time seven readings with minor variations were identified.

3 Shiʿi Muslims base their laws on their own collections of traditions, most importantly, those of al-Kulayni (d. 940) and al-Qummi (d. 991), which include reports of the words and deeds of Shiʿi Imams, i.e., leaders of the community whose legitimacy stems from their being descendants of the prophet Muhammad through his daughter Fatima and son-in-law ʿAli.

4 Nasir al-Din Al-Baydawi, *Minhaj al-Wusul ila ʿIlm al-Usul* (Cairo: Matbaʿah Kurdistan alʿIlmiyyah, 1325), p. 3. I am grateful to Ahmad Hasan (*Principles of Islamic Jurisprudence*, Islamabad, Pakistan: Islamic Research Institute, 1993), I, p. 22, n. 11, for the reference to al-Baydawi.

5 Debate continues among scholars regarding the authenticity of legal texts attributed to the earliest legists. See, e.g., Norman Calder's *Studies in Early Muslim Jurisprudence* (Oxford: Clarendon Press, 1993) where he discussed the importance of distinguishing between texts actually attributable to the authors under whose names they appear, and texts similarly attributed but which have been elaborated on by later scholars within the authors' schools of thought. For our introductory purposes the nuances involved in this and similar distinctions are not significant. We shall follow the standard attribution of the legal canon as laid out by Joseph Schacht in *An Introduction to Islam* (Oxford: Oxford University Press, 1964). We shall also rely, where possible, on texts available to English readers in translation, duly noting that there are multiple editions of some of the formative texts and that some of the translations are more felicitous than others.

6 This usage was pointed out by Fazlur Rahman in *Islamic Methodology in History* (Islamabad: Islamic Research Institute, 1965), p. 13.

7 Note is taken that certain contempory scholars dispute the impact of al-Shafiʿi's work in establishing the currently accepted order of roots of Islamic law. See, e.g., Wael Hallaq, "Was al-Shafiʿi the Master Architect of Islamic Jurisprudence?" *International Journal of Middle East Studies* 25 (1993): 587–605, and Norman Calder, *Studies in Early Muslim Jurisprudence*; see also John Burton, "Rewriting the Timetable of Early Islam," *Journal of the American Oriental Society* 15 (1995): 453–62. This argument need not concern us here.

8 Al-Shafiʿi, *al-Risalah* (Cairo, 1321), p. 7.

9 Not to be confused with the contemporary State of Israel.

10 Fazlur Rahman, *Islam* (Chicago: University of Chicago Press, 1979), p. 35.

3 INTELLECTUAL SOURCES OF THE LAW

1 For discussion of the difference between oral and literate modes of reasoning, see Walter J. Ong, *Orality and Literacy* (London and New York: Methuen, 1985).

2 Majid Khadduri, *Islamic Jurisprudence: Shafiʿi's Risala, Translated with an Introduction, Notes and Appendices* (Baltimore: The Johns Hopkins University Press, 1961), p. 287.

3 Ibid.

4 Ibid., p. 288.

5 Imam Malik ibn Anas, *Al-Muwatta of Imam Malik ibn Anas: The First Formulation of Islamic Law*, trans. Aisha Abdurrahman Bewley (London and New York: Kegan Paul International, 1989), pp. 353–54.

6 Ibid., pp. 363–64.

7 Ibid., p. 211.
8 Khadduri, pp. 291–92.
9 Ibid., p. 290.
10 Ibid., p. 305.
11 Ibid., p. 308.
12 Ibid.
13 Ibid., p. 310.
14 Ibid., p. 324.
15 Abu Ja'far Muhammad ibn Jarir al-Tabari, *Jami' al-bayan 'an ta'wil ay al-Qur'an*, ed. Mahmud Muhammad and Ahmad Muhammad Shakir (Cairo: Dal al-Ma'arif, 1374/1954–): vi, pp. 170–85. This summary is taken from Jane Dammen McAuliffe's excellent discussion in "Quranic Hermeneutics: The Views of al-Tabari and Ibn Kathir," in Andrew Rippin, ed. *Approaches to the History of the Interpretation of the Qur'an* (Oxford: Clarendon Press, 1988) pp. 46–62.
16 McAuliffe's translation, ibid., p. 51.
17 Malik, *Al-Muwatta,* p. 344.
18 Al-Shafi'i, *Risala,* p. 123.
19 Ibid., pp. 123–24.
20 Ibid.
21 Ibid., p. 127.
22 Ibid., p. 210 ff.
23 Ibid., pp. 313–14.
24 Ibid., p. 292.
25 Ibid., p. 305.
26 Malik *Al-Muwatta,* p. 197.
27 Ibid., p. 296.
28 Ibid.
29 Quoted by Maxime Rodinson in *Mohammed*, trans. Anne Carter (New York: Pantheon Books, 1971), p. 286, from Jahiz, *Kitab al-Bayan wa-t-tabyin*, ed. Harun (Cairo, 1367/1948), II, pp. 31ff. Interestingly, as Rodinson notes, there are numerous versions of this speech, some of which exclude the claim that Arabs are not superior to non-Arabs. See, e.g., the one reported by Muhammad Husayn Haykal in *The Life of Muhammad*, trans. Isma'il Ragi A. al-Faruqi (Plainfield, IN: American Trust Publications, 1995), p. 487.
30 It would carry us far afield to do more than point out that the comparison of Judaic, Islamic, and Christian modes of legal thought, the possibility of a shared rationality, awaits attention. Gratian's *Decretum Concordia Discordantium Canonum* (*c.* 1140) so far as we know has never been brought into alignment, for purposes of comparison and contrast, with the classical Islamic and Judaic counterparts – and, we assert, they do constitute counterparts.

4 WORKING OF LAW: INSTITUTIONS

1 Translated from Abu Yusuf's *Kitab al-Kharaj* (Book of Taxation) by B. Lewis in *Islam: From the Prophet Muhammad to the Capture of Constantinople*, Vol. I: *Politics and War* (New York: Harper & Row, 1974), pp. 154–55.
2 Ibid., pp. 152–54.
3 Ibid., p. 155.
4 Ibid.
5 N.J. Coulson, *A History of Islamic Law* (Edinburgh: Edinburgh University Press, 1964), p. 37.
6 In Marshall G. S. Hodgson's analysis, the dynastic families had seized control of

the central political power of the Muslim empire (the army and the treasury that supported it) before there was any theory of political legitimacy in Islam. But by the tenth century, regional principalities had emerged and while they were generally content to pay nominal allegiance to the Baghdad caliphate, they posed a challenge to the central caliphate's real power. Hodgson says, "The caliphate itself was in question, in a world ruled by arbitrary amirs [princes], and the caliphate had proved willing to turn to Shar'i principles in its crisis. Hence the scholars set about developing the theory of a *siyasah shar'iyyah*, Shar'i political order." See *The Venture of Islam*, Vol. II: *The Expansion of Islam in the Middle Periods* (Chicago and London: The University of Chicago Press, 1974), p. 55. It should be noted, however, that even in al-Mawardi's formulation, the term "imamate" is used, rather than "caliphate". The terms are interchangeable in this context.

7 This account is taken from pp. 3–6, 14–15, and 19–20 of al-Mawardi's *Al-Ahkam al-Sultaniyya*, translated by Bernard Lewis in *Islam*, Vol. I: *Politics and War*, pp. 171–79.

8 Ibid.

9 Muhammad al-Juwayni, *Ghiyath al-Umama*. Iskandariyya, 1979: 274–75: "If the sultan does not reach the degree of ijtihad, then the jurists are to be followed and the sultan will provide them with help, power, and protection." Quoted by Wael Hallaq, "Was the Gate of Ijtihad Closed?" in *International Journal of Middle East Studies* 16 (1984):13.

10 Translated from al-Mawardi's *Al-Ahkam al-Sultaniyya* by Bernard Lewis in *Islam*, Vol. I: *Politics and War*, p. 177.

11 Translated from Abu Yusuf's *Kitab al-Kharaj* by Lewis, *Islam*, Vol. I, p. 159.

12 Ibid., p. 155.

13 Imam Malik ibn Anas, *Al-Muwatta' of Imam Malik ibn Anas: The First Formulation of Islamic Law*, trans Aisha Abdurrahman Bewley (London: Kegan Paul International, 1989), p. 344.

14 Majid Khadduri, *Islamic Jurisprudence: Shafi'i's Risala, Translated with an Introduction, Notes, and Appendices* (Baltimore: The Johns Hopkins University Press, 1961), pp. 105–06.

5 WORKING OF LAW: PERSONNEL

1 Imam Malik Ibn Anas, *Al-Muwatta of Imam Malik ibn Anas: The First Formulation of Islamic Law*, trans. Aisha Abdurrahman Bewley (London and New York: Kegan Paul International, 1989), p. 296.

2 Ibid.

3 Ibid., p. 422.

4 Majid Khadduri, *Islamic Jurisprudence: Shafi'i's Risala, Translated with an Introduction, Notes, and Appendices* (Baltimore: The Johns Hopkins University Press, 1961), p. 306.

5 Ibid.

6 Ibid., p. 307.

7 Ibid., p. 306.

8 Ibid., p. 81.

9 Ibid., p. 82.

10 Ibid., p. 87.

11 Ibid., p. 99.

12 Translated from Mawardi's *Al-Ahkam al-Sultaniyya* by Bernard Lewis, *Islam from the Prophet Muhammad to the Capture of Constantinople*, Vol. II: *Religion and Society* (New York, Hagerstown, San Francisco, London: Harper Torchbooks, 1974), p. 41.

13 Ibid., p. 40.
14 Ibid.
15 Ibid., p. 41.
16 Ibid., p. 42.
17 Ibid.
18 Translated from Muhammad ibn al-Harith al-Khushani, *Kitab al-Qudat bi-Qurtuba* by Bernard Lewis, *Islam*, Vol. II, p. 44–45.
19 Mawardi in Lewis, *Islam*, Vol. II, p. 42.
20 Ibid., p. 40.

6 DISPROPORTIONS

1 We plan a source-book to amplify the comparison and contrast in these specific areas of law and others.
2 Imam Malik ibn Anas, *Al-Muwatta,* p. 190.
3 Ibid., pp. 190–91.
4 Ibid., p. 323.
5 Joseph Schacht, *An Introduction to Islamic Law* (Oxford: Clarendon Press, 1982), p. 130.
6 Imam Malik ibn Anas, *Al-Muwatta,* p. 321.
7 Ibid., p. 321.
8 Ibid.
9 Ibid., p. 320.
10 Ibid., pp. 320–21.
11 Ibid., p. 321.
12 Majid Khadduri, *Islamic Jurisprudence: Shafi'i's Risala* (Baltimore: The Johns Hopkins University Press, 1961), pp. 143–44.
13 Ibid., p. 322.
14 Ibid., p. 321.
15 Ibid.
16 Ibid., p. 327.
17 Ibid.
18 Ibid., p. 332.
19 Ibid., p. 333.
20 Ibid., pp. 339–40.
21 Ibid., p. 339.
22 Ibid., p. 340.
23 Paul V. McC. Flesher, *Oxen, Women, or Citizens? Slaves in the System of the Mishnah* (Atlanta: Scholars Press for Brown Judaic Studies, 1999), p. 1.
24 Ibid.
25 Ibid., pp. 7–8.
26 Ibid, p. 62.
27 Ibid., p. 67.
28 Imam Malik ibn Anas, *Al-Muwatta*, pp. 39–40.
29 Majid Khadduri, *Islamic Jurisprudence: Shafi'i's Risala*, pp. 166–67.
30 Imam Malik ibn Anas, *Al-Muwatta*, p. 132.
31 Ibid., p. 134.
32 Ibid., p. 135.
33 Ibid., p. 130.
34 Ibid., p. 128.
35 Ibid., p. 129.
36 Ibid., p. 143.

37 Ibid., p. 147.
38 Ibid., p. 150.

7 UNIQUE CATEGORIES

1 This is an account of the classical theology and law of Judaism, so we do not take up those contemporary Judaisms that treat the State of Israel within the framework of their theology, the national-religious Zionist movement, Mizrachi, for one example, American Reform and Conservative Judaisms, for another; nor do we deal with contemporary Judaisms that altogether reject Zionism as anti-Judaic, identified with certain groups within Hasidism, for instance, or the contemporary Judaisms that do not accord religious significance to the State of Israel but accept the State and its support for their institutions. None of these complications has any bearing upon our task.
2 Majid Khadduri, *Islamic Jurisprudence: Shafi'i's Risala* (Baltimore: The Johns Hopkins University Press, 1961), p. 126.
3 Ibid., pp. 133–34.
4 The usage is generally traced to hadith reports. See discussion by A. Abel, "Dar al-Islam" in *Encyclopedia of Islam*, new edition (Leiden: E.J. Brill, 1963), Vol. II, p. 127.
5 Fazlur Rahman, *Islam and Modernity: Transformation of an Intellectual Tradition* (Chicago and London: The University of Chicago Press, 1982), pp. 7–8.
6 See, e.g., Ibn Hazm, *Kitab al-Fasl fi'l-Milal wa'l-Awha' wa'l-Nihal* (Cairo, 1321, IV), p. 135.
7 Imam Malik ibn Anas, *Al-Muwatta of Imam Malik ibn Anas: The First Formulation of Islamic Law*, trans. Aisha Abdurrahman Bewley (London and New York: Kegan Paul International, 1989), pp. 173–4.
8 Ibid., p. 173.
9 Ibid., p. 176.
10 Ibid., p. 180.
11 Ibid.
12 Khadduri, *Islamic Jurisprudence: Shafi'i's Risala*, p. 82.
13 Ibid. pp. 82–86.
14 See Tamara Sonn, "Political Authority in Classical Islamic Thought", *The American Journal of Islamic Social Sciences* 13(3) (Autumn 1996):309–24.
15 Malik, *Al-Muwatta,* p. 174.
16 Ibn Abi Zayd al-Qayrawani, "The Laws of Holy War" in John Alden Williams (ed.) *Themes of Islamic Civilization* (Berkeley, Los Angeles, London: University of California Press, 1971), p. 266.
17 Malik, *Al-Muwatta,* p. 174.
18 Ibid., p. 175.
19 Ibn Abi Zayd al-Qayrawani, "The Laws of Holy War" in Alden Williams (ed.) *Themes of Islamic Civilization*, pp. 266–67.
20 Malik, *Al-Muwatta,* p. 183.
21 Muslim b. Hajjaj al-Qushayri al-Naysaburi, *al-Sahih*, trans. 'Abdul Hamid Siddiqi (Lahore: Sh. Muhammad Ashraf, 1973), III, p. 942.
22 Al-Shaybani, "On Calling to Islam in Battle" in Alden (ed.) *Themes of Islamic Civilization*, p. 277.
23 See Sonn, "Political Authority".
24 Al-Shaybani, "On Calling to Islam in Battle" in Alden (ed.) *Themes of Islamic Civilization*, p. 277.
25 In Shi'i law the role of the legal scholar differs from that in Sunni Islam. Whereas

Sunni law is expressed in the texts and anyone willing to pursue the rigorous education involved may become a legal scholar, in Shi'i Islam God continues to guide the community through descendants of Prophet Muhammad through his cousin and son-in-law, 'Ali, in his marriage to Muhammad's daughter, Fatimah. In this context, there may be a counterpart for the notion of "meeting God" in the study of law. For a discussion of the Shi'i notion of the imamate, see Abdulaziz Sachedina, *Islamic Messianism: The Idea of Mahdi in Twelver Shi'ism* (Albany, NY: State University of New York Press, 1981).

26 Muhammad 'Abduh, *Theology of Unity*, trans. Kenneth Cragg and Ishaq Masa'ad (London: George Allen & Unwin, 1966), p. 141.

27 N. J. Coulson, *A History of Islamic Law* (Edinburgh: University Press, 1964), p. 37.

28 In Marshall G. S. Hodgson's analysis, the dynastic families had seized control of the central political power of the Muslim empire (the army and the treasury that supported it) before there was any theory of political legitimacy in Islam. But by the tenth century, regional principalities had emerged and while they were generally content to pay nominal allegiance to the Baghdad caliphate, they posed a challenge to the central caliphate's real power. Hodgson says, "The caliphate itself was in question, in a world ruled by arbitrary amirs [princes], and the caliphate had proved willing to turn to Shar'i principles in its crisis. Hence the scholars set about developing the theory of a *sihasah shar'iyyah*, Shar'i political order." See *The Venture of Islam*, Vol. II: *The Expansion of Islam in the Middle Periods* (Chicago and London: The University of Chicago Press, 1974), p. 55. It should be noted that even in al-Mawardi's formulation, the term "imamate" is used rather than "caliphate". Scholars agree, however, that the terms are interchangeable in this context.

29 The following account is taken from pp. 3–6, 14–15, and 19–20 of al-Mawardi's *Al-Ahkam al-Sultaniyya*, translated by Bernard Lewis in *Islam*, Vol. I: *Politics and War* (New York, Hagerstown, San Francisco, London: Harper Torchbooks, 1974), pp. 171–79.

30 Muhammad al-Juwayni, *Ghiyath al-Umama* (Iskandariyya, 1979), pp. 274–75: "If the sultan does not reach the degree of ijtihad, then the jurists are to be followed and the sultan will provide them with help, power, and protection." Quoted by Wael Hallaq, "Was the Gate of Ijtihad Closed?", *International Journal of Middle East Studies* 16 (1984):13.

31 Nevertheless, al-Mawardi notes that the caliph may delegate the following four kinds of authority:

1 Those who have unlimited authority of unlimited scope. These are the viziers [ministers], for they are entrusted with all public affairs without specific attribution.

2 Those who have unlimited authority of limited scope. These are the provincial and district governors, whose authority is unlimited within the specific areas assigned to them.

3 Those who have limited authority of unlimited scope. These are the chief qadi [judge], the commander of the armies, the commandant of the frontier fortresses, the intendant of land tax, and the collector of alms, each of whom has unlimited authority in the specific functions assigned to him.

4 Those with limited authority of limited scope, such as the qadi or a town or district, the local intendant of land tax, collector of tithes, the frontier commandant, or the army commander, every one of whom has limited authority of limited scope.

32 See Ibn Taymiyya, *Majmu'at al-Rasa'il al-Kubra*, ed. Muhammad 'Ali Subayh, 1966. Vol. I, p. 312ff.
33 Ibn Taymiyya, *Raf' al-Malam 'an al-A'immah al-A'lam*, ed. M. H. al-Faqqi (Cairo: Matba'at al-Sunnah al-Muhammadiyyah, 1958), p. 9.
34 Majid Khadduri, *The Islamic Law of Nations: Shaybani's Siyar* (Baltimore: The Johns Hopkins University Press, 1966), p. 10.
35 Wael B. Hallaq, "Was the Gate of Ijtihad Closed?", p. 5.
36 See Tamara Sonn, *Interpreting Islam: Bandali Jawzi's Islamic Intellectual History* (New York: Oxford University Press, 1996), pp. 23–37.
37 Hamilton A. R. Gibb, *Studies on the Civilization of Islam*, ed. Stanford J. Shaw and William R. Polk (Boston: Beacon Press, 1962), p. 115.
38 Ibid, p. 117.

8 EPILOGUE

1 Majid Khadduri, *The Islamic Law of Nations: Shaybani's Siyar* (Baltimore: The Johns Hopkins University Press, 1966), pp. 152–54.
2 See Taqiyy al-Din Ahmad Ibn Taymiyya, *Al-Fatawa al-Kubra* (Cairo: Dar al-Kutub al-Haditha, 1966), Vol. I, p. 484.

INDEX